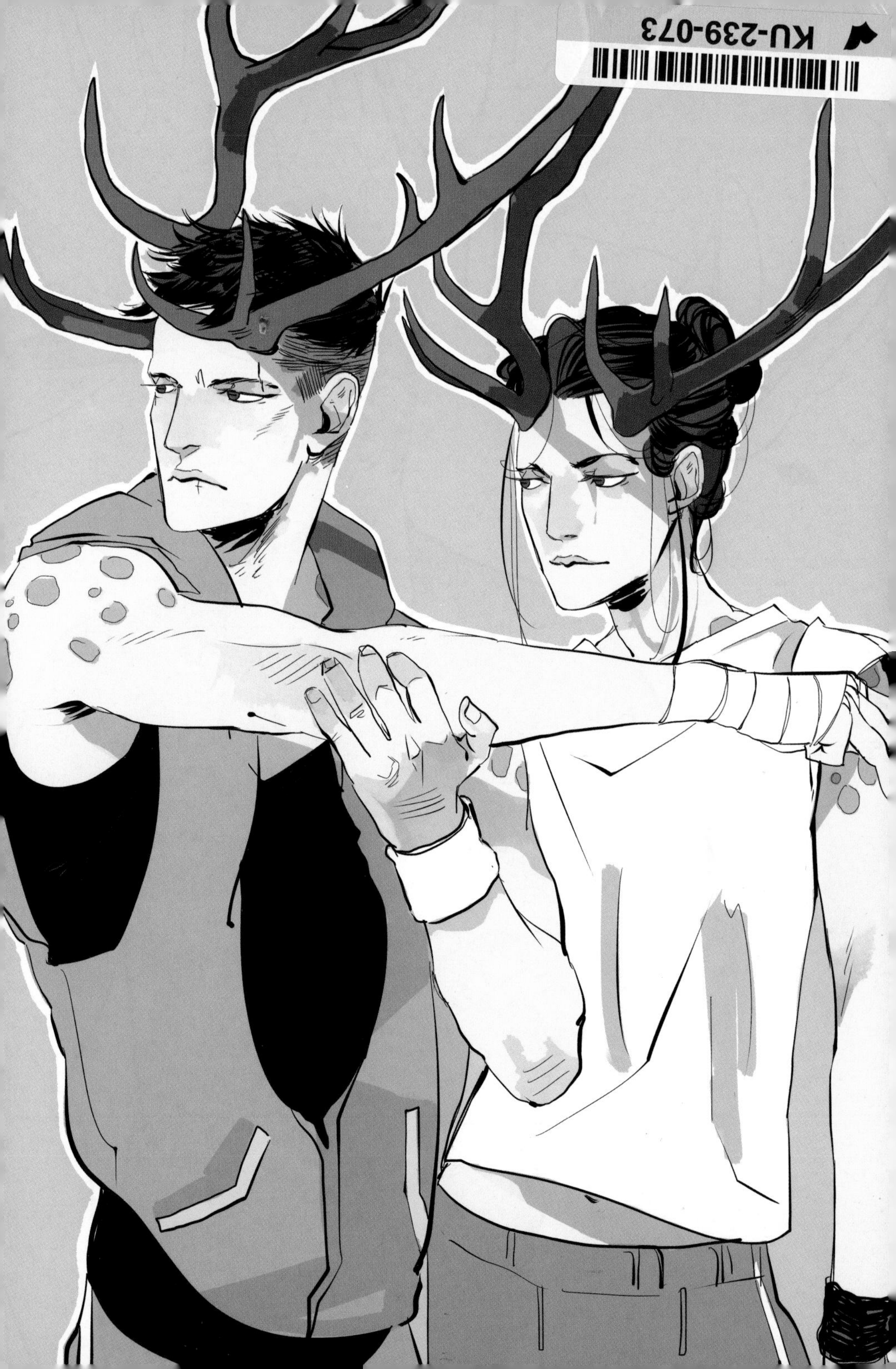

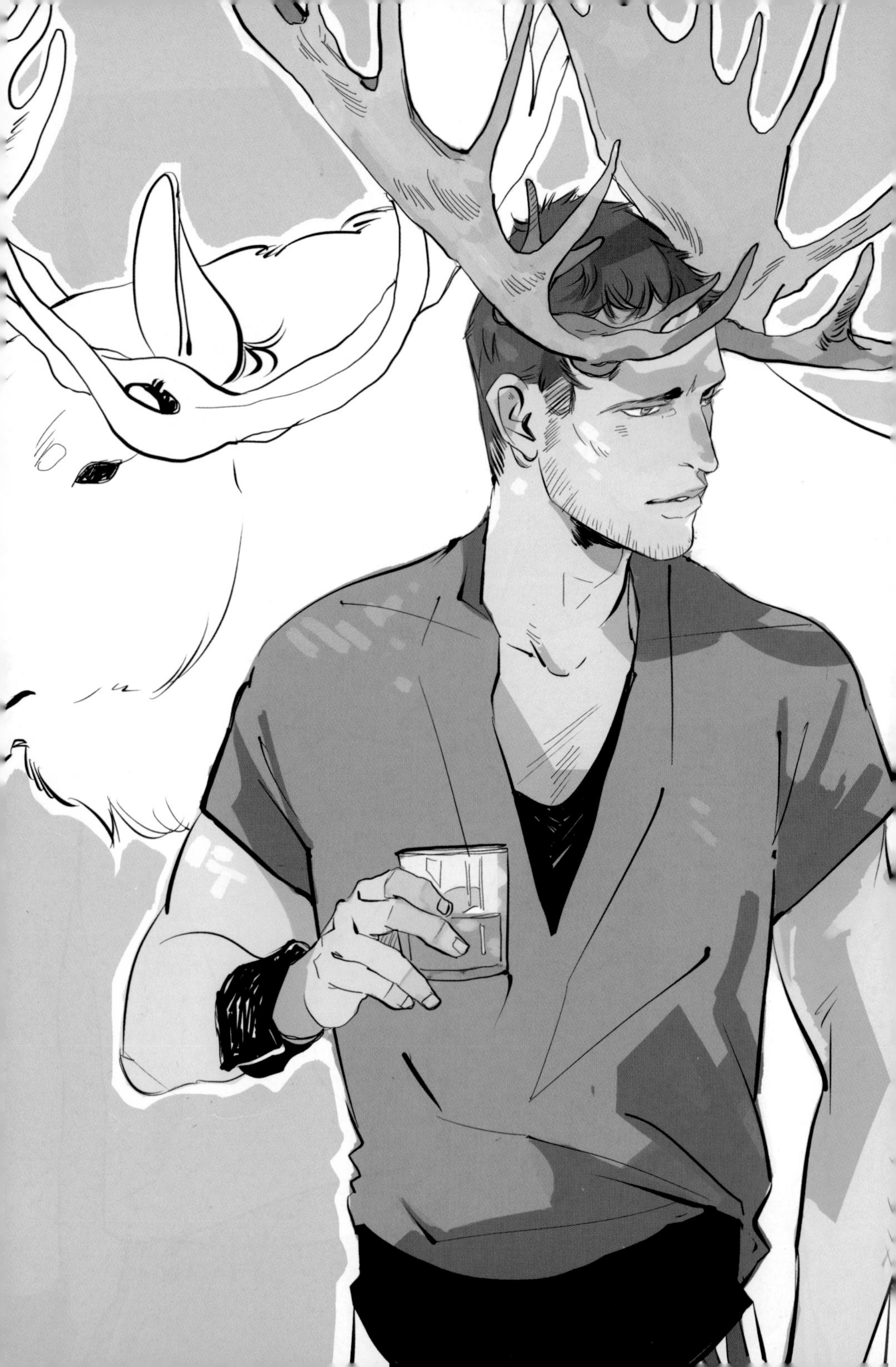

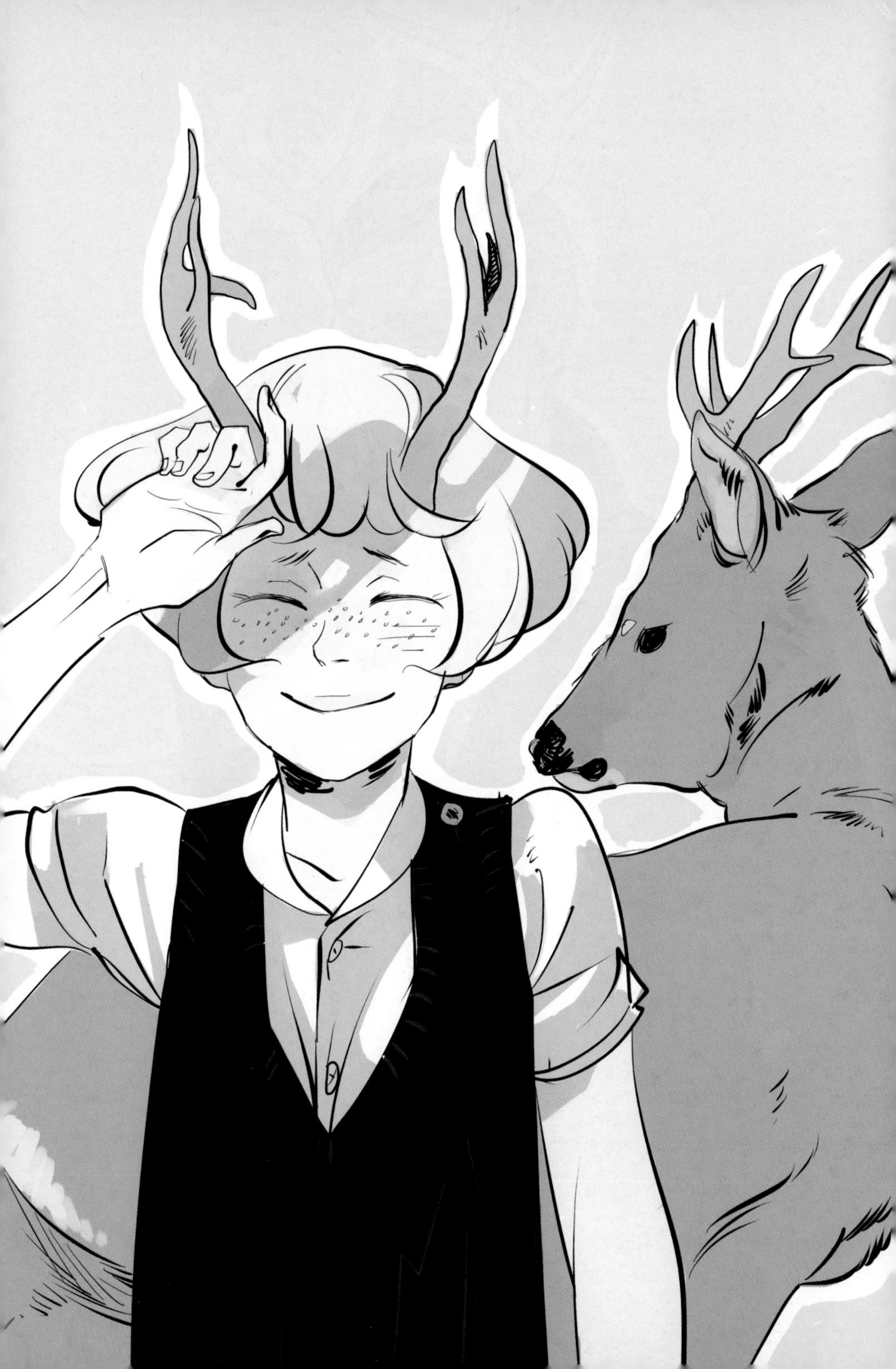

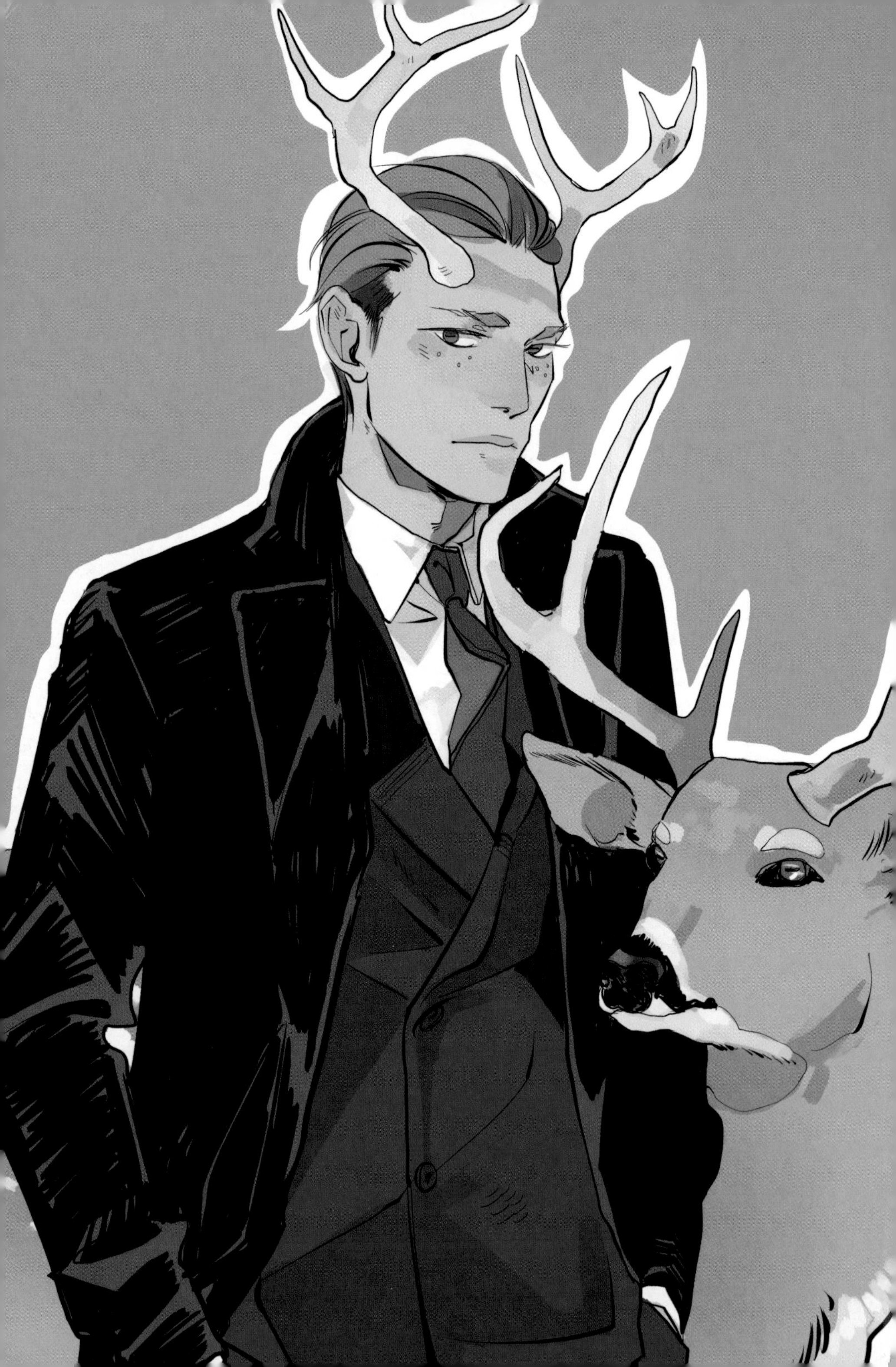

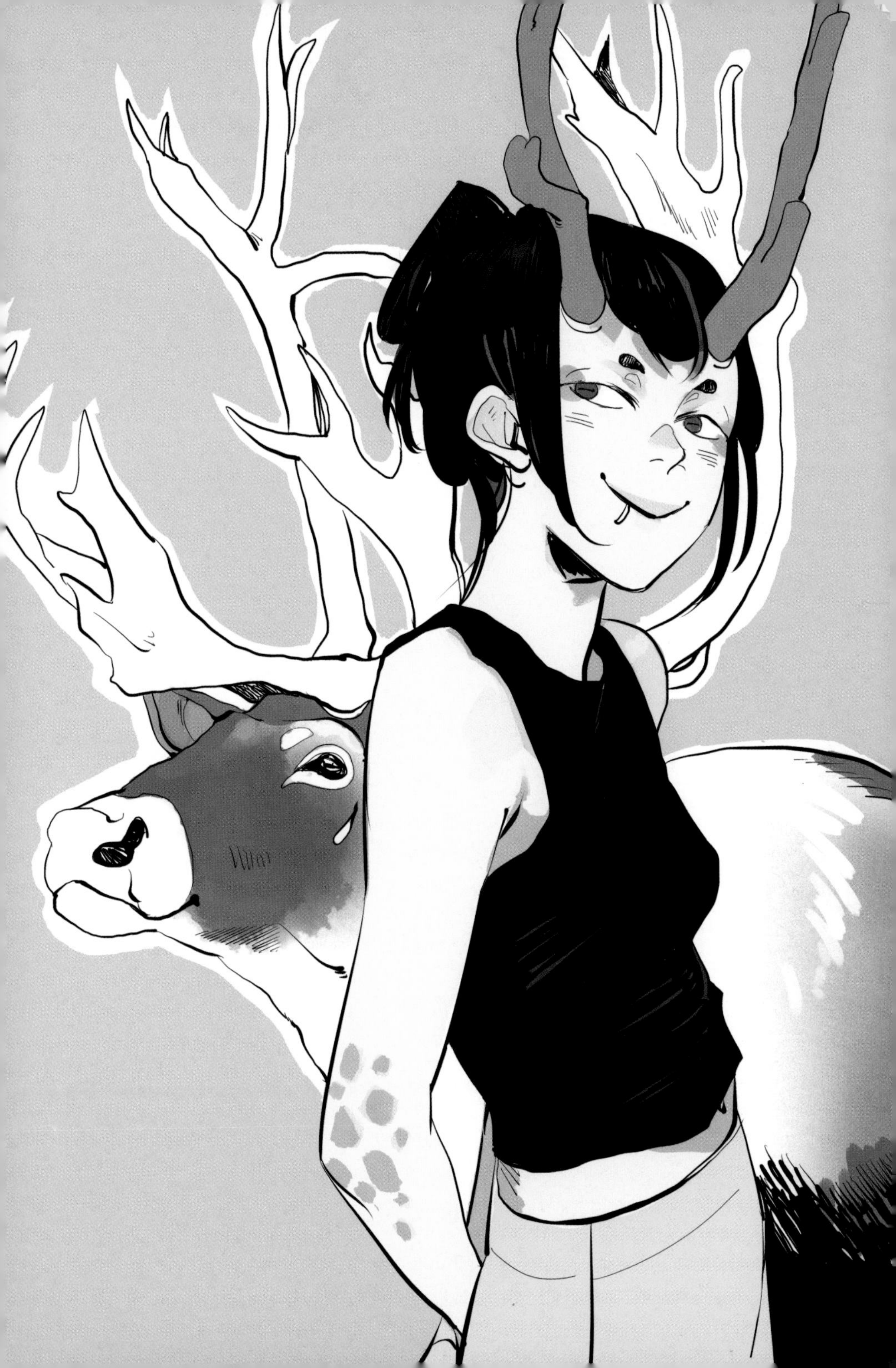

Contents

DEDICATED TO GRANDMA JEAN,
WHO MAY HAVE THOUGHT THIS STORY WAS STRANGE
BUT WOULD HAVE BEEN PROUD OF ME ANYWAY.

Reindeer Boy

Cassandra Jean

Yen Press
1290 Avenue of the Americas
New York, NY 10104

Visit us!
❄ yenpress.com
❄ facebook.com/yenpress
❄ twitter.com/yenpress
❄ yenpress.tumblr.com
❄ instagram.com/yenpress

First Yen Press Edition: December 2016

Yen Press is an imprint of Yen Press, LLC.
The Yen Press name and logo are trademarks of Yen Press, LLC.

The publisher is not responsible for websites (or their content)
that are not owned by the publisher.

Library of Congress Control Number: 2016955395

ISBNs: 978-0-316-38418-6 (paperback)
978-0-316-38415-5 (ebook)

10 9 8 7 6 5 4 3 2 1

BVG

Printed in the United States of America

Chapter 1

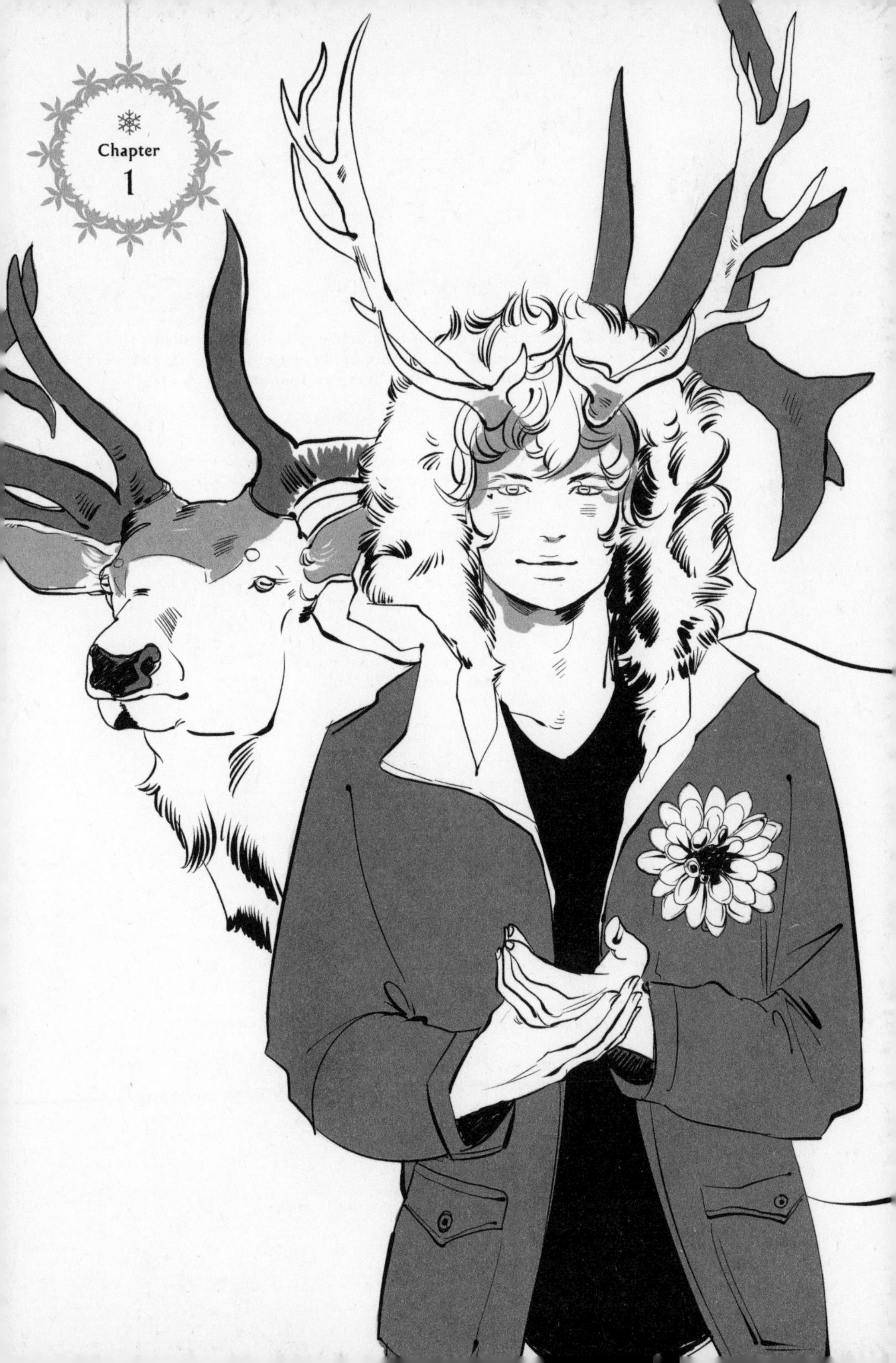

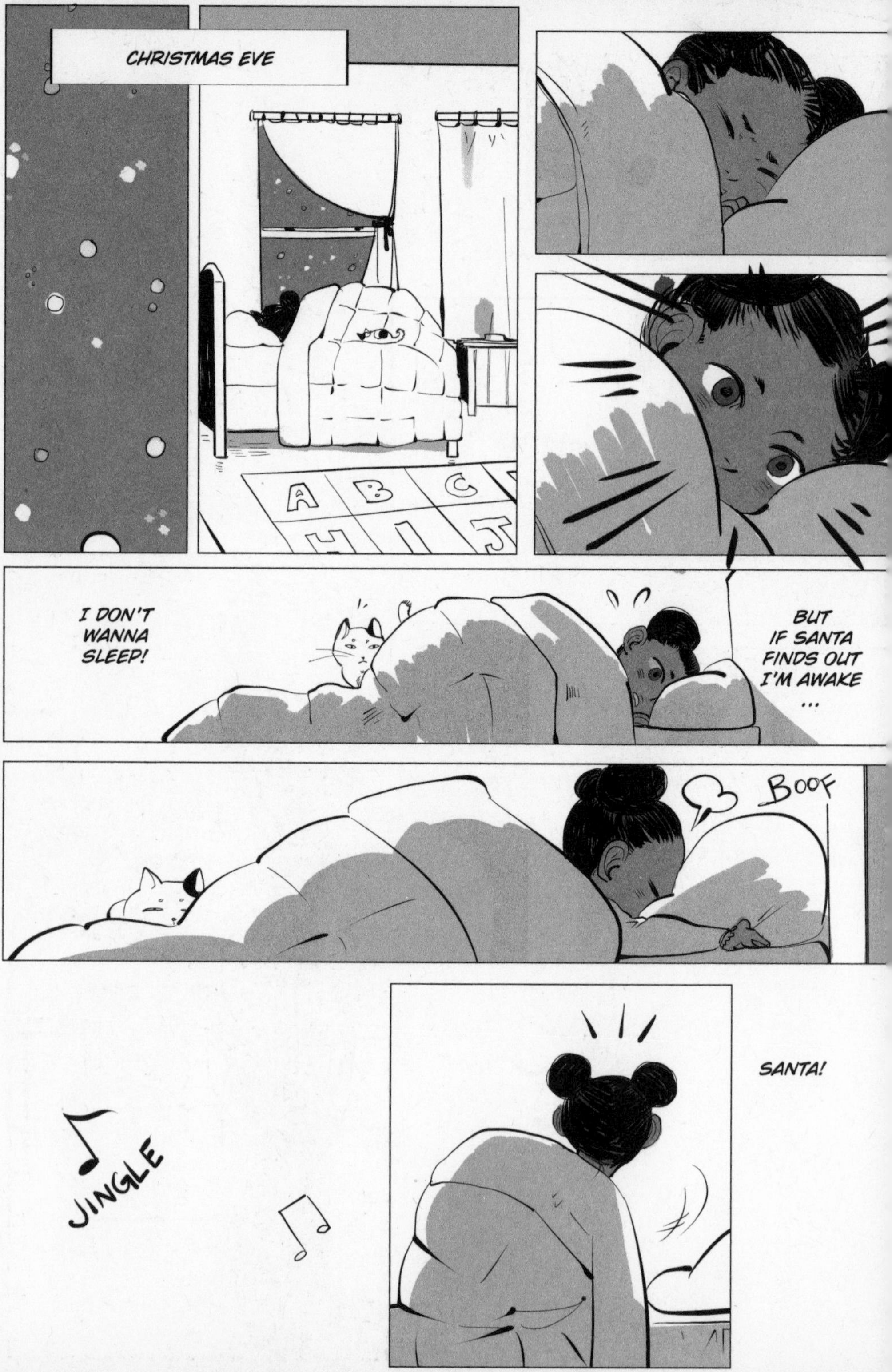
CHRISTMAS EVE
I DON'T WANNA SLEEP!
BUT IF SANTA FINDS OUT I'M AWAKE ...
BOOF
JINGLE
SANTA!

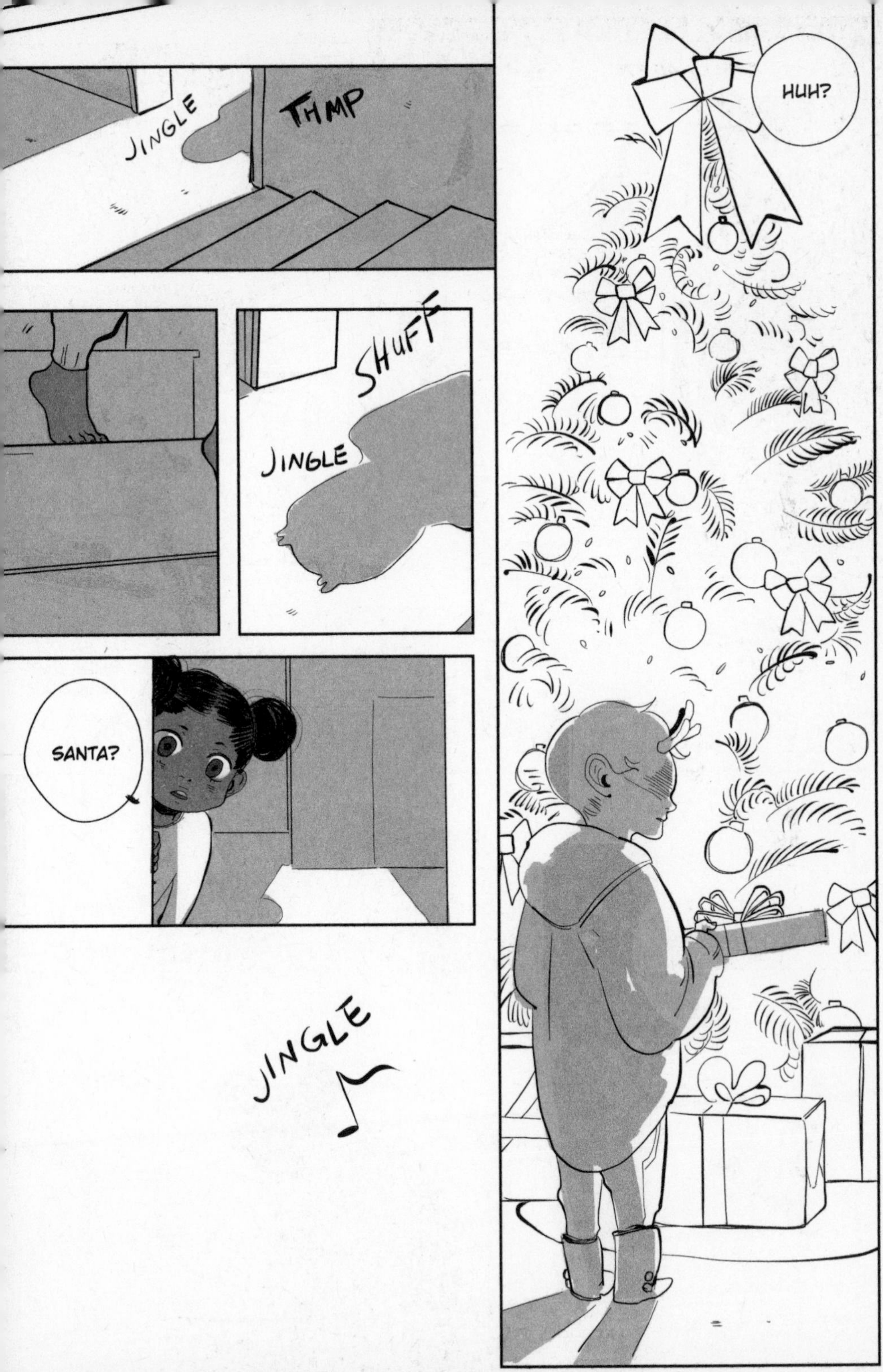
JINGLE
THMP
SHUFF
JINGLE
SANTA?
JINGLE
HUH?

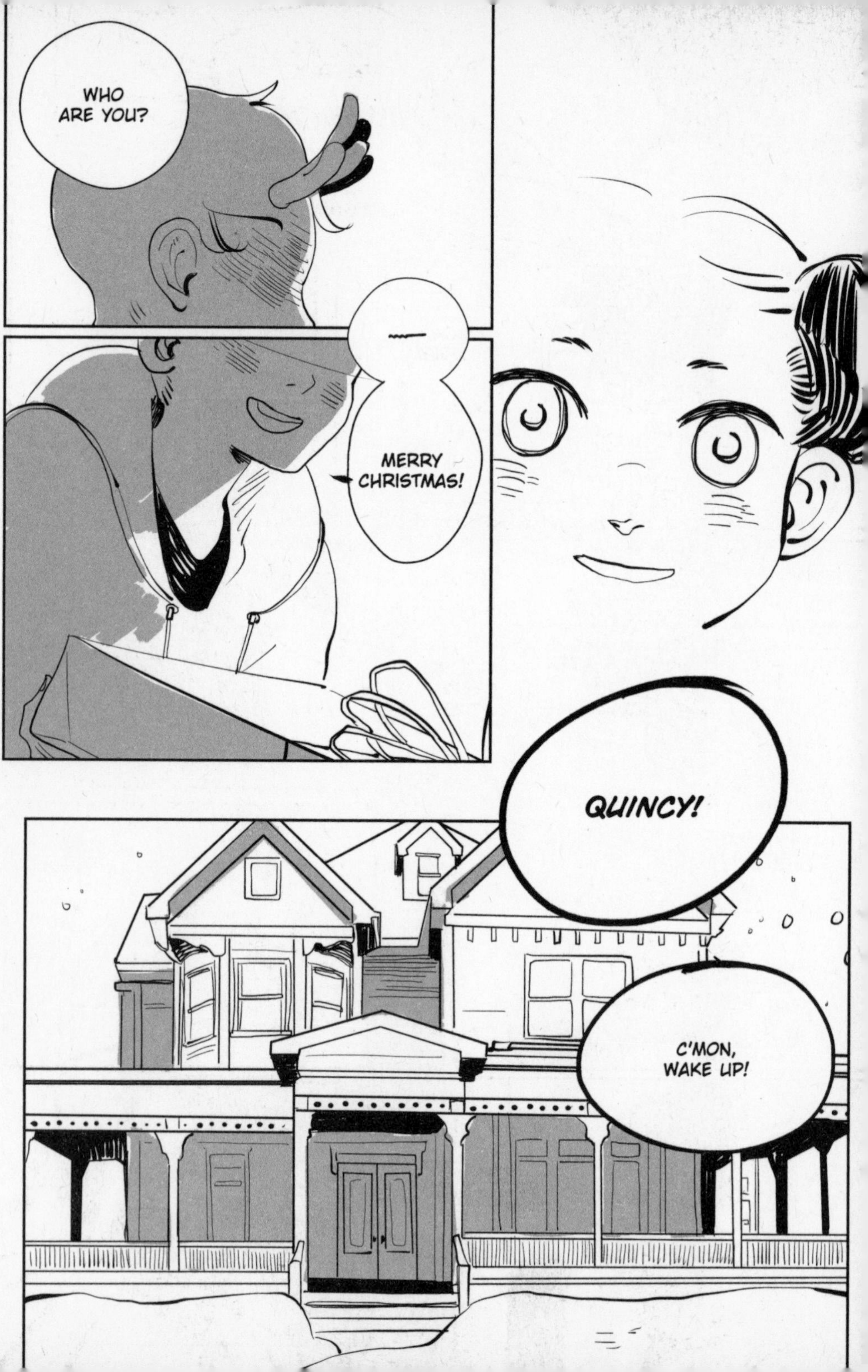
WHO ARE YOU?
MERRY CHRISTMAS!
QUINCY!
C'MON, WAKE UP!

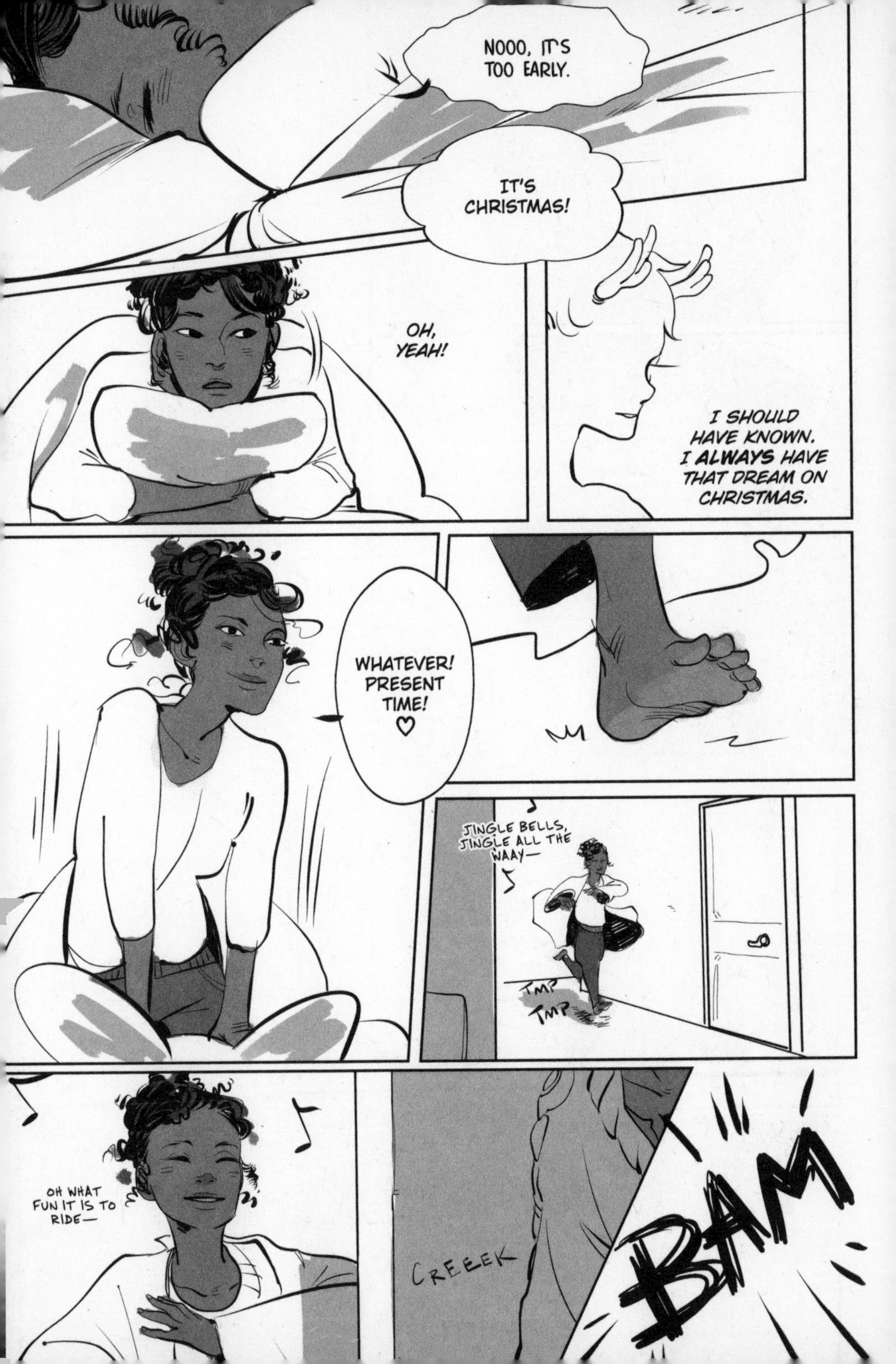
NOOO, IT'S TOO EARLY.
IT'S CHRISTMAS!
OH, YEAH!
I SHOULD HAVE KNOWN. I **ALWAYS** HAVE THAT DREAM ON CHRISTMAS.
WHATEVER! PRESENT TIME! ♡
JINGLE BELLS, JINGLE ALL THE WAAY—
TMP
TMP
OH WHAT FUN IT IS TO RIDE—
CREEEK
BAM

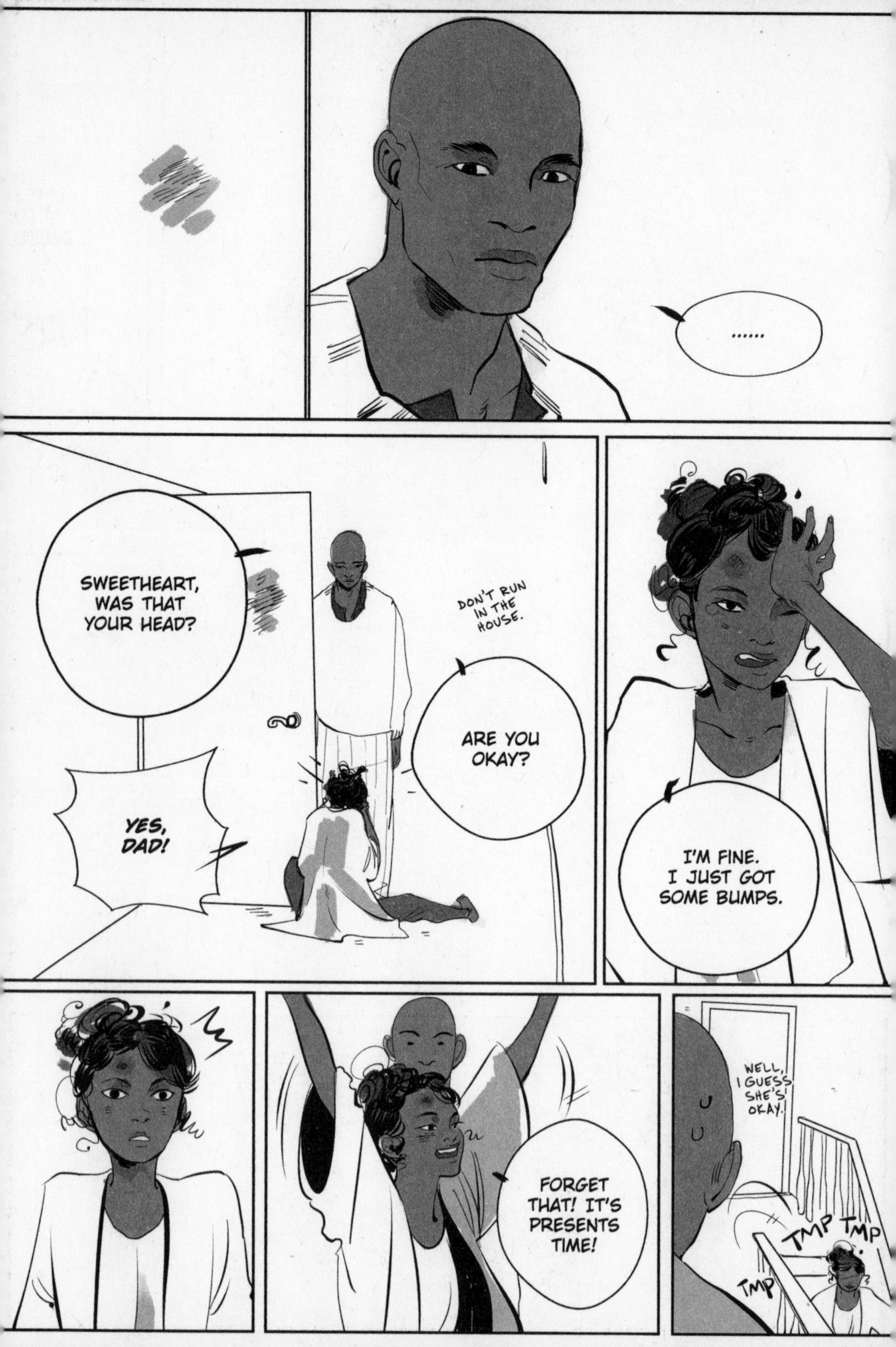
......
SWEETHEART, WAS THAT YOUR HEAD?
YES, DAD!
DON'T RUN IN THE HOUSE.
ARE YOU OKAY?
I'M FINE. I JUST GOT SOME BUMPS.
FORGET THAT! IT'S PRESENTS TIME!
WELL, I GUESS SHE'S OKAY.
TMP TMP
TMP

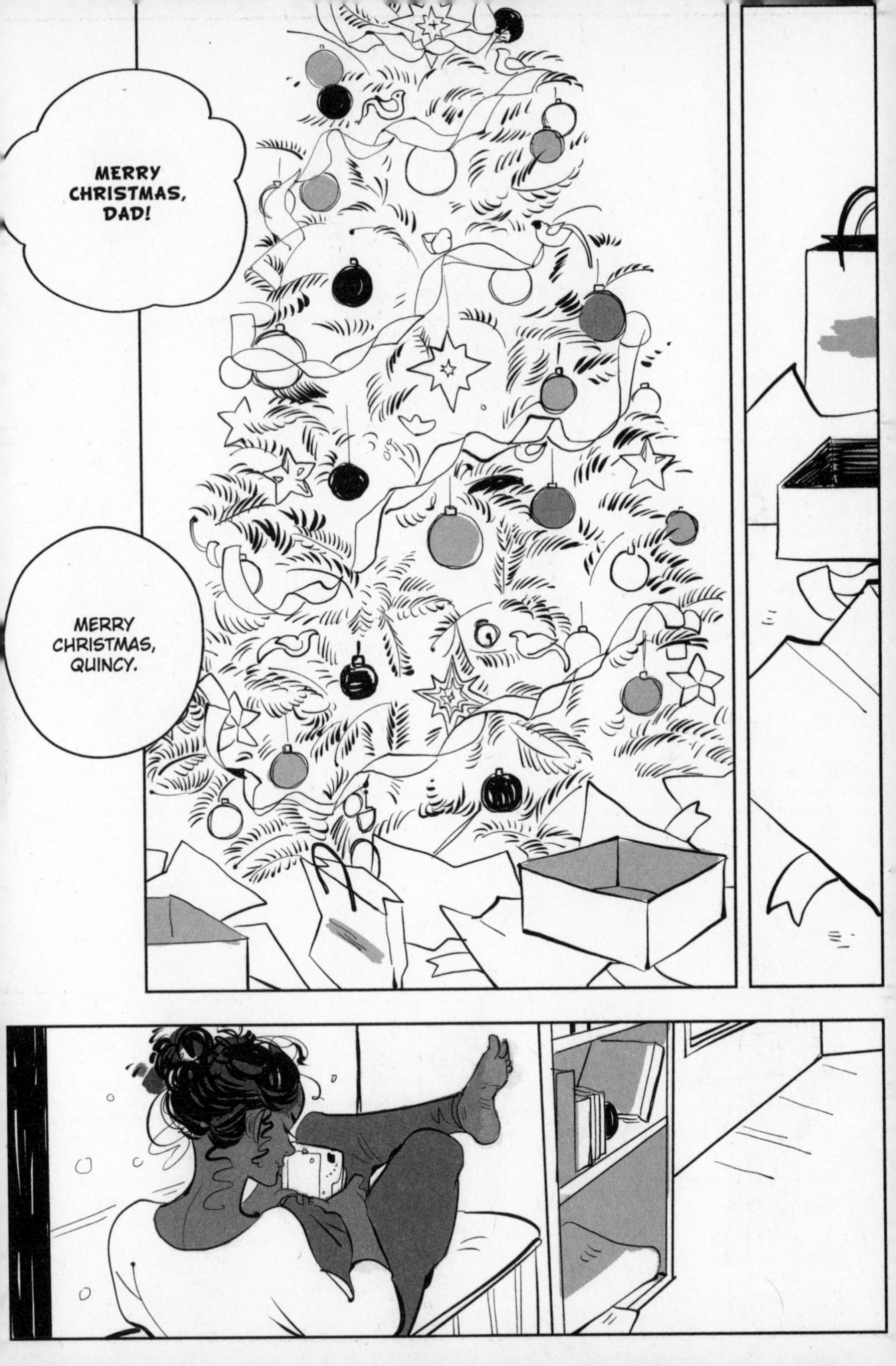
MERRY CHRISTMAS, DAD!
MERRY CHRISTMAS, QUINCY.

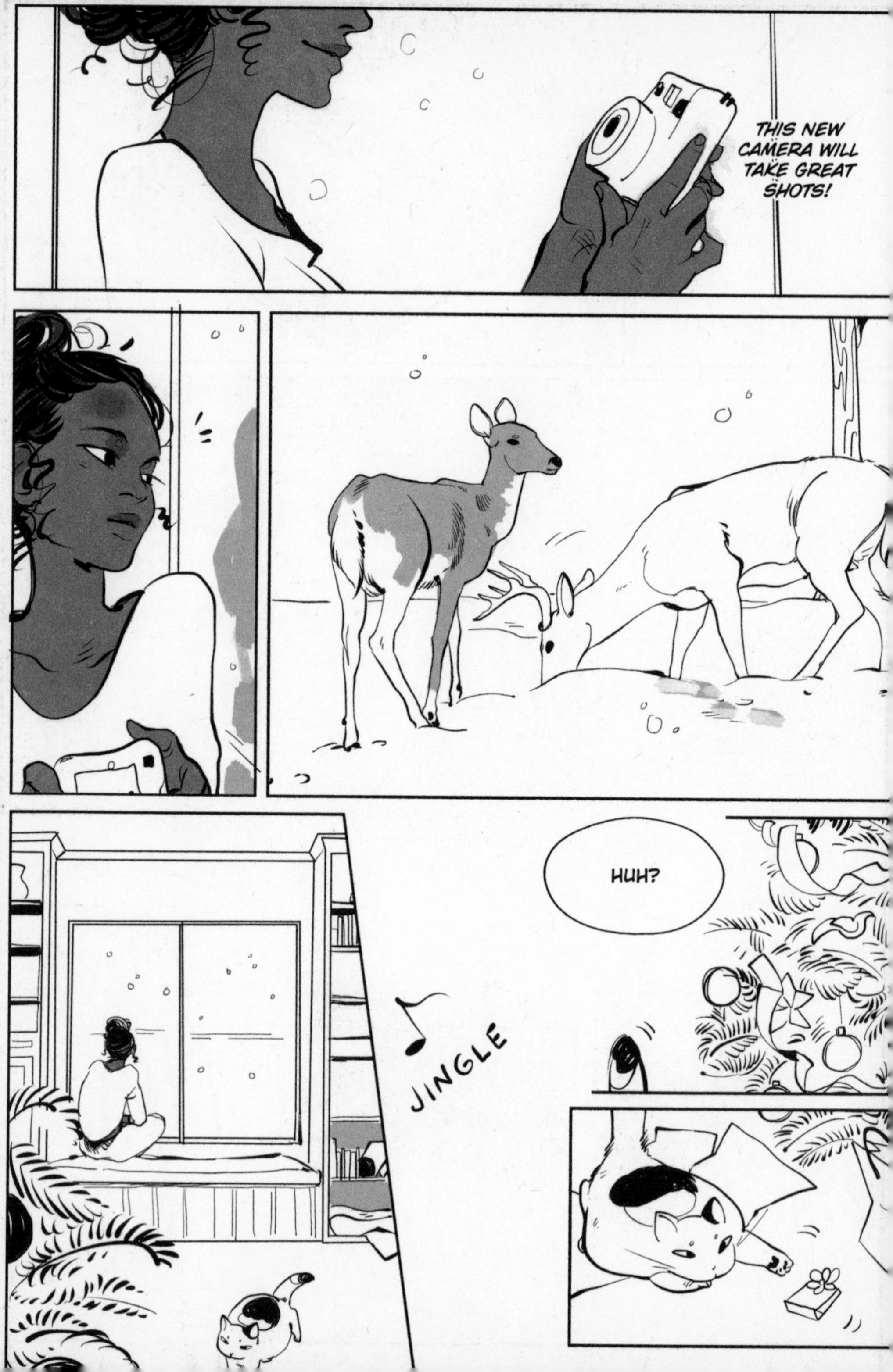
THIS NEW CAMERA WILL TAKE GREAT SHOTS!
JINGLE
HUH?

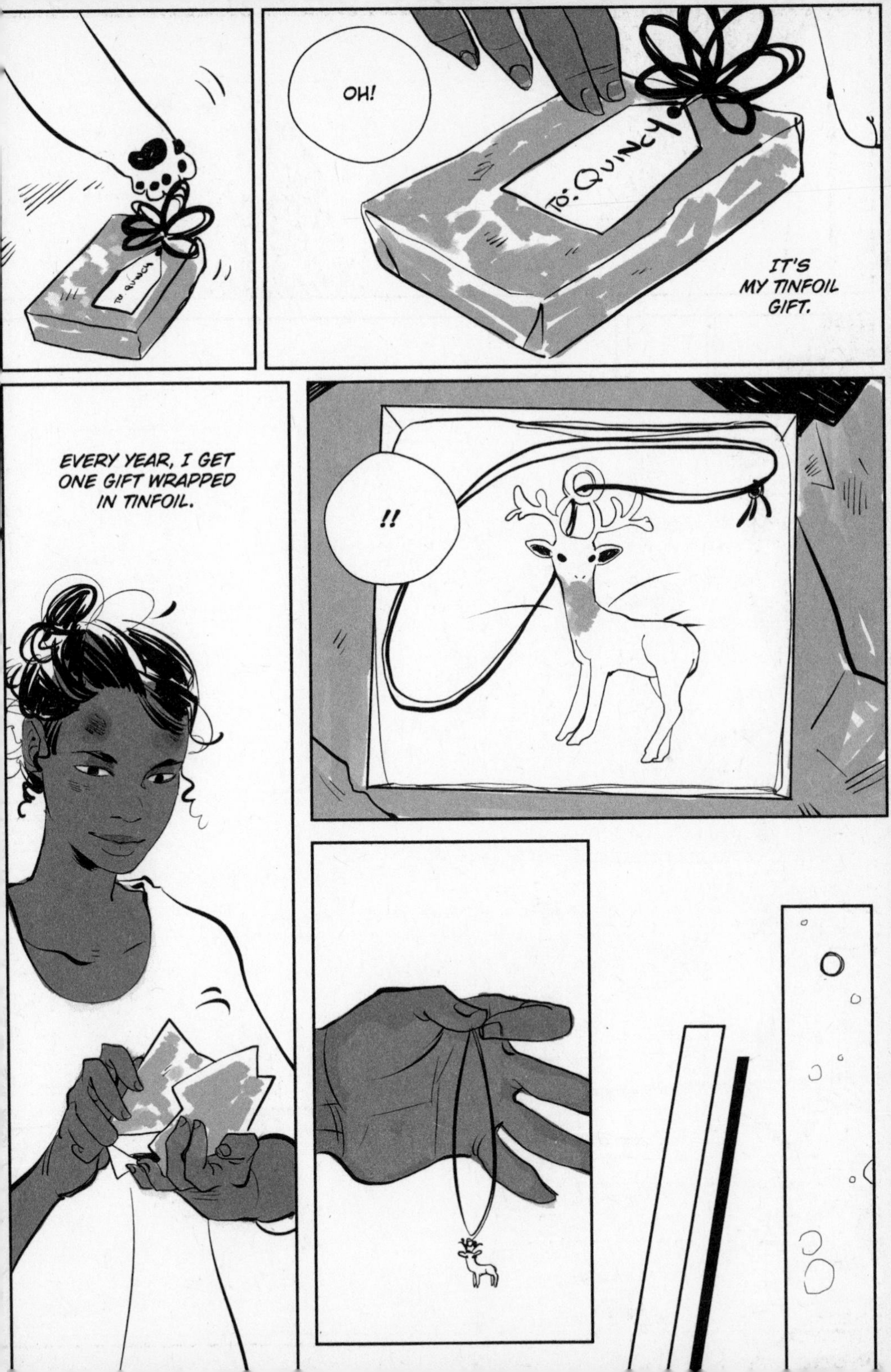
TO: QUINCY
OH!
TO: QUINCY
IT'S MY TINFOIL GIFT.
EVERY YEAR, I GET ONE GIFT WRAPPED IN TINFOIL.
!!

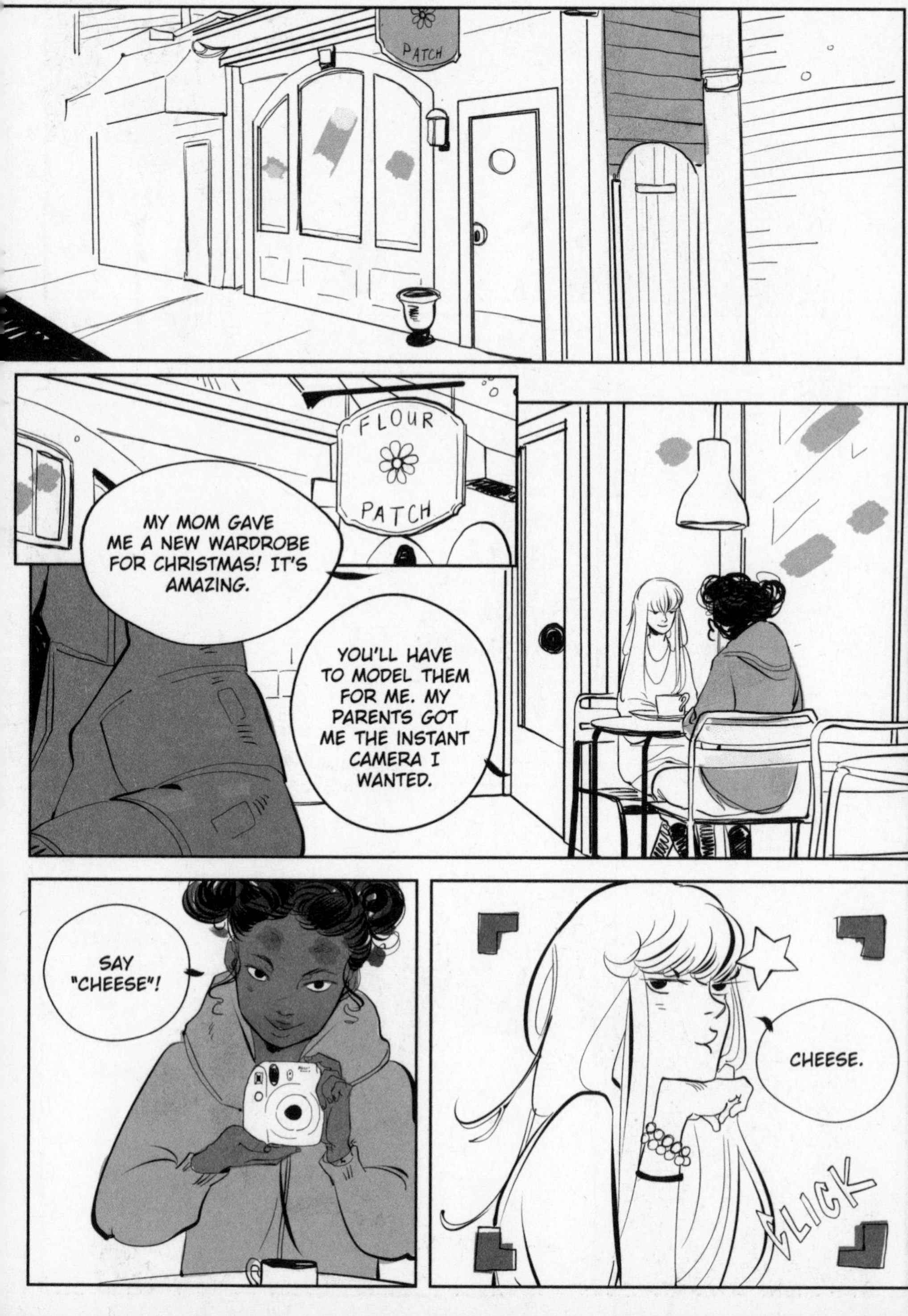
PATCH
FLOUR PATCH
MY MOM GAVE ME A NEW WARDROBE FOR CHRISTMAS! IT'S AMAZING.
YOU'LL HAVE TO MODEL THEM FOR ME. MY PARENTS GOT ME THE INSTANT CAMERA I WANTED.
SAY "CHEESE"!
CHEESE.
CLICK

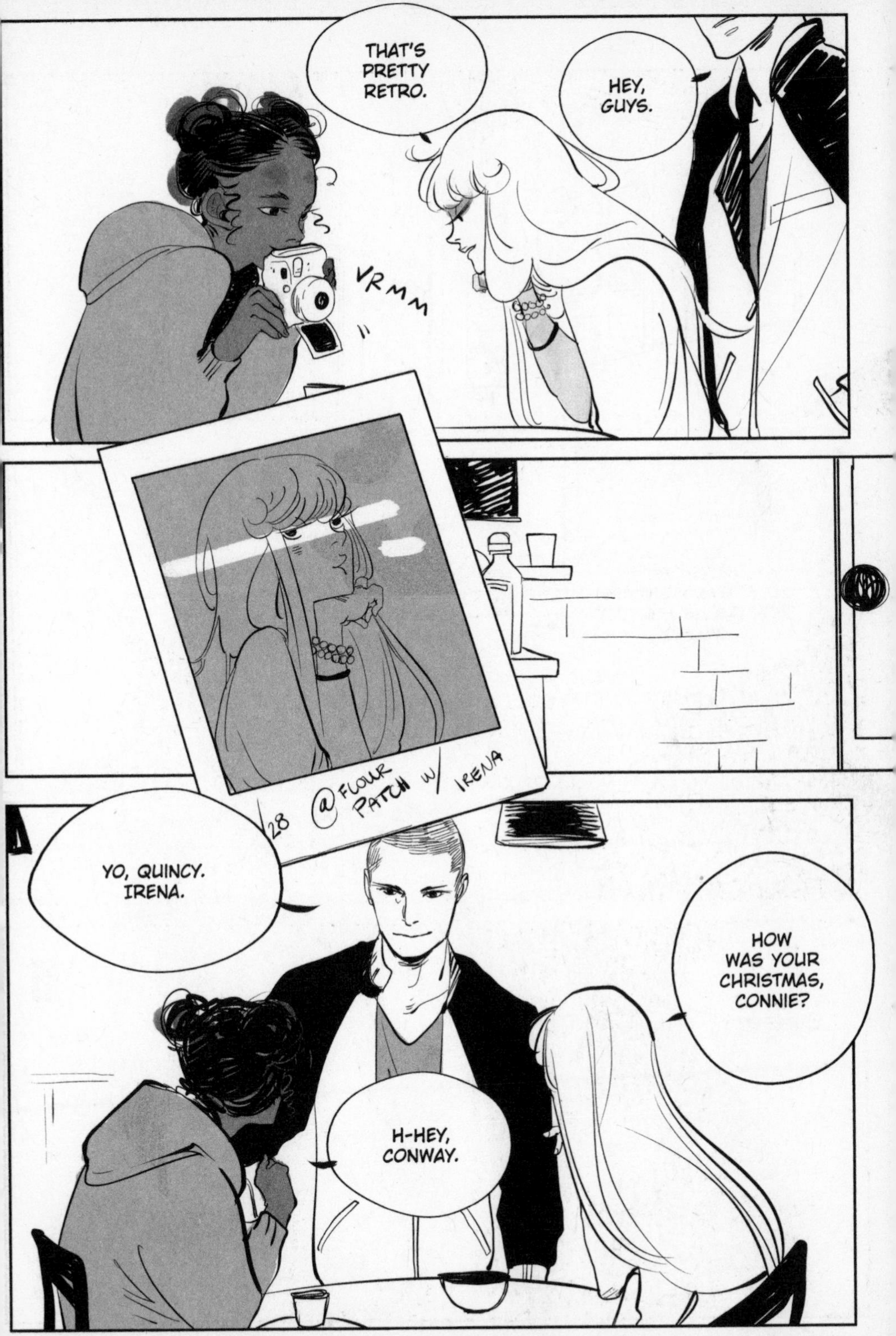
THAT'S PRETTY RETRO.
HEY, GUYS.
VRMM
@FLOUR PATCH w/ IRENA
28
YO, QUINCY. IRENA.
HOW WAS YOUR CHRISTMAS, CONNIE?
H-HEY, CONWAY.

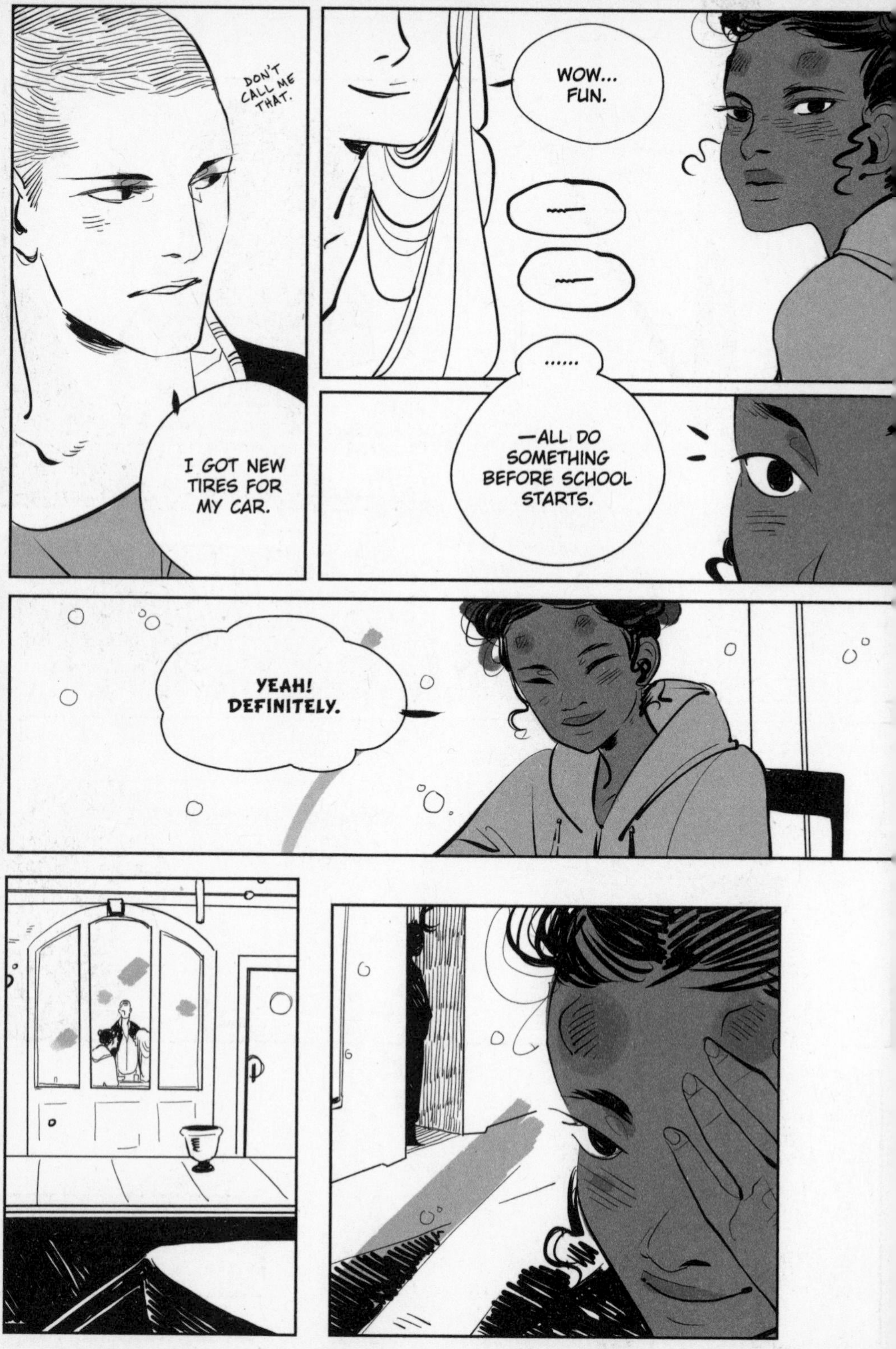
DON'T CALL ME THAT.
I GOT NEW TIRES FOR MY CAR.
WOW... FUN.
—
—
......
—ALL DO SOMETHING BEFORE SCHOOL STARTS.
YEAH! DEFINITELY.

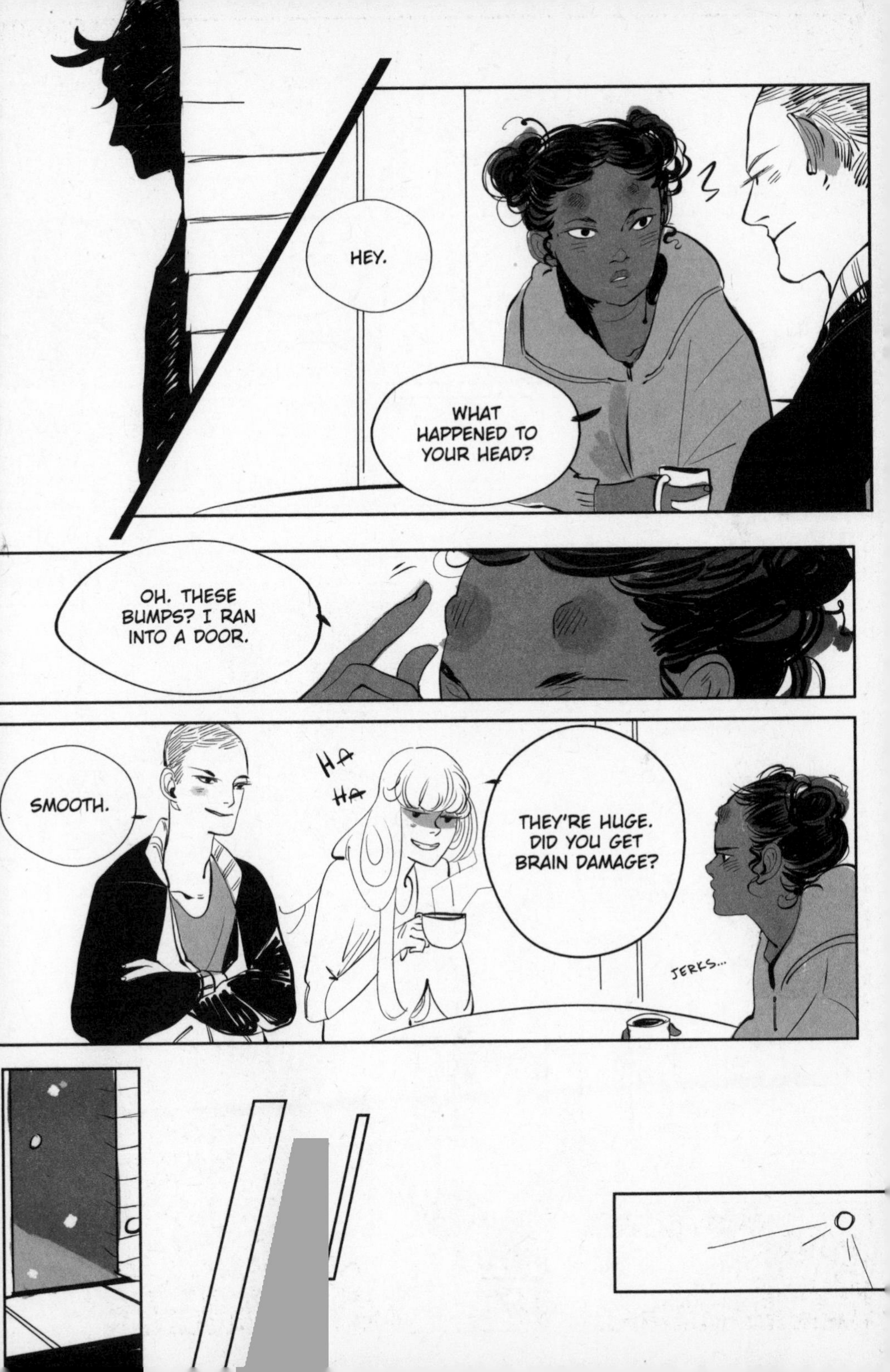
HEY.
WHAT HAPPENED TO YOUR HEAD?
OH. THESE BUMPS? I RAN INTO A DOOR.
SMOOTH.
HA HA
THEY'RE HUGE. DID YOU GET BRAIN DAMAGE?
JERKS...

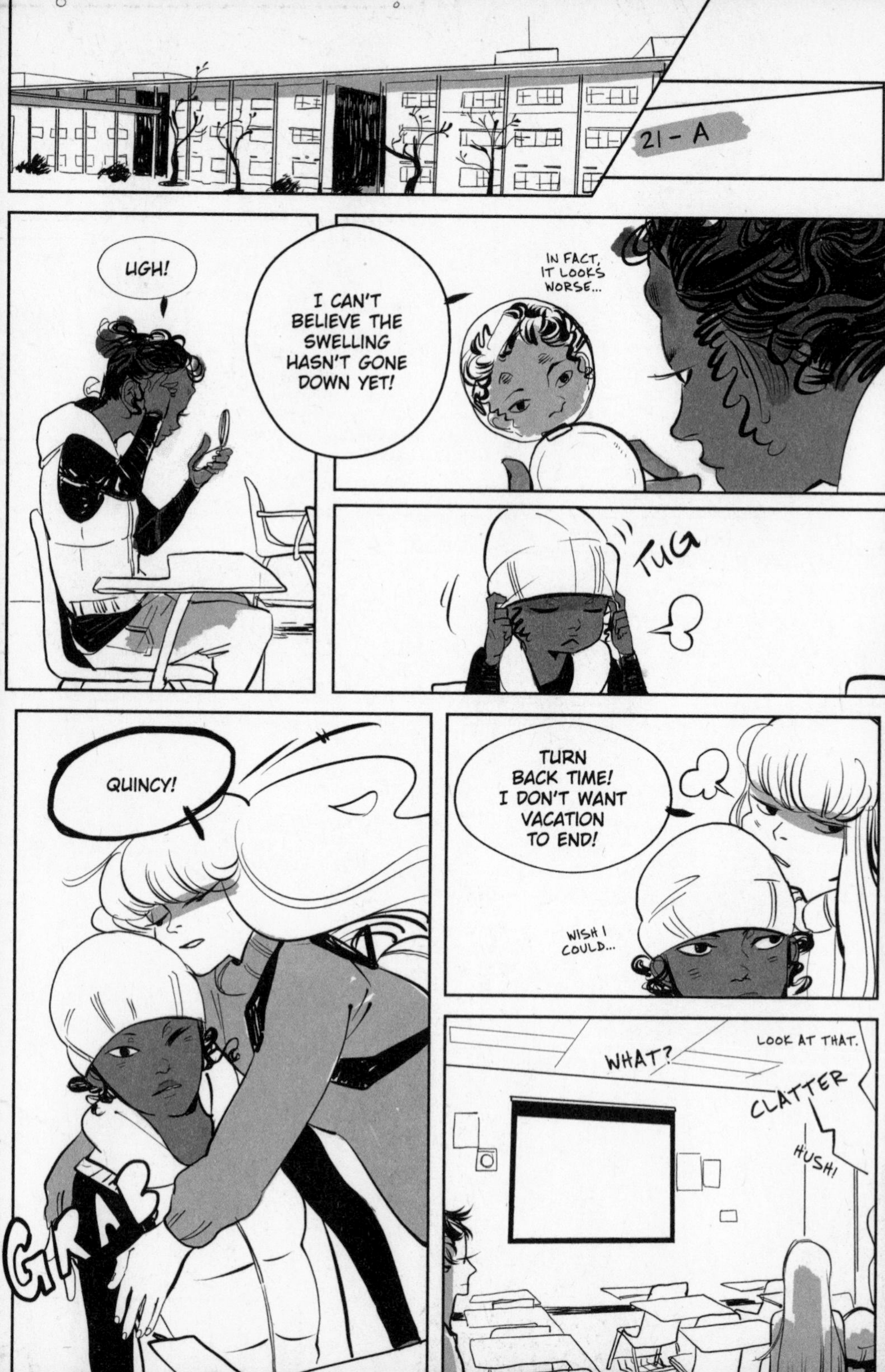
21 - A
UGH!
I CAN'T BELIEVE THE SWELLING HASN'T GONE DOWN YET!
IN FACT, IT LOOKS WORSE...
TUG
QUINCY!
GRAB
TURN BACK TIME! I DON'T WANT VACATION TO END!
WISH I COULD...
WHAT?
LOOK AT THAT.
CLATTER
HUSH!

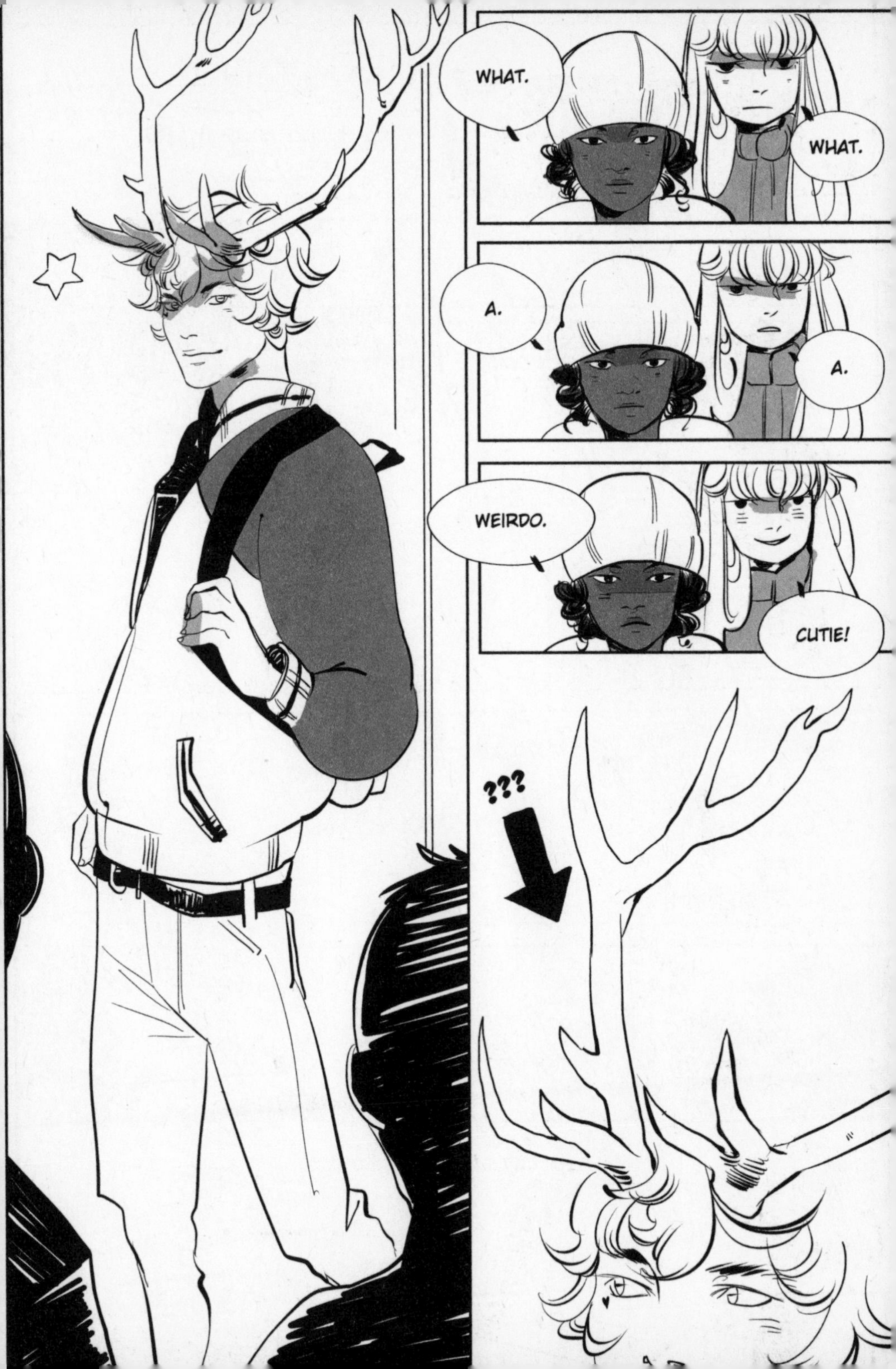
WHAT.
WHAT.
A.
A.
WEIRDO.
CUTIE!
???

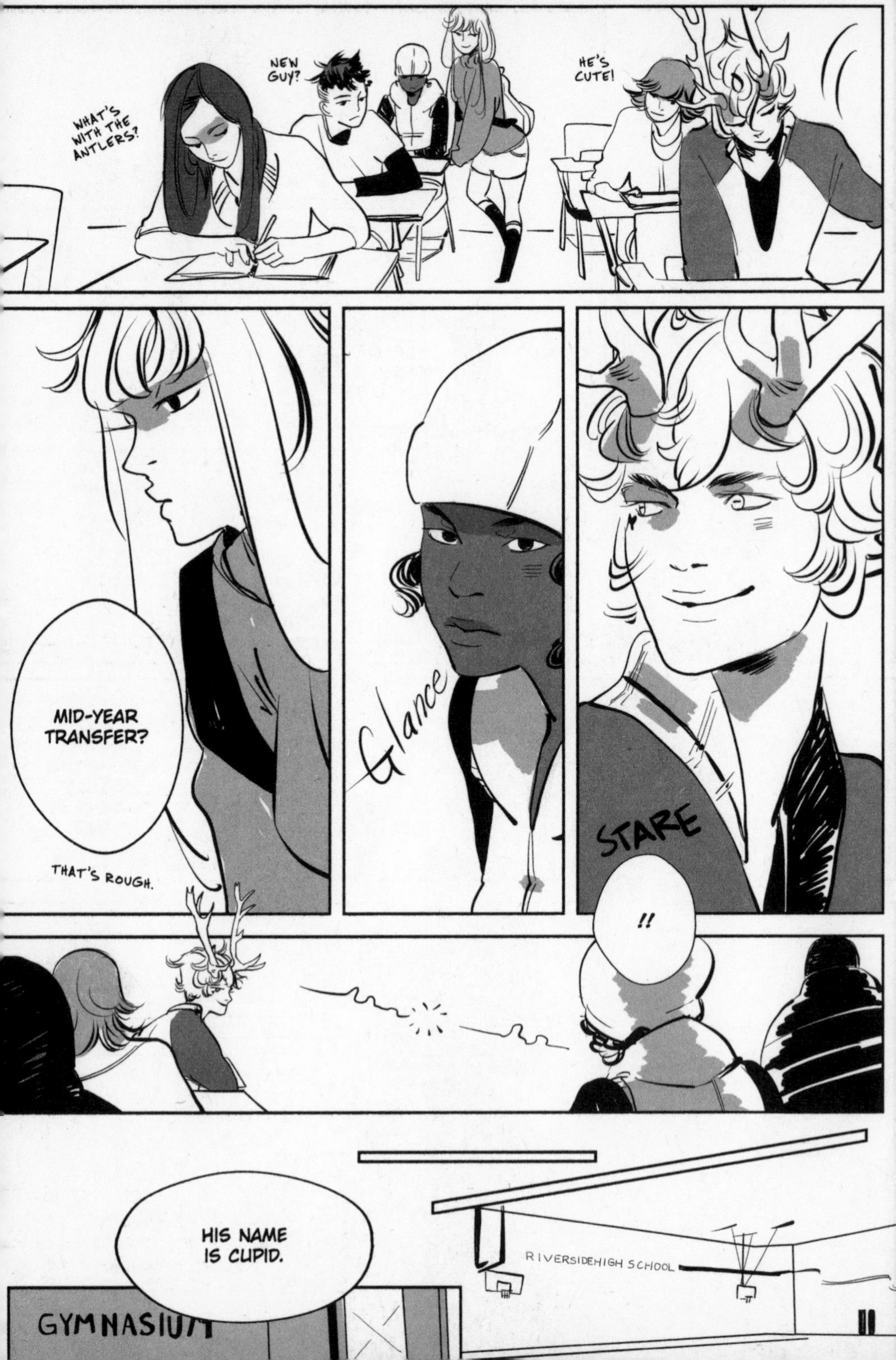
WHAT'S WITH THE ANTLERS?
NEW GUY?
HE'S CUTE!
MID-YEAR TRANSFER?
THAT'S ROUGH.
Glance
STARE
!!
HIS NAME IS CUPID.
RIVERSIDEHIGH SCHOOL
GYMNASIUM

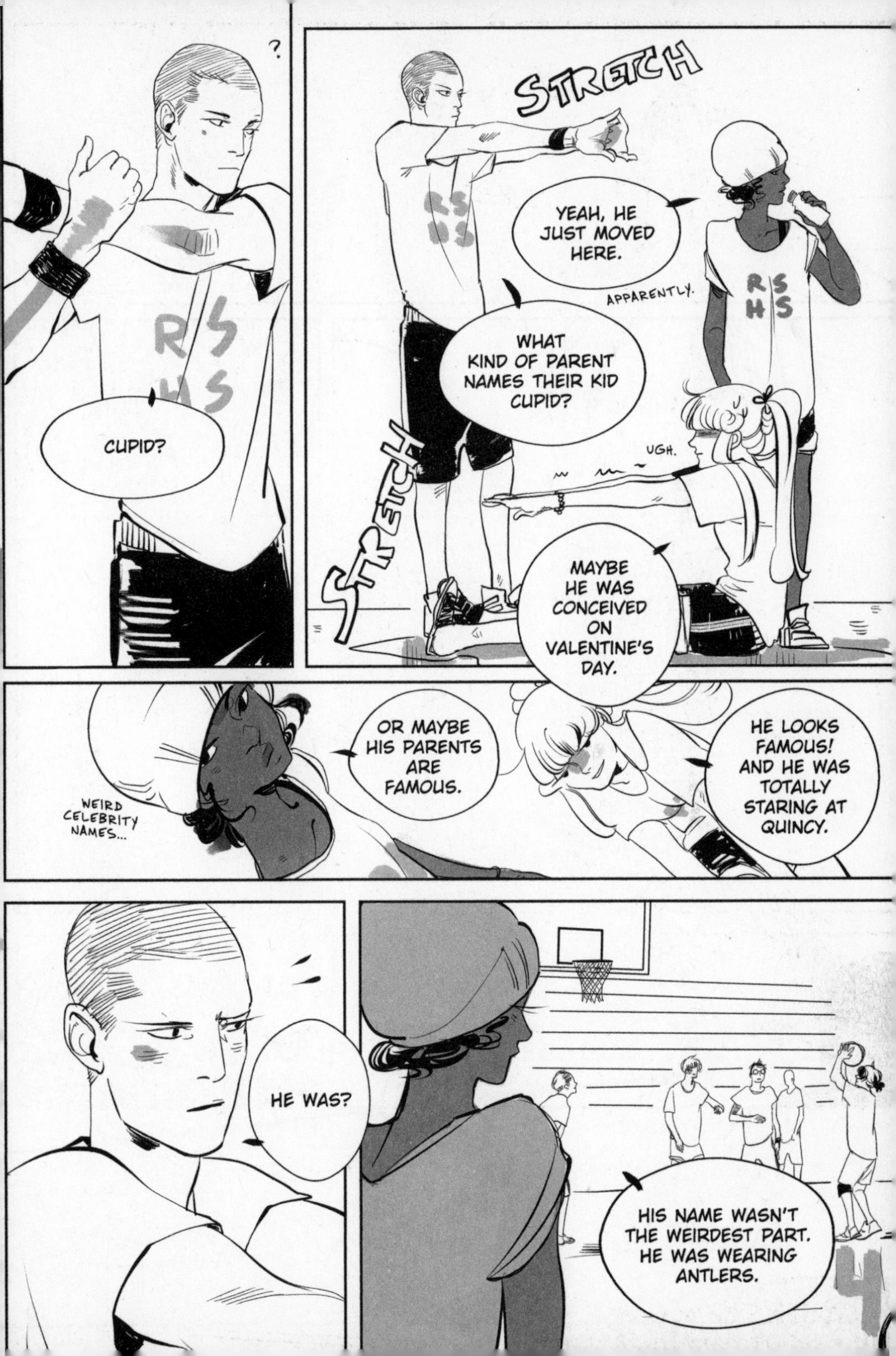
?
CUPID?
STRETCH
YEAH, HE JUST MOVED HERE.
APPARENTLY.
WHAT KIND OF PARENT NAMES THEIR KID CUPID?
STRETCH
UGH.
MAYBE HE WAS CONCEIVED ON VALENTINE'S DAY.
WEIRD CELEBRITY NAMES...
OR MAYBE HIS PARENTS ARE FAMOUS.
HE LOOKS FAMOUS! AND HE WAS TOTALLY STARING AT QUINCY.
HE WAS?
HIS NAME WASN'T THE WEIRDEST PART. HE WAS WEARING ANTLERS.

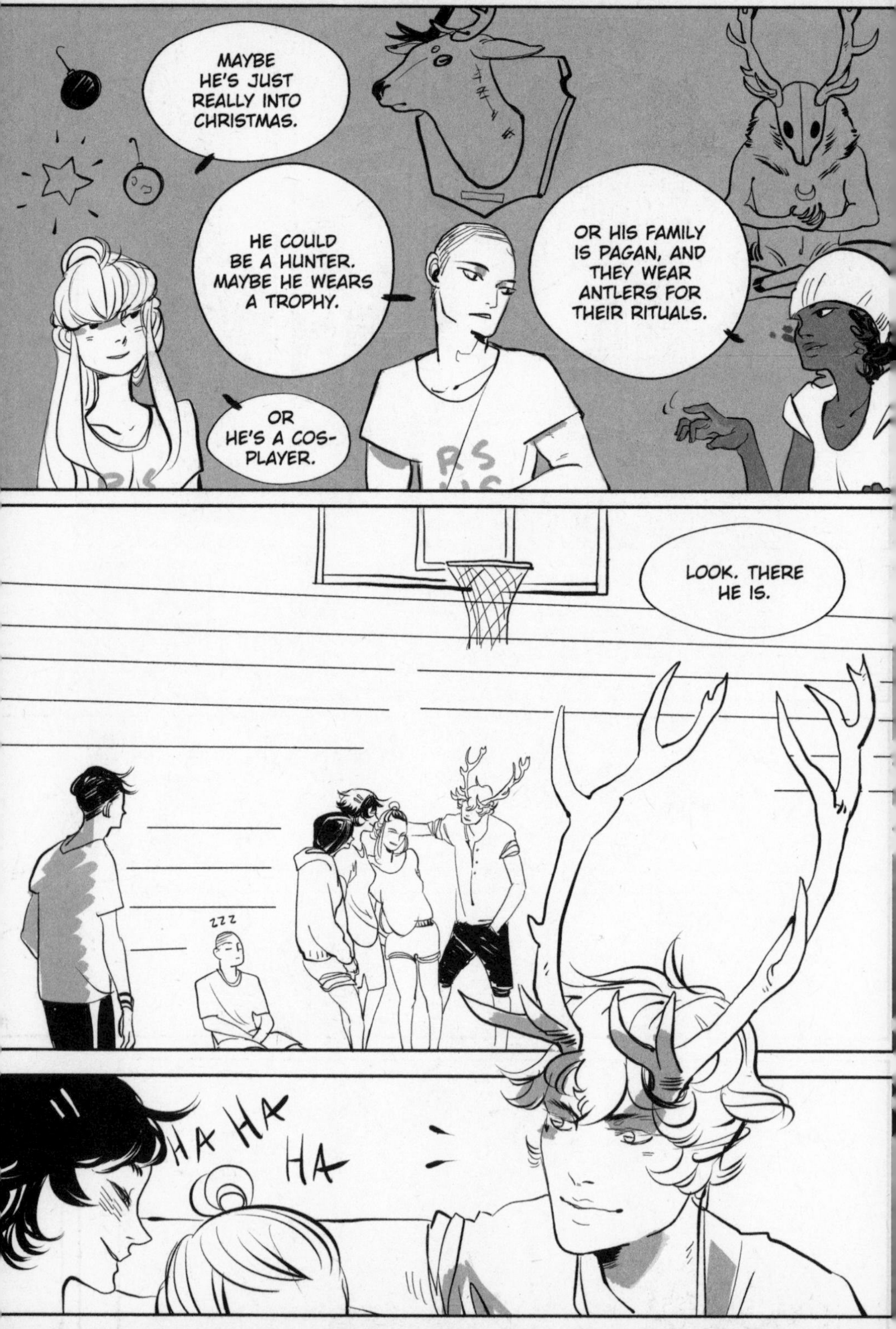
MAYBE HE'S JUST REALLY INTO CHRISTMAS.
HE COULD BE A HUNTER. MAYBE HE WEARS A TROPHY.
OR HE'S A COS-PLAYER.
OR HIS FAMILY IS PAGAN, AND THEY WEAR ANTLERS FOR THEIR RITUALS.
LOOK. THERE HE IS.
ZZZ
HA HA HA

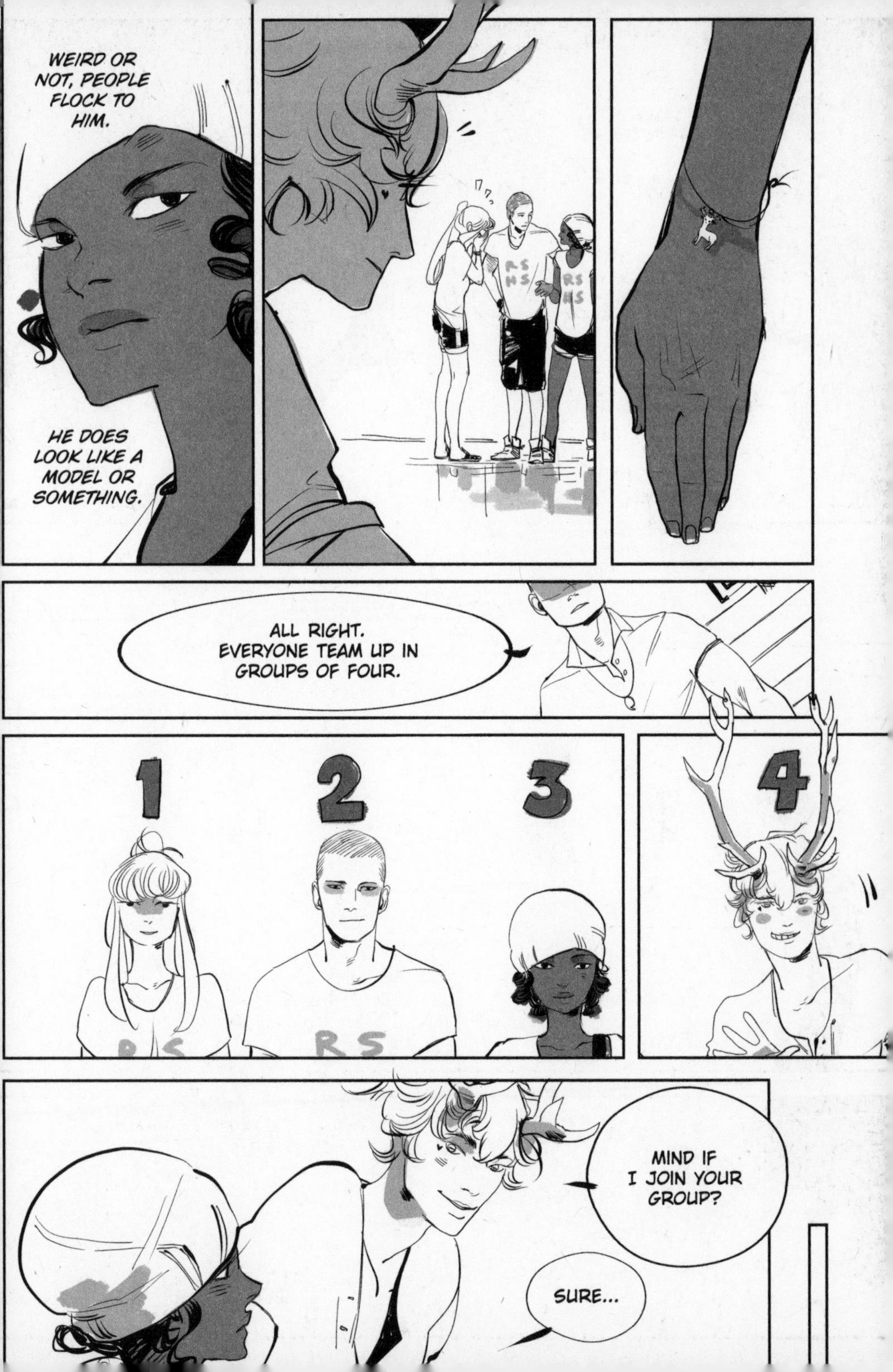
WEIRD OR NOT, PEOPLE FLOCK TO HIM.
HE DOES LOOK LIKE A MODEL OR SOMETHING.
ALL RIGHT. EVERYONE TEAM UP IN GROUPS OF FOUR.
1
2
3
4
MIND IF I JOIN YOUR GROUP?
SURE...

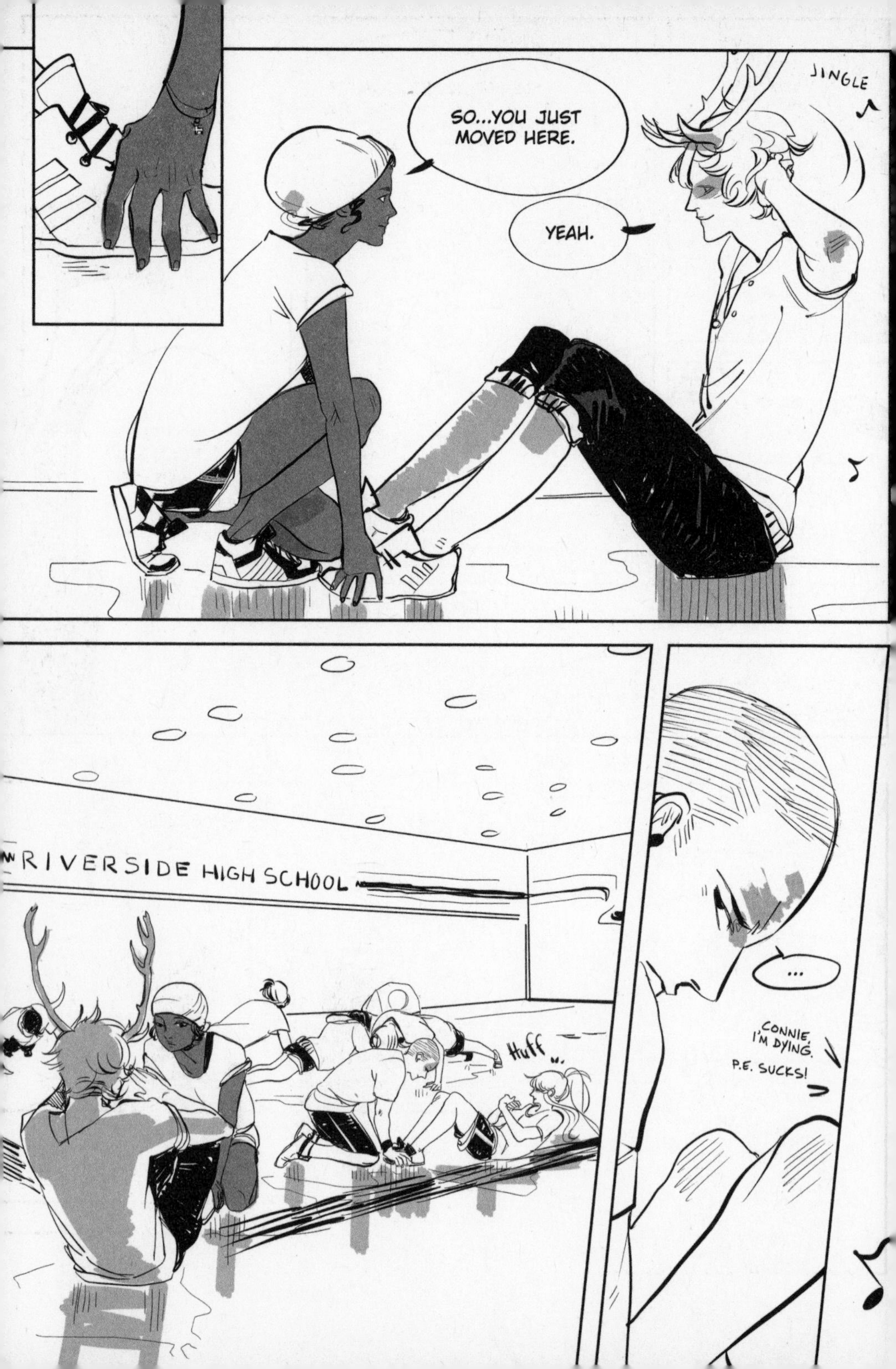
SO...YOU JUST MOVED HERE.
YEAH.
JINGLE
RIVERSIDE HIGH SCHOOL
Huff..
...
CONNIE, I'M DYING.
P.E. SUCKS!

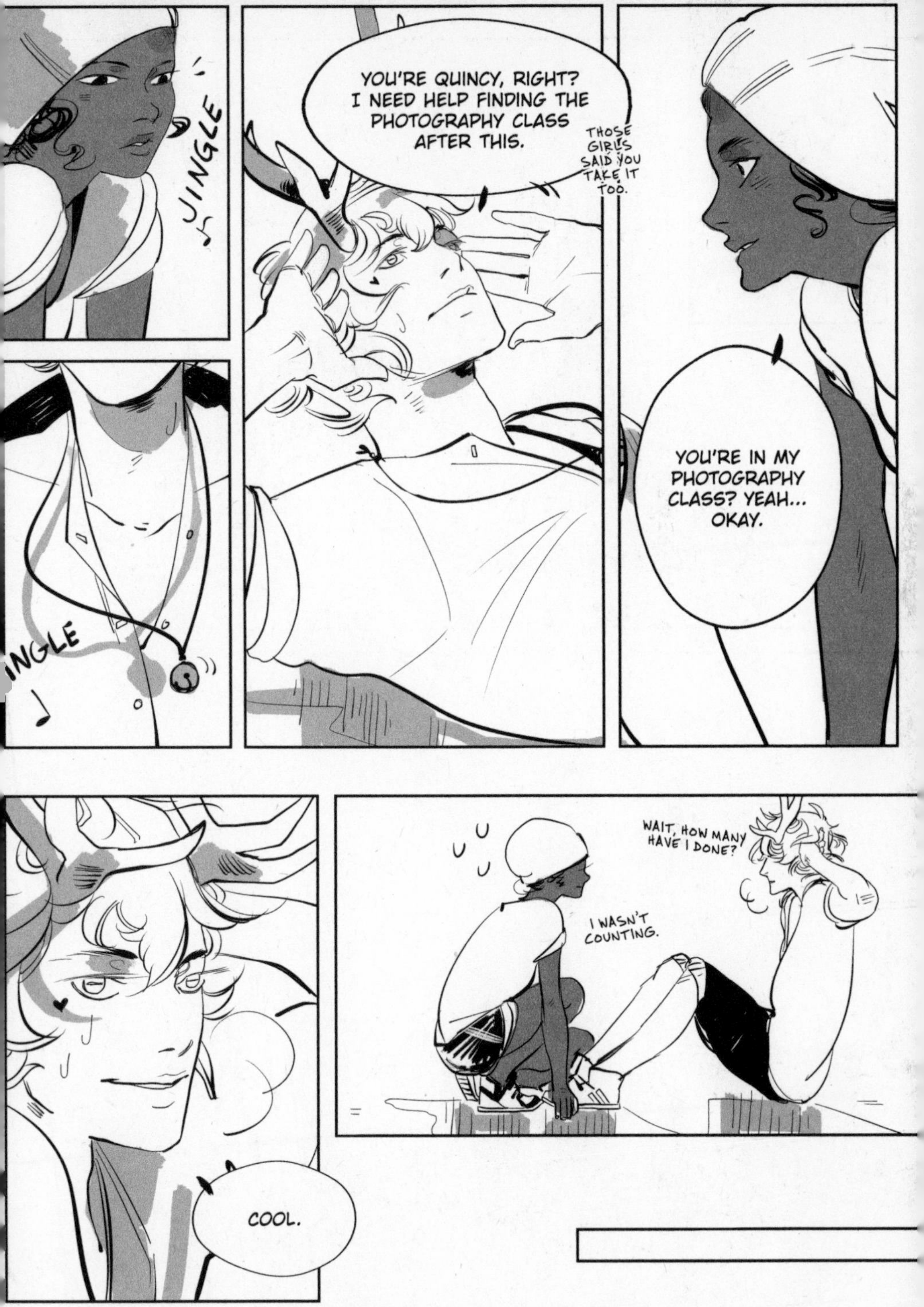
JINGLE
YOU'RE QUINCY, RIGHT? I NEED HELP FINDING THE PHOTOGRAPHY CLASS AFTER THIS.
THOSE GIRLS SAID YOU TAKE IT TOO.
YOU'RE IN MY PHOTOGRAPHY CLASS? YEAH... OKAY.
INGLE
COOL.
WAIT, HOW MANY HAVE I DONE?
I WASN'T COUNTING.

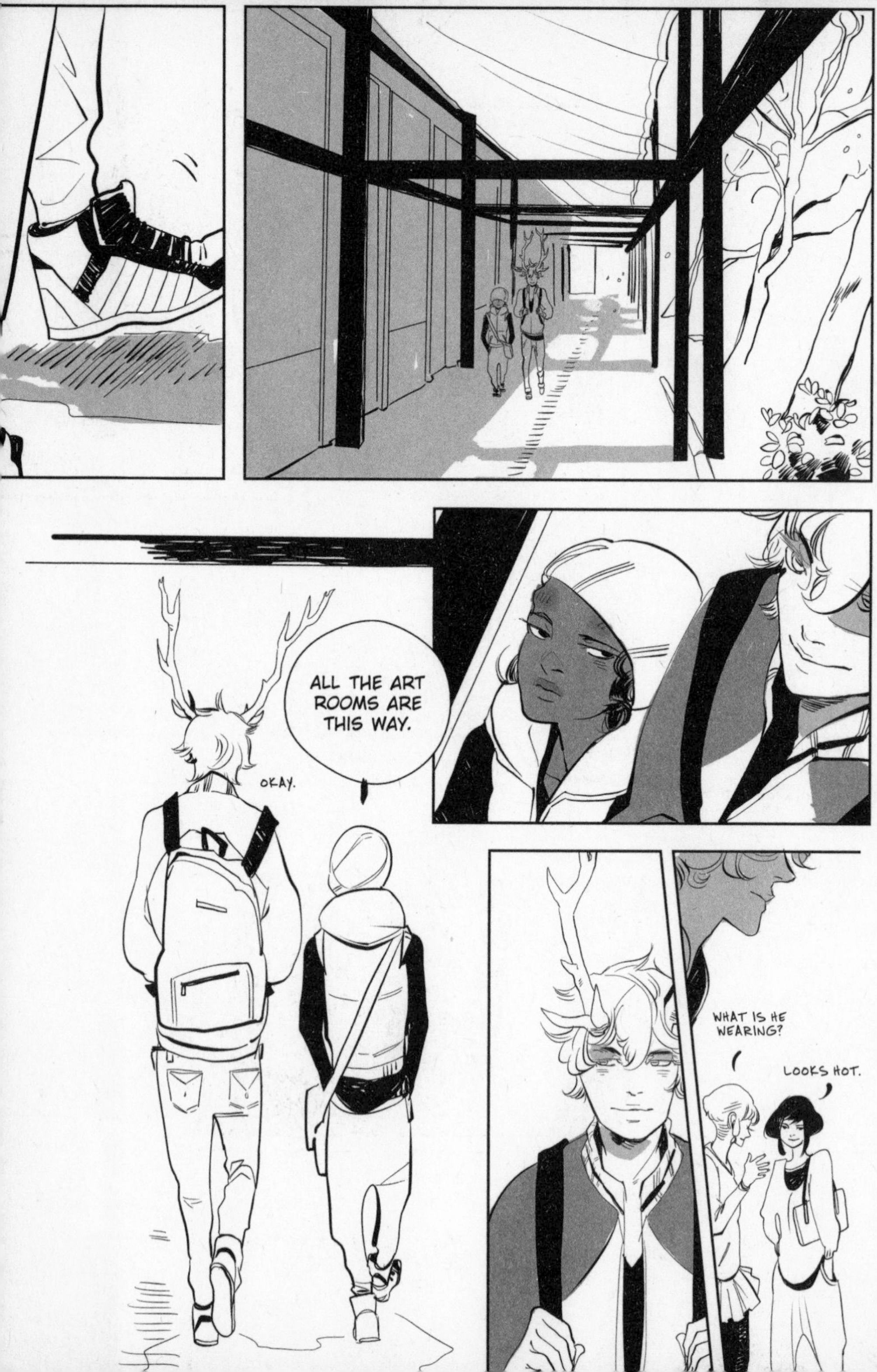
ALL THE ART ROOMS ARE THIS WAY.
OKAY.
WHAT IS HE WEARING?
LOOKS HOT.

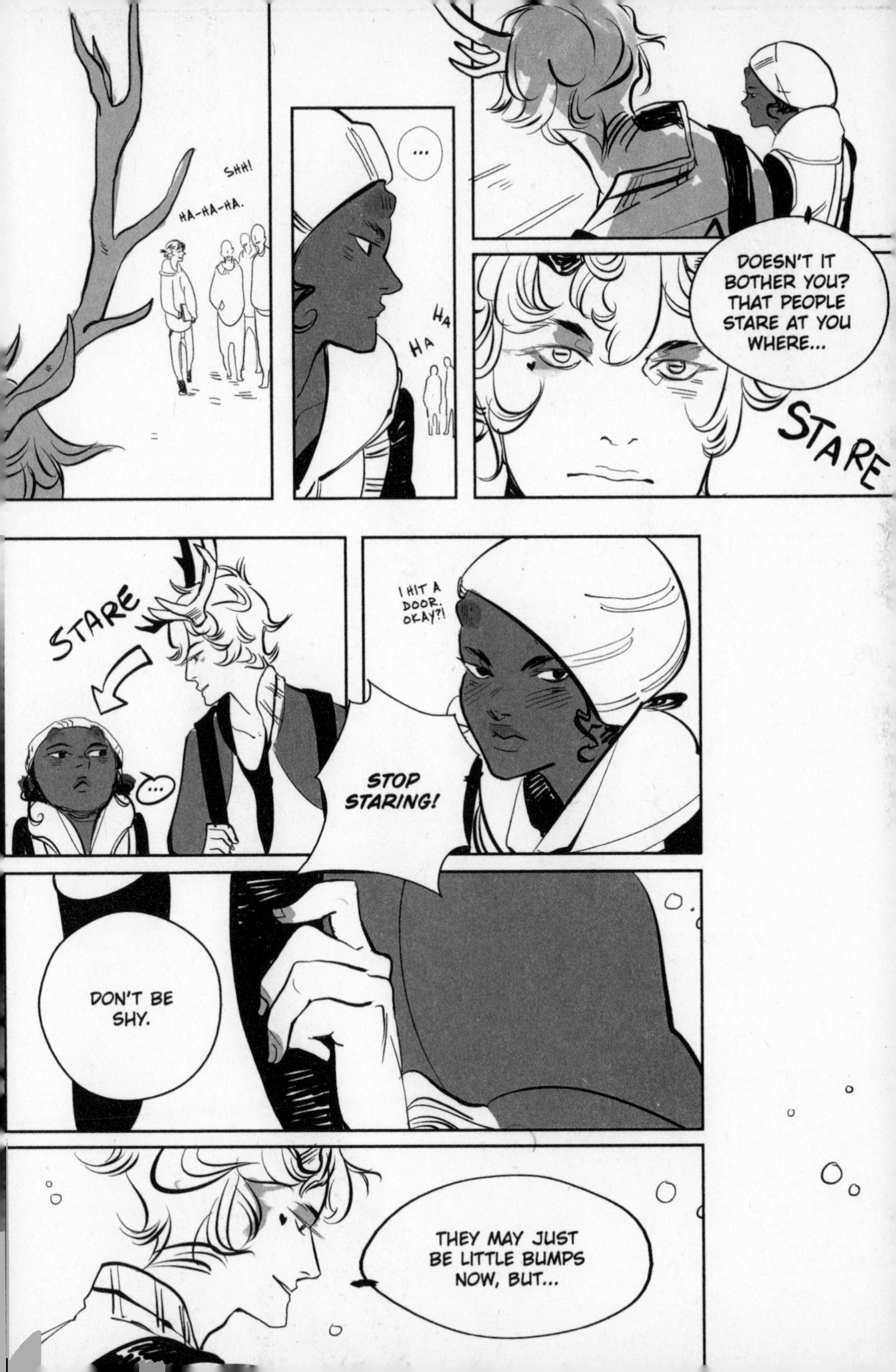
SHH!
HA-HA-HA.
...
HA
HA
DOESN'T IT BOTHER YOU? THAT PEOPLE STARE AT YOU WHERE...
STARE
STARE
...
I HIT A DOOR. OKAY?!
STOP STARING!
DON'T BE SHY.
THEY MAY JUST BE LITTLE BUMPS NOW, BUT...

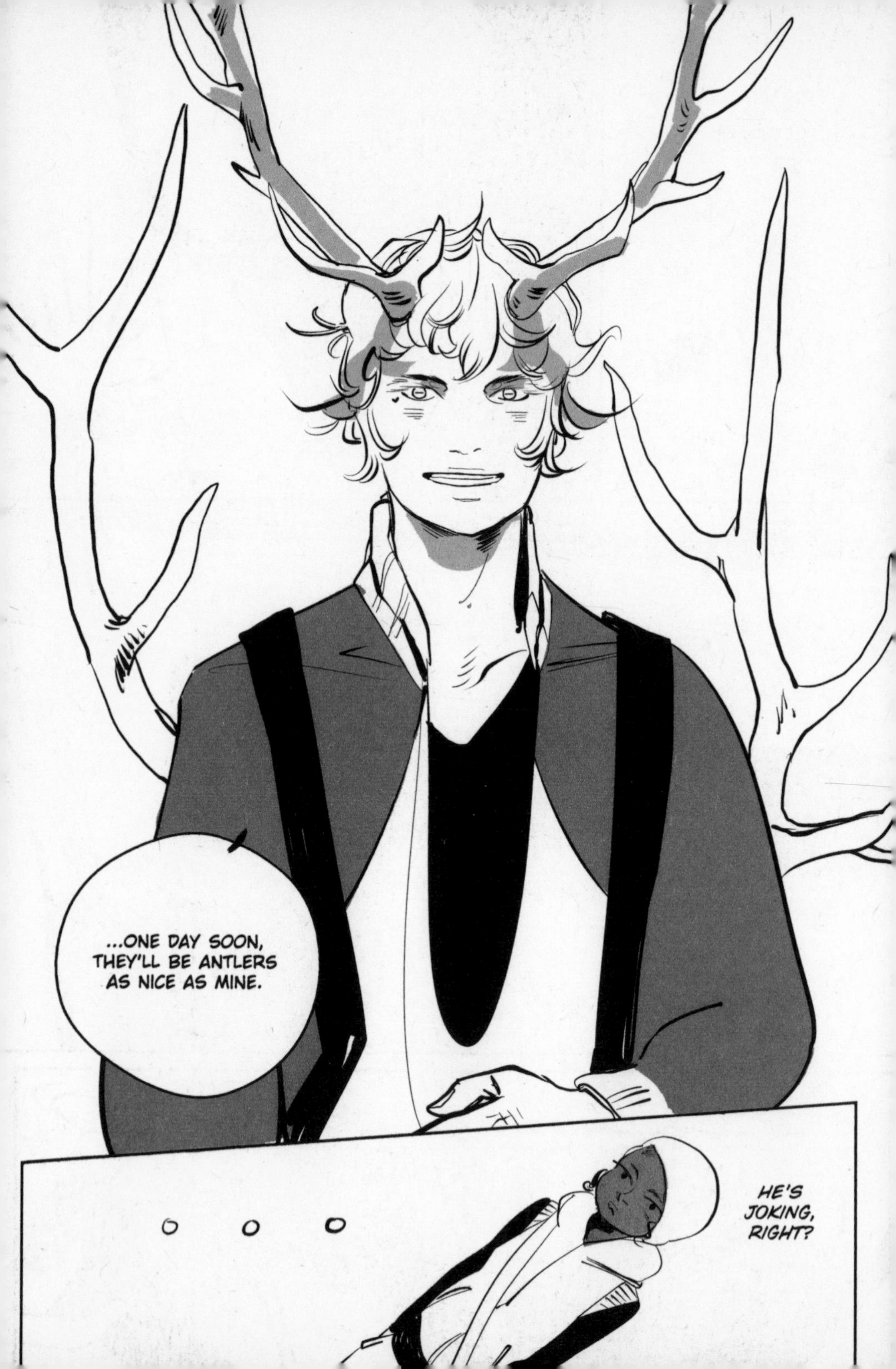
...ONE DAY SOON, THEY'LL BE ANTLERS AS NICE AS MINE.
O O O
HE'S JOKING, RIGHT?

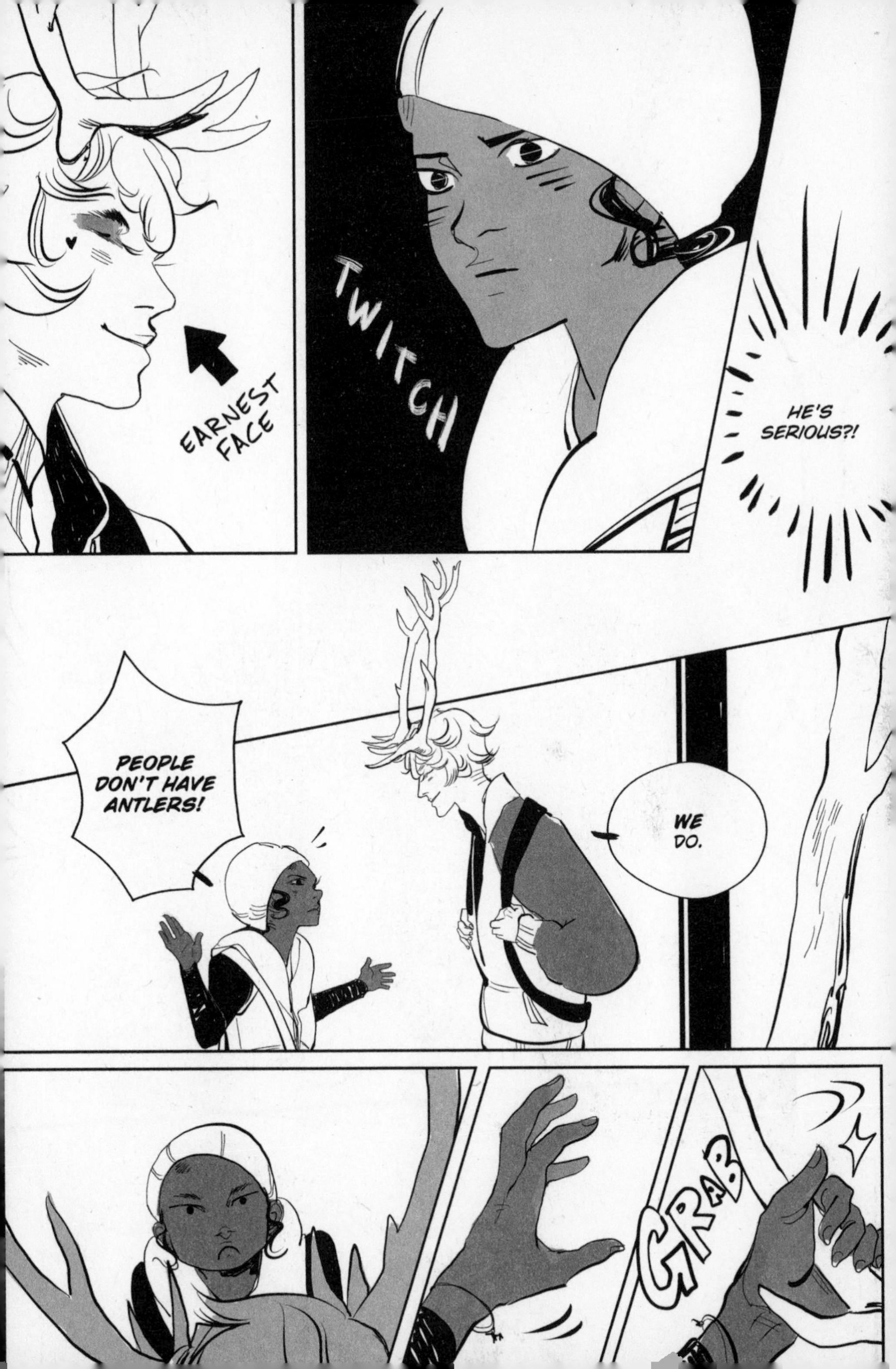
EARNEST FACE
TWITCH
HE'S SERIOUS?!
PEOPLE DON'T HAVE ANTLERS!
WE DO.
GRAB

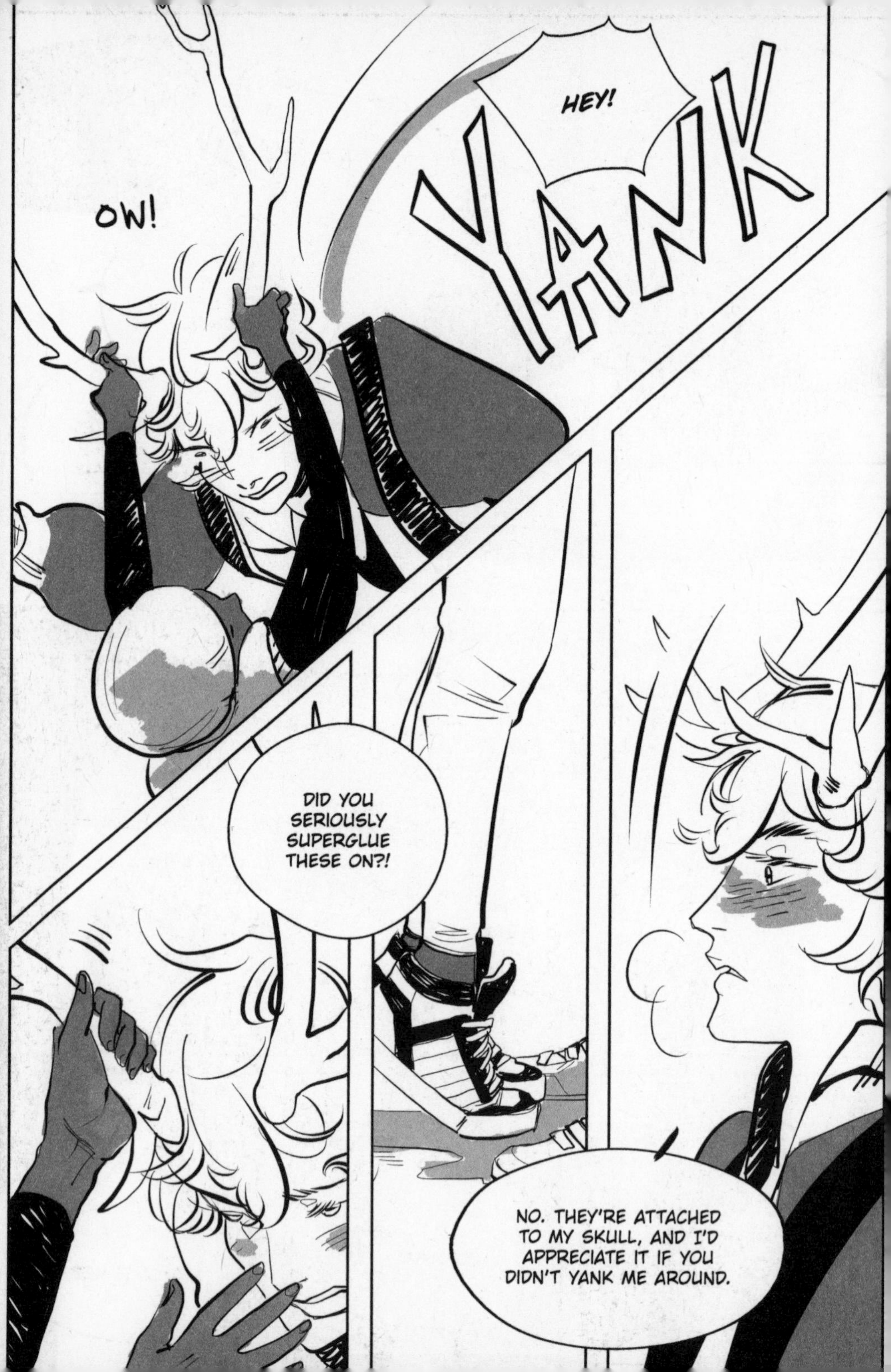
OW!
HEY!
YANK
DID YOU SERIOUSLY SUPERGLUE THESE ON?!
NO. THEY'RE ATTACHED TO MY SKULL, AND I'D APPRECIATE IT IF YOU DIDN'T YANK ME AROUND.

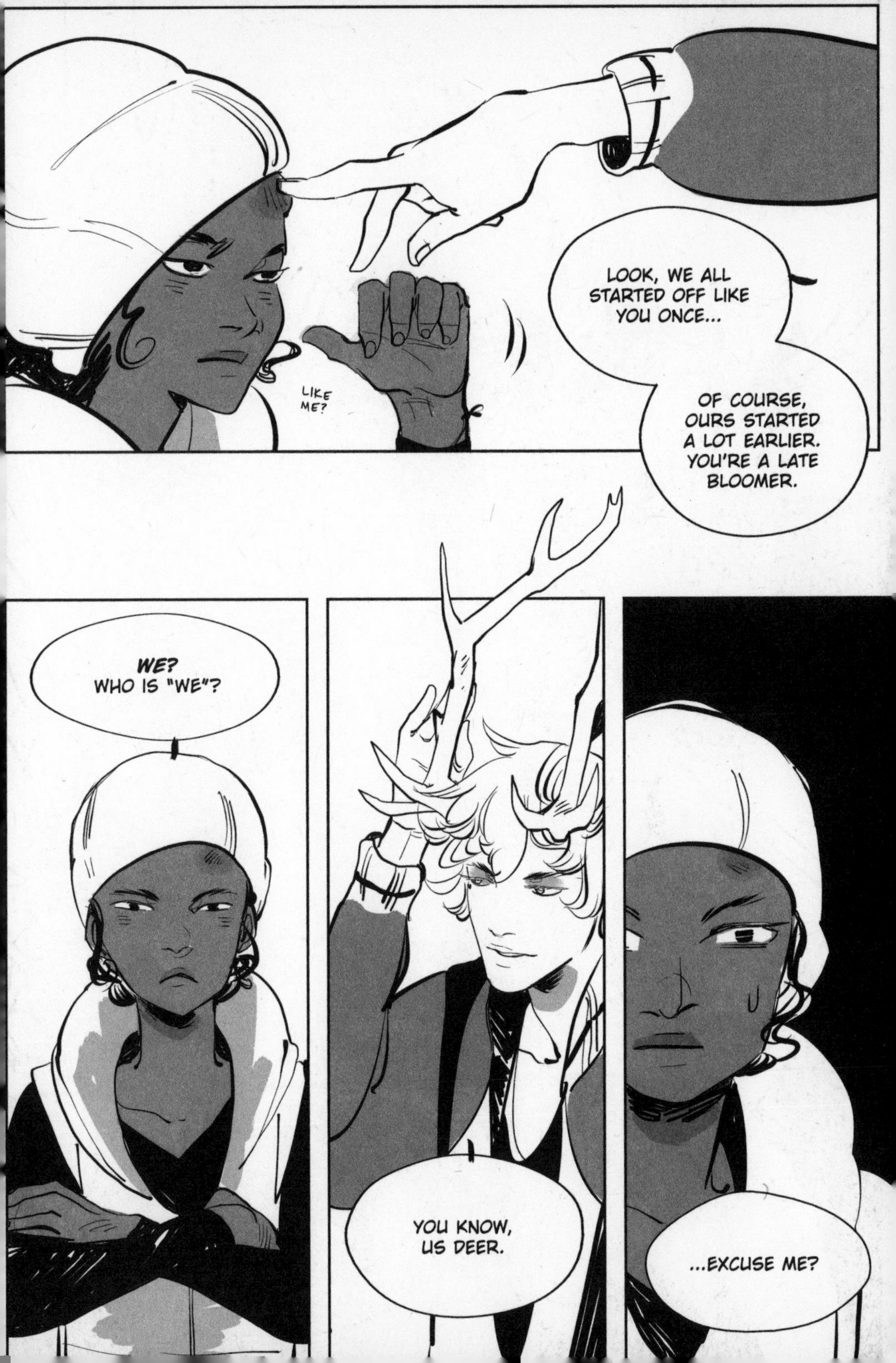
LIKE ME?
LOOK, WE ALL STARTED OFF LIKE YOU ONCE...
OF COURSE, OURS STARTED A LOT EARLIER. YOU'RE A LATE BLOOMER.
WE? WHO IS "WE"?
YOU KNOW, US DEER.
...EXCUSE ME?

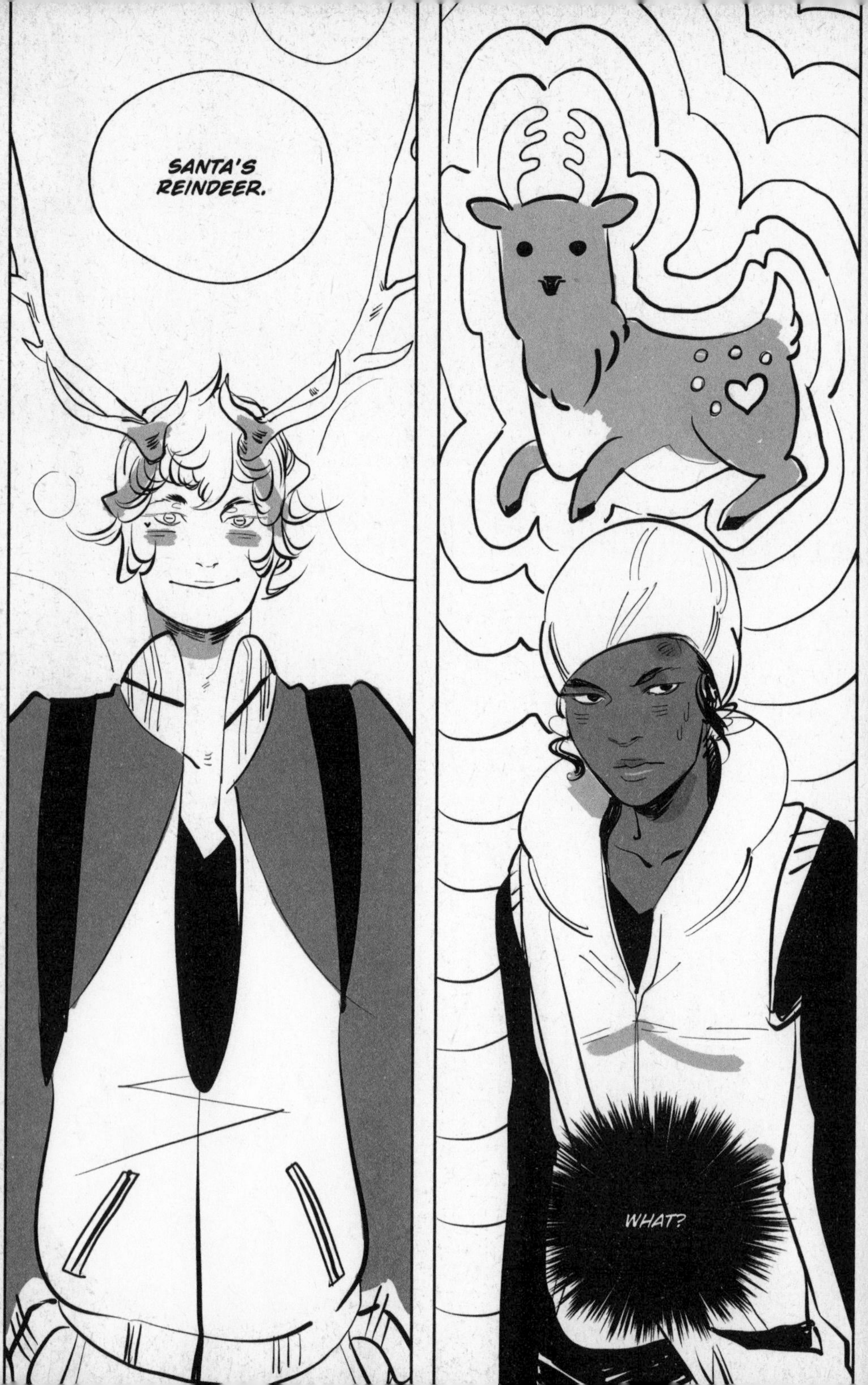
SANTA'S REINDEER.
WHAT?

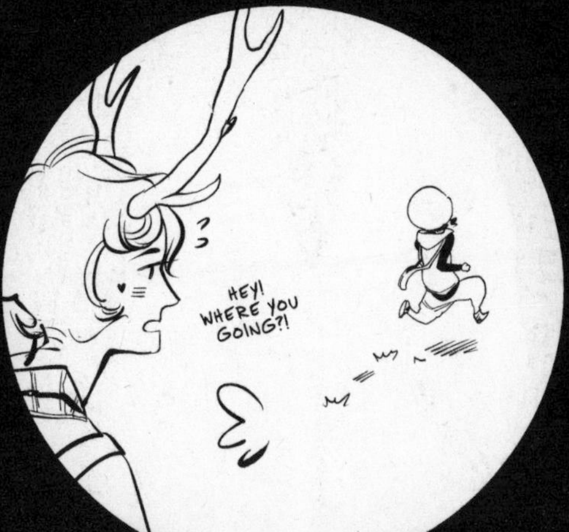
HEY! WHERE YOU GOING?!

Reindeer
Boy

Chapter 2

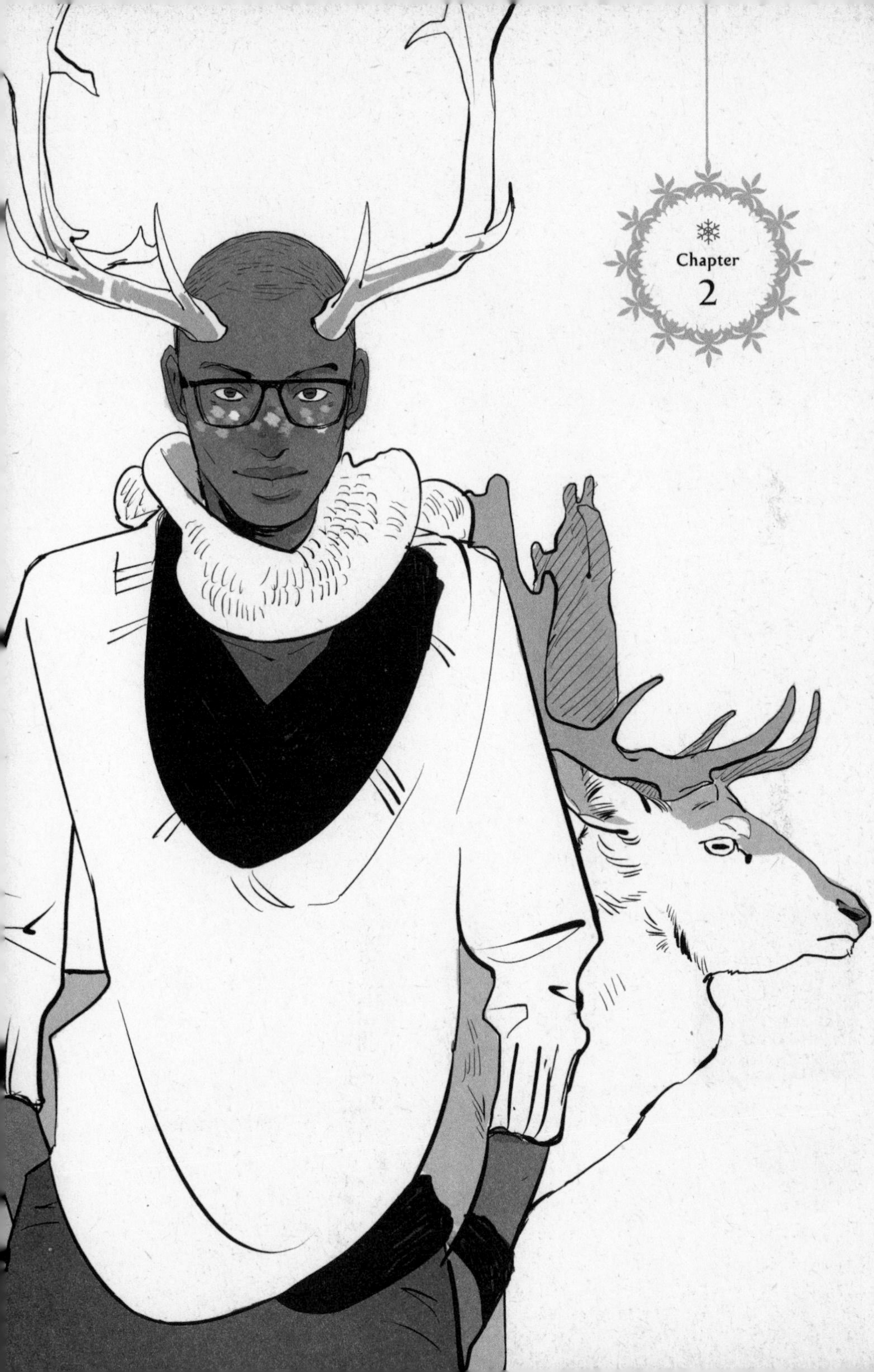

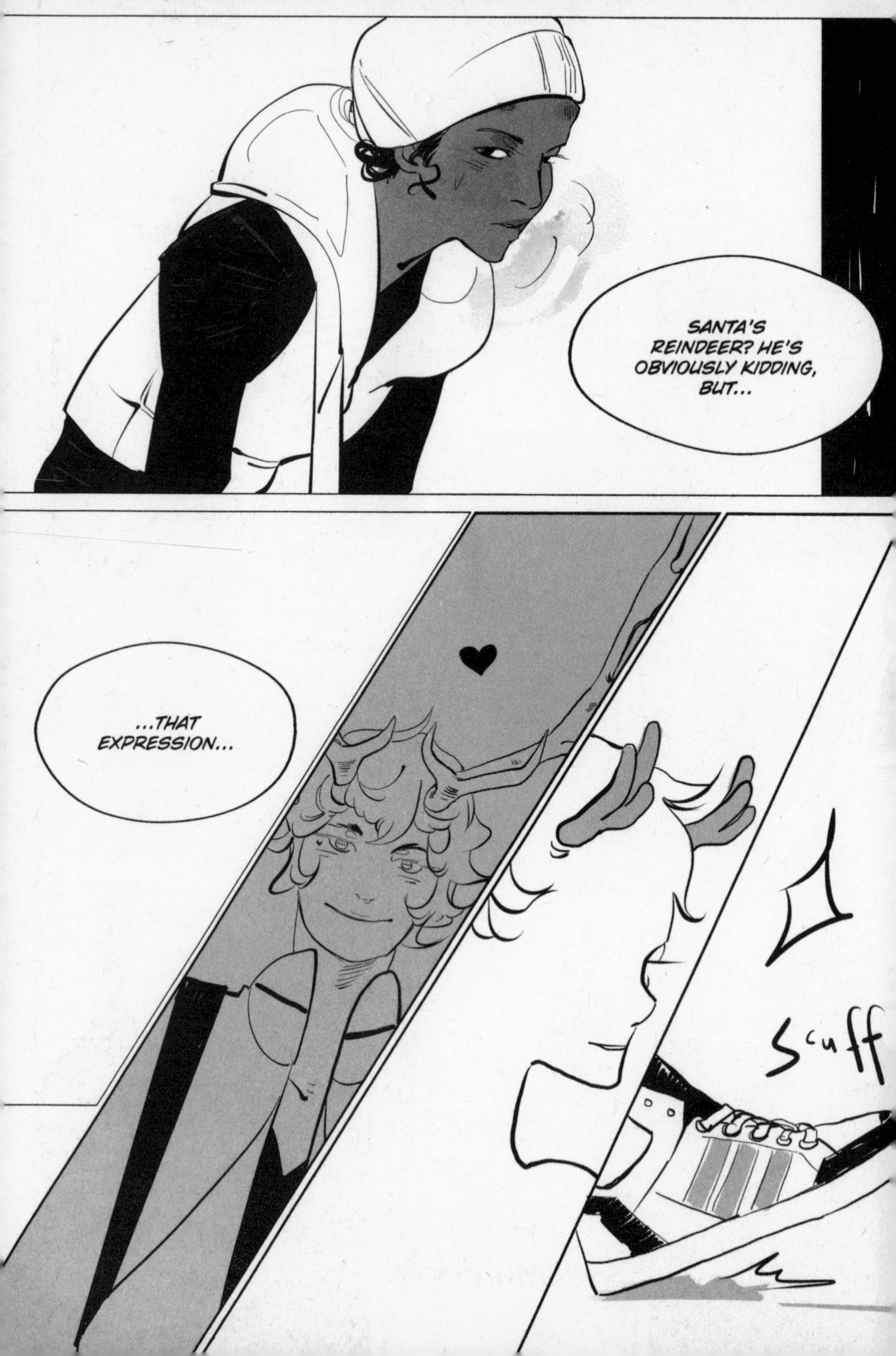
SANTA'S REINDEER? HE'S OBVIOUSLY KIDDING, BUT...
...THAT EXPRESSION...
Scuff

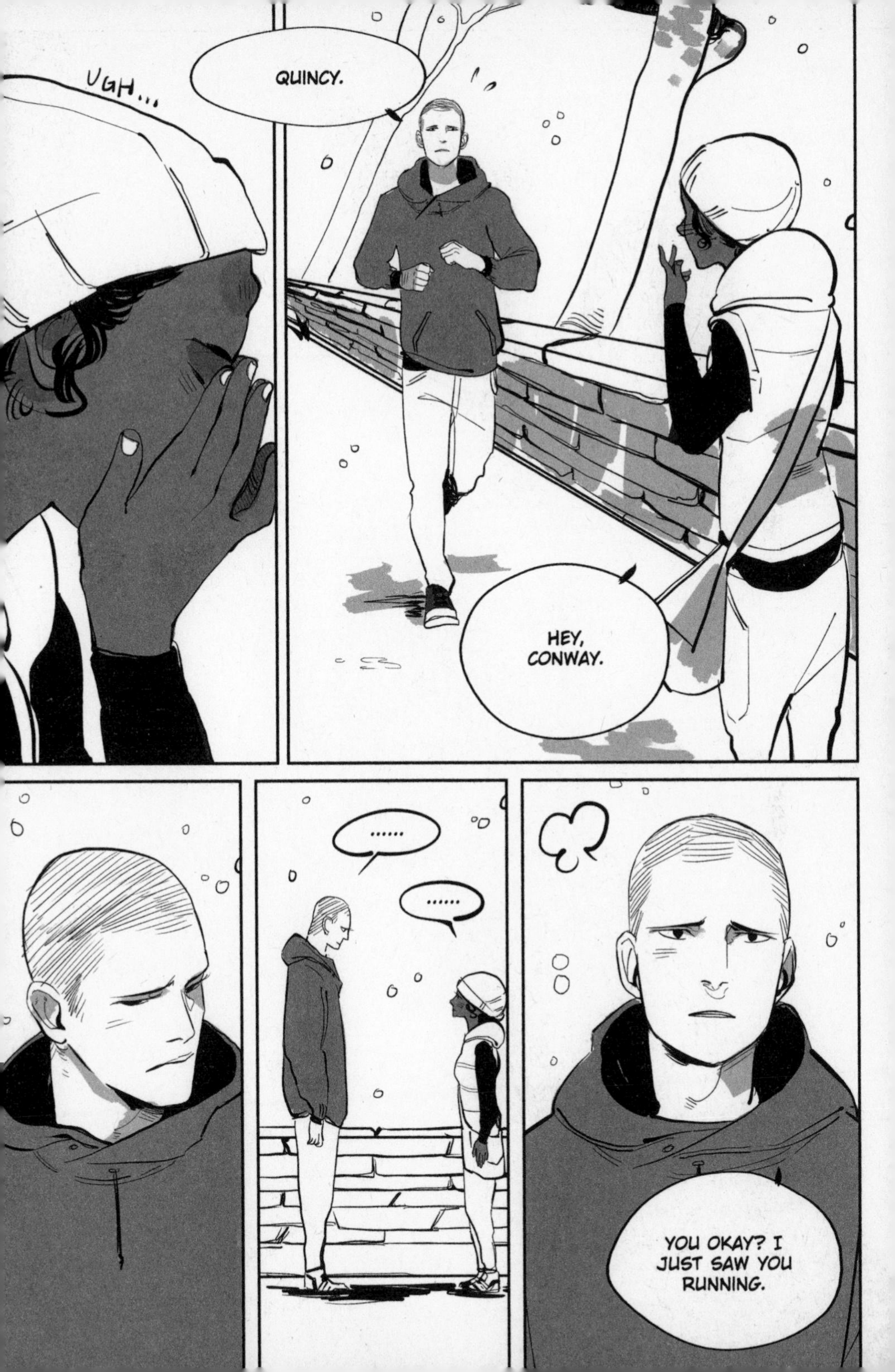
UGH...
QUINCY.
HEY, CONWAY.
......
......
YOU OKAY? I JUST SAW YOU RUNNING.

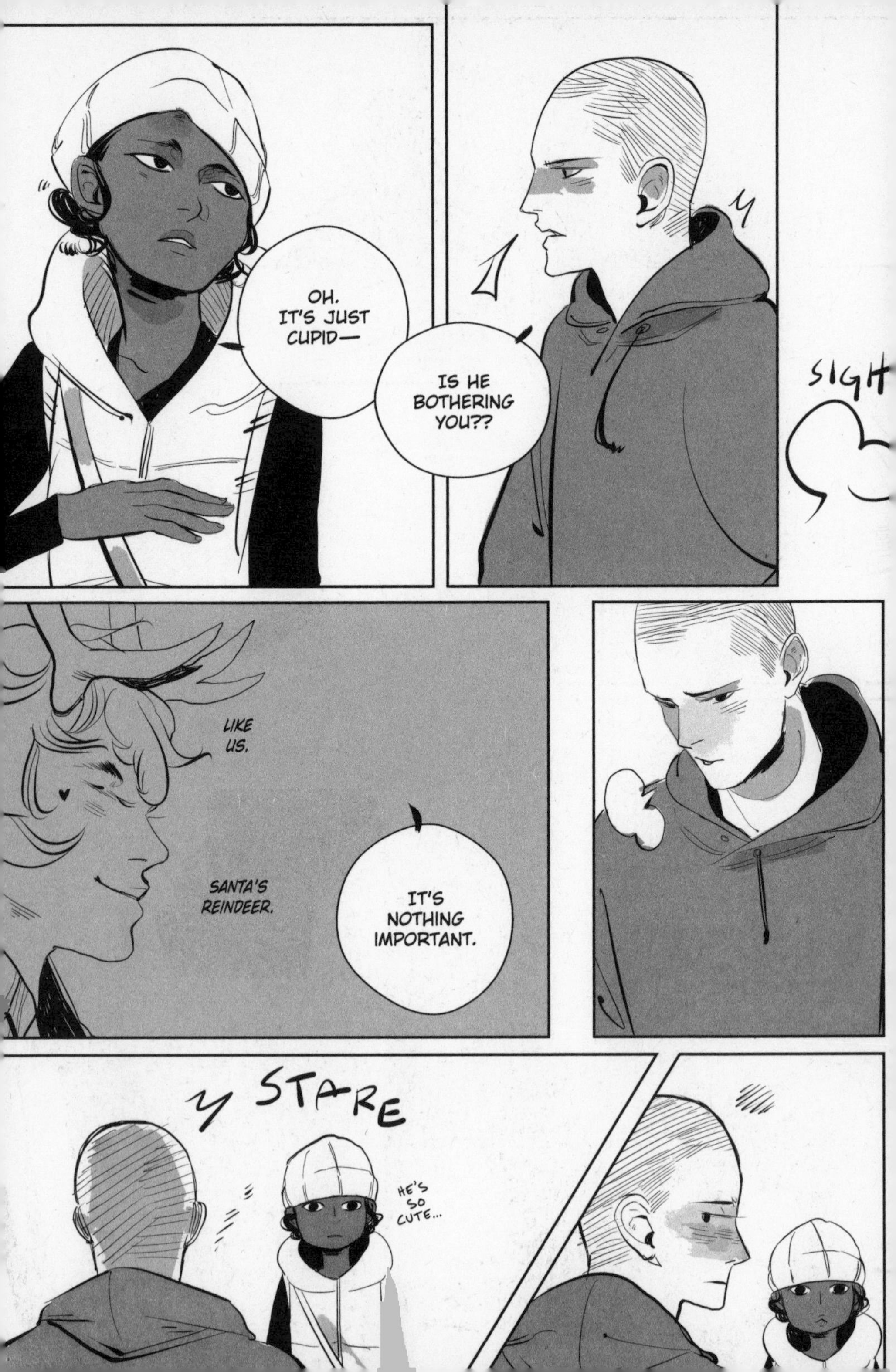
OH. IT'S JUST CUPID—
IS HE BOTHERING YOU??
SIGH
LIKE US.
SANTA'S REINDEER.
IT'S NOTHING IMPORTANT.
STARE
HE'S SO CUTE...

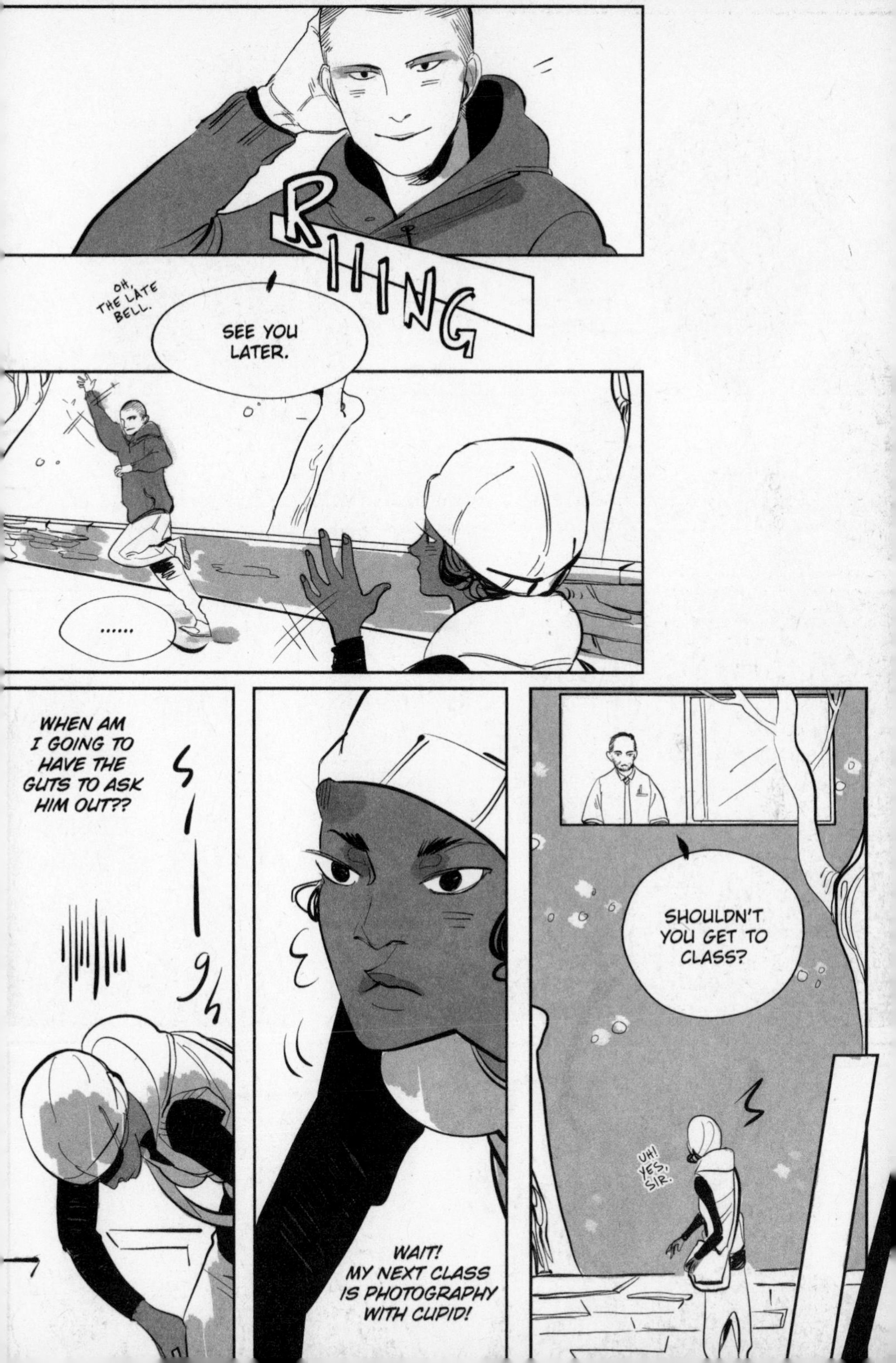

RIIING
OH, THE LATE BELL.
SEE YOU LATER.
......
WHEN AM I GOING TO HAVE THE GUTS TO ASK HIM OUT??
WAIT! MY NEXT CLASS IS PHOTOGRAPHY WITH CUPID!
SHOULDN'T YOU GET TO CLASS?
UH! YES, SIR.

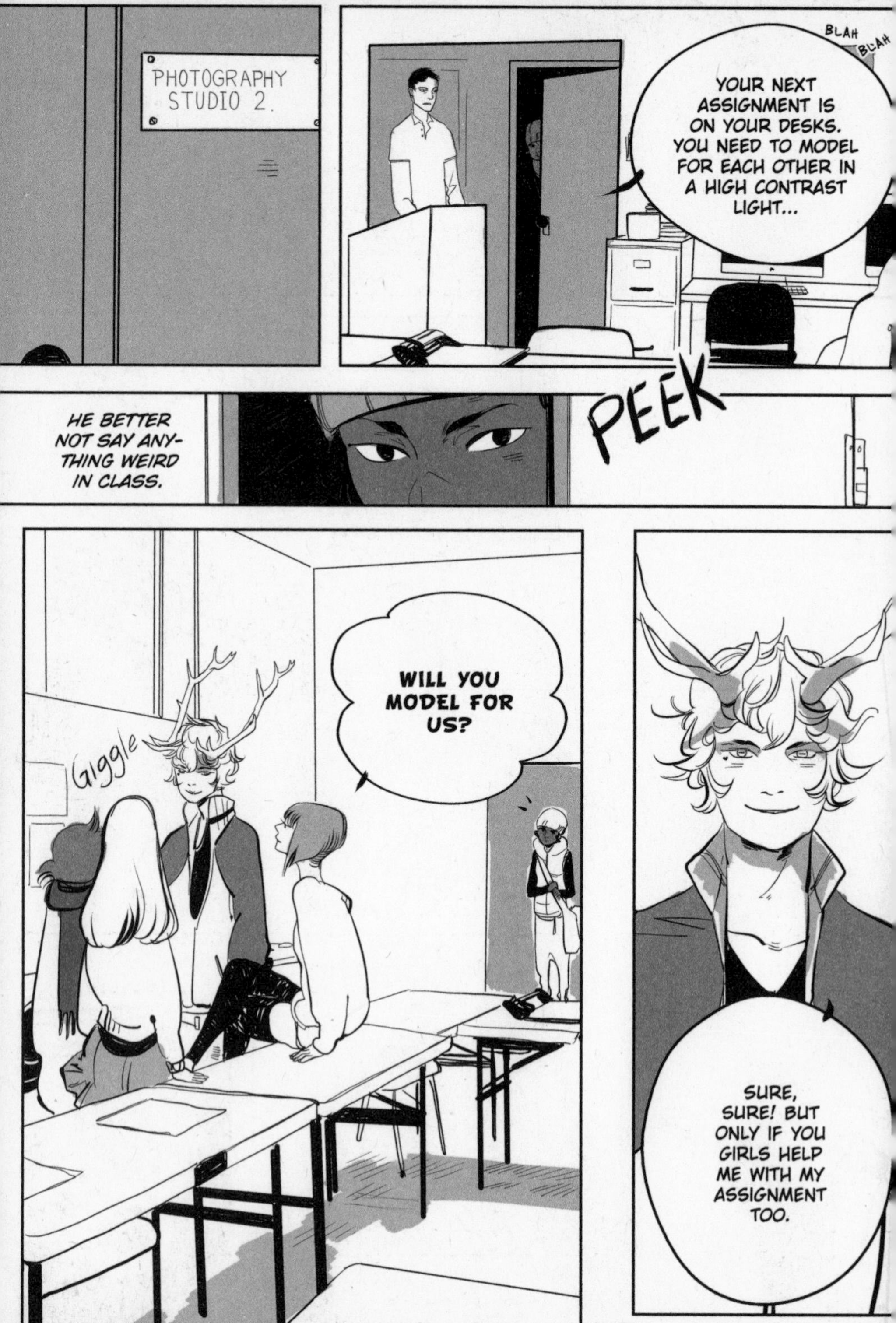
PHOTOGRAPHY STUDIO 2.
BLAH BLAH
YOUR NEXT ASSIGNMENT IS ON YOUR DESKS. YOU NEED TO MODEL FOR EACH OTHER IN A HIGH CONTRAST LIGHT...
HE BETTER NOT SAY ANY-THING WEIRD IN CLASS.
PEEK
Giggle
WILL YOU MODEL FOR US?
SURE, SURE! BUT ONLY IF YOU GIRLS HELP ME WITH MY ASSIGNMENT TOO.

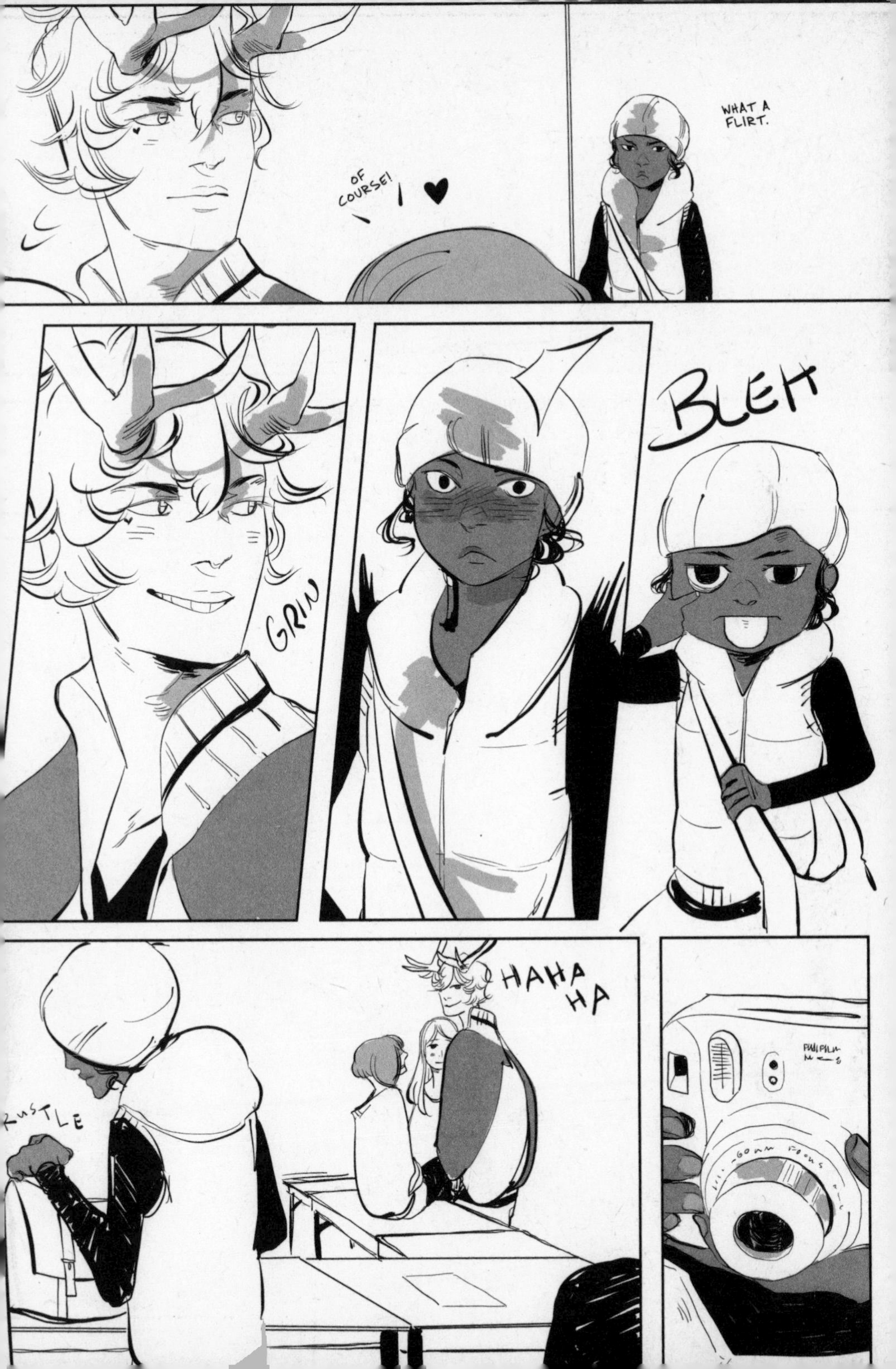
OF COURSE! ♥
WHAT A FLIRT.
GRIN
BLEH
RUSTLE
HAHA HA

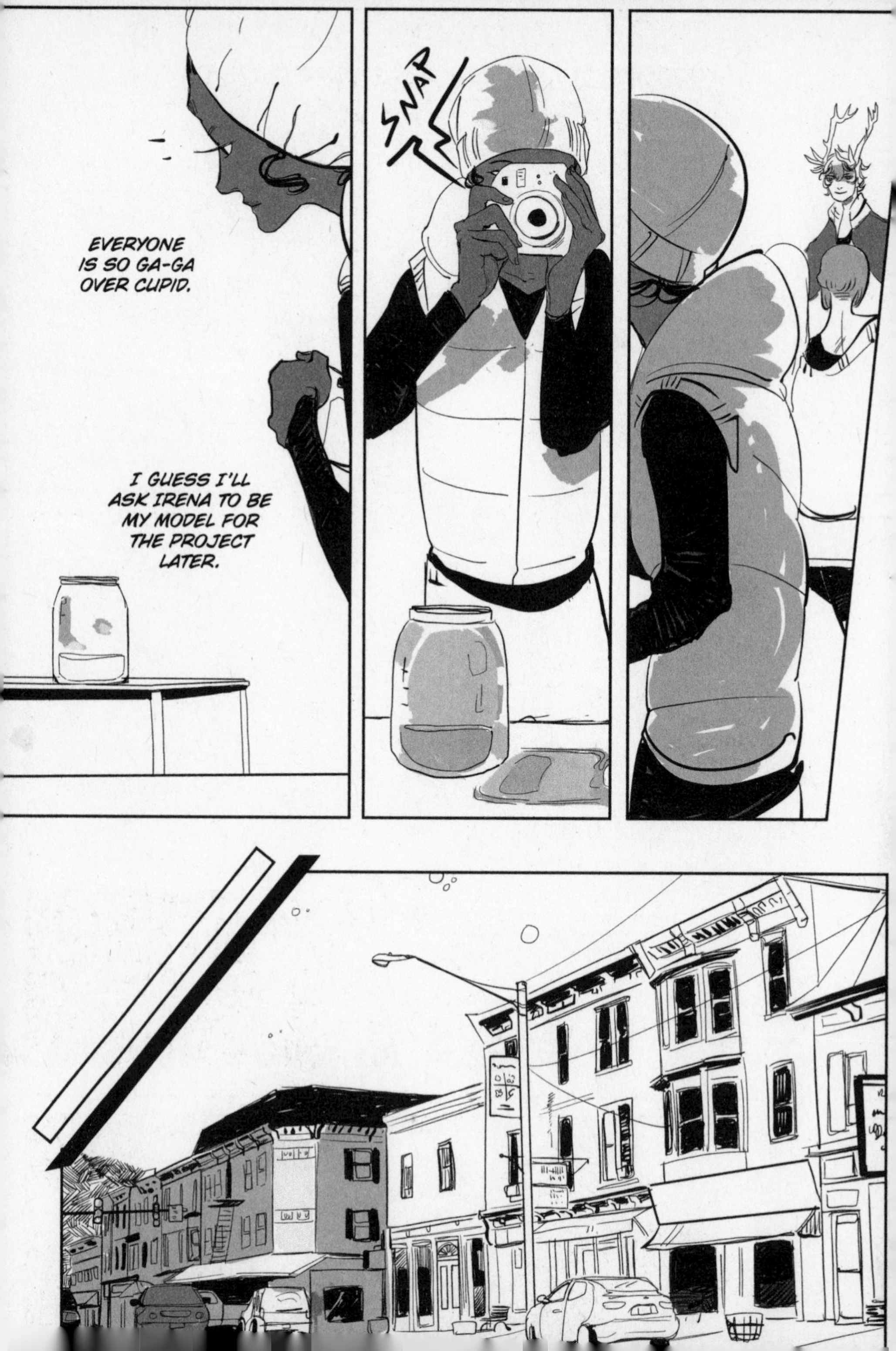
EVERYONE IS SO GA-GA OVER CUPID.
I GUESS I'LL ASK IRENA TO BE MY MODEL FOR THE PROJECT LATER.
SNAP

THE FLOWER SHOP

HELLO, GIRLS.

HI, MS. SANTOS.

HUH?

I WENT TO THE POST OFFICE EARLIER. EVERYONE WAS GOSSIPING ABOUT CUPID.

AT THE RATE HE'S GOING...

MY PACKAGE! THAT WAS FAST.

...HE'LL CHARM THE PANTS OFF EVERYONE IN TOWN.

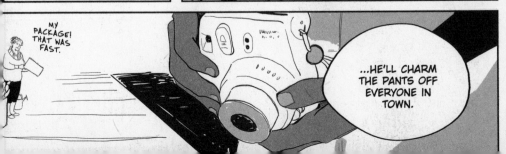

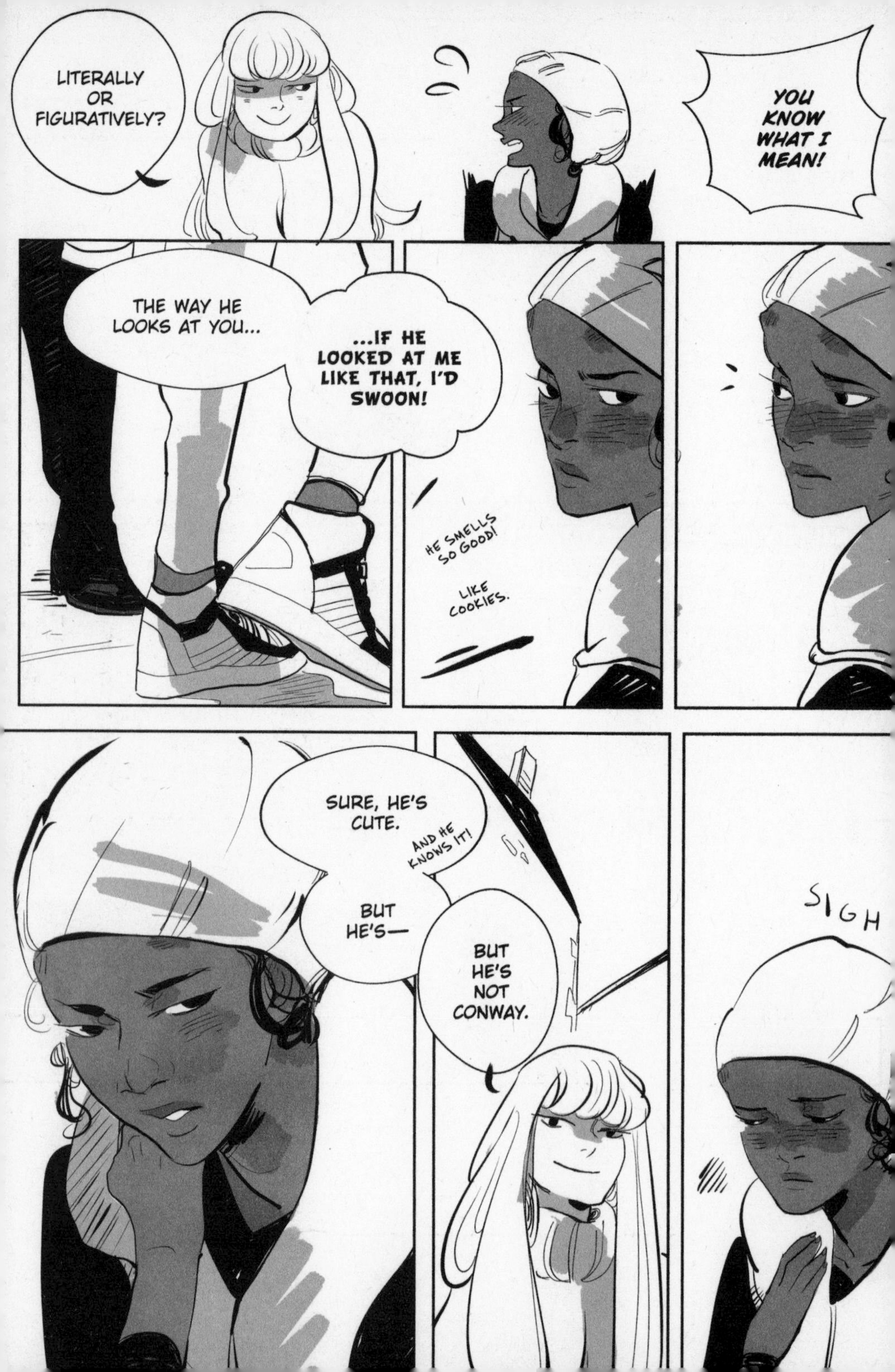
LITERALLY OR FIGURATIVELY?
YOU KNOW WHAT I MEAN!
THE WAY HE LOOKS AT YOU...
...IF HE LOOKED AT ME LIKE THAT, I'D SWOON!
HE SMELLS SO GOOD!
LIKE COOKIES.
SURE, HE'S CUTE.
AND HE KNOWS IT!
BUT HE'S—
BUT HE'S NOT CONWAY.
SIGH

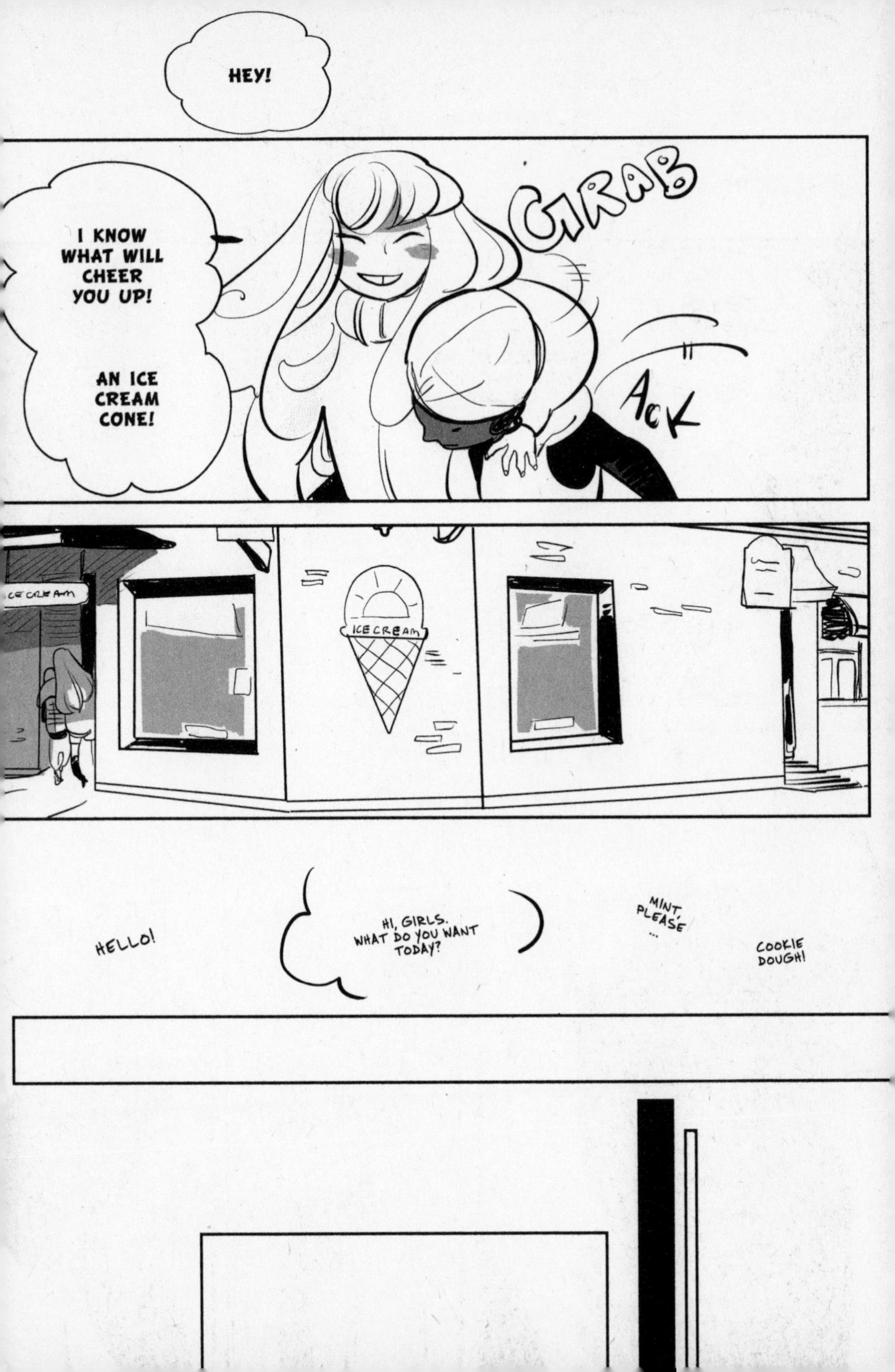

HEY!
I KNOW WHAT WILL CHEER YOU UP!
AN ICE CREAM CONE!
GRAB
ACK
ICE CREAM
ICE CREAM
HELLO!
HI, GIRLS. WHAT DO YOU WANT TODAY?
MINT, PLEASE ...
COOKIE DOUGH!

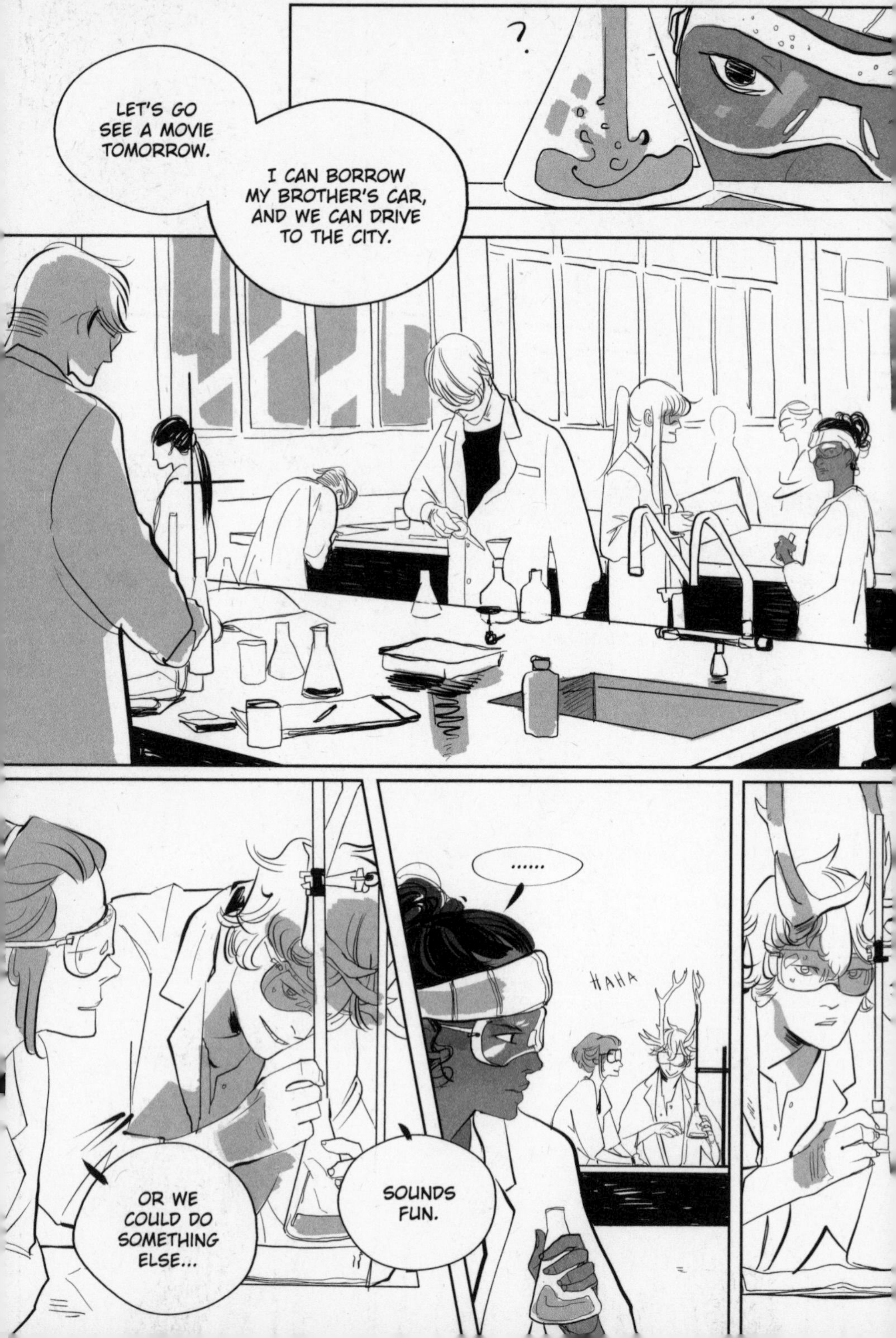
LET'S GO SEE A MOVIE TOMORROW.
I CAN BORROW MY BROTHER'S CAR, AND WE CAN DRIVE TO THE CITY.
?
OR WE COULD DO SOMETHING ELSE...
......
HAHA
SOUNDS FUN.

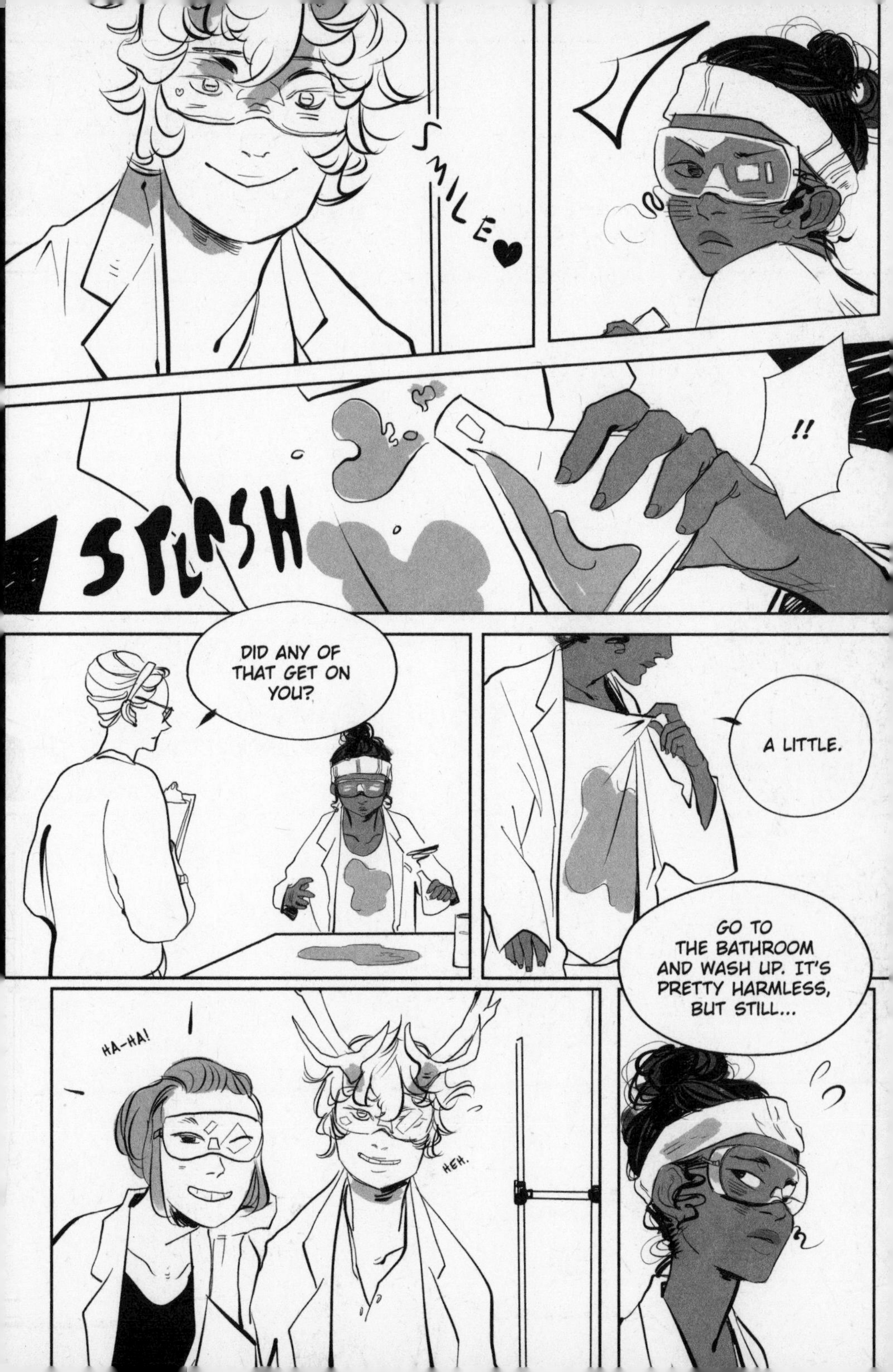
SMILE♥
STPLASH
!!
DID ANY OF THAT GET ON YOU?
A LITTLE.
HA-HA!
HEH.
GO TO THE BATHROOM AND WASH UP. IT'S PRETTY HARMLESS, BUT STILL...

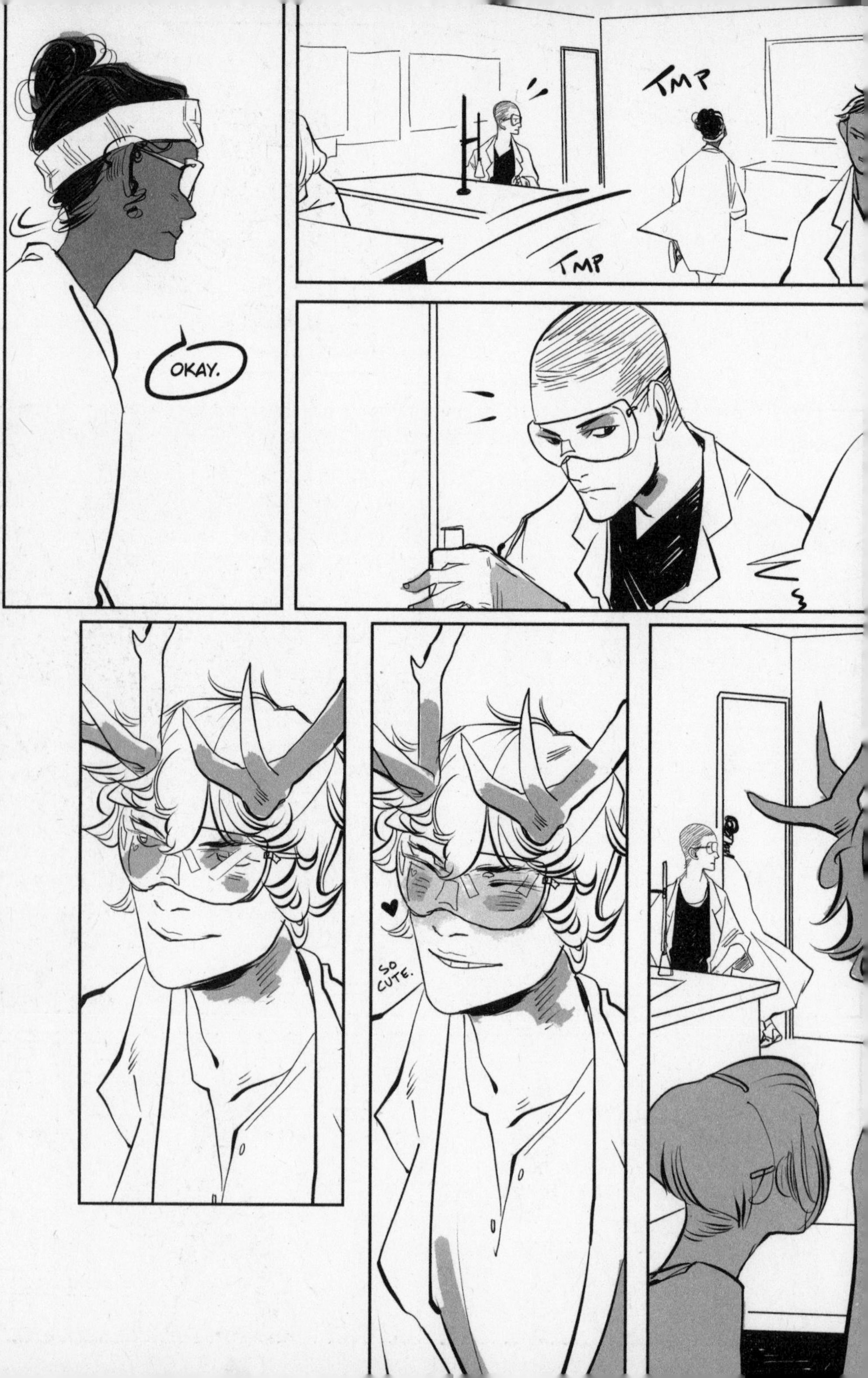
OKAY.
TMP
TMP
SO CUTE.

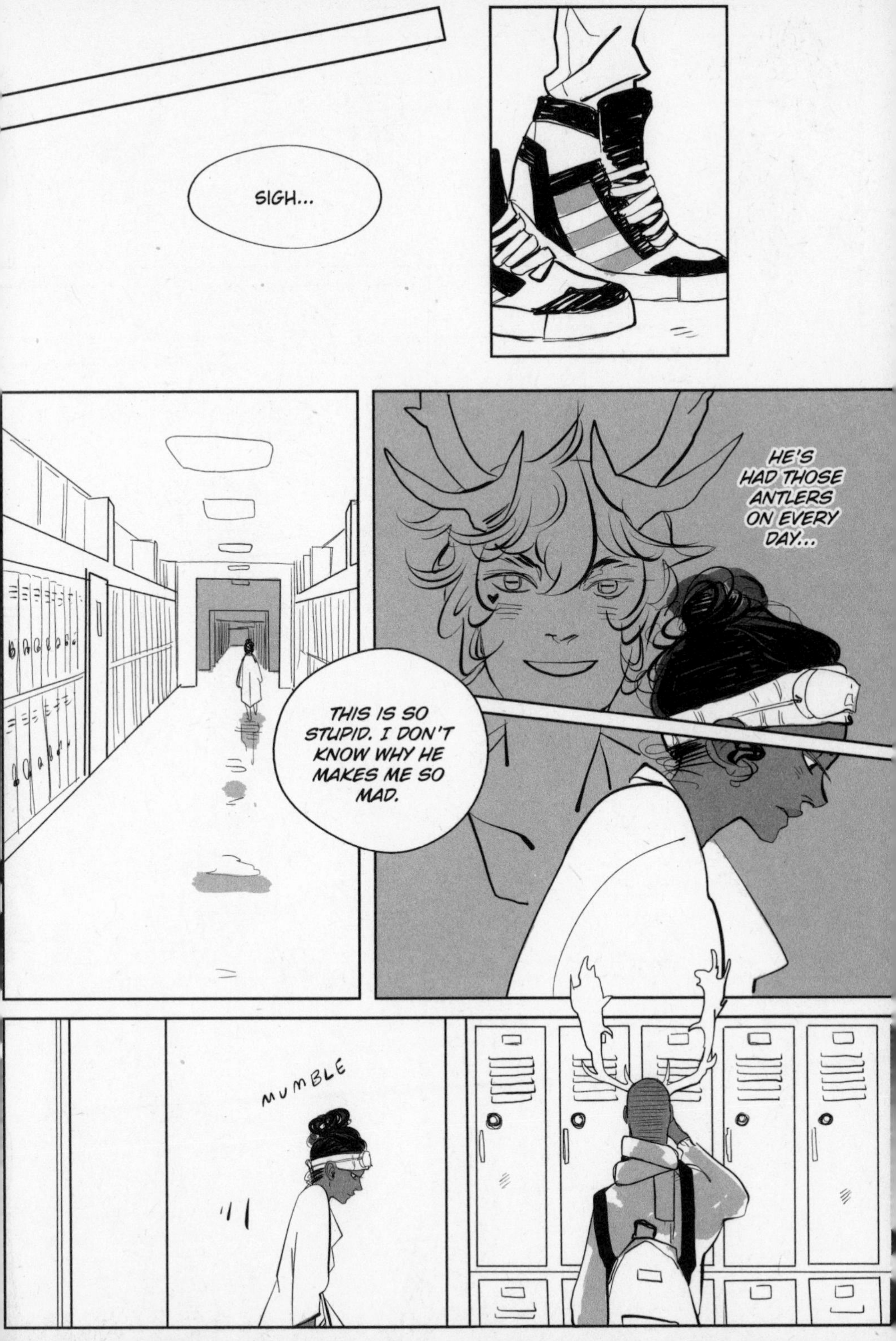

SIGH...
HE'S HAD THOSE ANTLERS ON EVERY DAY...
THIS IS SO STUPID. I DON'T KNOW WHY HE MAKES ME SO MAD.
MUMBLE

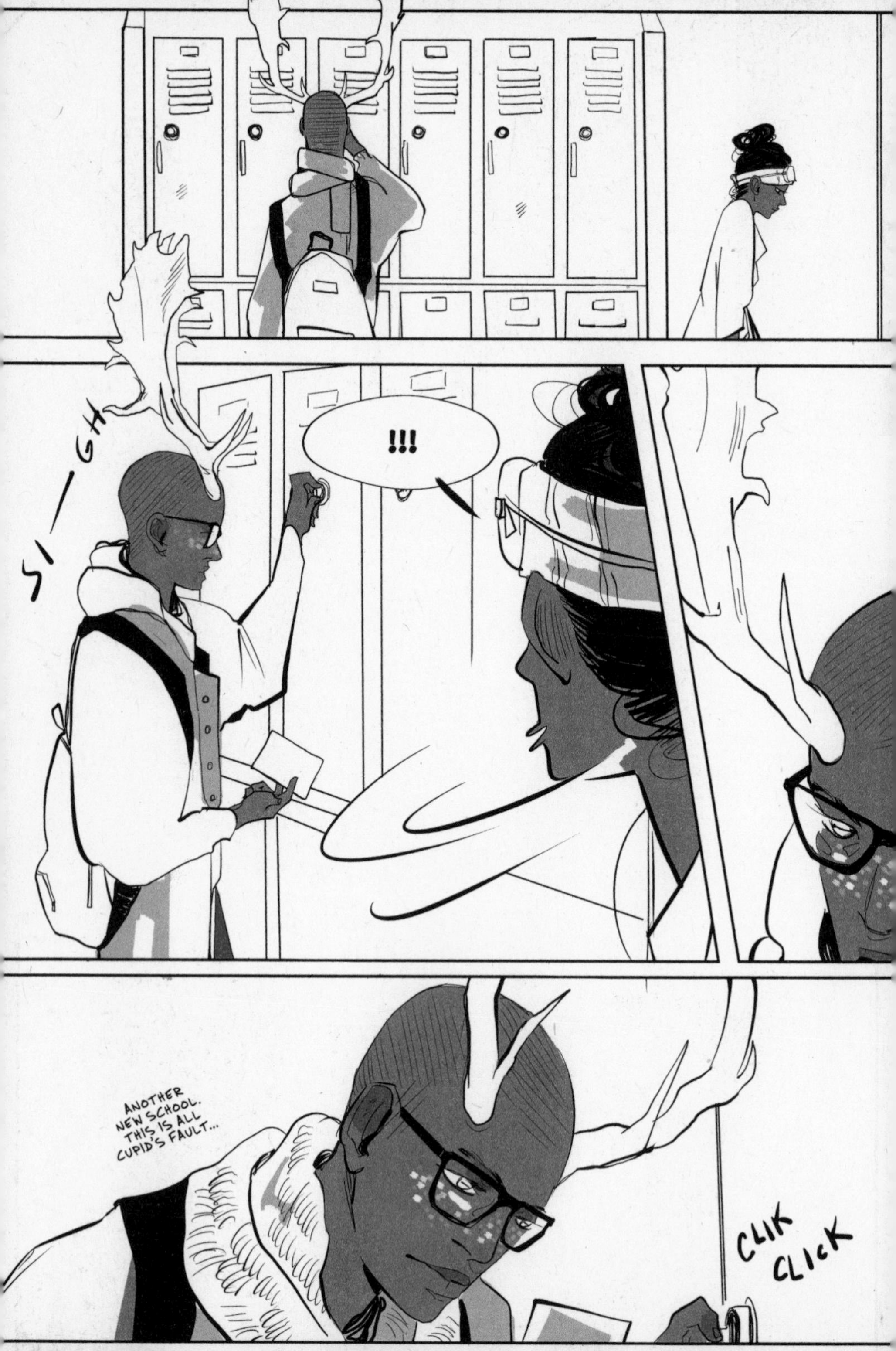
SI—GH
!!!
ANOTHER NEW SCHOOL. THIS IS ALL CUPID'S FAULT...
CLIK
CLICK

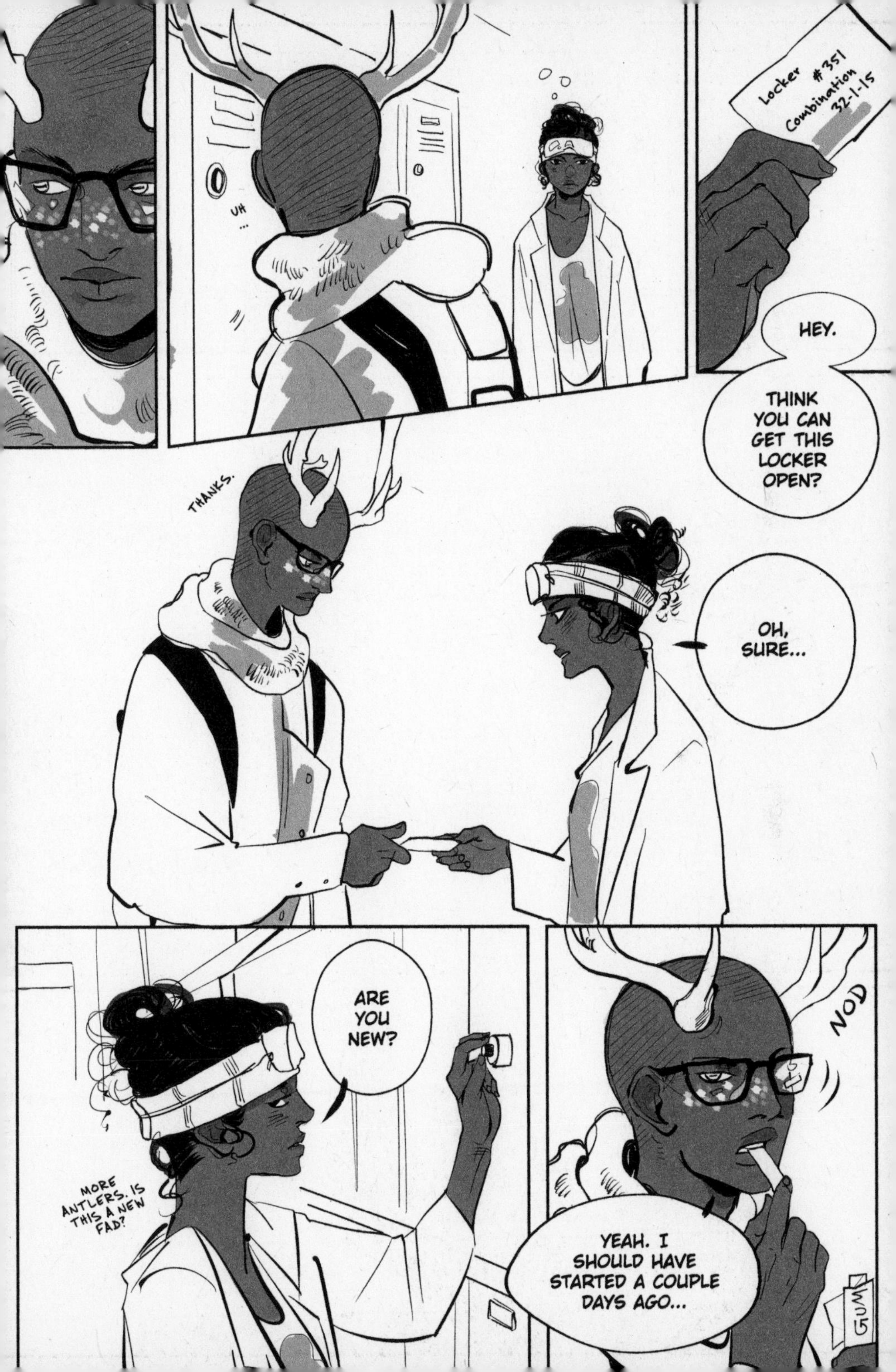
UH ...
Locker #351 Combination 32-1-15
HEY.
THINK YOU CAN GET THIS LOCKER OPEN?
THANKS.
OH, SURE...
ARE YOU NEW?
MORE ANTLERS. IS THIS A NEW FAD?
NOD
YEAH. I SHOULD HAVE STARTED A COUPLE DAYS AGO...
GUM

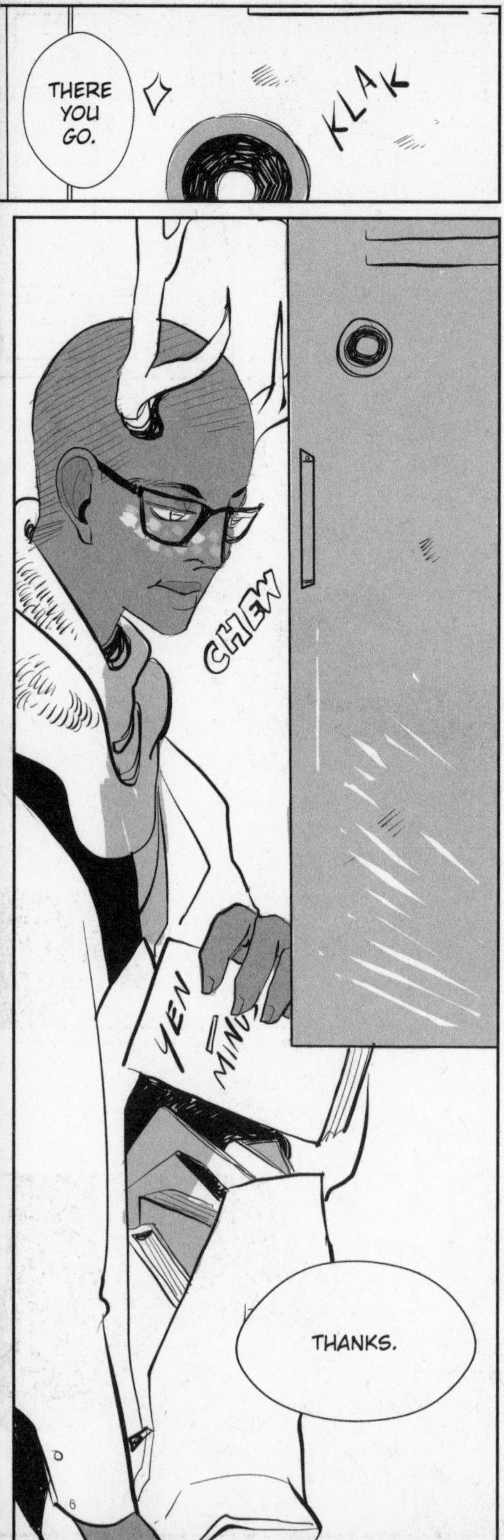
THERE YOU GO.
KLAK
CHEW
YEN — MINUS
THANKS.

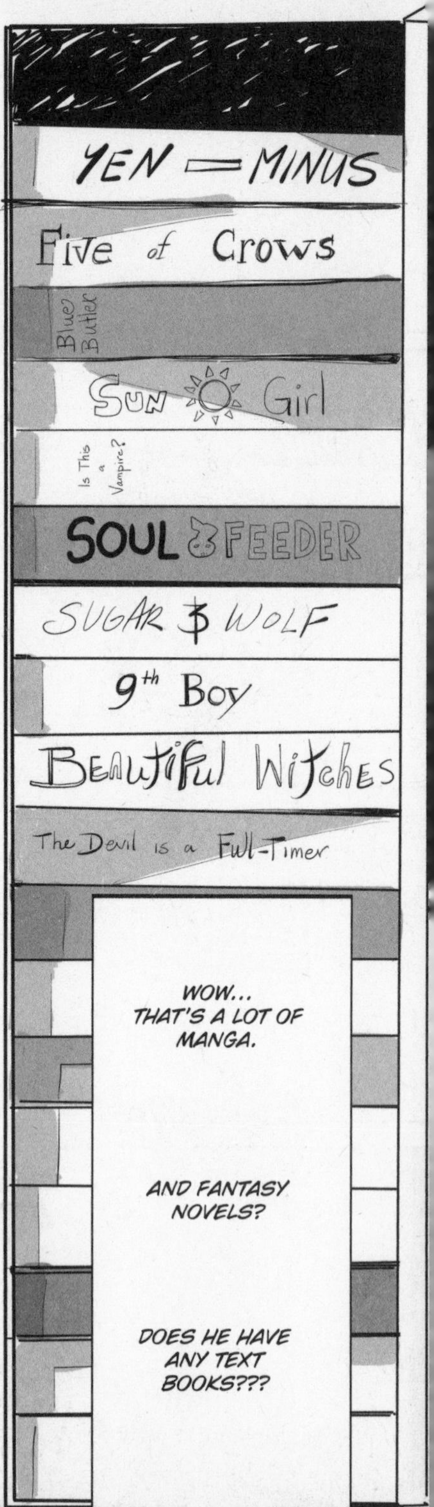
YEN — MINUS
Five of Crows
Blue Butler
Sun Girl
Is This a Vampire?
SOUL FEEDER
SUGAR & WOLF
9th Boy
Beautiful Witches
The Devil is a Full-Timer
WOW... THAT'S A LOT OF MANGA.
AND FANTASY NOVELS?
DOES HE HAVE ANY TEXT BOOKS???

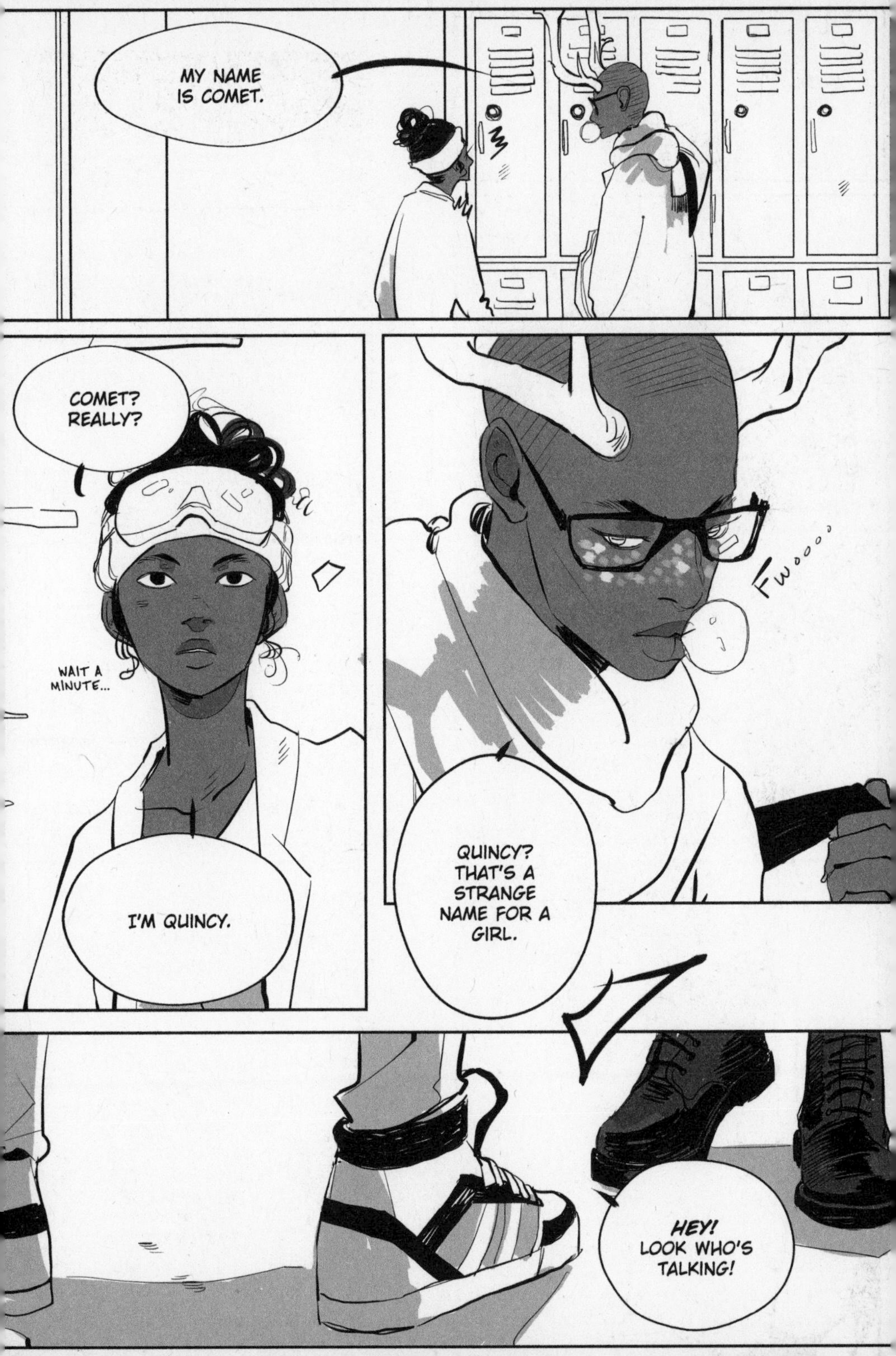
MY NAME IS COMET.
COMET? REALLY?
WAIT A MINUTE...
I'M QUINCY.
Fwooooo
QUINCY? THAT'S A STRANGE NAME FOR A GIRL.
HEY! LOOK WHO'S TALKING!

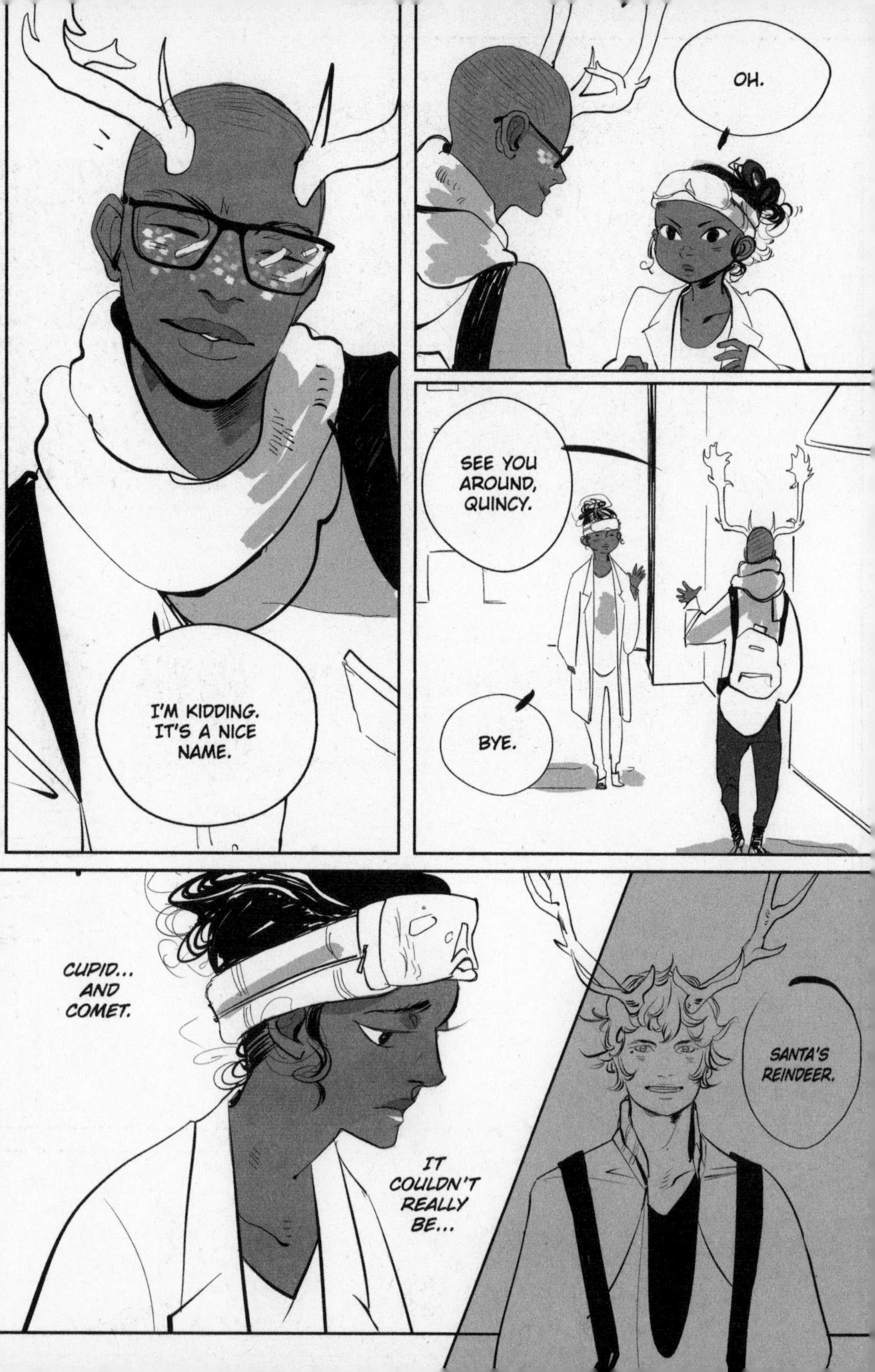
I'M KIDDING. IT'S A NICE NAME.
OH.
SEE YOU AROUND, QUINCY.
BYE.
CUPID... AND COMET.
IT COULDN'T REALLY BE...
SANTA'S REINDEER.

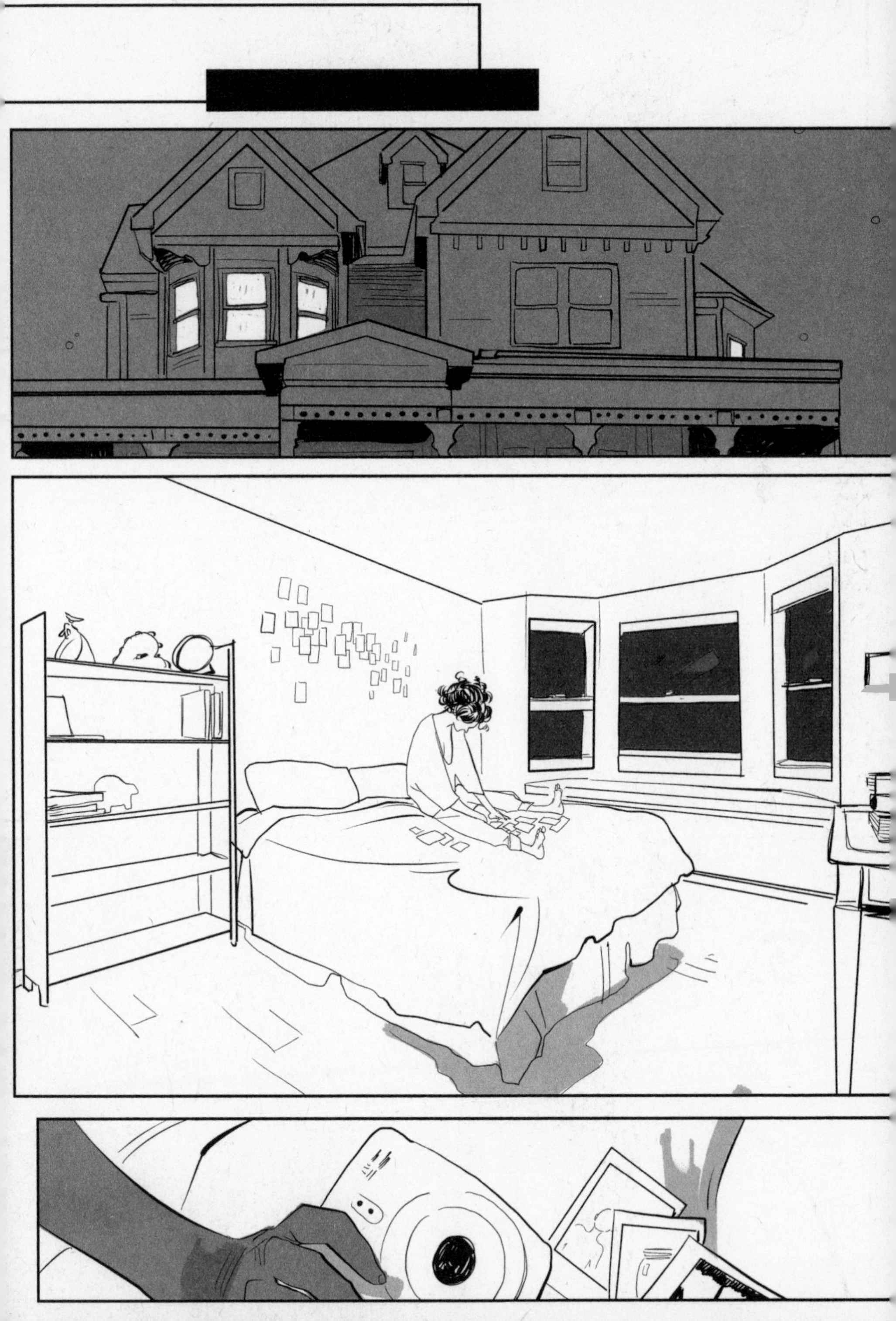

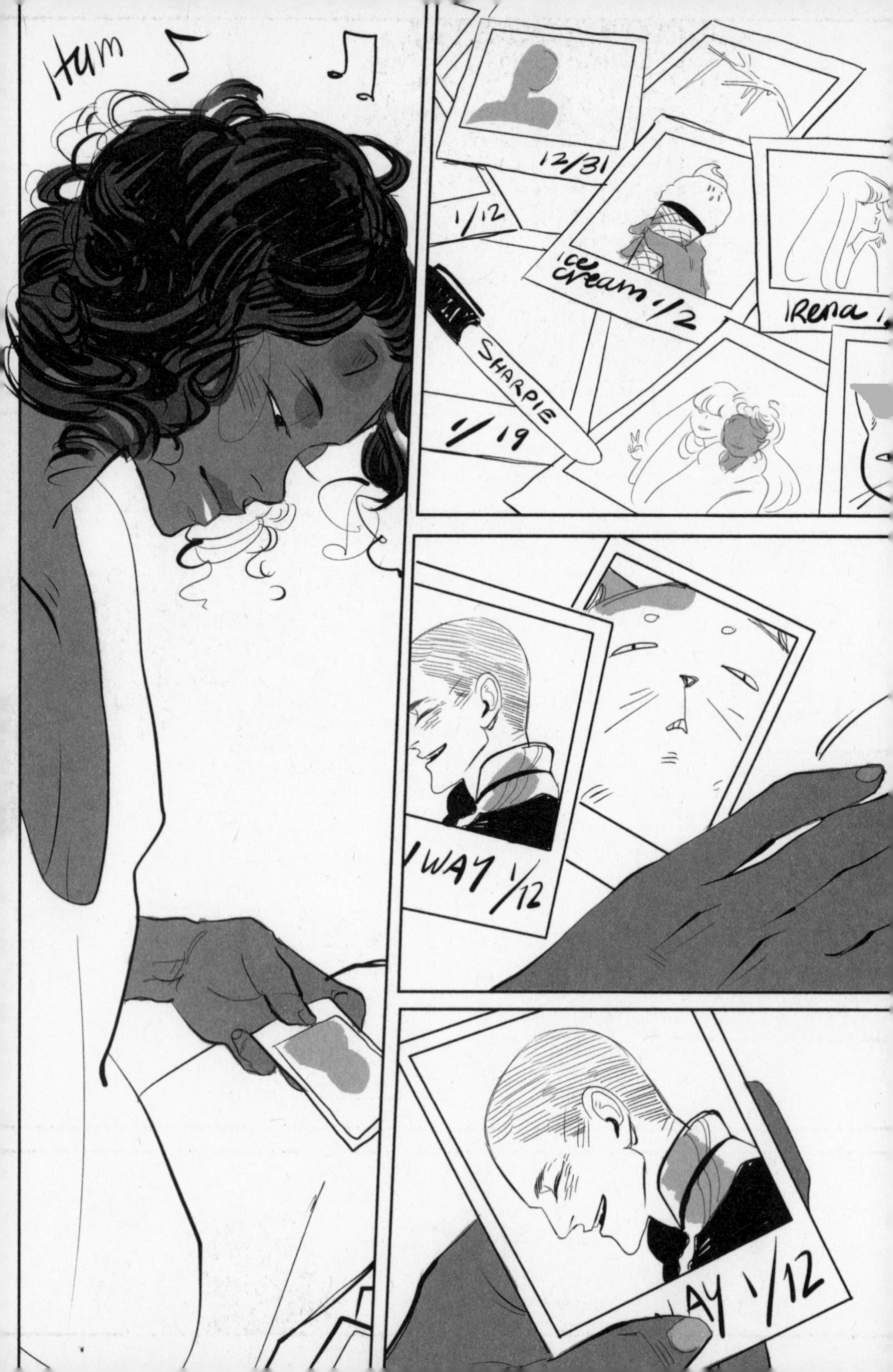
Hum
12/31
1/12
Ice Cream 1/2
Rena
SHARPIE
1/19
WAY 1/12
AY 1/12

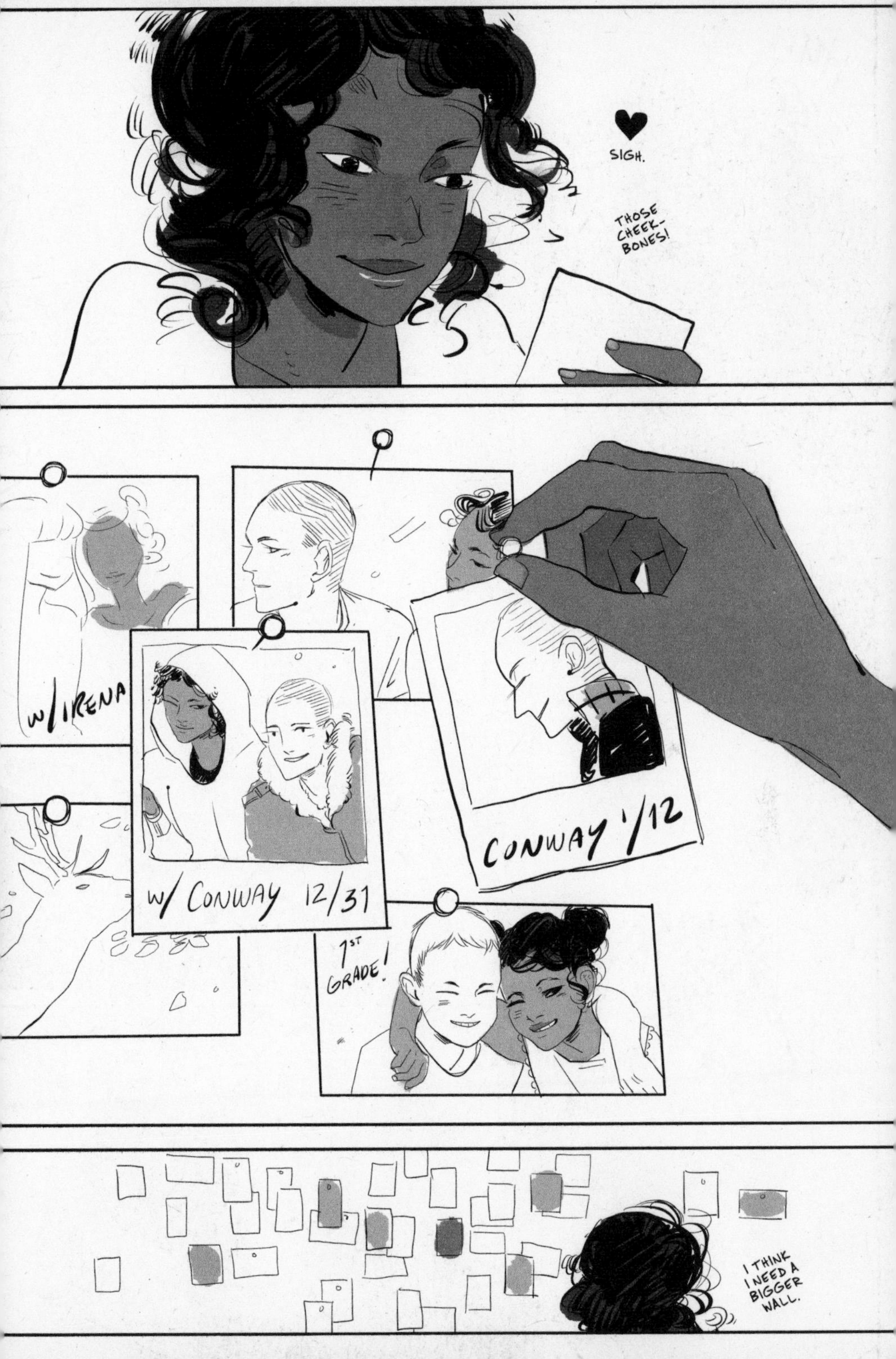
SIGH.
THOSE CHEEK-BONES!
W/IRENA
w/ CONWAY 12/31
CONWAY 1/12
1ST GRADE!
I THINK I NEED A BIGGER WALL.

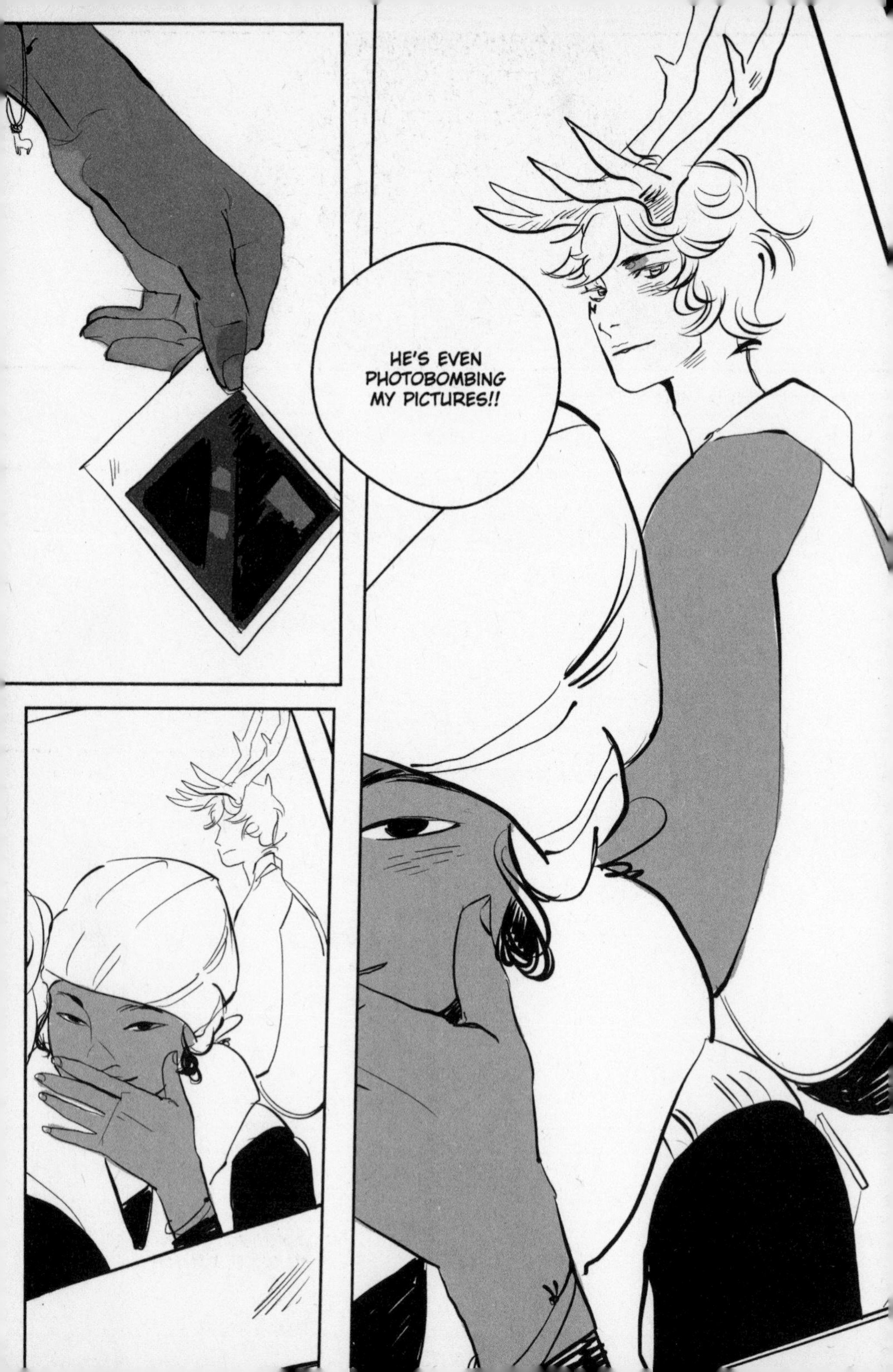
HE'S EVEN PHOTOBOMBING MY PICTURES!!

I KNOW I'M BEING UNREASONABLE.

SO WHY...?

WHY DOES HE MAKE ME
FEEL SO ANXIOUS...?

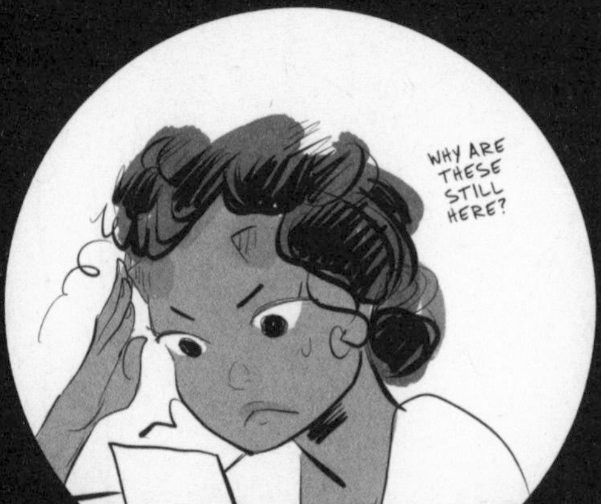
WHY ARE THESE STILL HERE?

Chapter 3

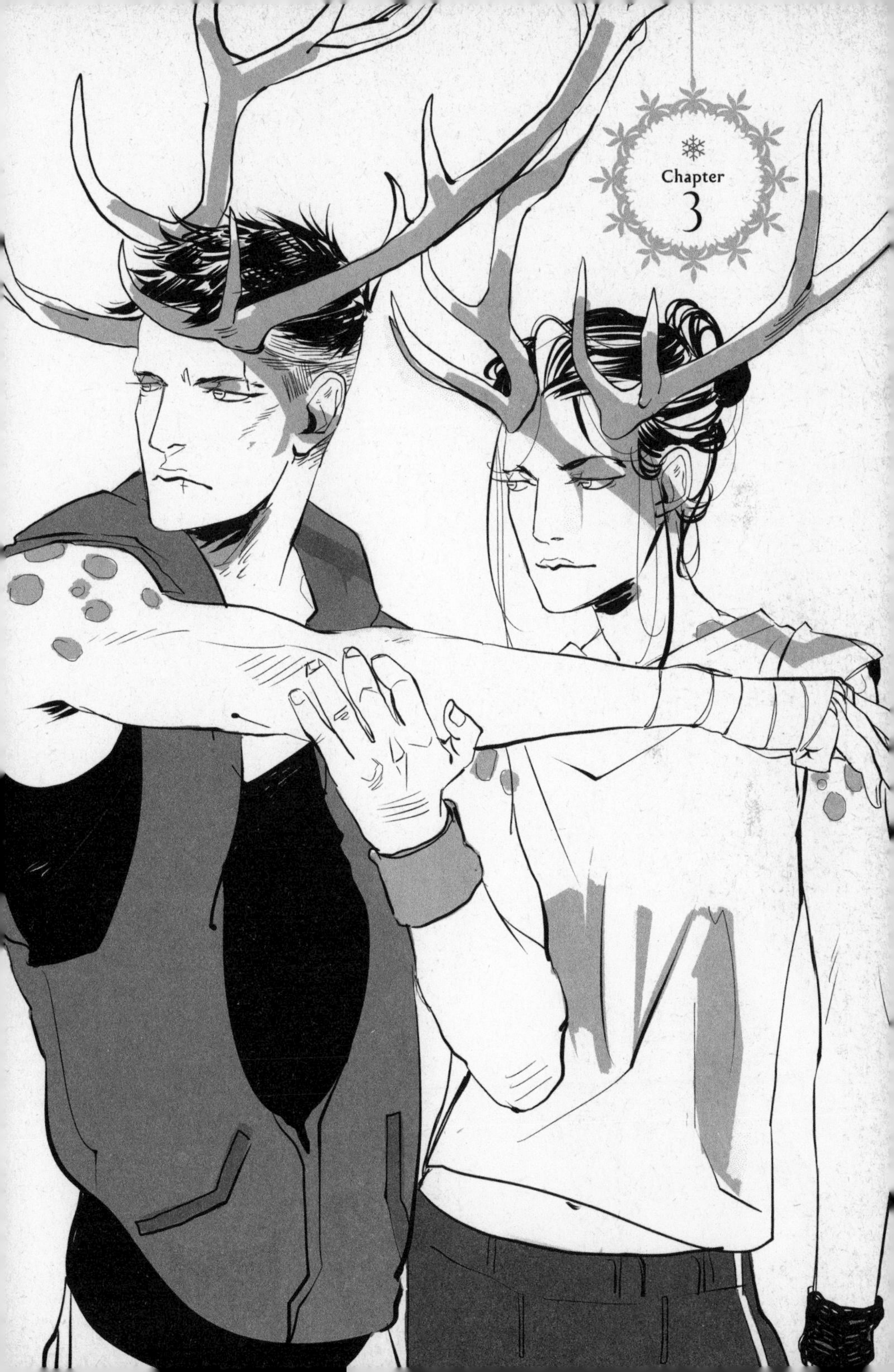

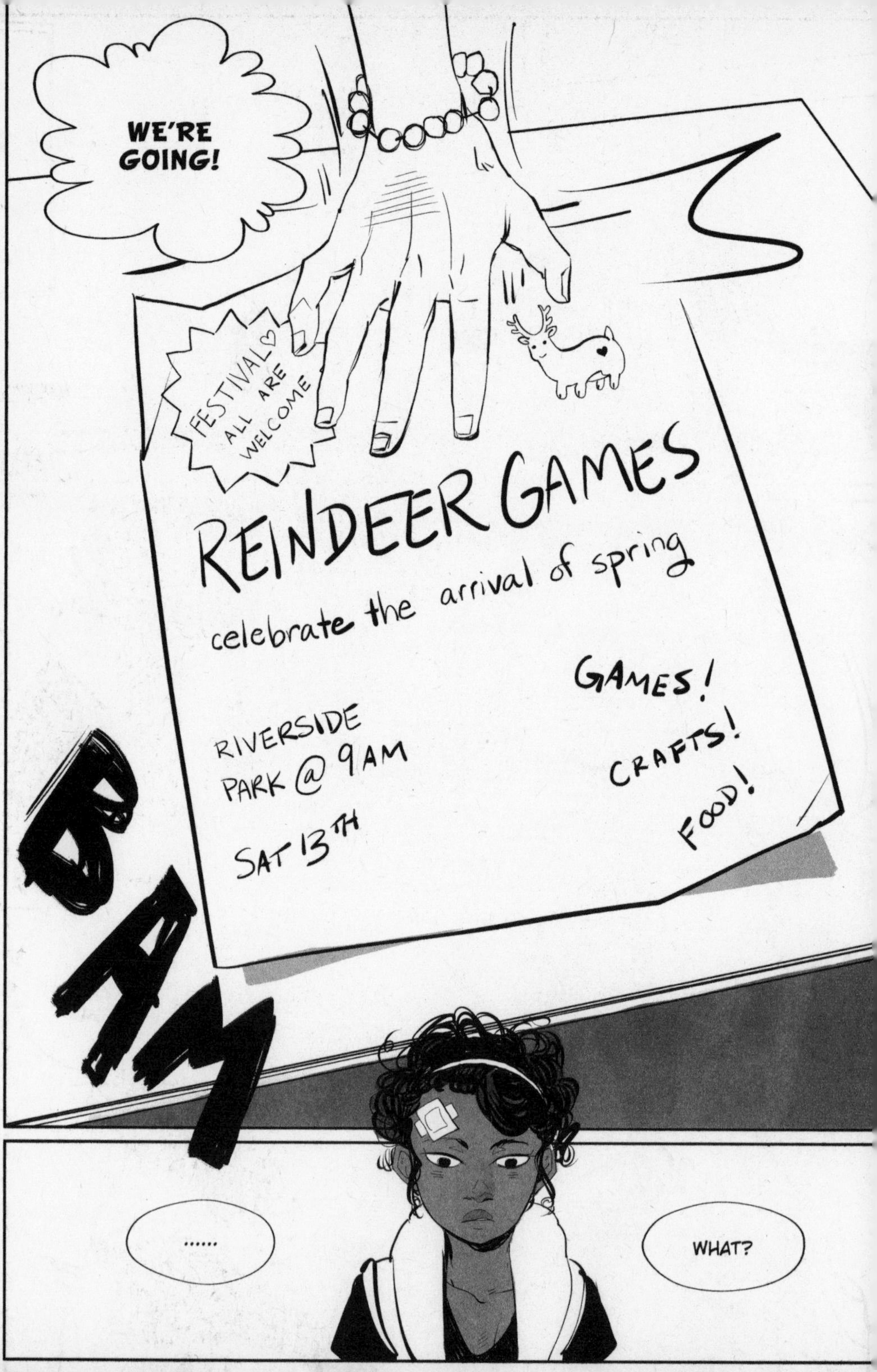
WE'RE GOING!
FESTIVAL♡ ALL ARE WELCOME
REINDEER GAMES
celebrate the arrival of spring
RIVERSIDE PARK @ 9AM
SAT 13TH
GAMES!
CRAFTS!
FOOD!
BAM
......
WHAT?

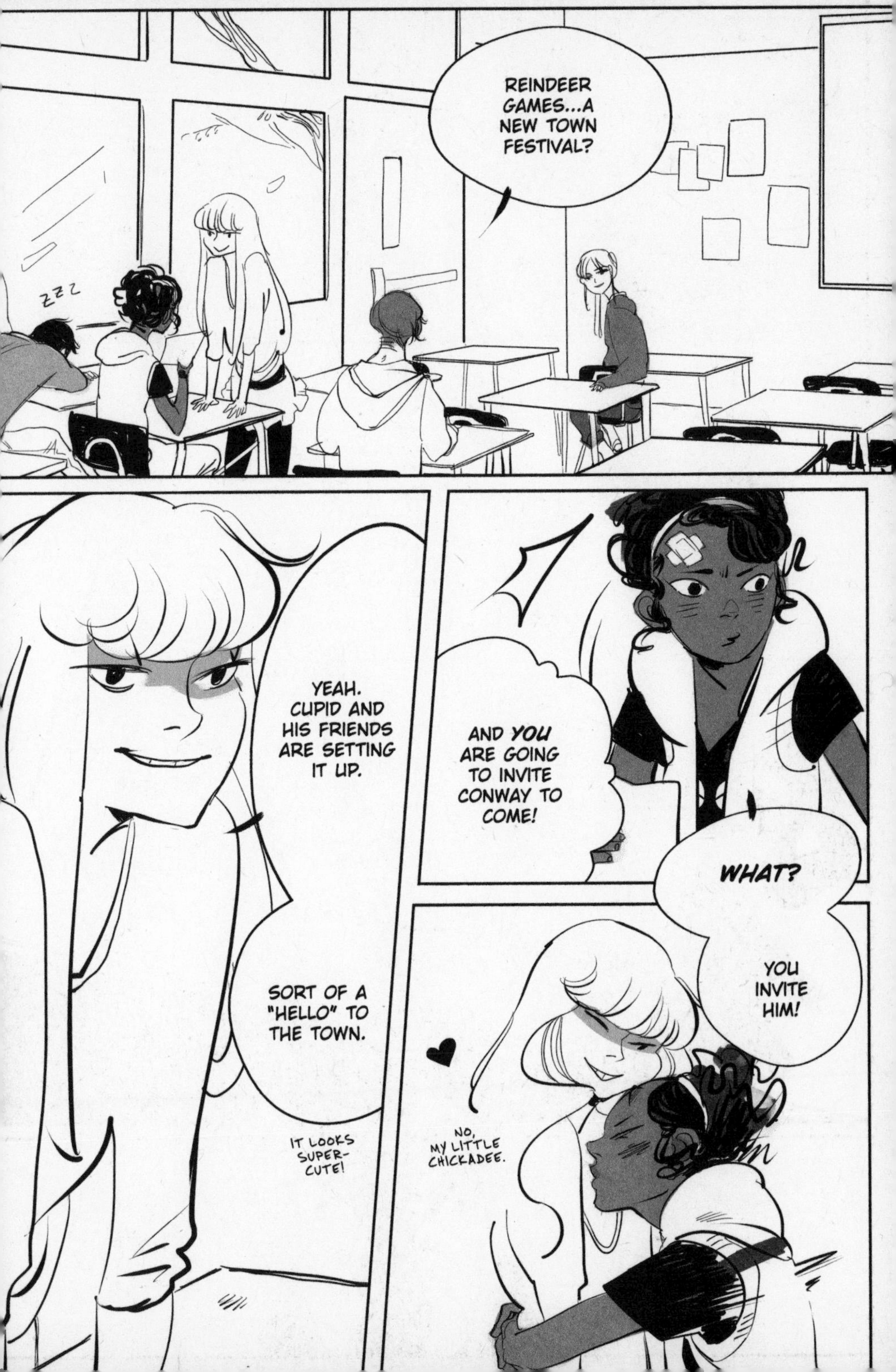
REINDEER GAMES...A NEW TOWN FESTIVAL?
ZZZ
YEAH. CUPID AND HIS FRIENDS ARE SETTING IT UP.
SORT OF A "HELLO" TO THE TOWN.
IT LOOKS SUPER-CUTE!
AND *YOU* ARE GOING TO INVITE CONWAY TO COME!
WHAT?
YOU INVITE HIM!
NO, MY LITTLE CHICKADEE.

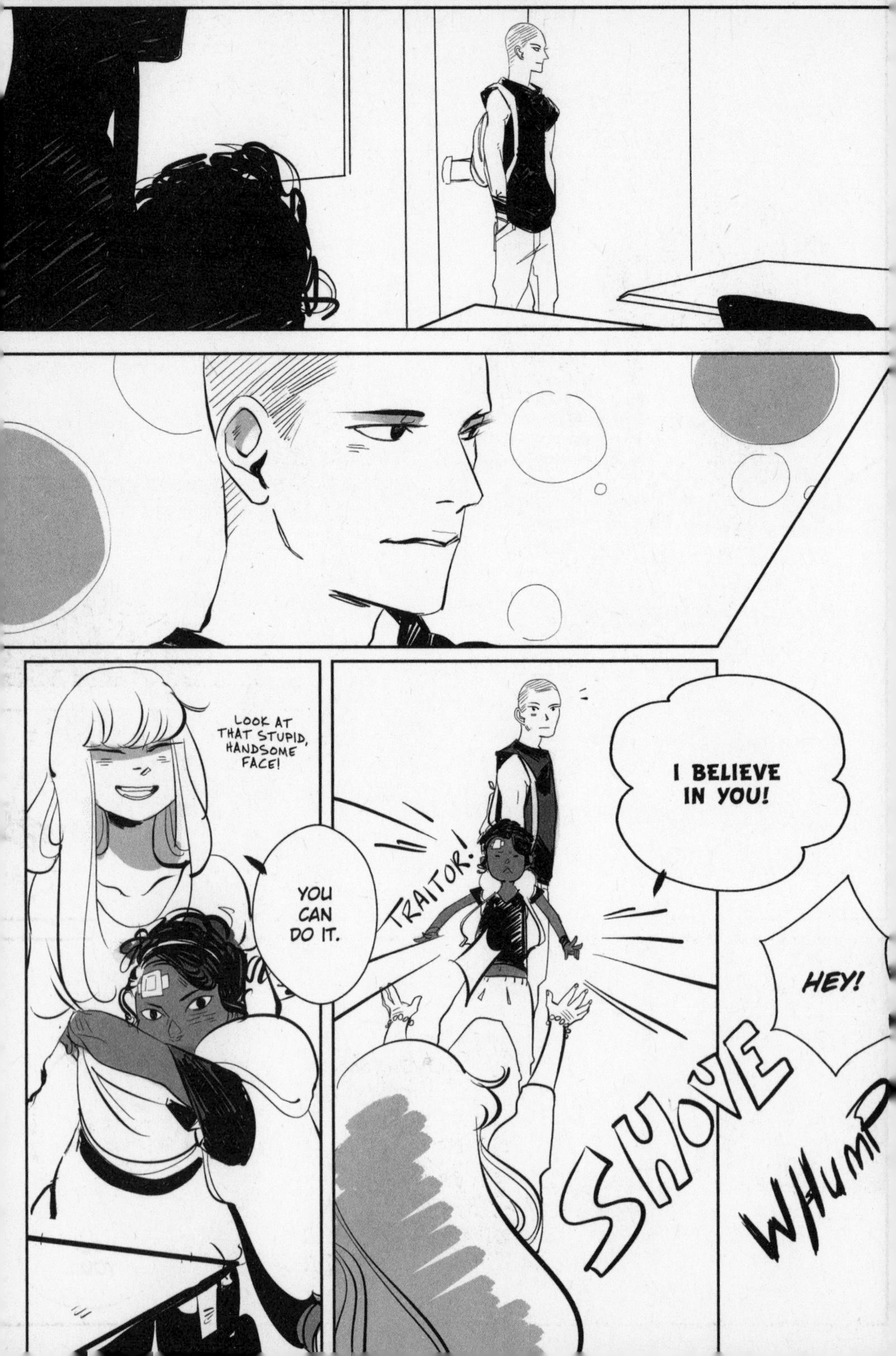
LOOK AT THAT STUPID, HANDSOME FACE!
YOU CAN DO IT.
TRAITOR!
I BELIEVE IN YOU!
HEY!
SHOVE
WHUMP

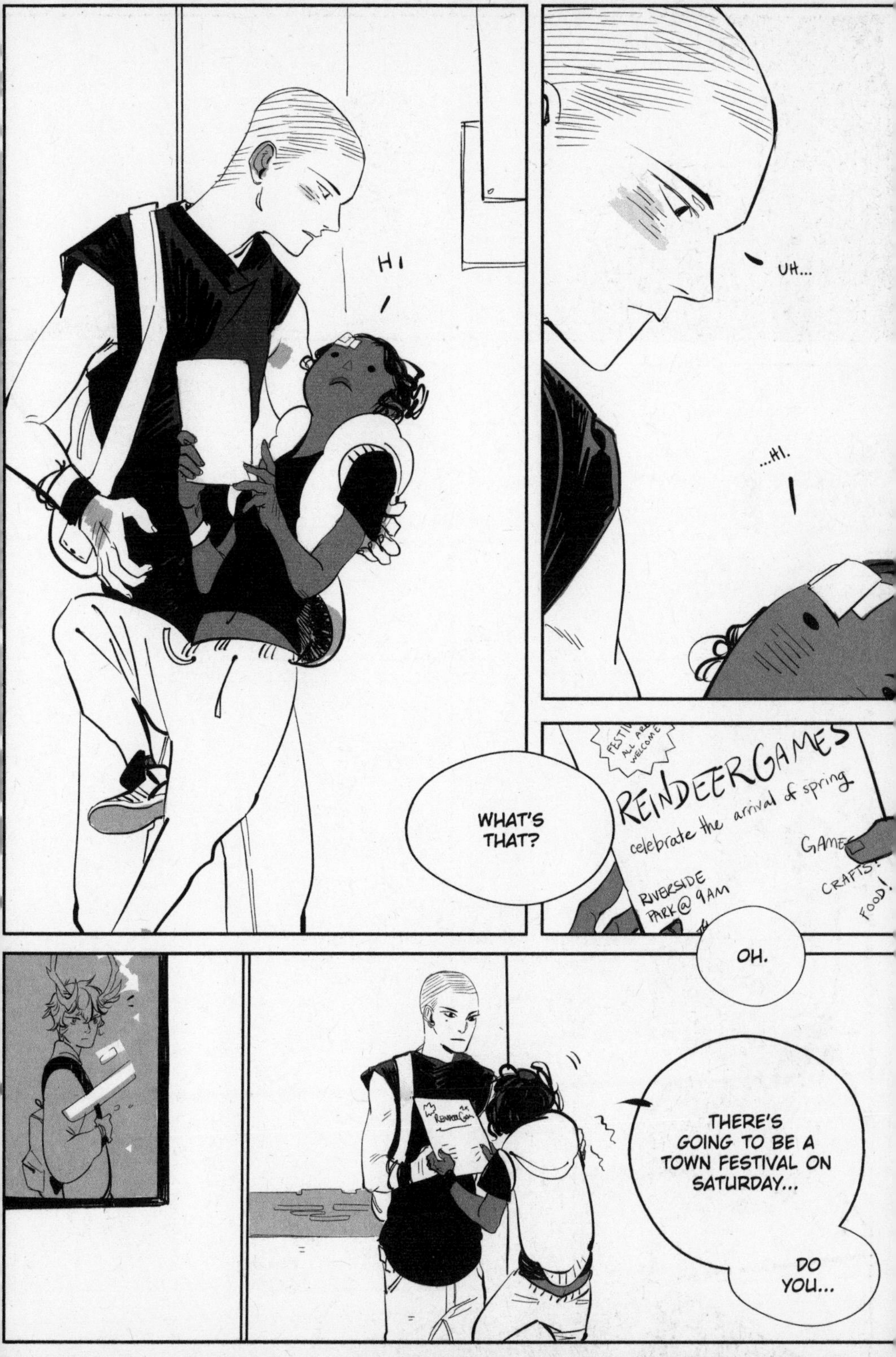
HI
UH...
...HI.
WHAT'S THAT?
FESTIV
ALL AR
WELCOME
REINDEERGAMES
celebrate the arrival of spring
GAMES
CRAFTS!
FOOD!
RIVERSIDE PARK @ 9AM
OH.
THERE'S GOING TO BE A TOWN FESTIVAL ON SATURDAY...
DO YOU...

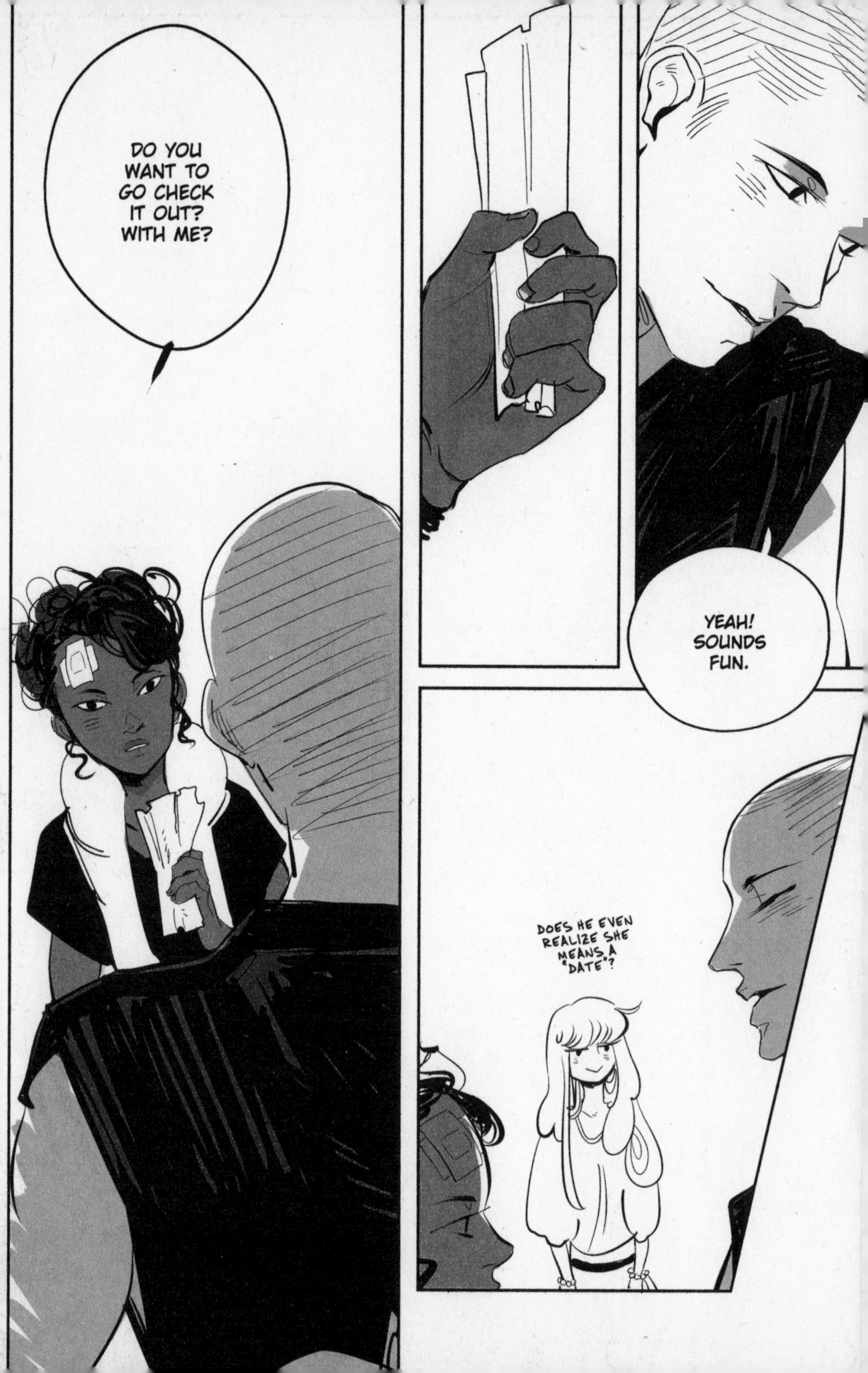
DO YOU WANT TO GO CHECK IT OUT? WITH ME?
YEAH! SOUNDS FUN.
DOES HE EVEN REALIZE SHE MEANS A "DATE"?

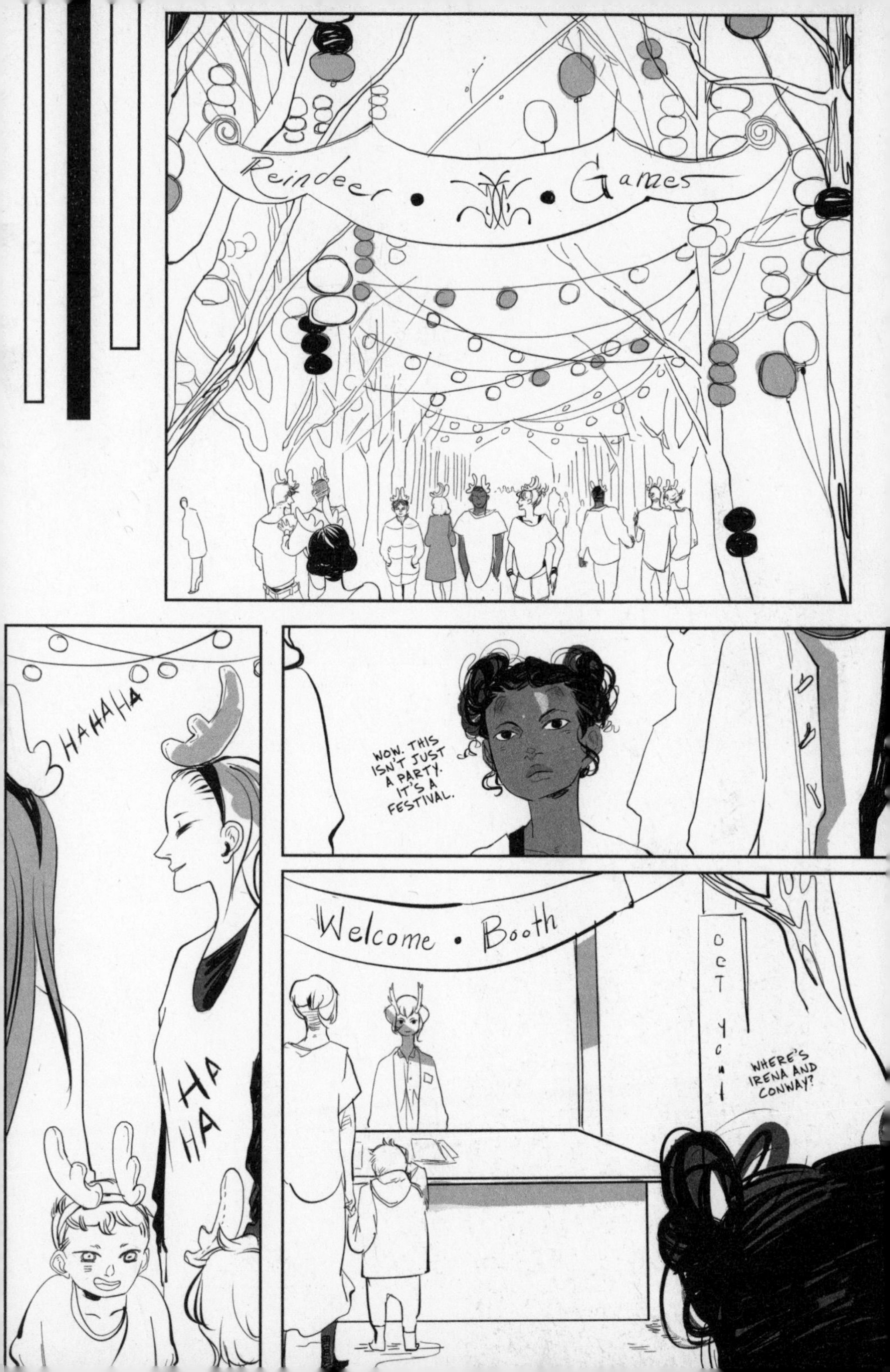
Reindeer • Games
HAHAHA
HA HA
WOW. THIS ISN'T JUST A PARTY. IT'S A FESTIVAL.
Welcome • Booth
WHERE'S IRENA AND CONWAY?

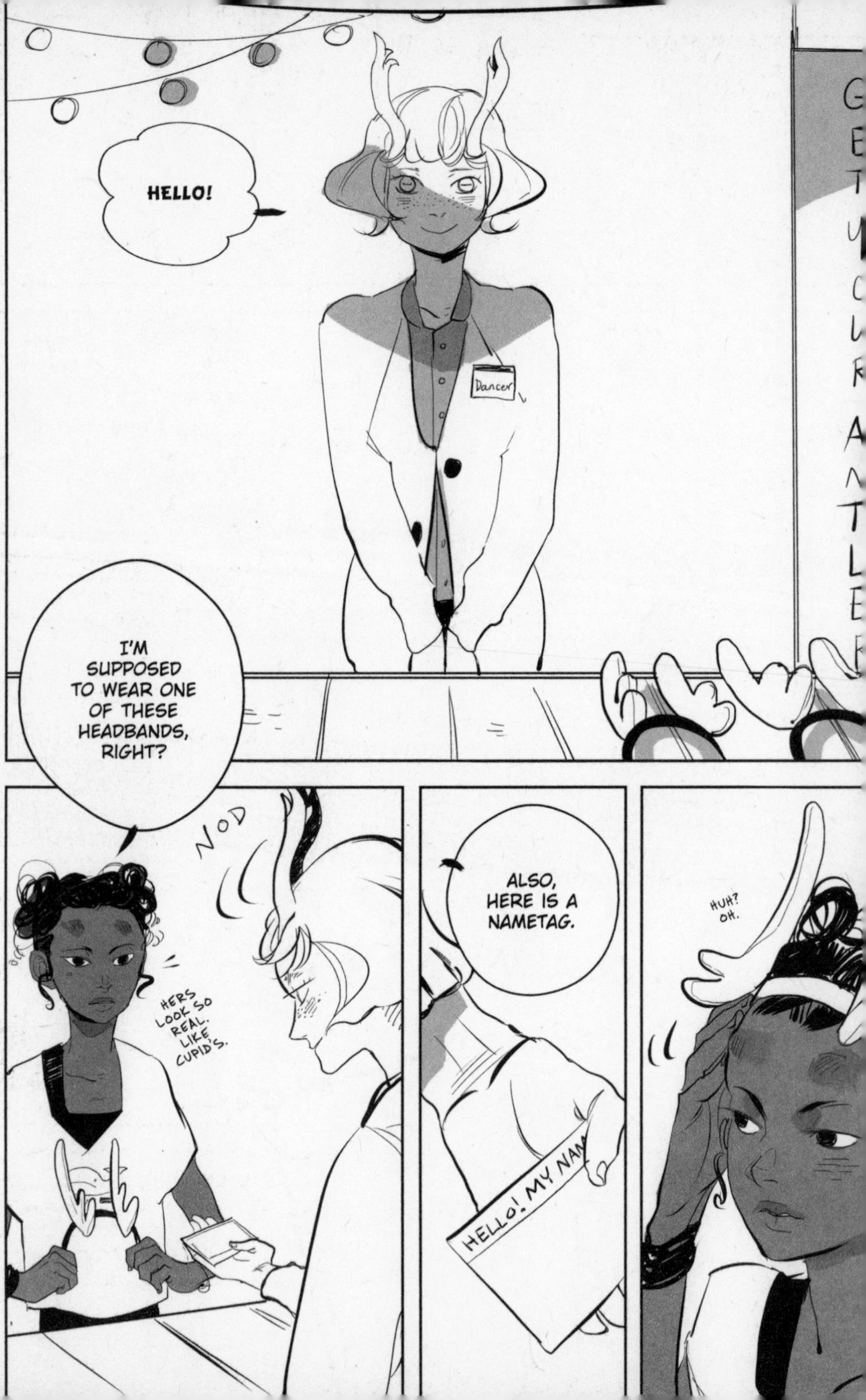
HELLO!
Dancer
GET YOUR ANTLER
I'M SUPPOSED TO WEAR ONE OF THESE HEADBANDS, RIGHT?
NOD
HERS LOOK SO REAL. LIKE CUPID'S.
ALSO, HERE IS A NAMETAG.
HELLO! MY NAM
HUH? OH.

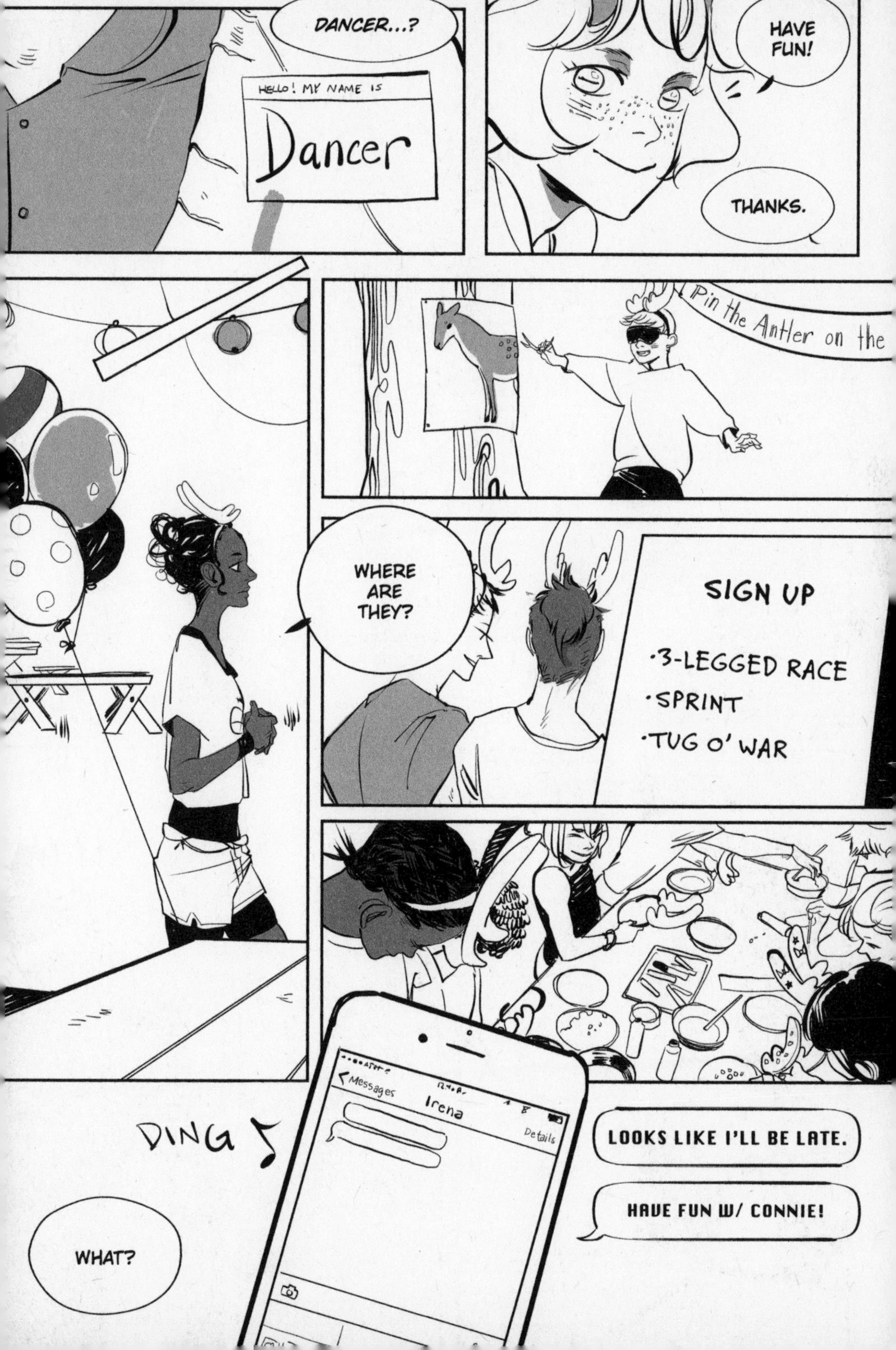
DANCER...?
HELLO! MY NAME IS
Dancer
HAVE FUN!
THANKS.
Pin the Antler on the
WHERE ARE THEY?
SIGN UP
·3-LEGGED RACE
·SPRINT
·TUG O' WAR
DING
Messages
Irena
Details
LOOKS LIKE I'LL BE LATE.
HAVE FUN W/ CONNIE!
WHAT?

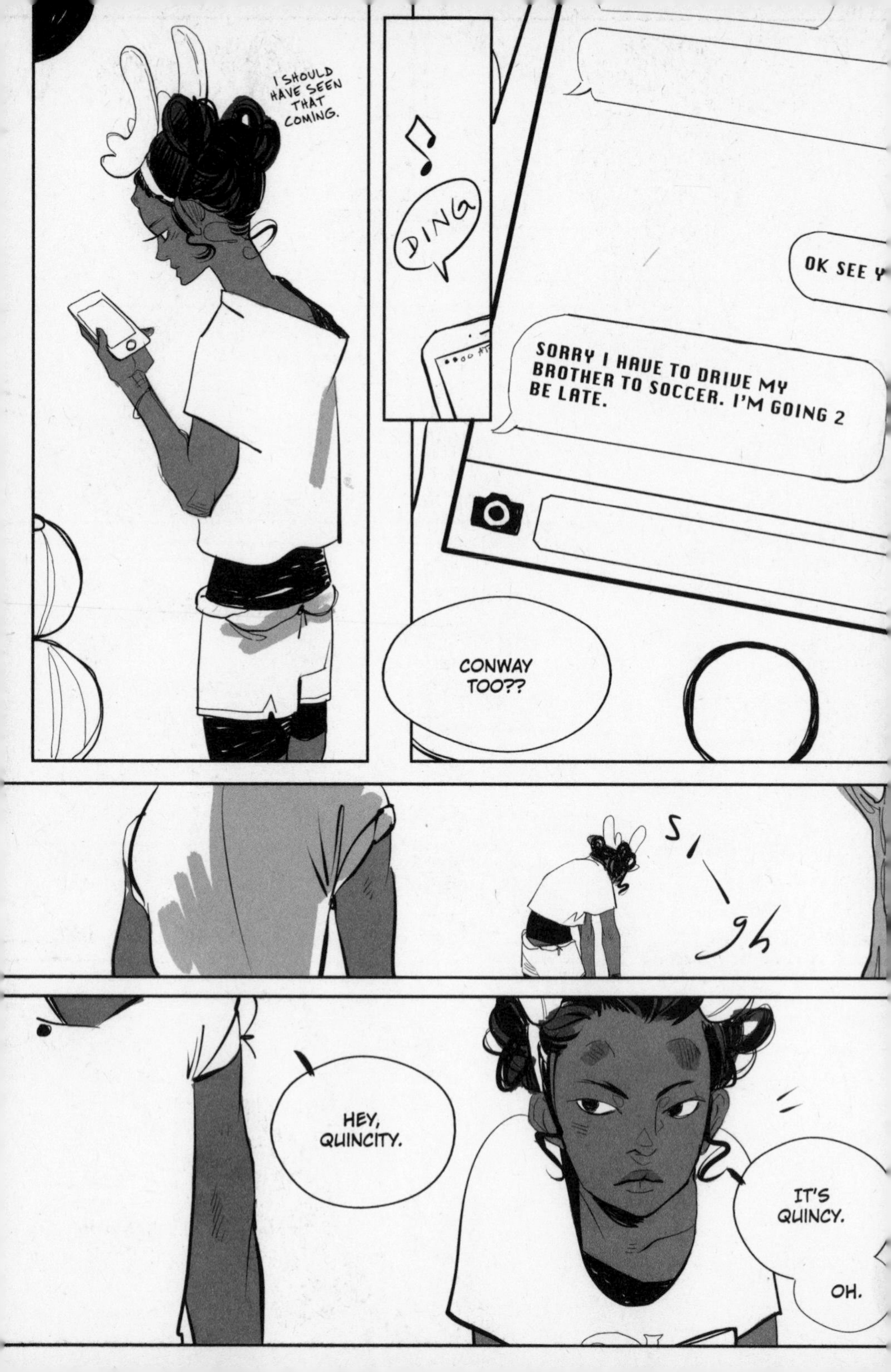
I SHOULD HAVE SEEN THAT COMING.
DING
OK SEE Y
SORRY I HAVE TO DRIVE MY BROTHER TO SOCCER. I'M GOING 2 BE LATE.
CONWAY TOO??
SIGH
HEY, QUINCITY.
IT'S QUINCY.
OH.

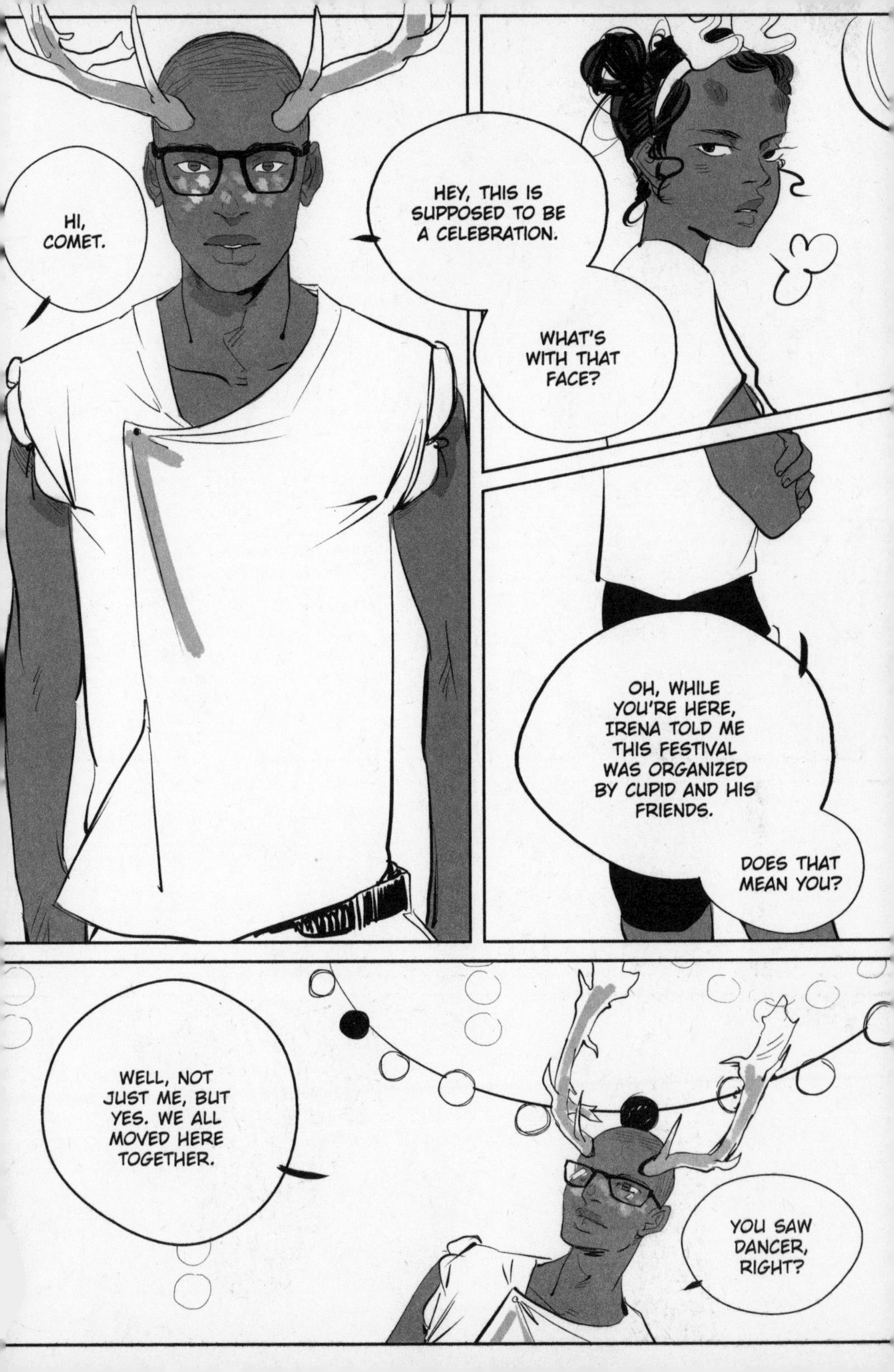
HI, COMET.
HEY, THIS IS SUPPOSED TO BE A CELEBRATION.
WHAT'S WITH THAT FACE?
OH, WHILE YOU'RE HERE, IRENA TOLD ME THIS FESTIVAL WAS ORGANIZED BY CUPID AND HIS FRIENDS.
DOES THAT MEAN YOU?
WELL, NOT JUST ME, BUT YES. WE ALL MOVED HERE TOGETHER.
YOU SAW DANCER, RIGHT?

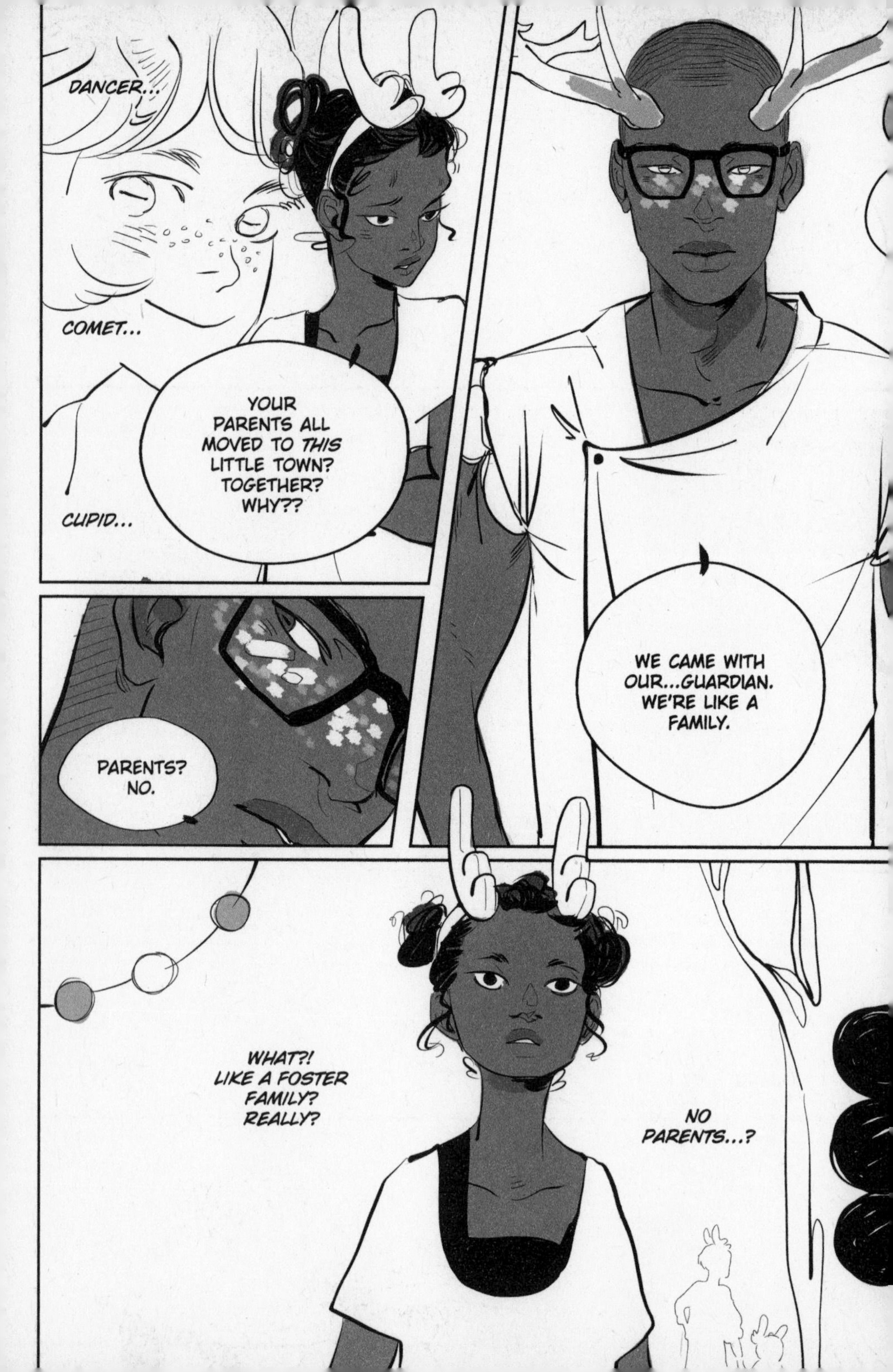
DANCER...
COMET...
CUPID...
YOUR PARENTS ALL MOVED TO *THIS* LITTLE TOWN? TOGETHER? WHY??
WE CAME WITH OUR...GUARDIAN. WE'RE LIKE A FAMILY.
PARENTS? NO.
WHAT?! LIKE A FOSTER FAMILY? REALLY?
NO PARENTS...?

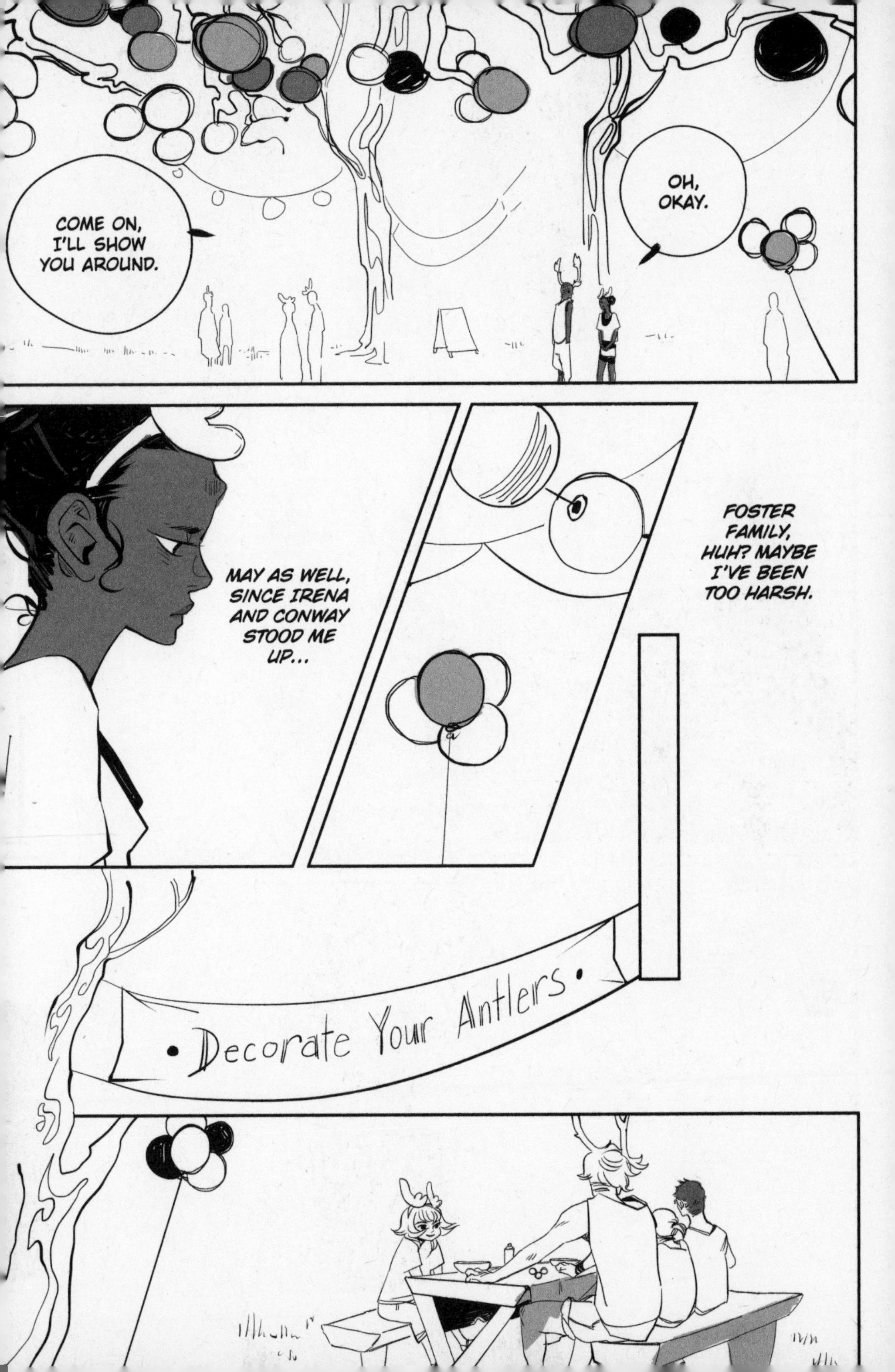
COME ON, I'LL SHOW YOU AROUND.
OH, OKAY.
MAY AS WELL, SINCE IRENA AND CONWAY STOOD ME UP...
FOSTER FAMILY, HUH? MAYBE I'VE BEEN TOO HARSH.
• Decorate Your Antlers •

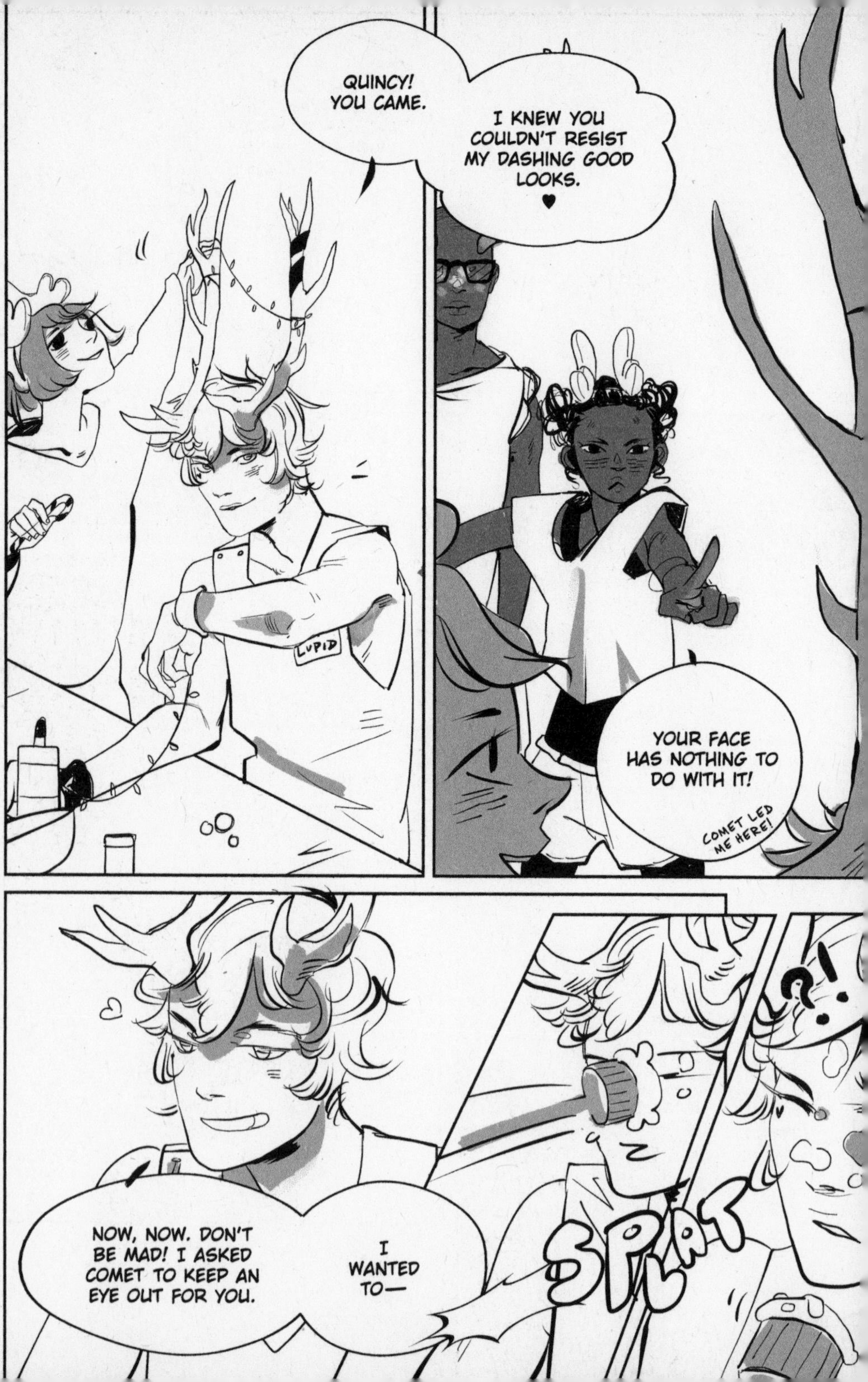
QUINCY! YOU CAME.
I KNEW YOU COULDN'T RESIST MY DASHING GOOD LOOKS. ♥
LUPID
YOUR FACE HAS NOTHING TO DO WITH IT!
COMET LED ME HERE!
NOW, NOW. DON'T BE MAD! I ASKED COMET TO KEEP AN EYE OUT FOR YOU.
I WANTED TO—
SPLAT
?!

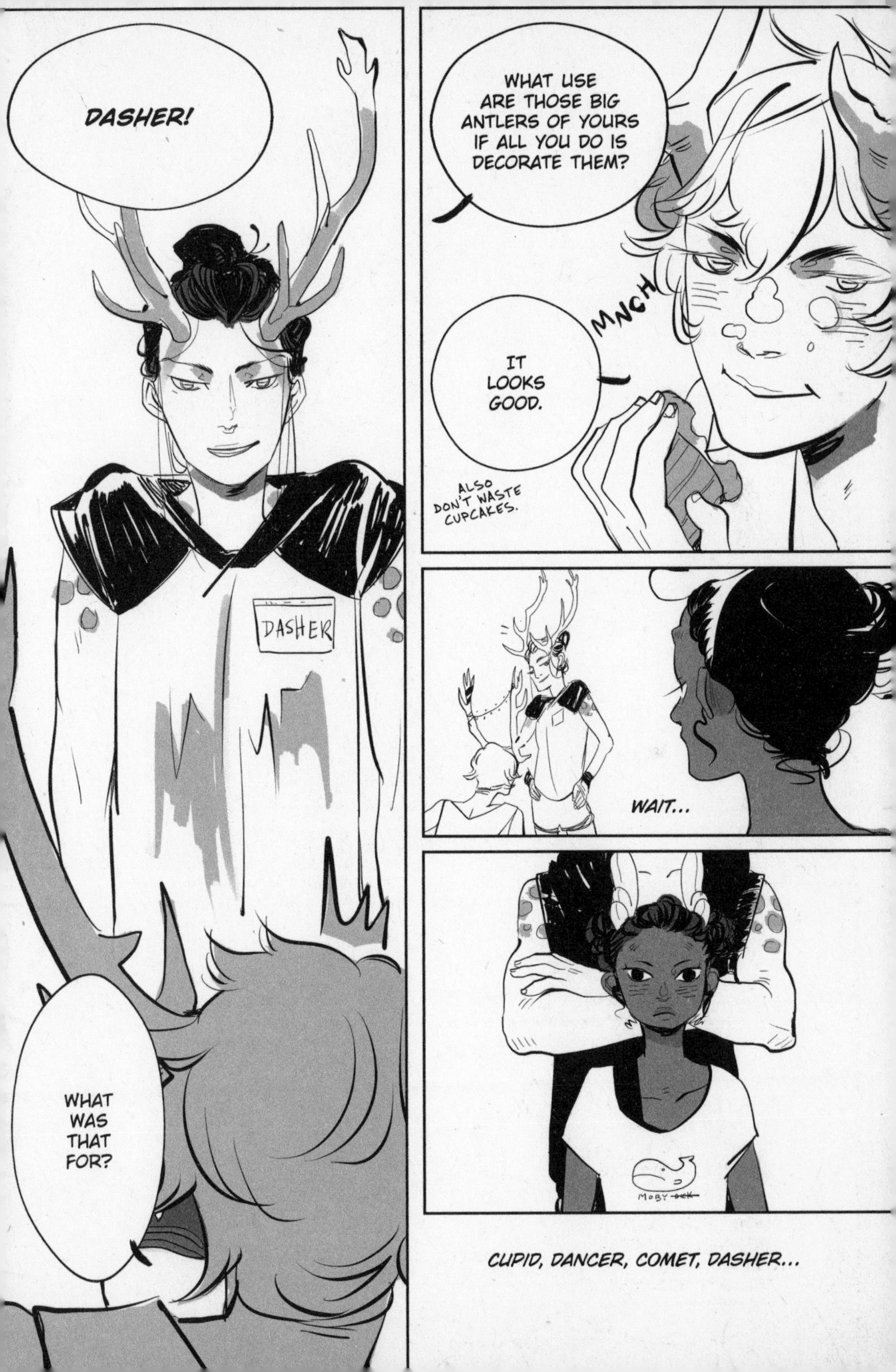
DASHER!
DASHER
WHAT WAS THAT FOR?
WHAT USE ARE THOSE BIG ANTLERS OF YOURS IF ALL YOU DO IS DECORATE THEM?
MNCH
IT LOOKS GOOD.
ALSO DON'T WASTE CUPCAKES.
WAIT...
MOBY
CUPID, DANCER, COMET, DASHER...

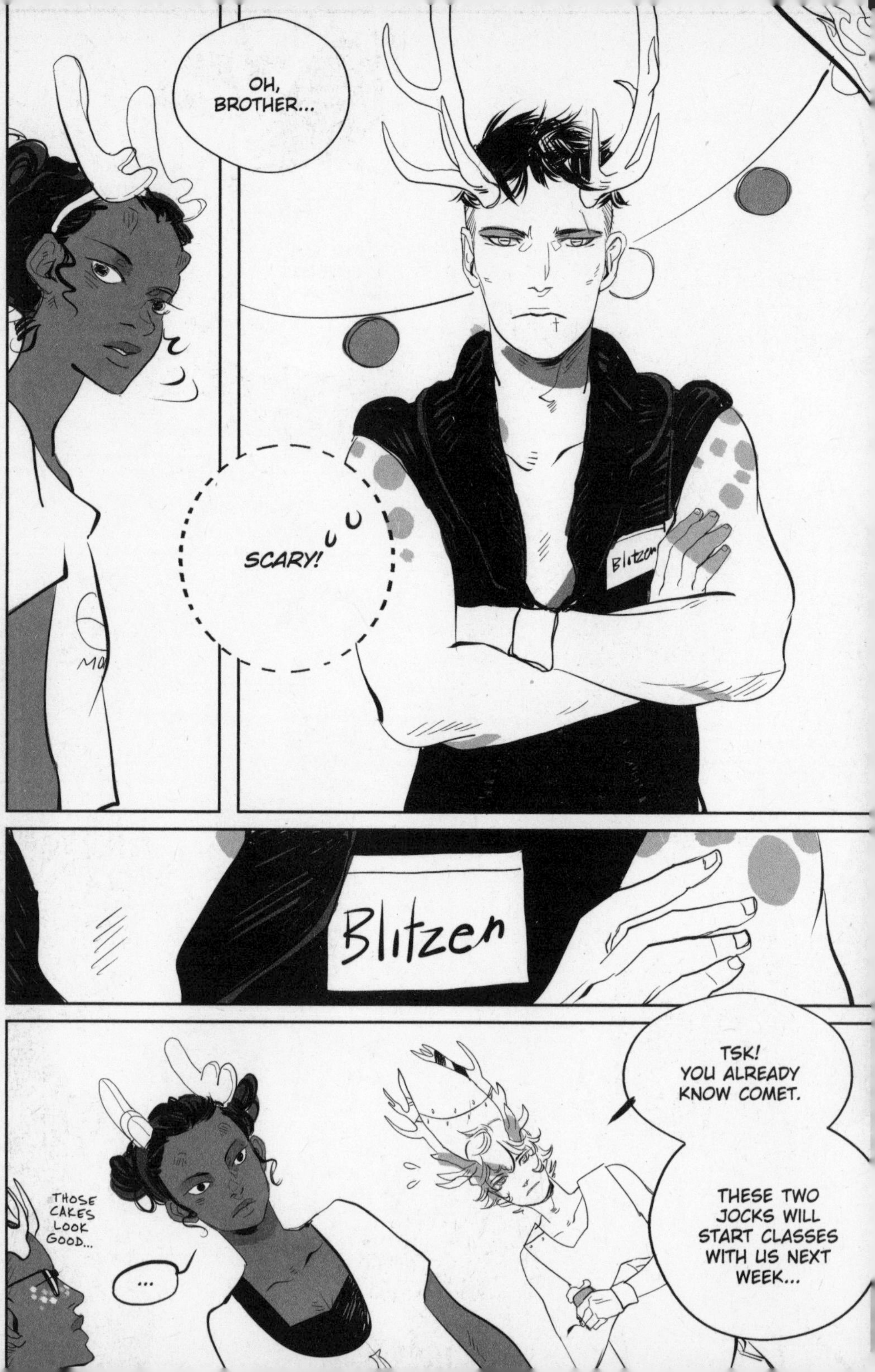
OH, BROTHER...
SCARY!
Blitzen
Blitzen
THOSE CAKES LOOK GOOD...
...
TSK! YOU ALREADY KNOW COMET.
THESE TWO JOCKS WILL START CLASSES WITH US NEXT WEEK...

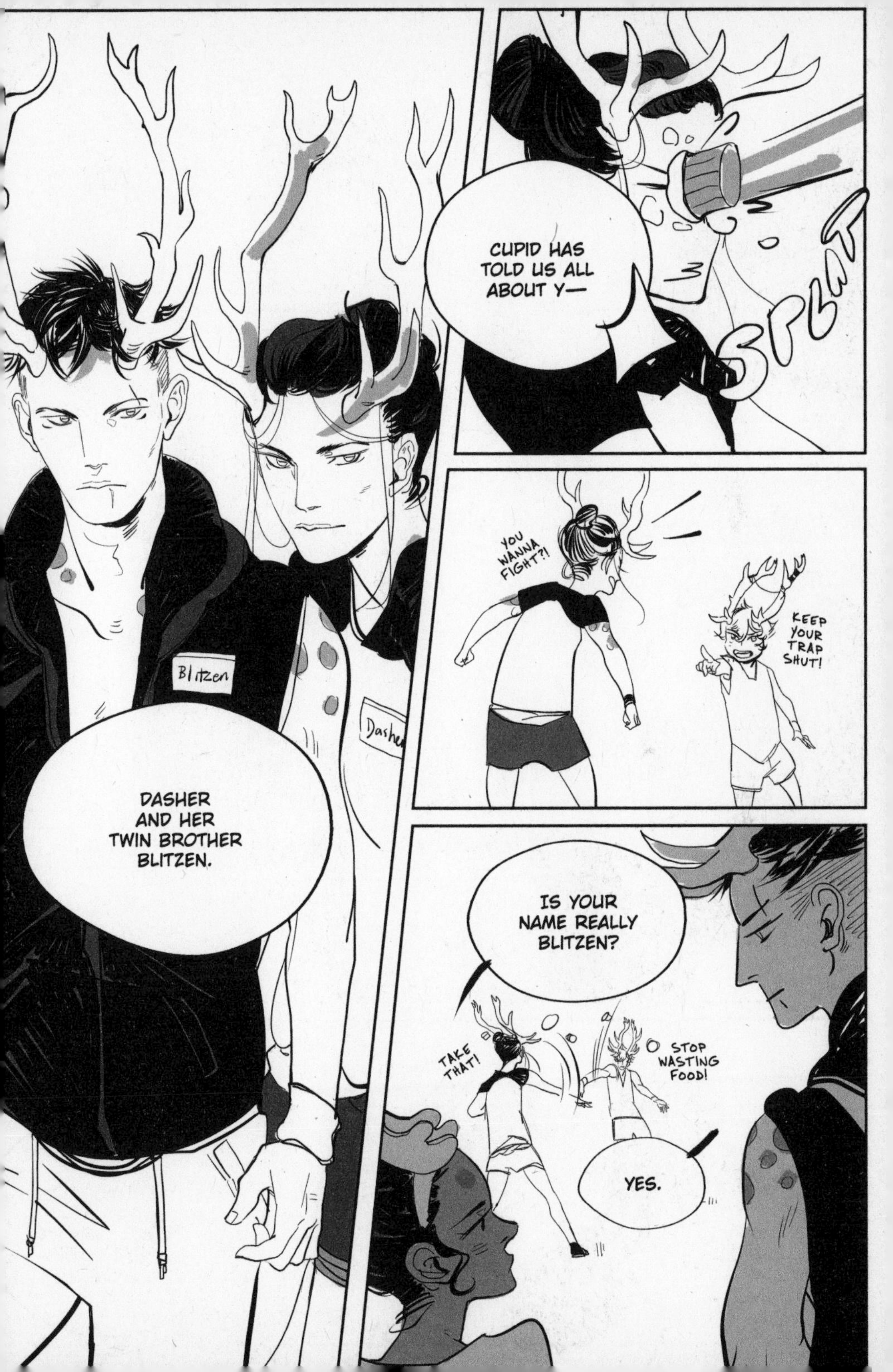
Blitzen
DASHER AND HER TWIN BROTHER BLITZEN.
CUPID HAS TOLD US ALL ABOUT Y—
SPLAT
YOU WANNA FIGHT?!
KEEP YOUR TRAP SHUT!
IS YOUR NAME REALLY BLITZEN?
TAKE THAT!
STOP WASTING FOOD!
YES.

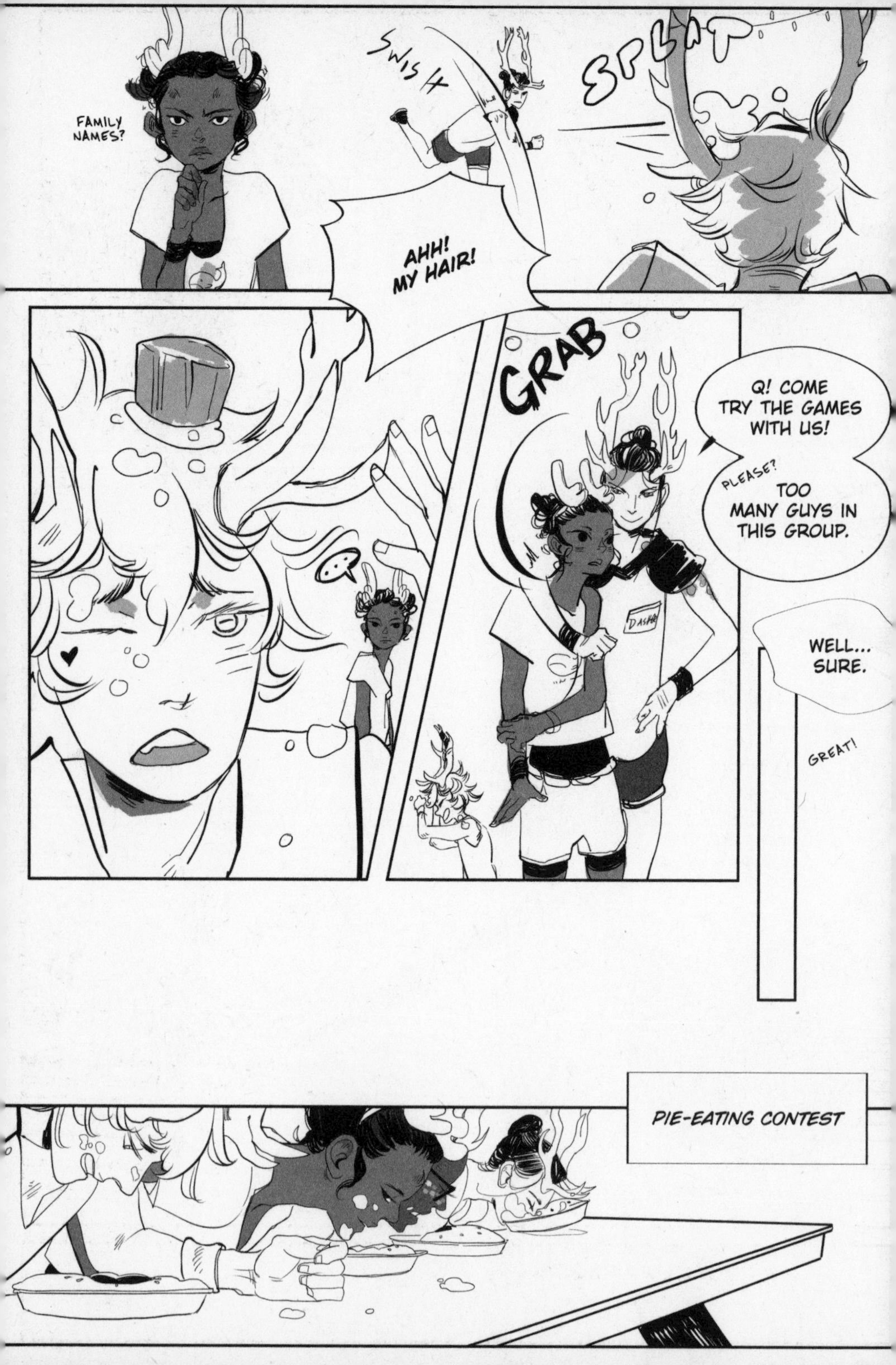
FAMILY NAMES?
SWISH
SPLAT
AHH! MY HAIR!
GRAB
Q! COME TRY THE GAMES WITH US!
PLEASE?
TOO MANY GUYS IN THIS GROUP.
WELL... SURE.
GREAT!
PIE-EATING CONTEST

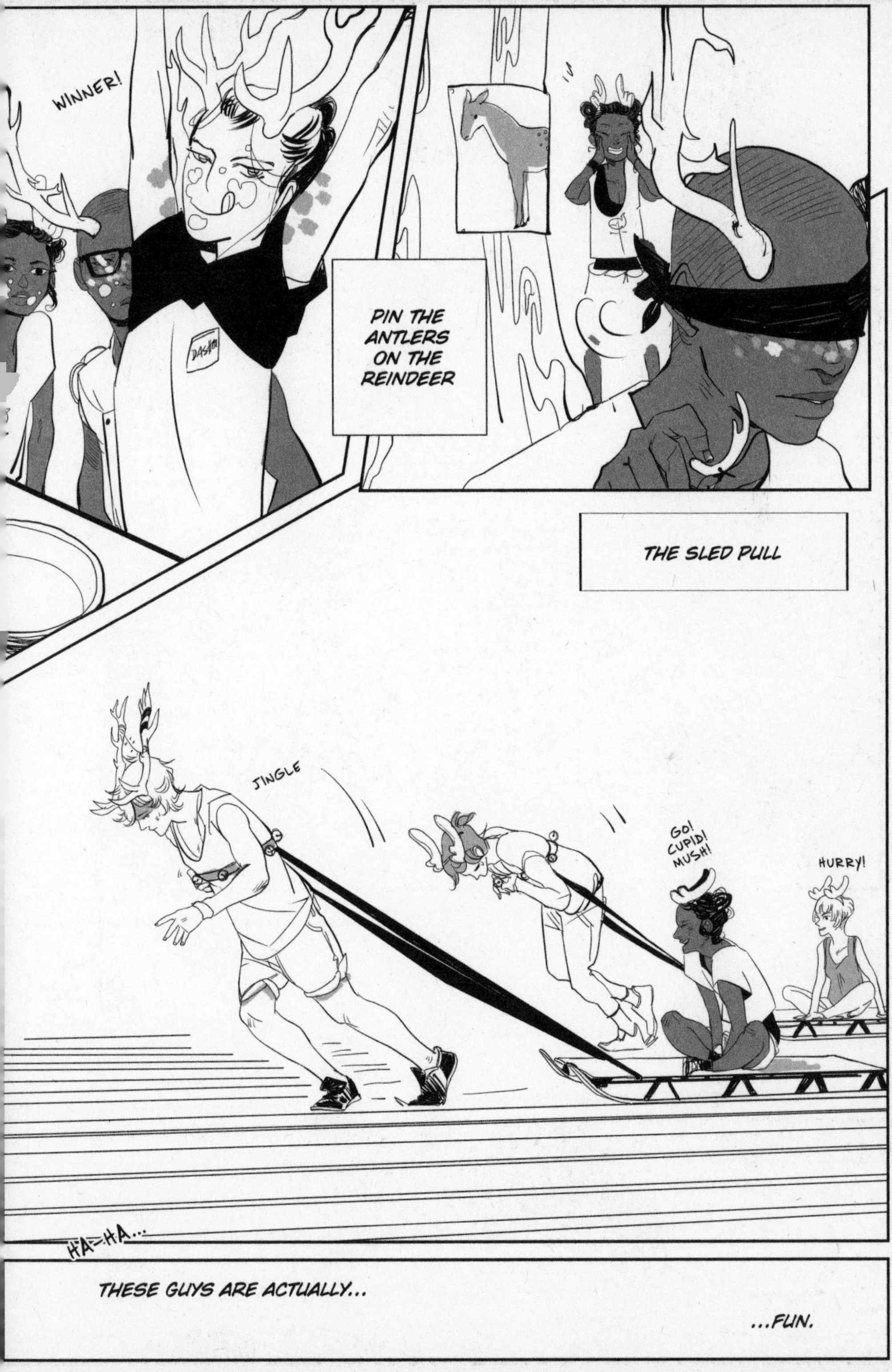
WINNER!
PIN THE ANTLERS ON THE REINDEER
THE SLED PULL
JINGLE
GO! CUPID! MUSH!
HURRY!
HA-HA...
THESE GUYS ARE ACTUALLY...
...FUN.

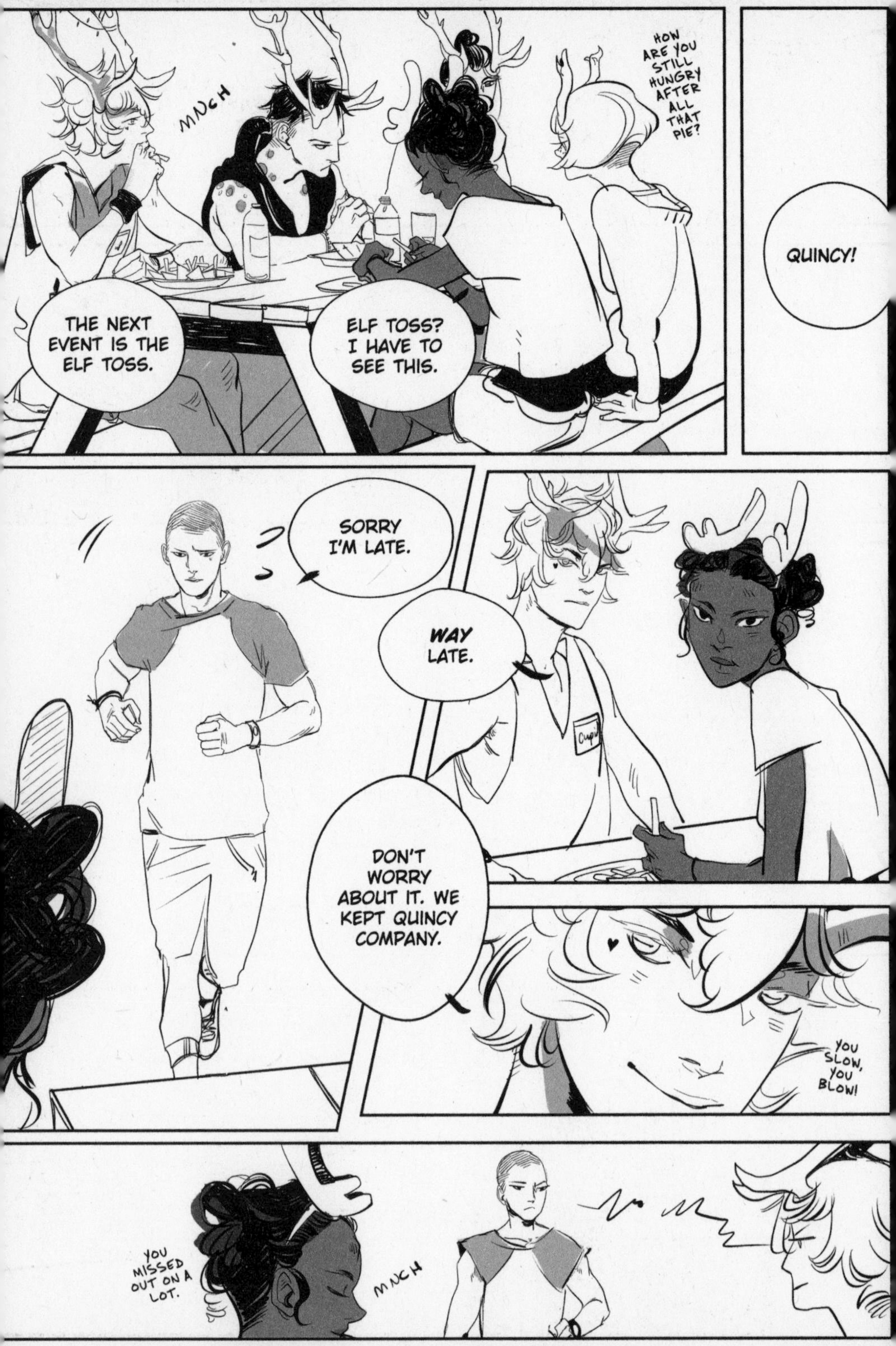
MNCH
HOW ARE YOU STILL HUNGRY AFTER ALL THAT PIE?
THE NEXT EVENT IS THE ELF TOSS.
ELF TOSS? I HAVE TO SEE THIS.
QUINCY!
SORRY I'M LATE.
WAY LATE.
DON'T WORRY ABOUT IT. WE KEPT QUINCY COMPANY.
YOU SLOW, YOU BLOW!
YOU MISSED OUT ON A LOT.
MNCH

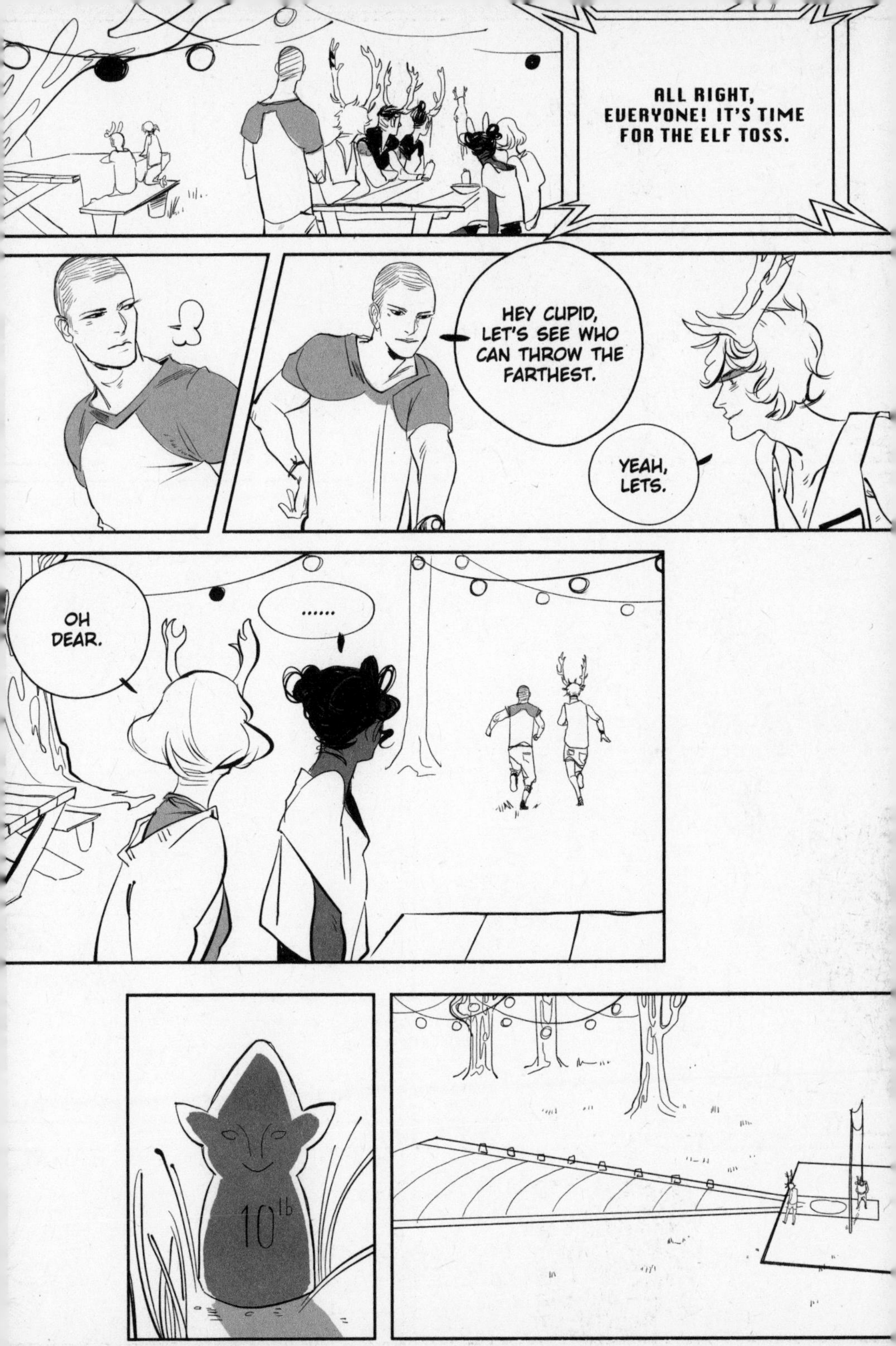
ALL RIGHT, EVERYONE! IT'S TIME FOR THE ELF TOSS.
HEY CUPID, LET'S SEE WHO CAN THROW THE FARTHEST.
YEAH, LETS.
OH DEAR.
......
10lb

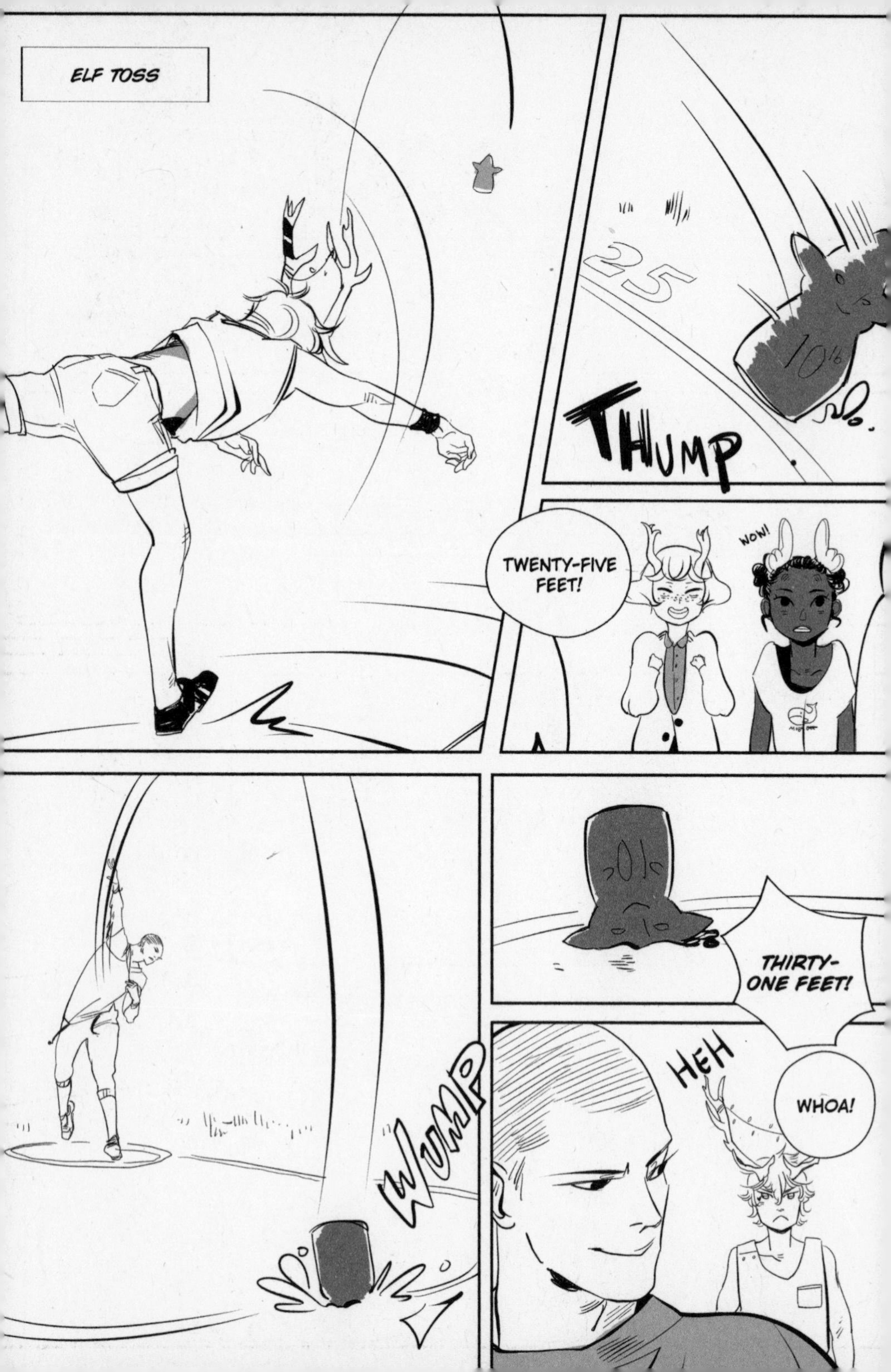
ELF TOSS
25
10lb
THUMP
TWENTY-FIVE FEET!
WOW!
THIRTY-ONE FEET!
WOMP
HEH
WHOA!

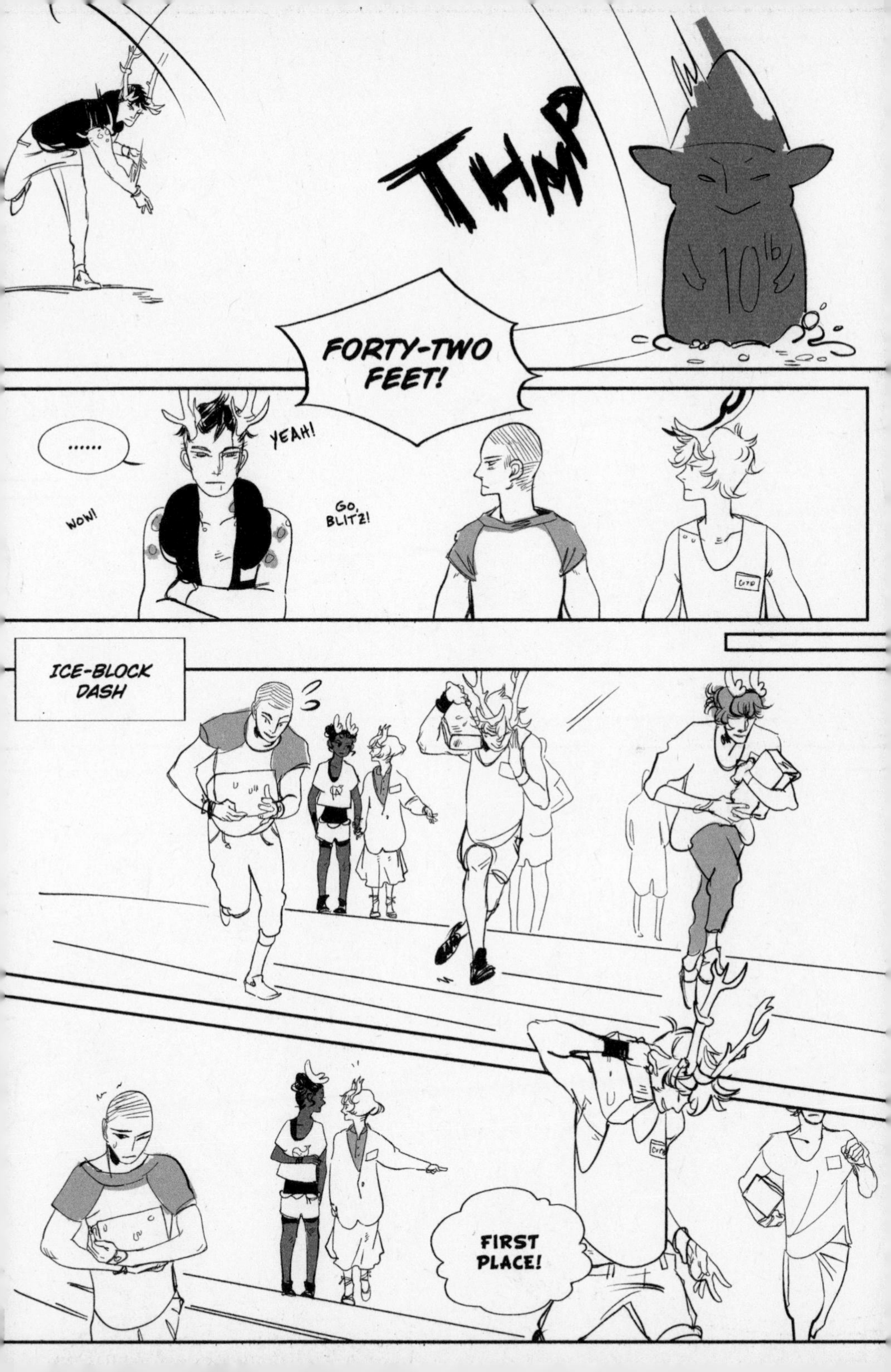
THMP
10lb
FORTY-TWO FEET!
......
YEAH!
WOW!
GO, BLITZ!
ICE-BLOCK DASH
FIRST PLACE!

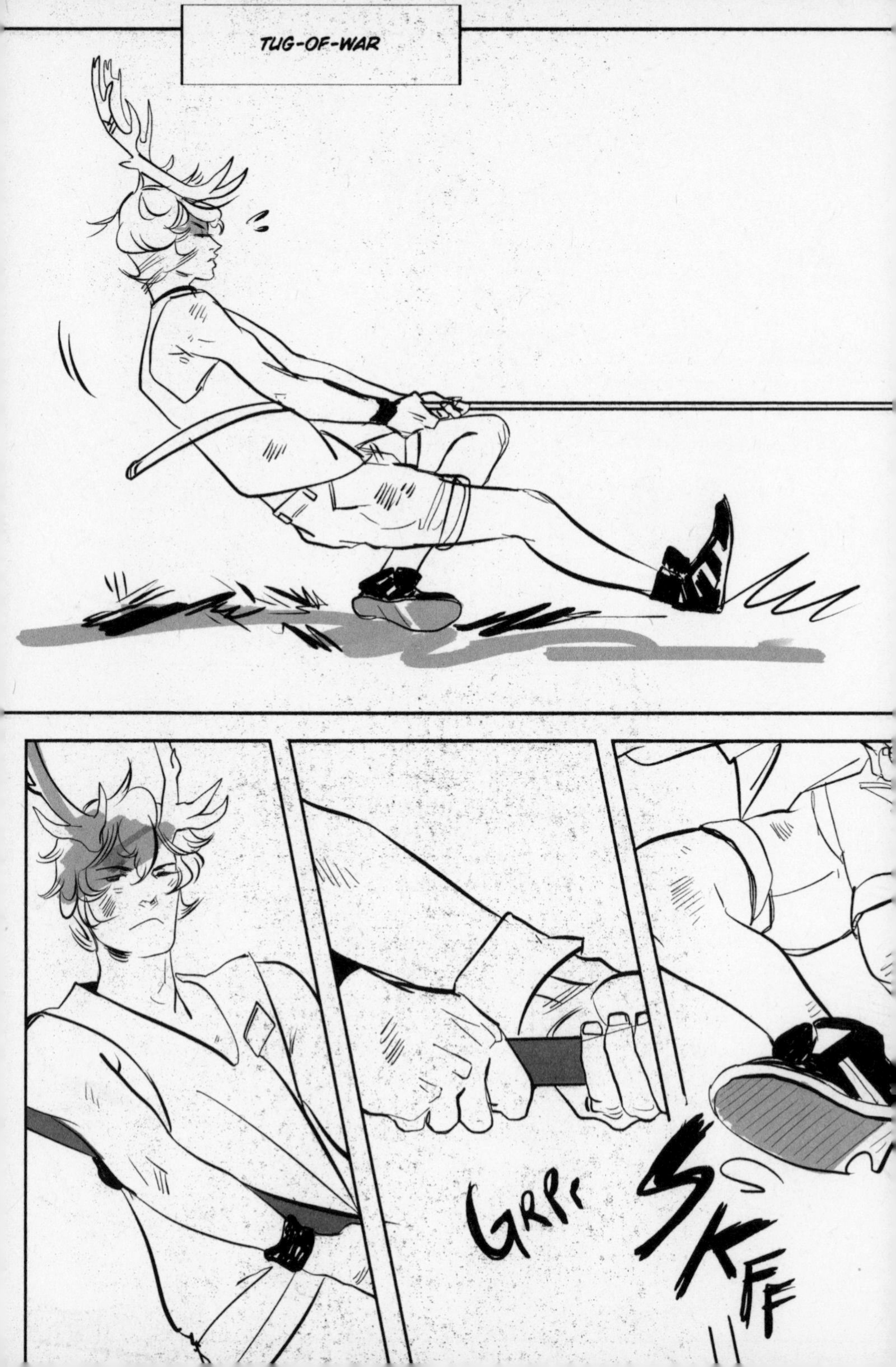
TUG-OF-WAR
GRPP
SKFF

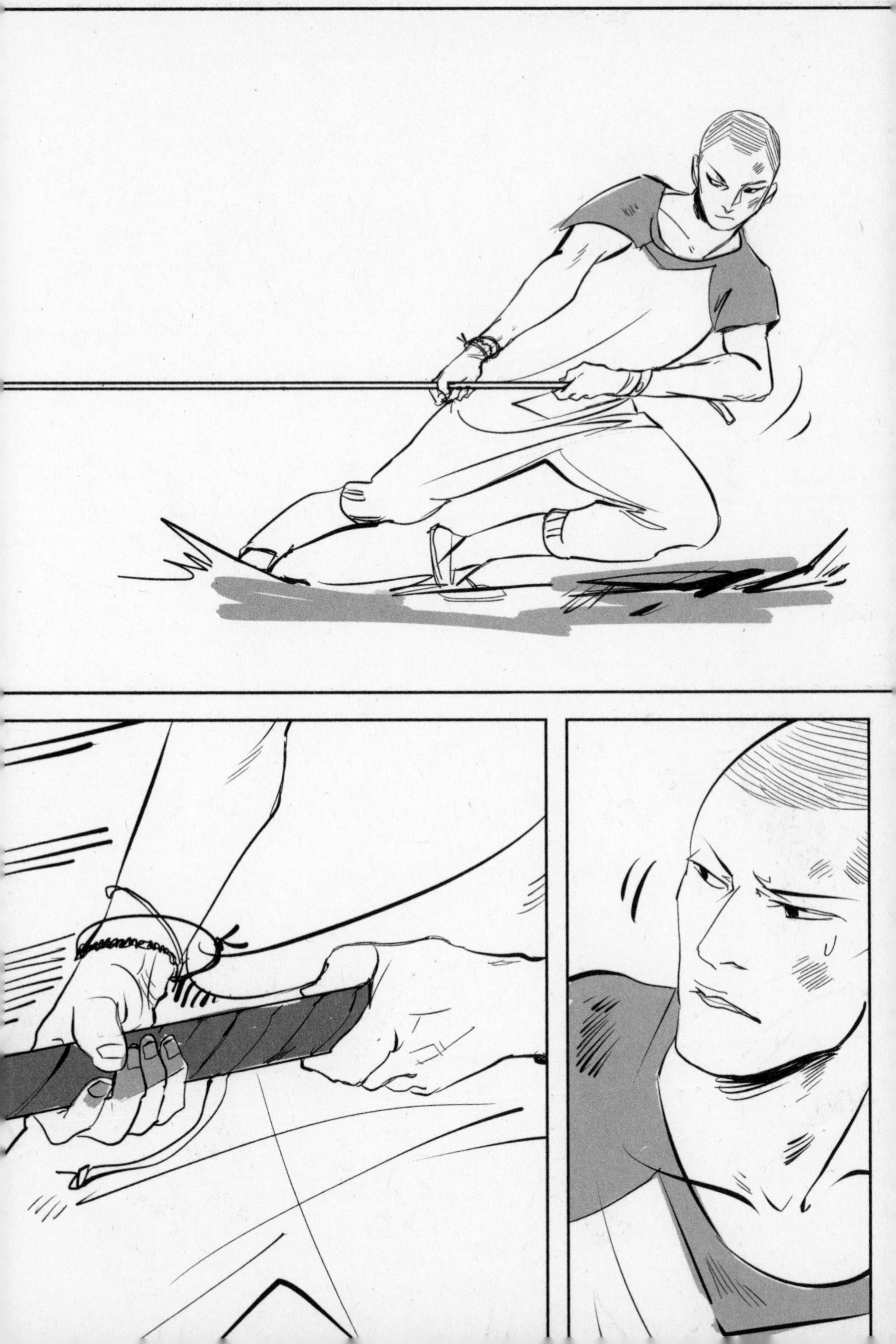

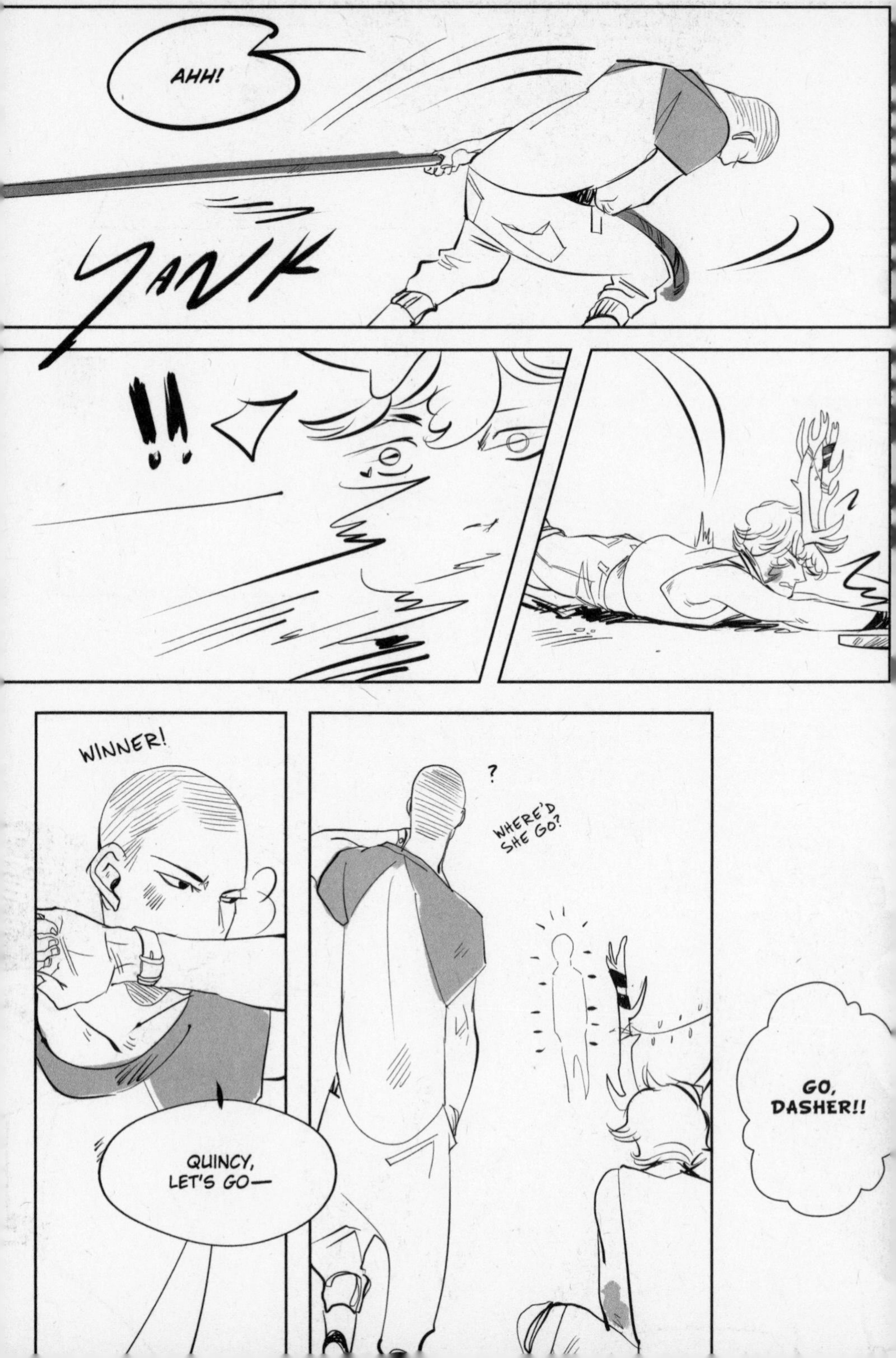
AHH!
YANK
!!
WINNER!
QUINCY, LET'S GO—
?
WHERE'D SHE GO?
GO, DASHER!!

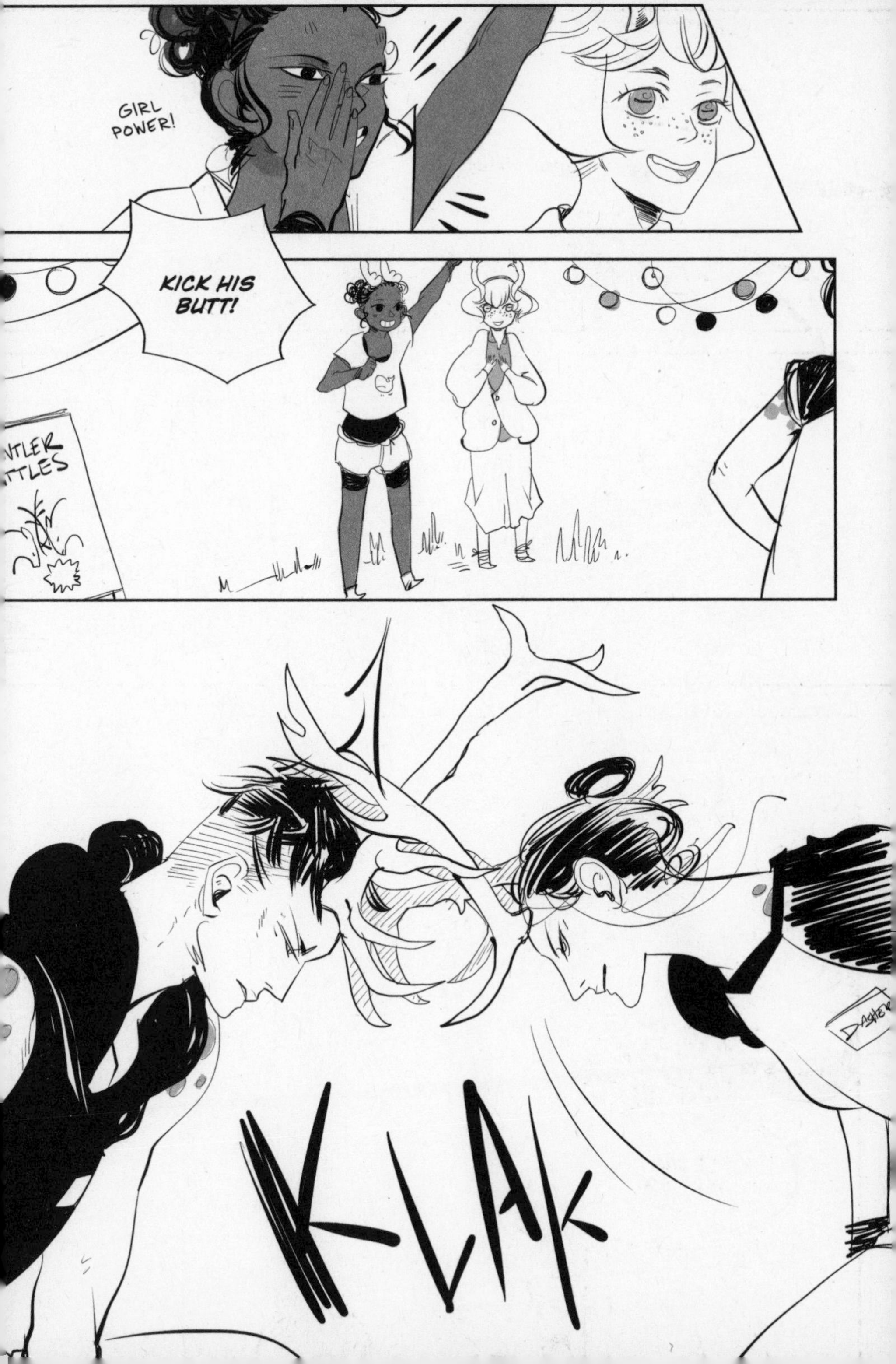
GIRL POWER!
KICK HIS BUTT!
NTLER
TTLES
DASHER
K-LAK

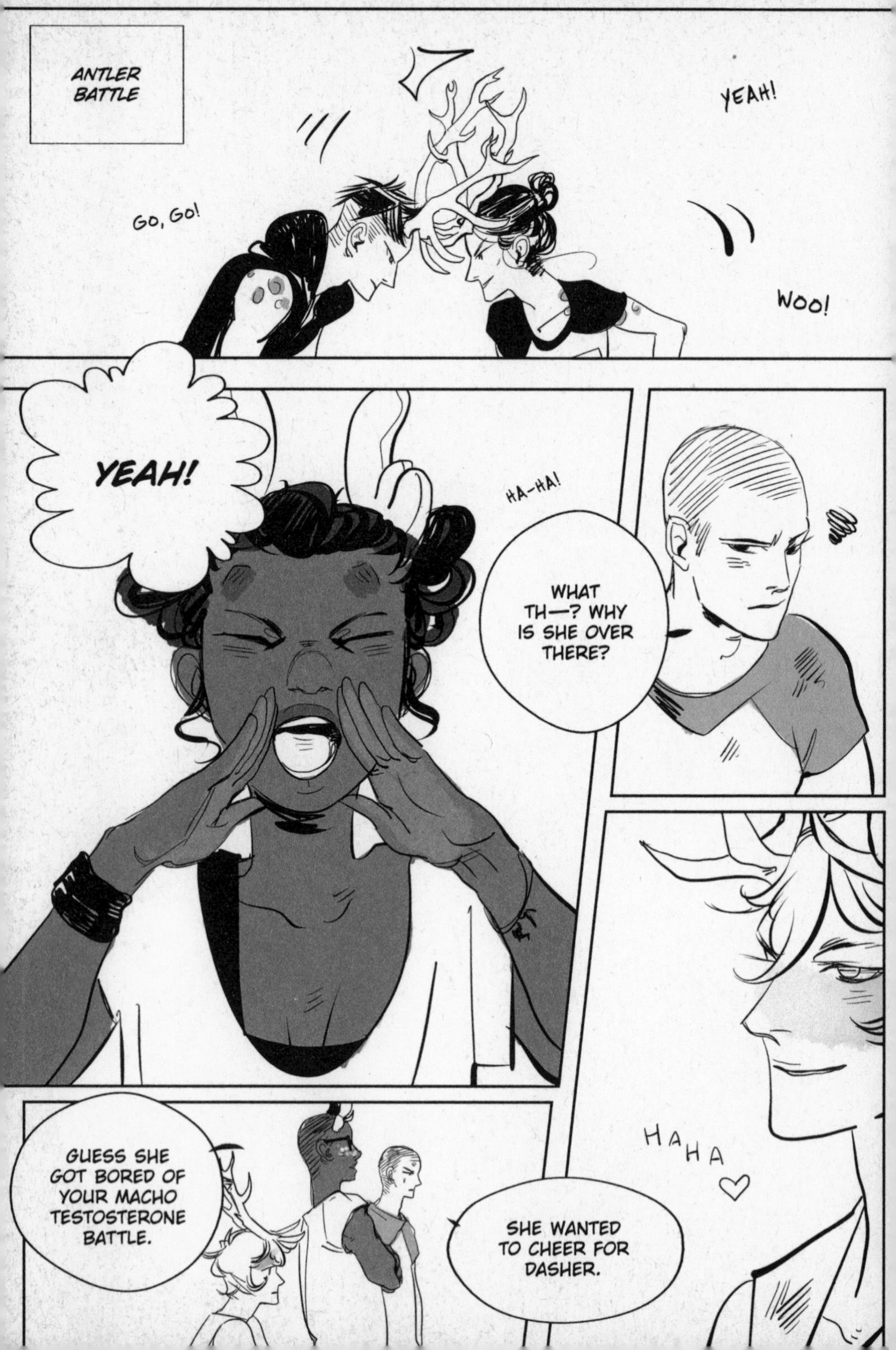
ANTLER BATTLE
GO, GO!
YEAH!
WOO!
YEAH!
HA-HA!
WHAT TH—? WHY IS SHE OVER THERE?
HAHA ♡
GUESS SHE GOT BORED OF YOUR MACHO TESTOSTERONE BATTLE.
SHE WANTED TO CHEER FOR DASHER.

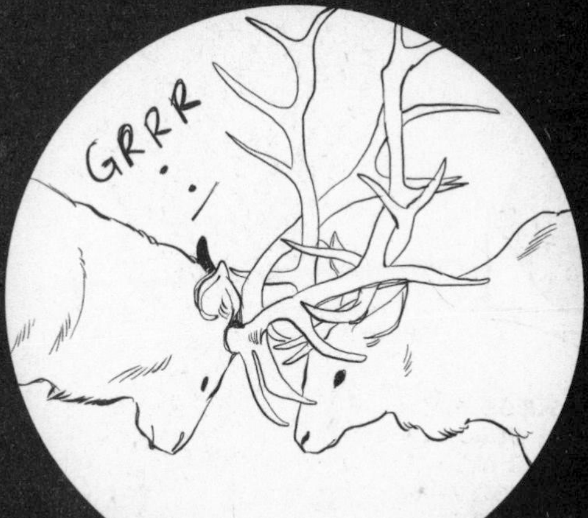
GRRR

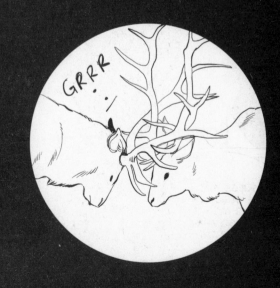

Reindeer Boy

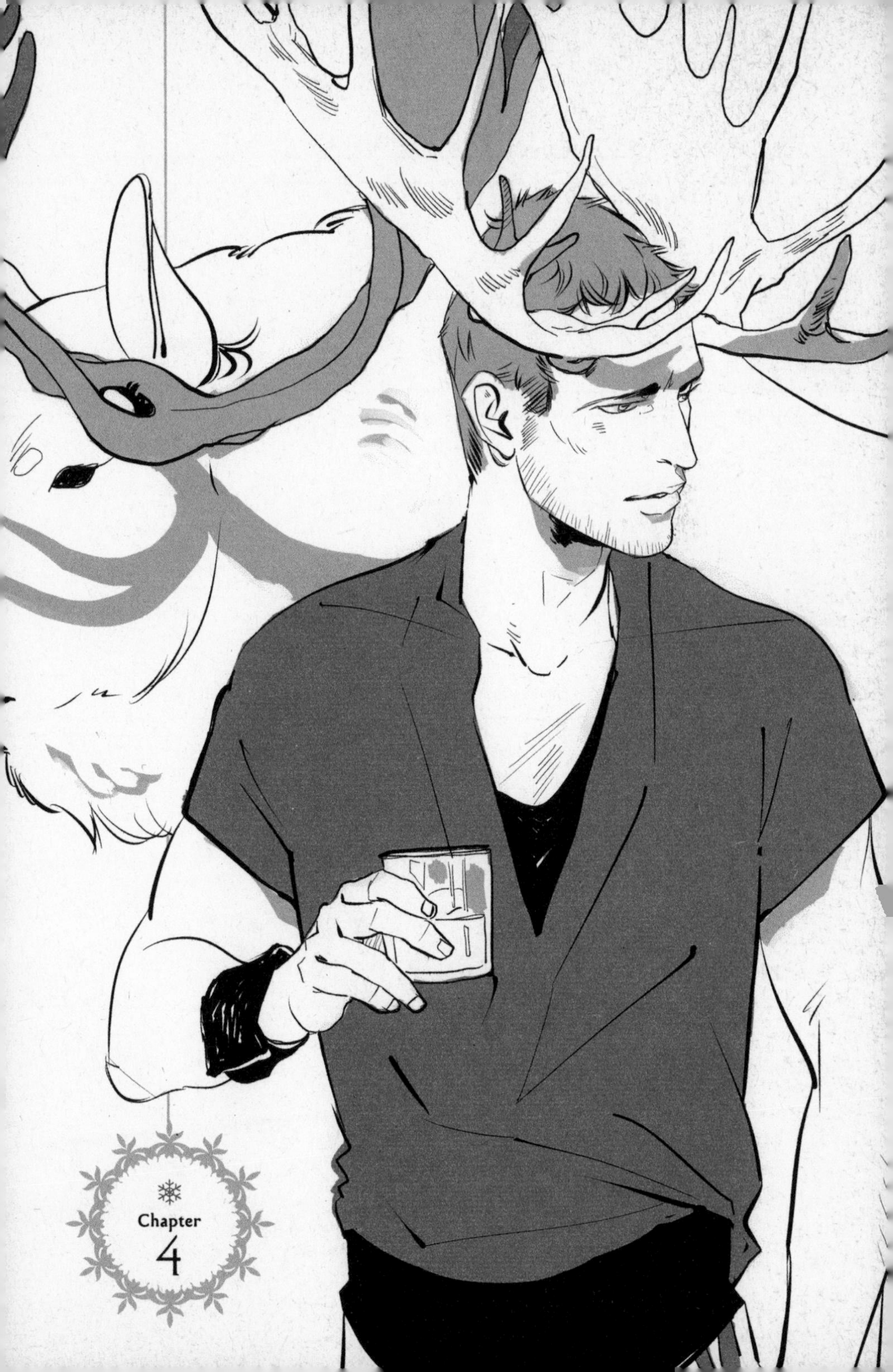

Chapter 4

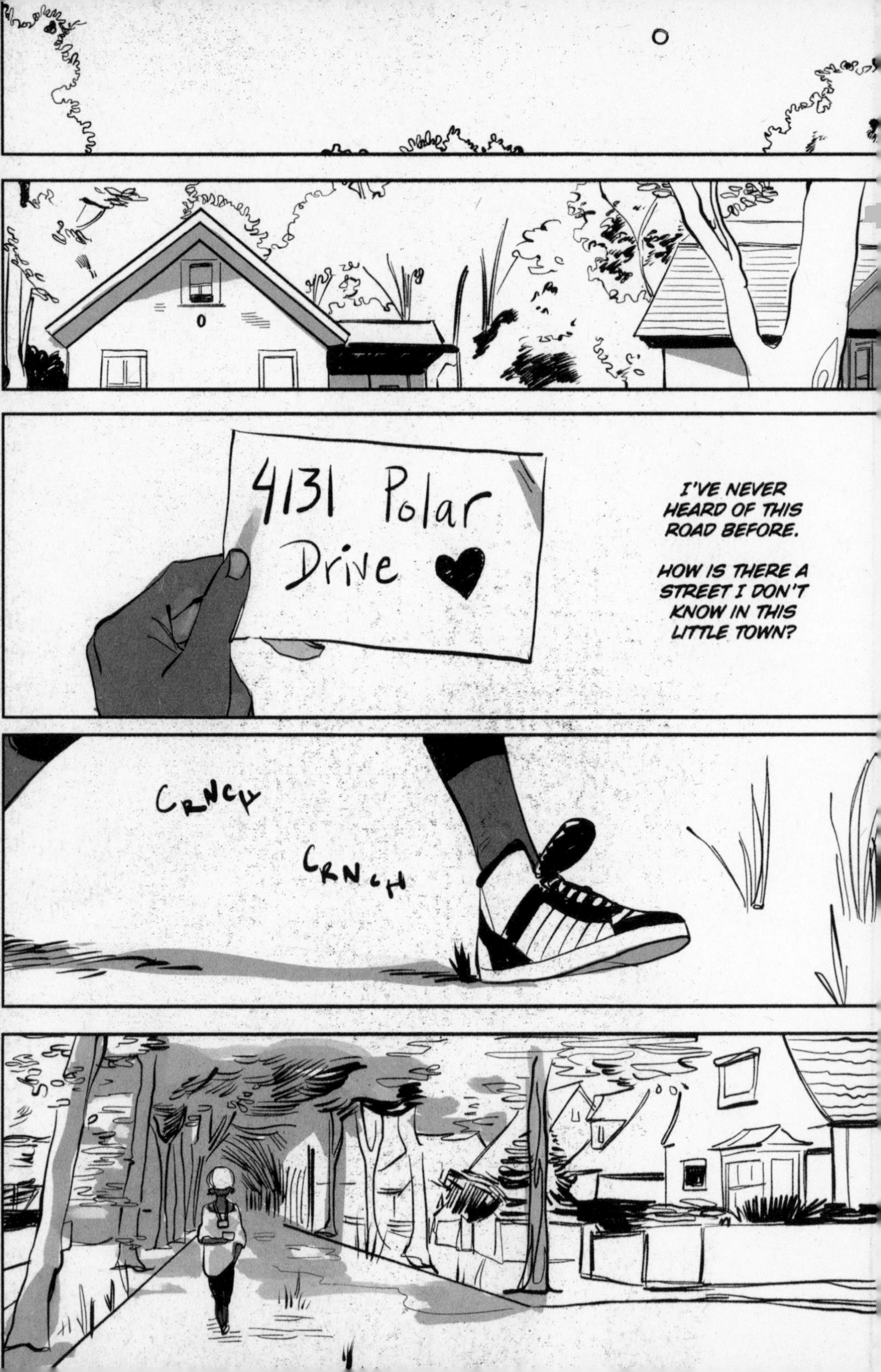
4131 Polar Drive ♥
I'VE NEVER HEARD OF THIS ROAD BEFORE.
HOW IS THERE A STREET I DON'T KNOW IN THIS LITTLE TOWN?
CRNCH
CRNCH

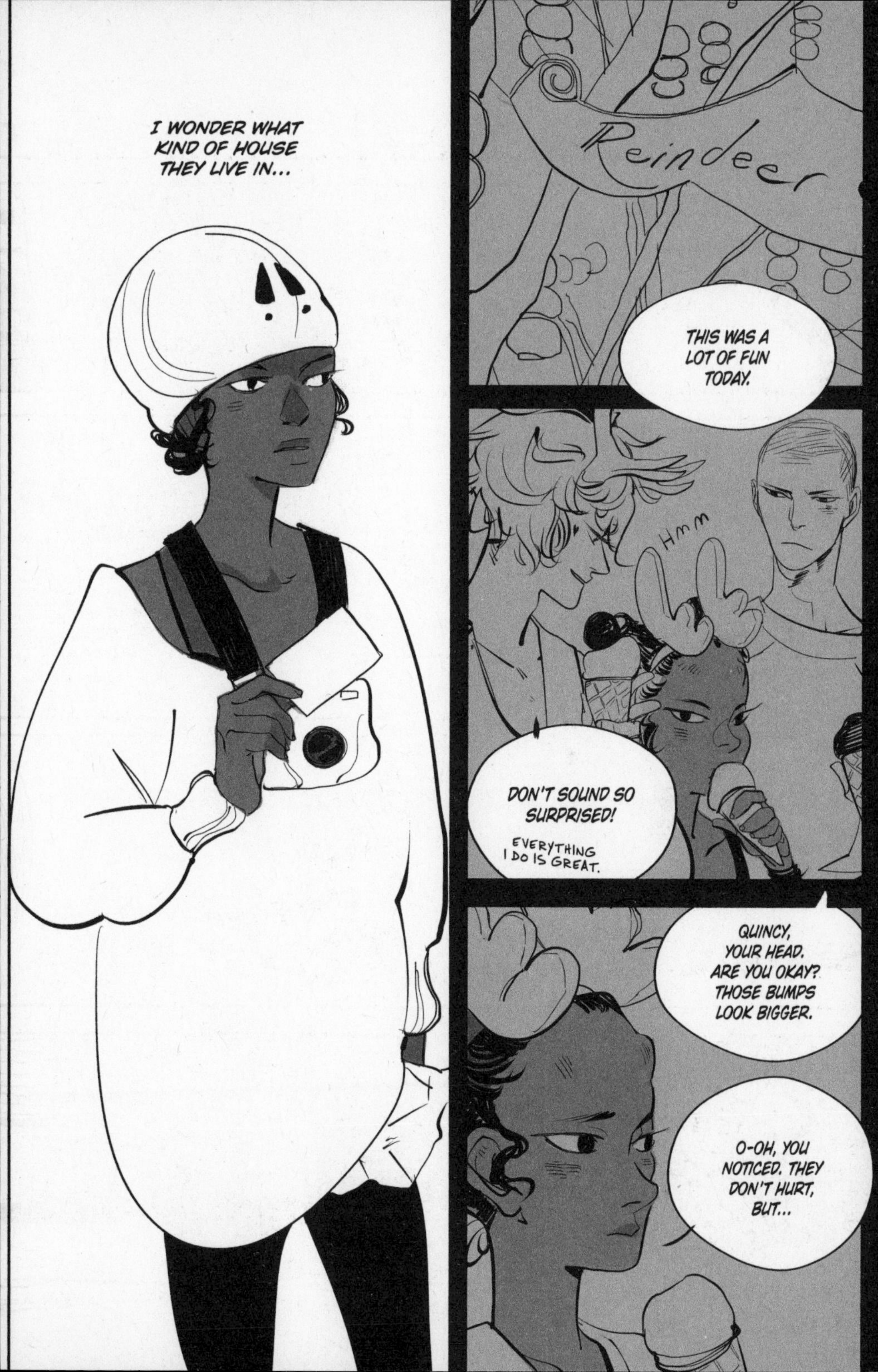
I WONDER WHAT KIND OF HOUSE THEY LIVE IN...
Reindeer
THIS WAS A LOT OF FUN TODAY.
HMM
DON'T SOUND SO SURPRISED!
EVERYTHING I DO IS GREAT.
QUINCY, YOUR HEAD. ARE YOU OKAY? THOSE BUMPS LOOK BIGGER.
O-OH, YOU NOTICED. THEY DON'T HURT, BUT...

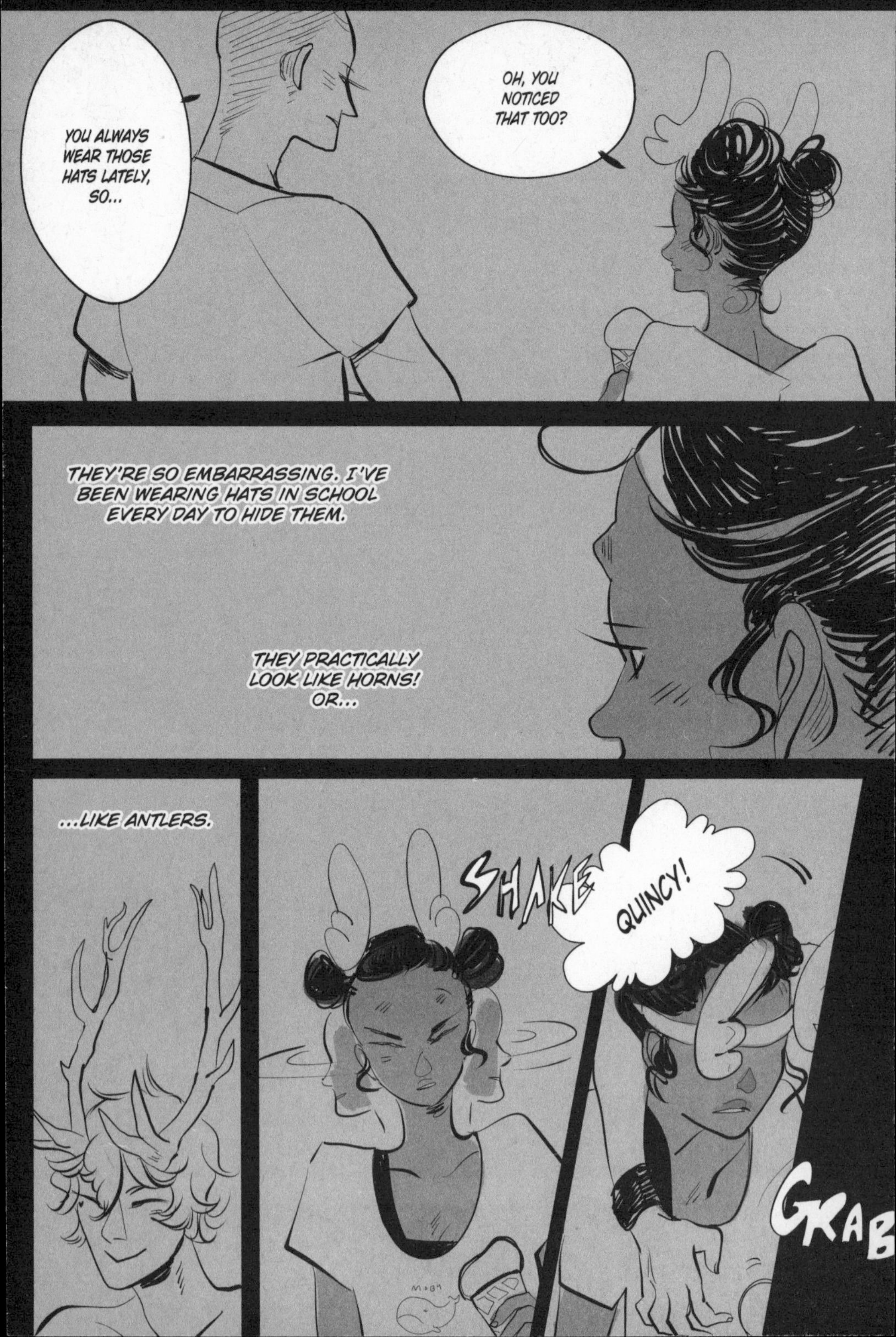
YOU ALWAYS WEAR THOSE HATS LATELY, SO...
OH, YOU NOTICED THAT TOO?
THEY'RE SO EMBARRASSING. I'VE BEEN WEARING HATS IN SCHOOL EVERY DAY TO HIDE THEM.
THEY PRACTICALLY LOOK LIKE HORNS! OR...
...LIKE ANTLERS.
SHAKE
QUINCY!
GRAB

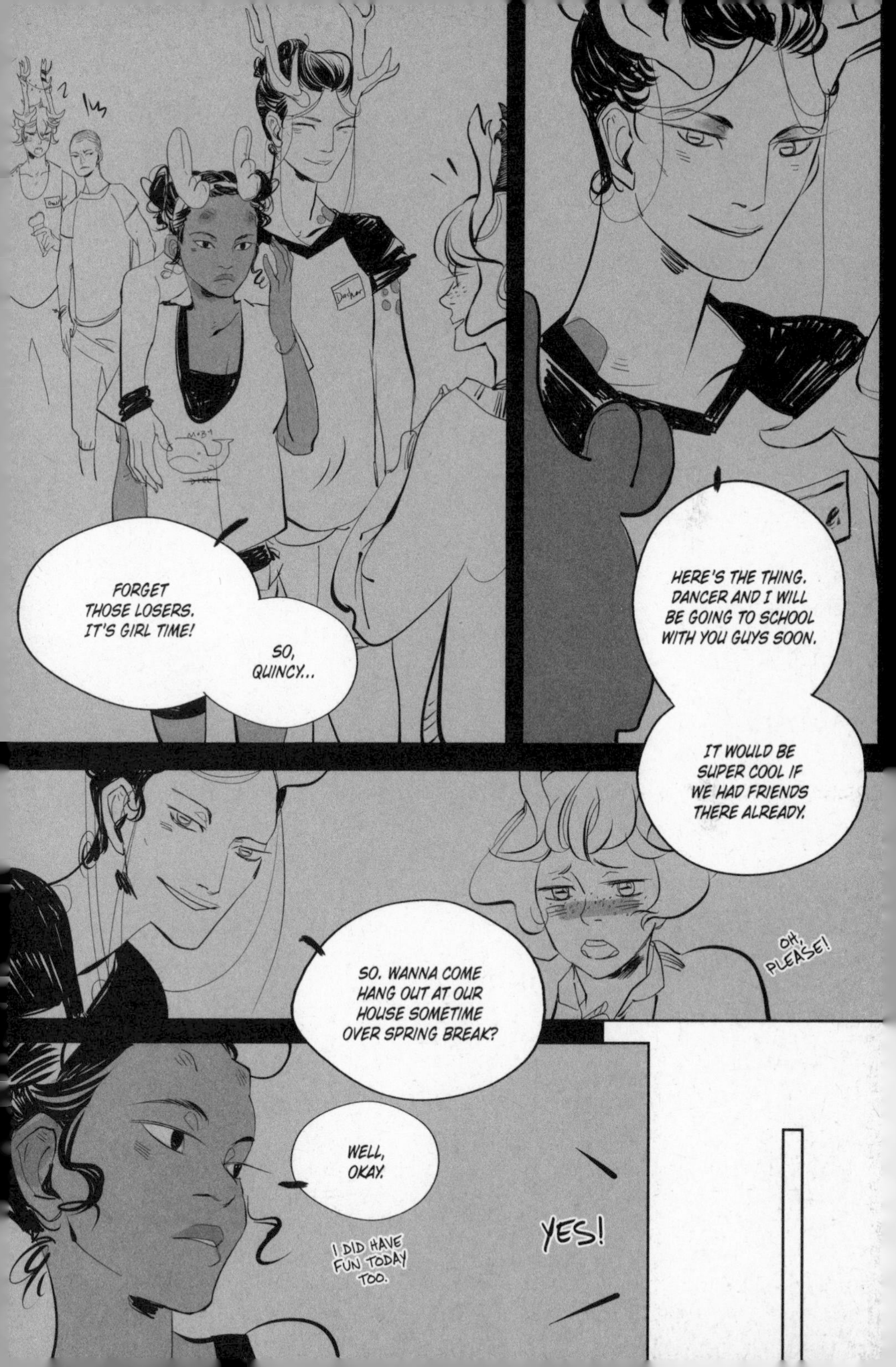
FORGET THOSE LOSERS. IT'S GIRL TIME!
SO, QUINCY...
HERE'S THE THING. DANCER AND I WILL BE GOING TO SCHOOL WITH YOU GUYS SOON.
IT WOULD BE SUPER COOL IF WE HAD FRIENDS THERE ALREADY.
SO. WANNA COME HANG OUT AT OUR HOUSE SOMETIME OVER SPRING BREAK?
OH, PLEASE!
WELL, OKAY.
I DID HAVE FUN TODAY TOO.
YES!

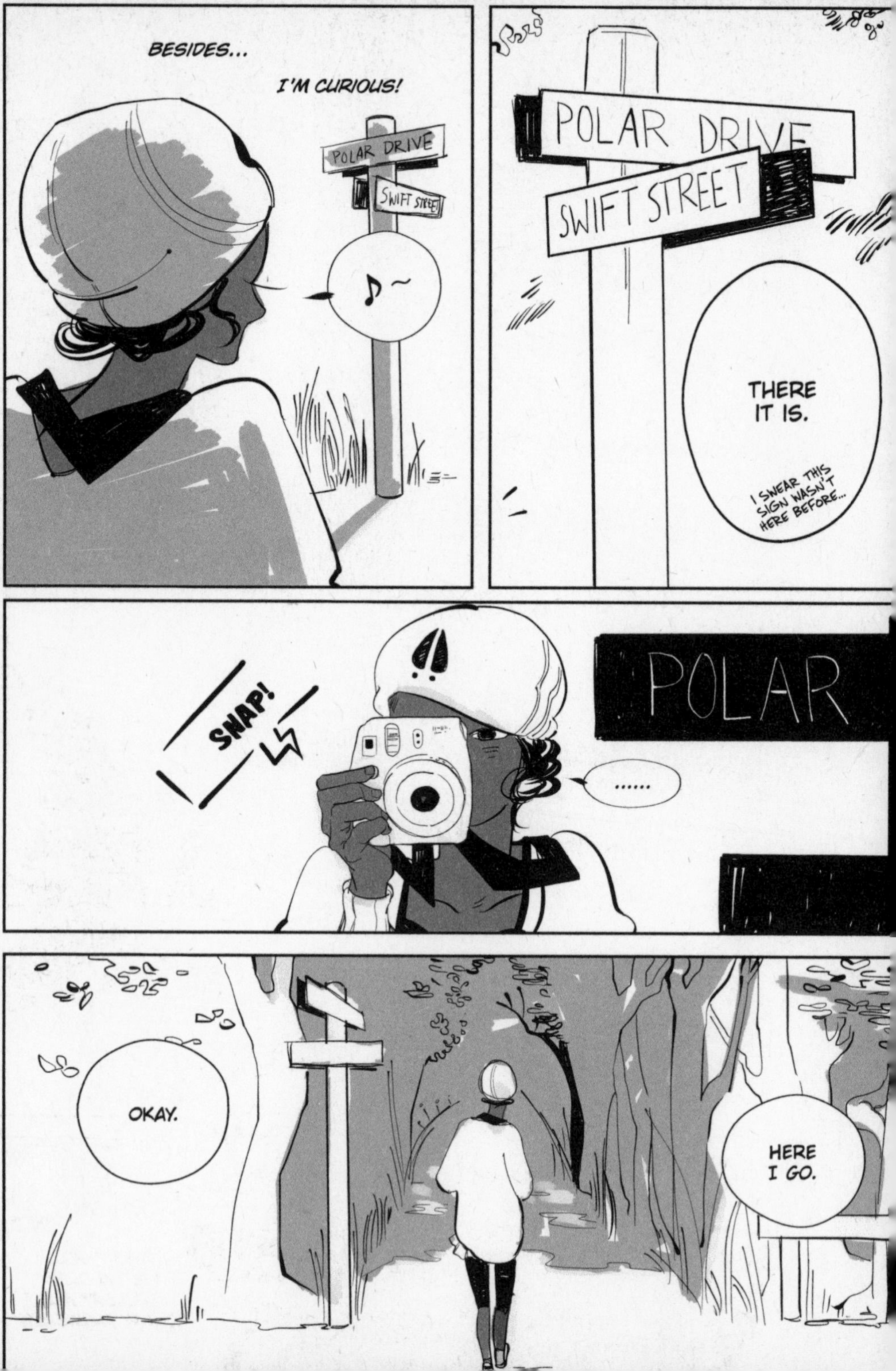
BESIDES...
I'M CURIOUS!
POLAR DRIVE
SWIFT STREET
♪~
POLAR DRIVE
SWIFT STREET
THERE IT IS.
I SWEAR THIS SIGN WASN'T HERE BEFORE...
SNAP!
......
POLAR
OKAY.
HERE I GO.

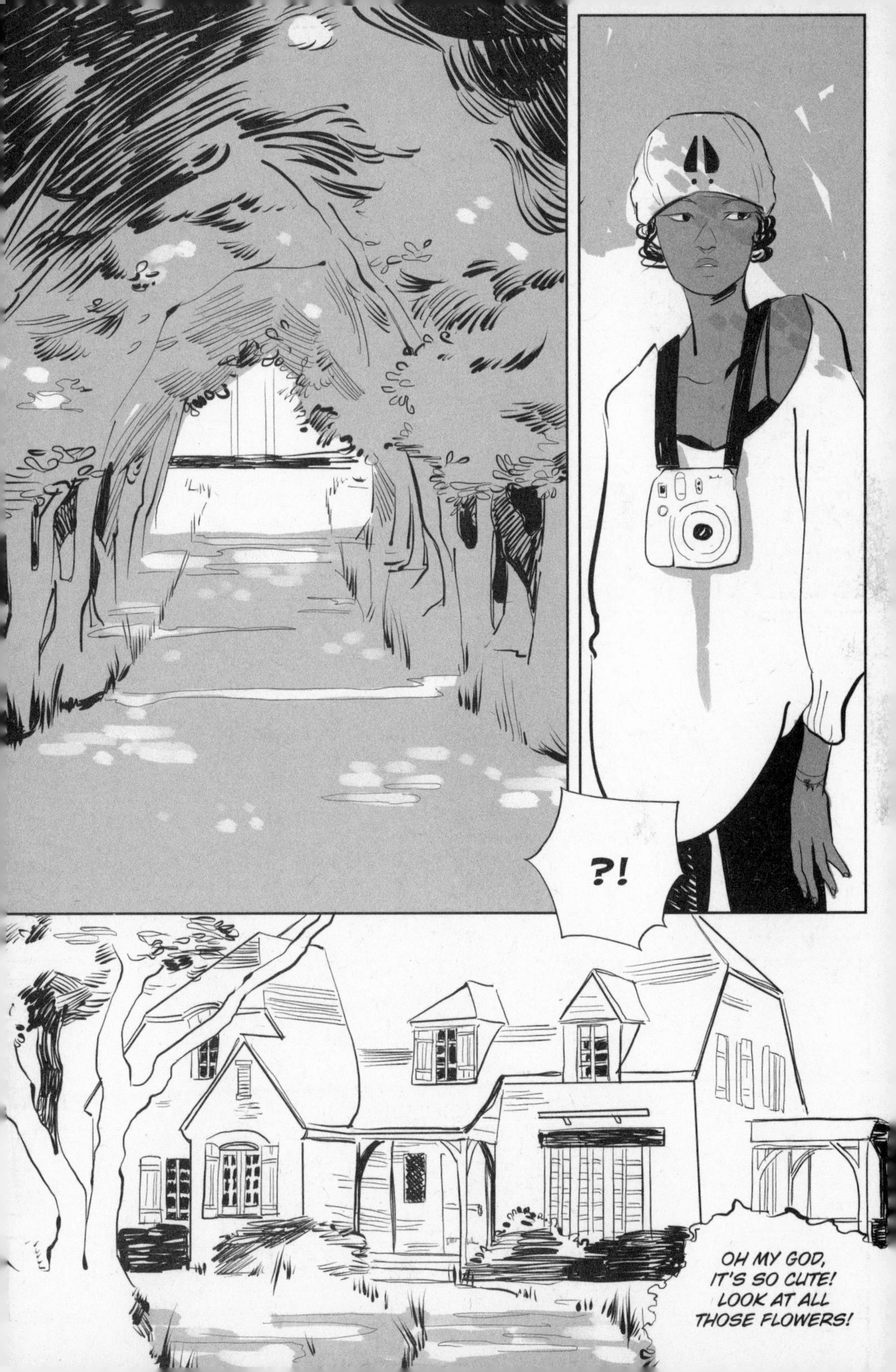
?!
OH MY GOD, IT'S SO CUTE! LOOK AT ALL THOSE FLOWERS!

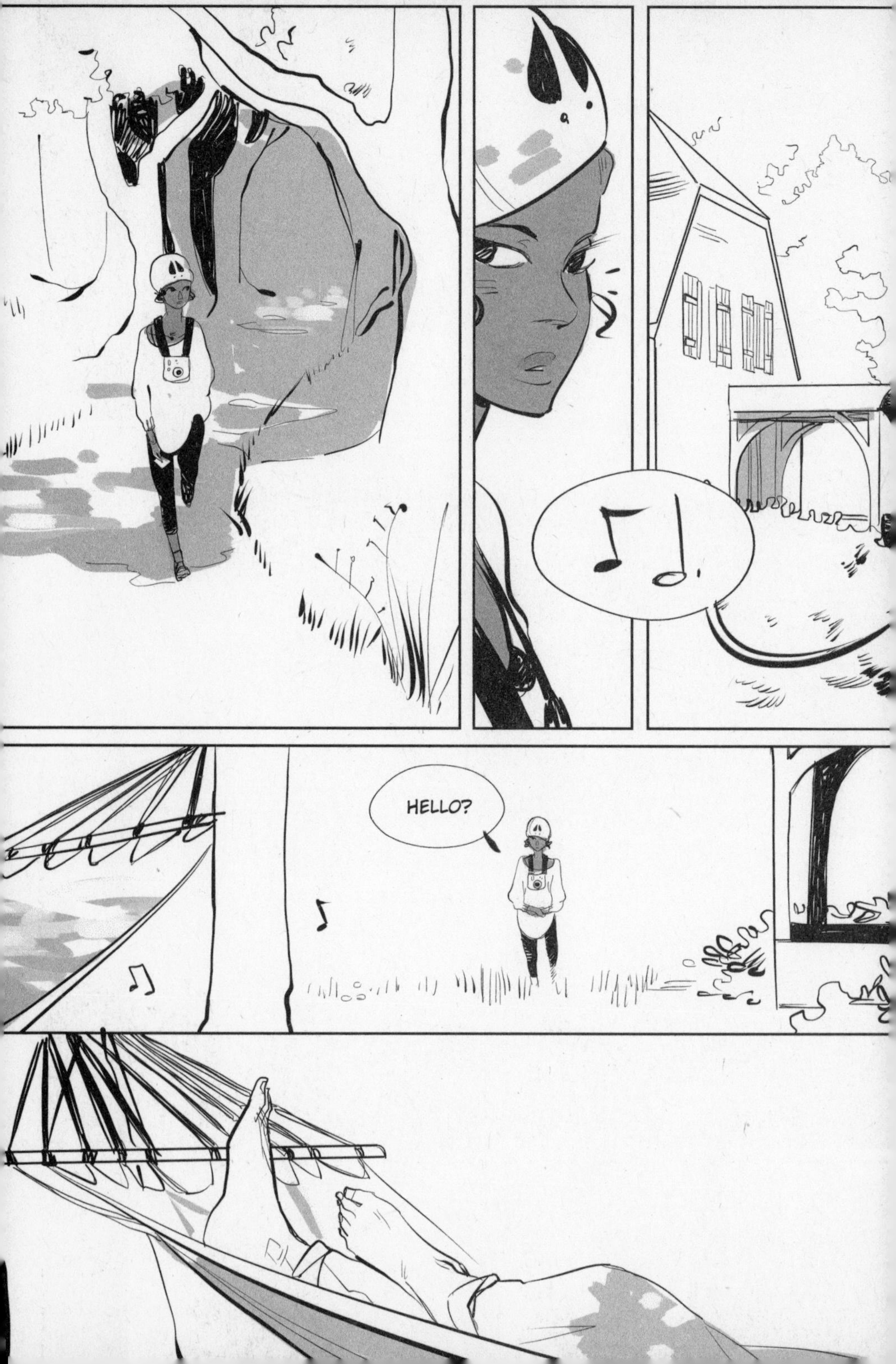
HELLO?

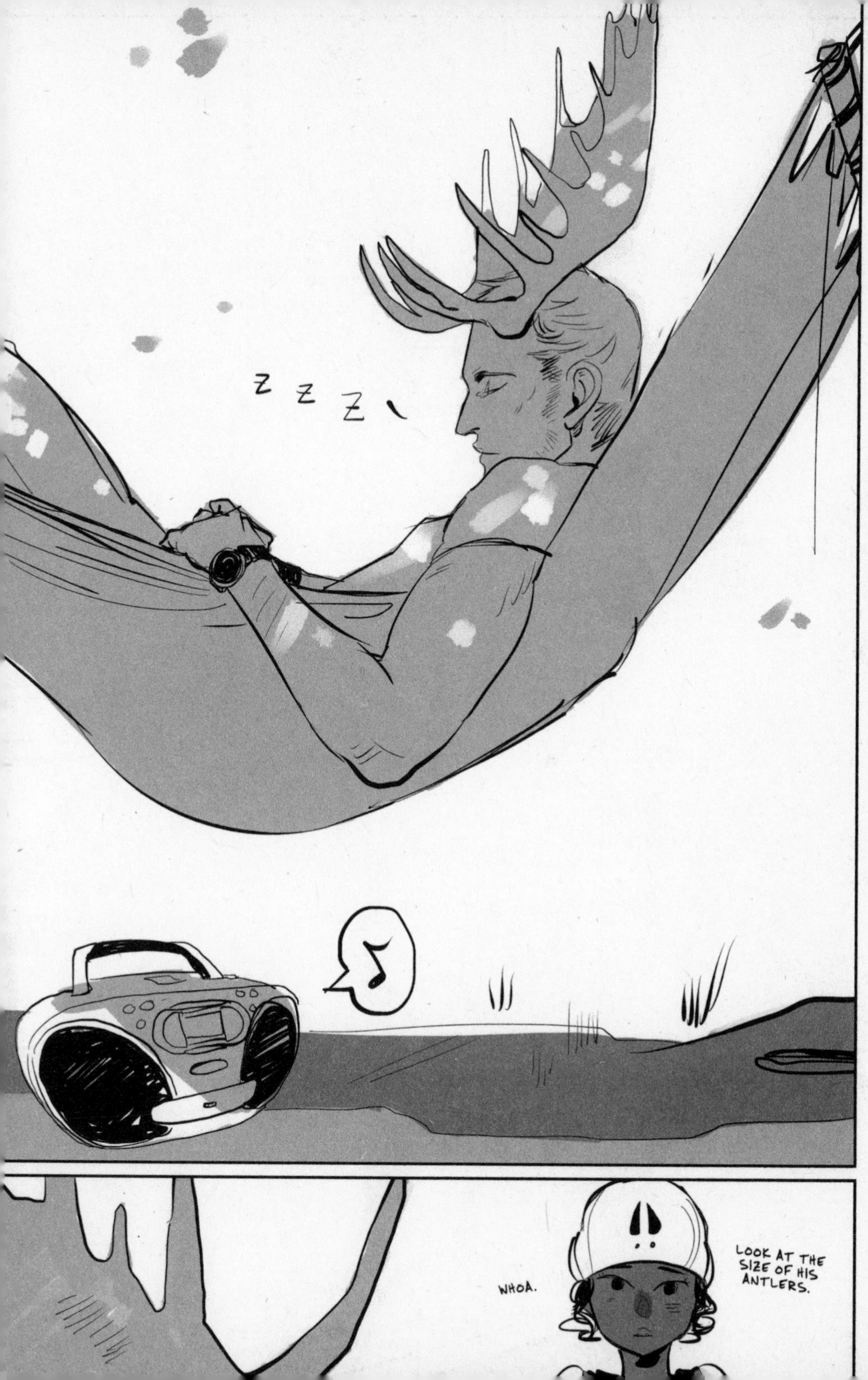
Z Z Z
WHOA.
LOOK AT THE SIZE OF HIS ANTLERS.

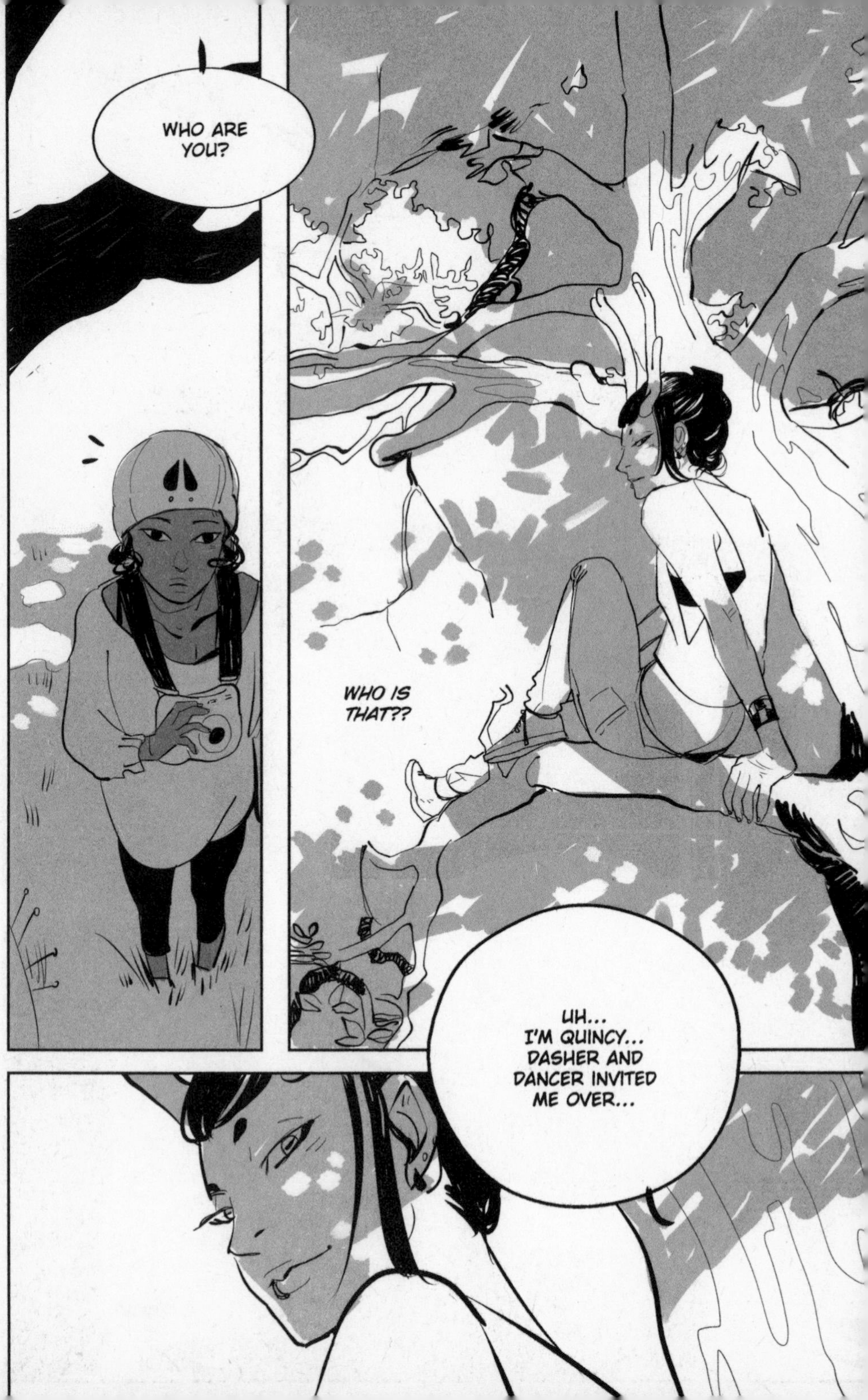
WHO ARE YOU?
WHO IS THAT??
UH... I'M QUINCY... DASHER AND DANCER INVITED ME OVER...

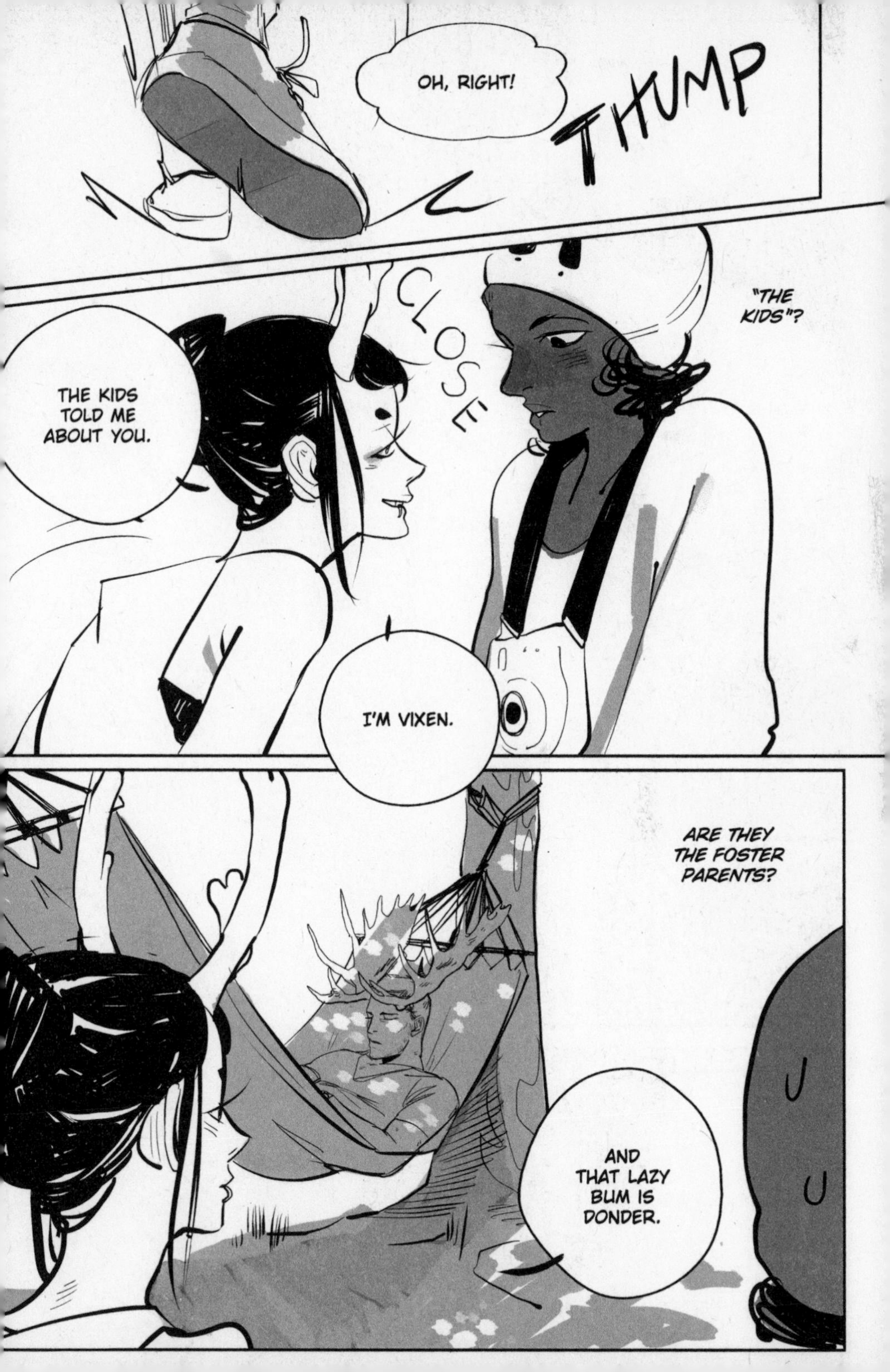

OH, RIGHT!
THUMP
THE KIDS TOLD ME ABOUT YOU.
CLOSE
"THE KIDS"?
I'M VIXEN.
ARE THEY THE FOSTER PARENTS?
AND THAT LAZY BUM IS DONDER.

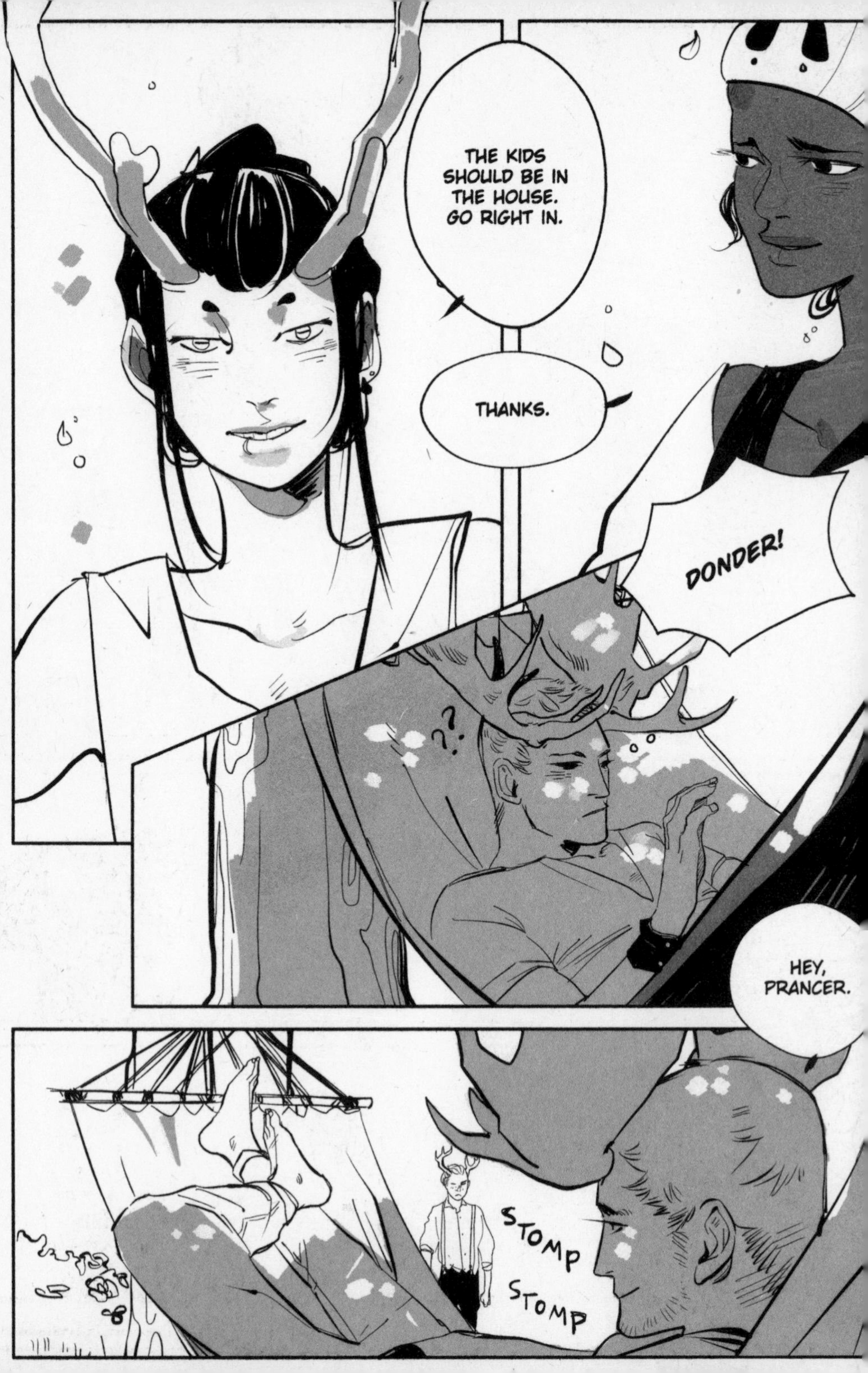
THE KIDS SHOULD BE IN THE HOUSE. GO RIGHT IN.
THANKS.
DONDER!
HEY, PRANCER.
STOMP
STOMP

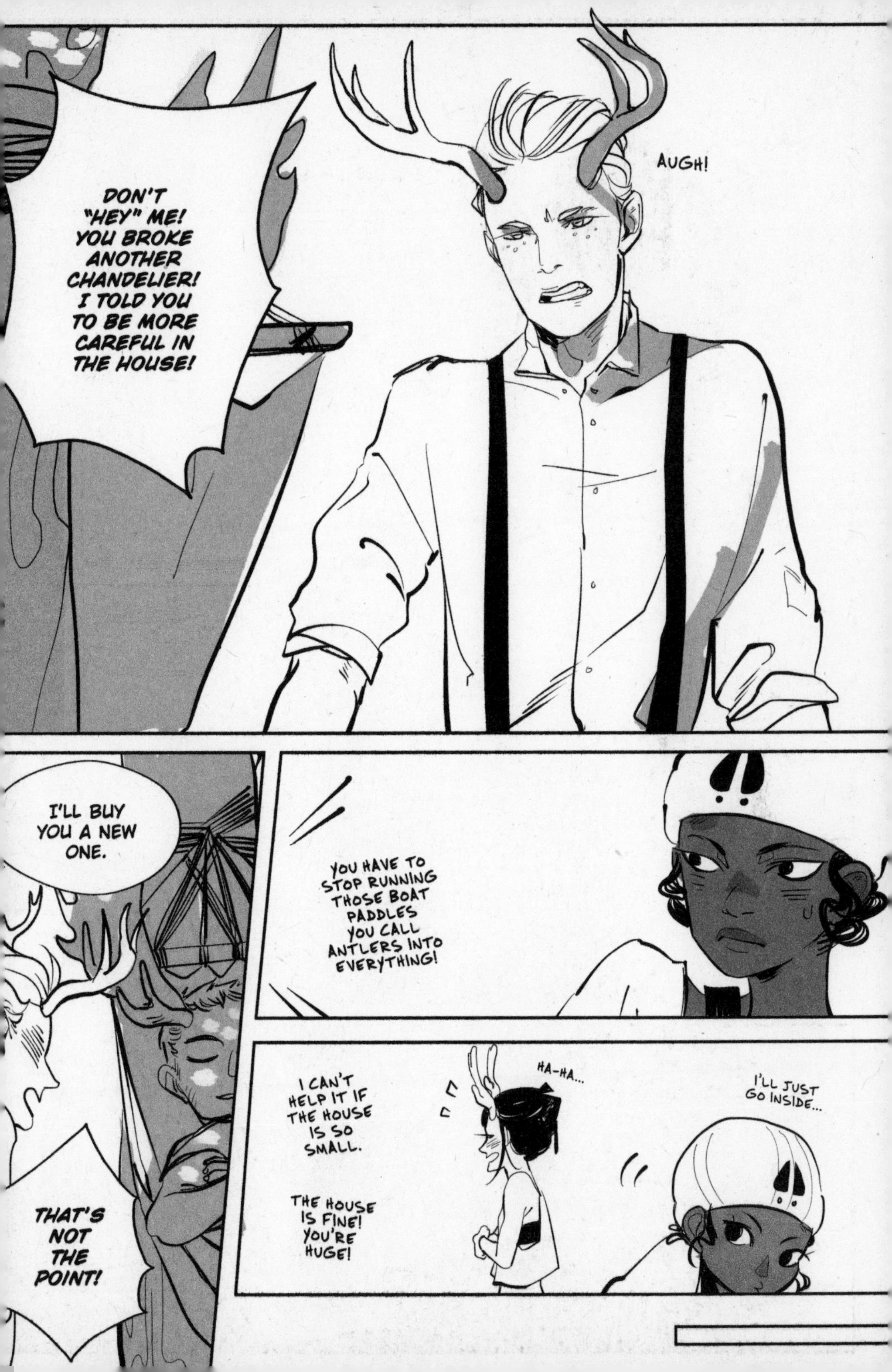
DON'T "HEY" ME! YOU BROKE ANOTHER CHANDELIER! I TOLD YOU TO BE MORE CAREFUL IN THE HOUSE!
AUGH!
I'LL BUY YOU A NEW ONE.
THAT'S NOT THE POINT!
YOU HAVE TO STOP RUNNING THOSE BOAT PADDLES YOU CALL ANTLERS INTO EVERYTHING!
I CAN'T HELP IT IF THE HOUSE IS SO SMALL.
THE HOUSE IS FINE! YOU'RE HUGE!
HA-HA...
I'LL JUST GO INSIDE...

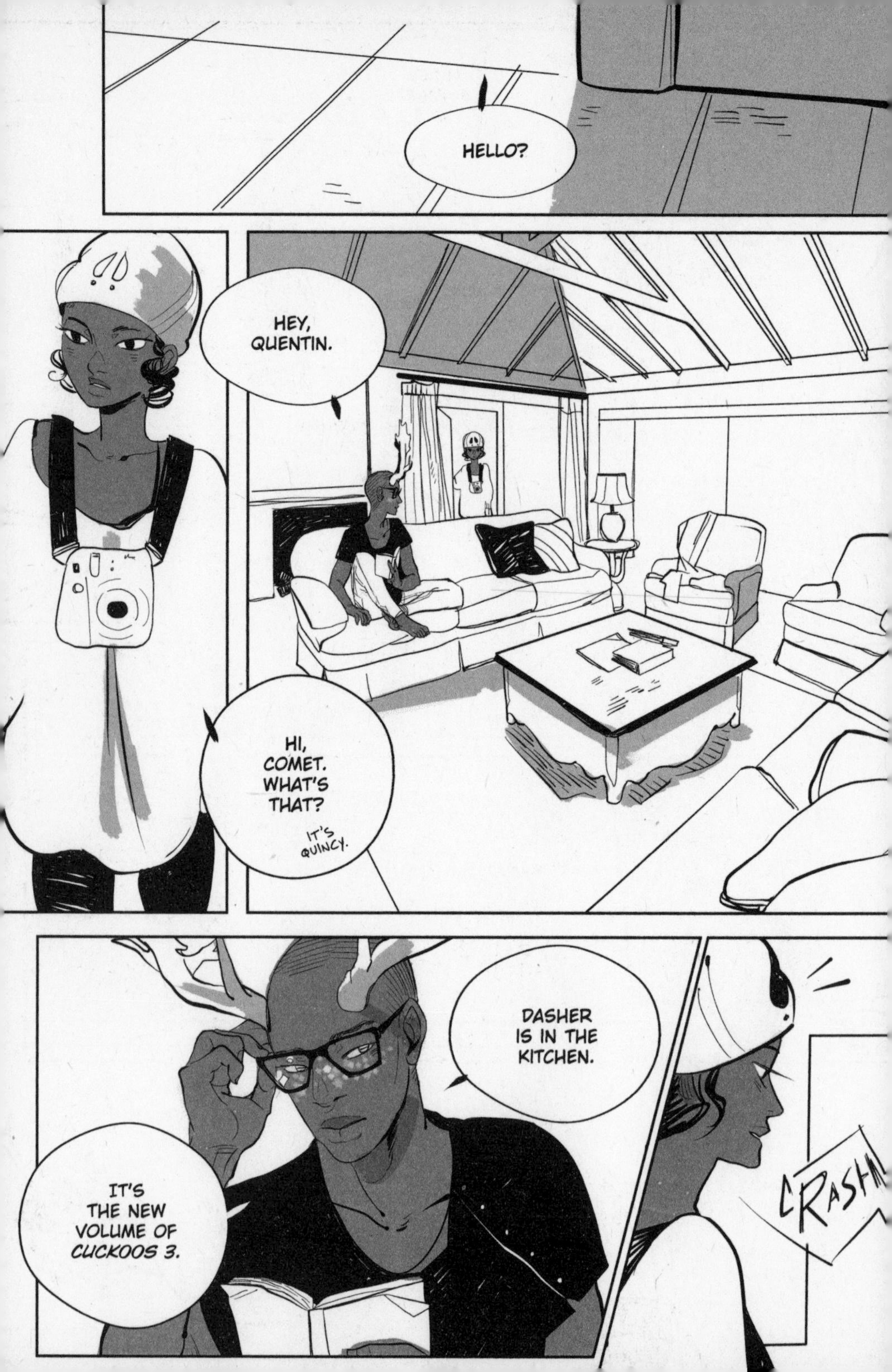
HELLO?
HEY, QUENTIN.
HI, COMET. WHAT'S THAT?
IT'S QUINCY.
IT'S THE NEW VOLUME OF *CUCKOOS 3.*
DASHER IS IN THE KITCHEN.
CRASH

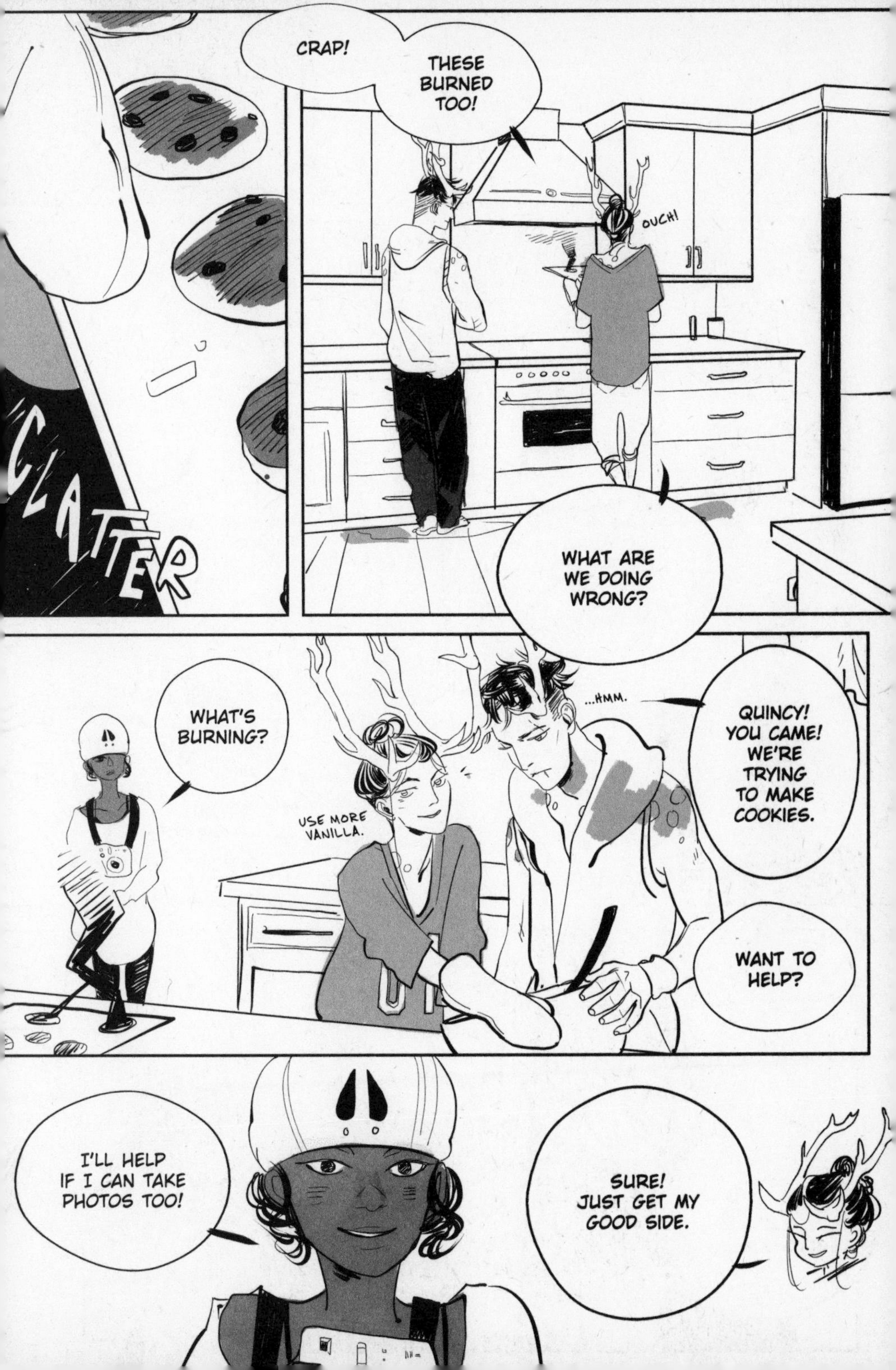
CLATTER
CRAP!
THESE BURNED TOO!
OUCH!
WHAT ARE WE DOING WRONG?
WHAT'S BURNING?
USE MORE VANILLA.
...HMM.
QUINCY! YOU CAME! WE'RE TRYING TO MAKE COOKIES.
WANT TO HELP?
I'LL HELP IF I CAN TAKE PHOTOS TOO!
SURE! JUST GET MY GOOD SIDE.

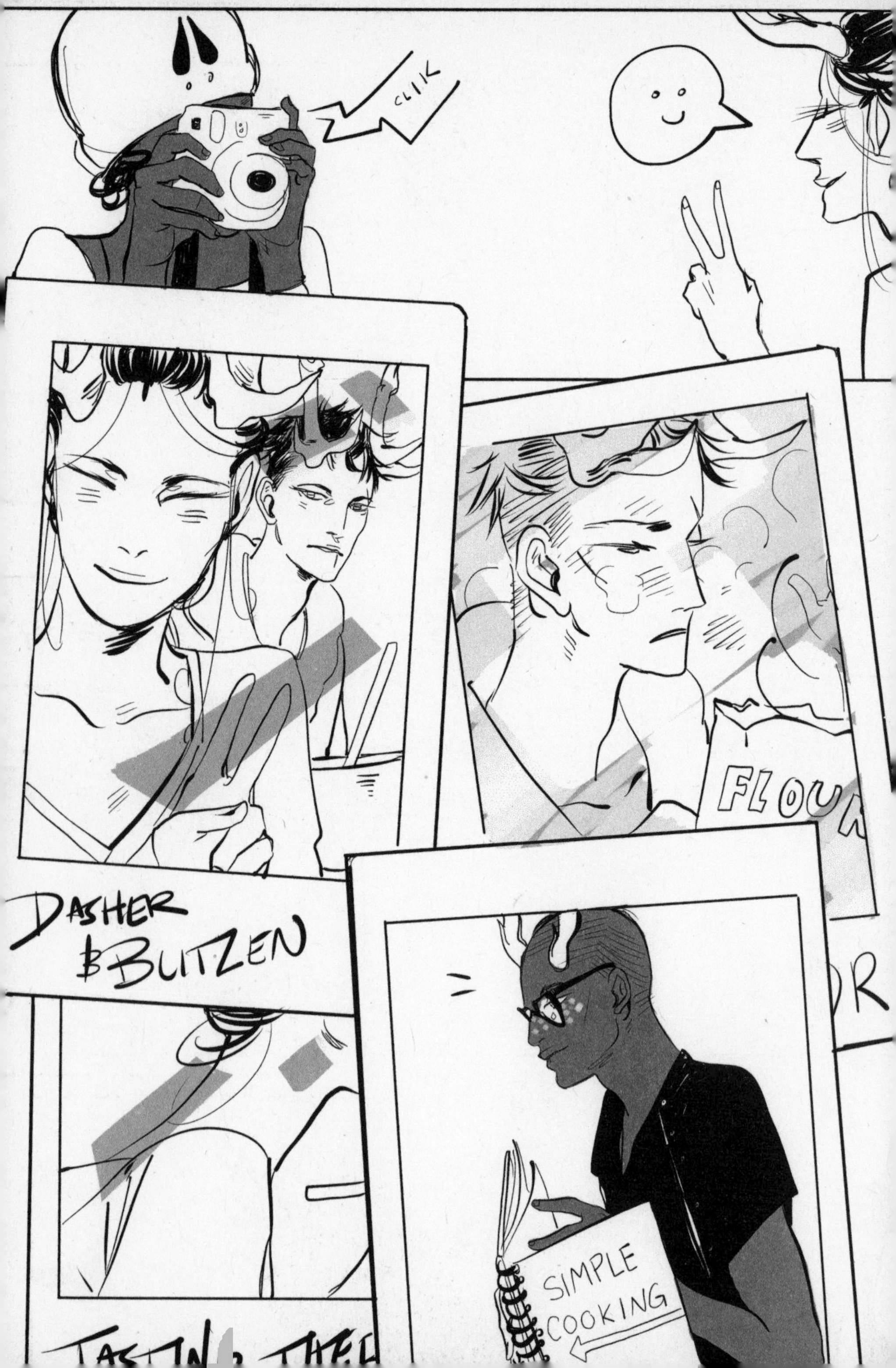
CLIK
DASHER & BLITZEN
FLOU
SIMPLE COOKING

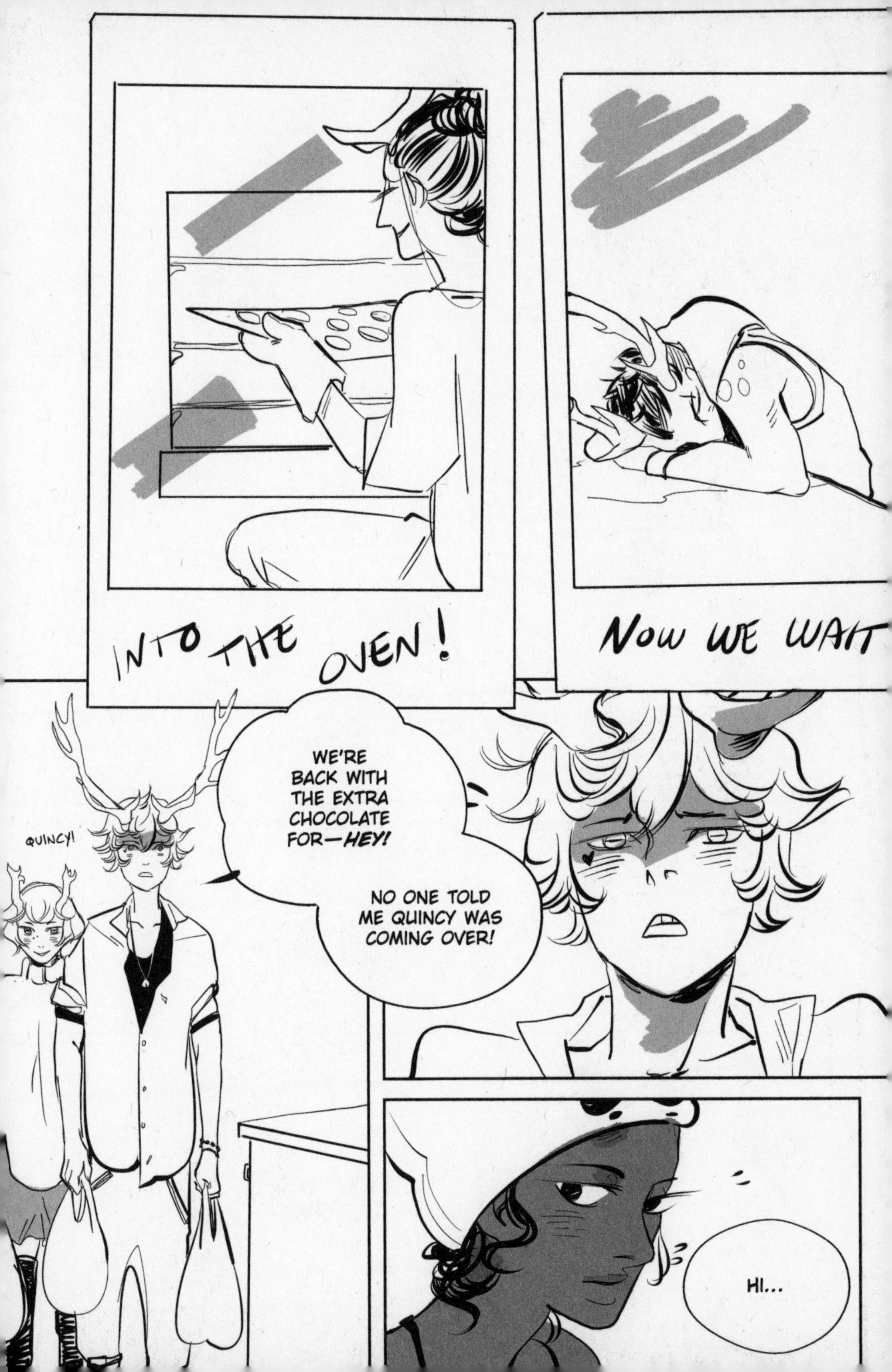
INTO THE OVEN!
NOW WE WAIT
QUINCY!
WE'RE BACK WITH THE EXTRA CHOCOLATE FOR—HEY!
NO ONE TOLD ME QUINCY WAS COMING OVER!
HI...

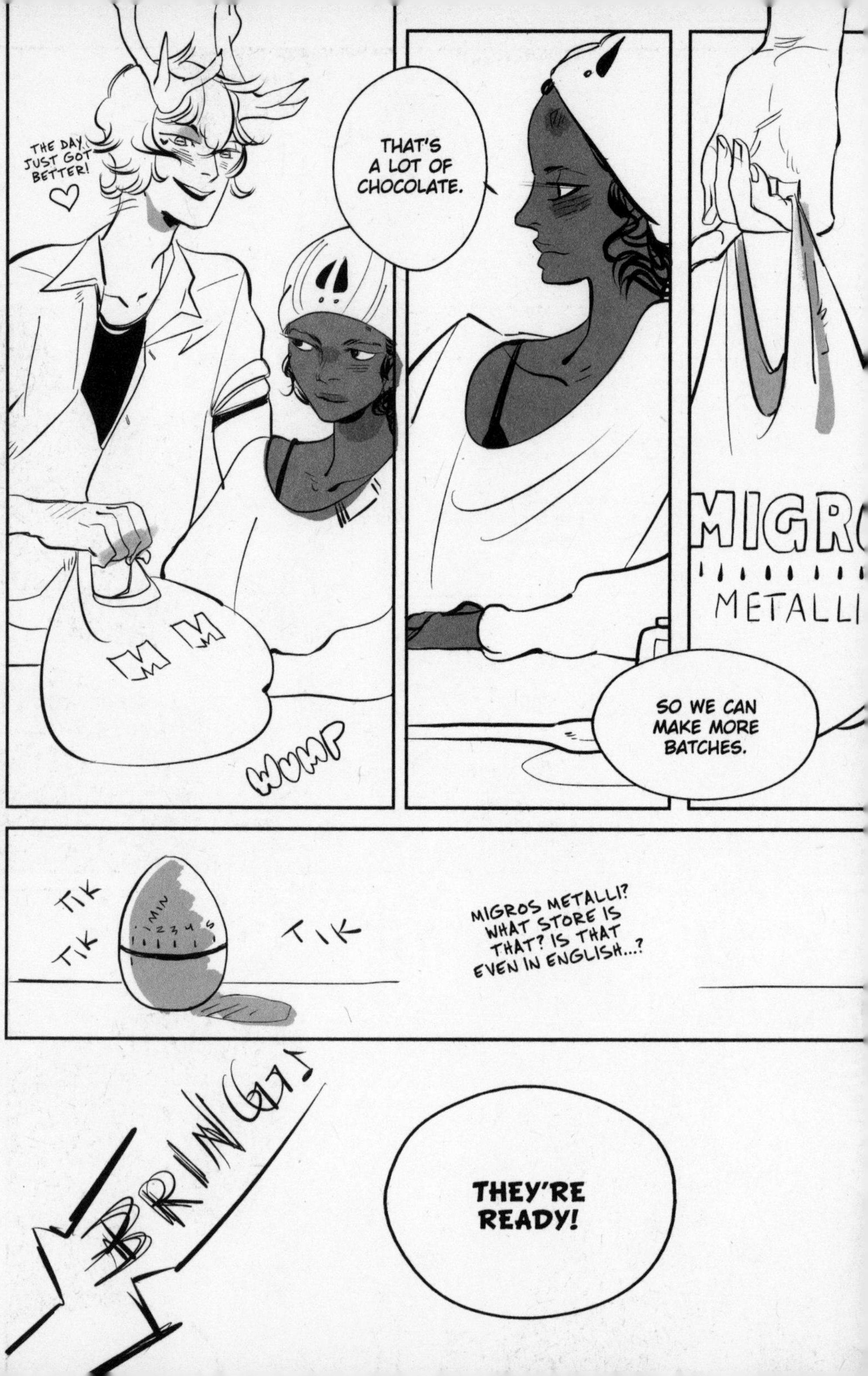
THE DAY JUST GOT BETTER! ♡
THAT'S A LOT OF CHOCOLATE.
WUMP
MIGRO
METALLI
SO WE CAN MAKE MORE BATCHES.
TIK
TIK
TIK
MIGROS METALLI? WHAT STORE IS THAT? IS THAT EVEN IN ENGLISH...?
BRINGG!
THEY'RE READY!

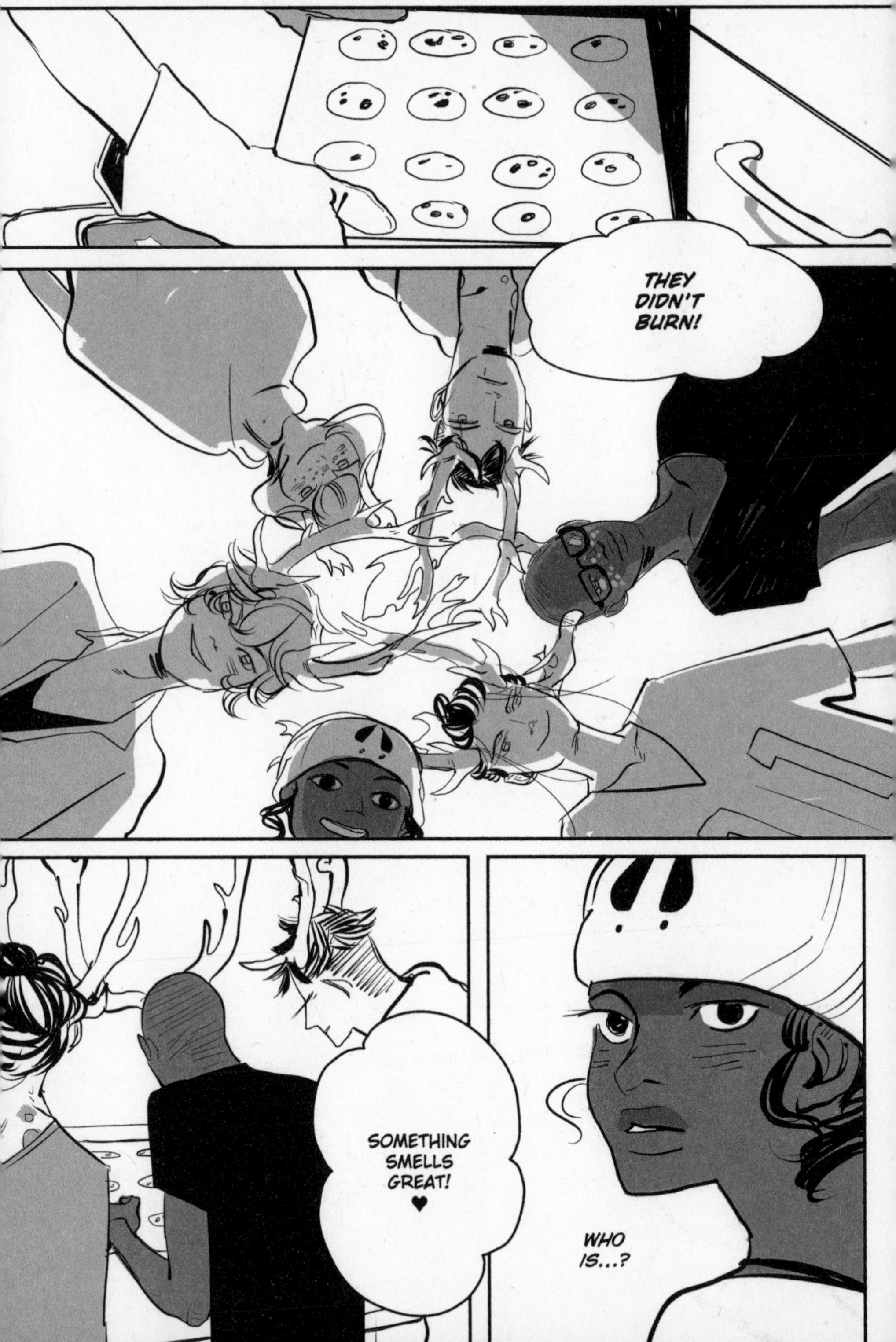
THEY DIDN'T BURN!
SOMETHING SMELLS GREAT! ♥
WHO IS...?

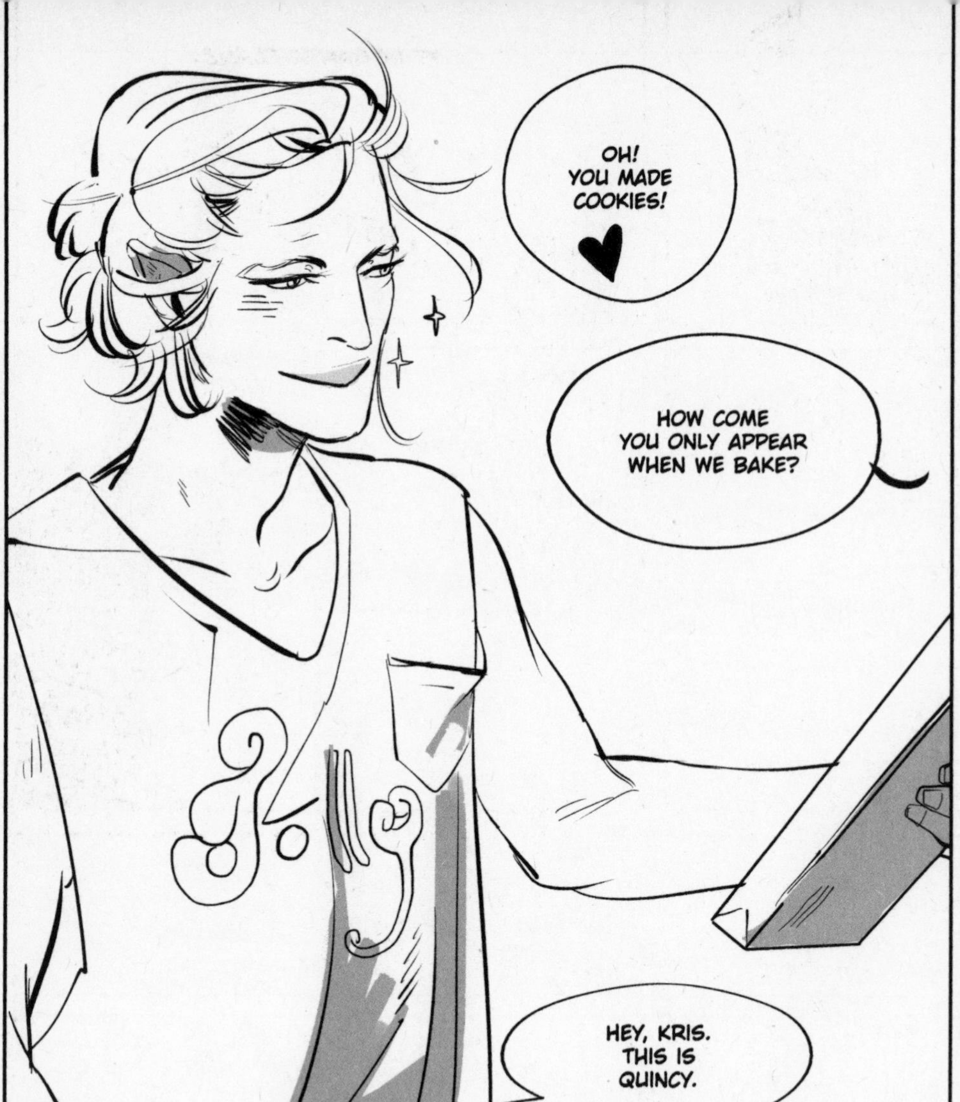
OH! YOU MADE COOKIES! ♥
HOW COME YOU ONLY APPEAR WHEN WE BAKE?
HEY, KRIS. THIS IS QUINCY.

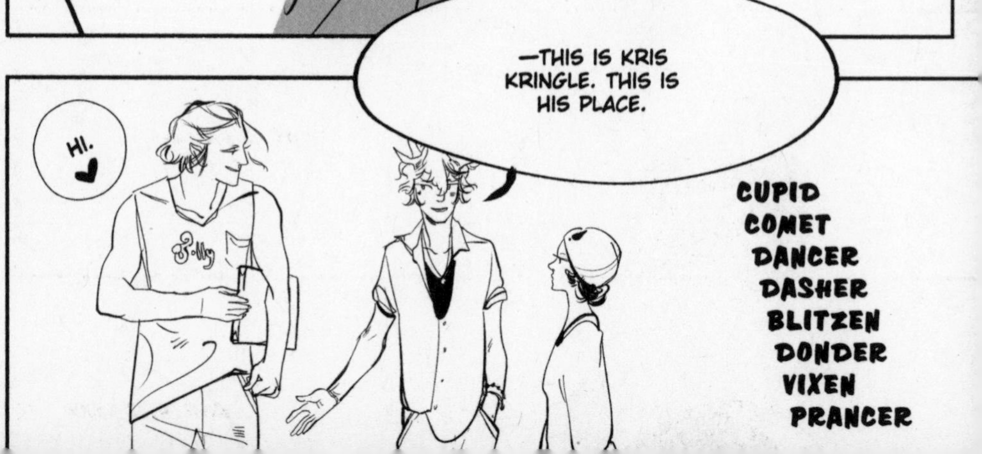
—THIS IS KRIS KRINGLE. THIS IS HIS PLACE.
HI. ♥
CUPID
COMET
DANCER
DASHER
BLITZEN
DONDER
VIXEN
PRANCER

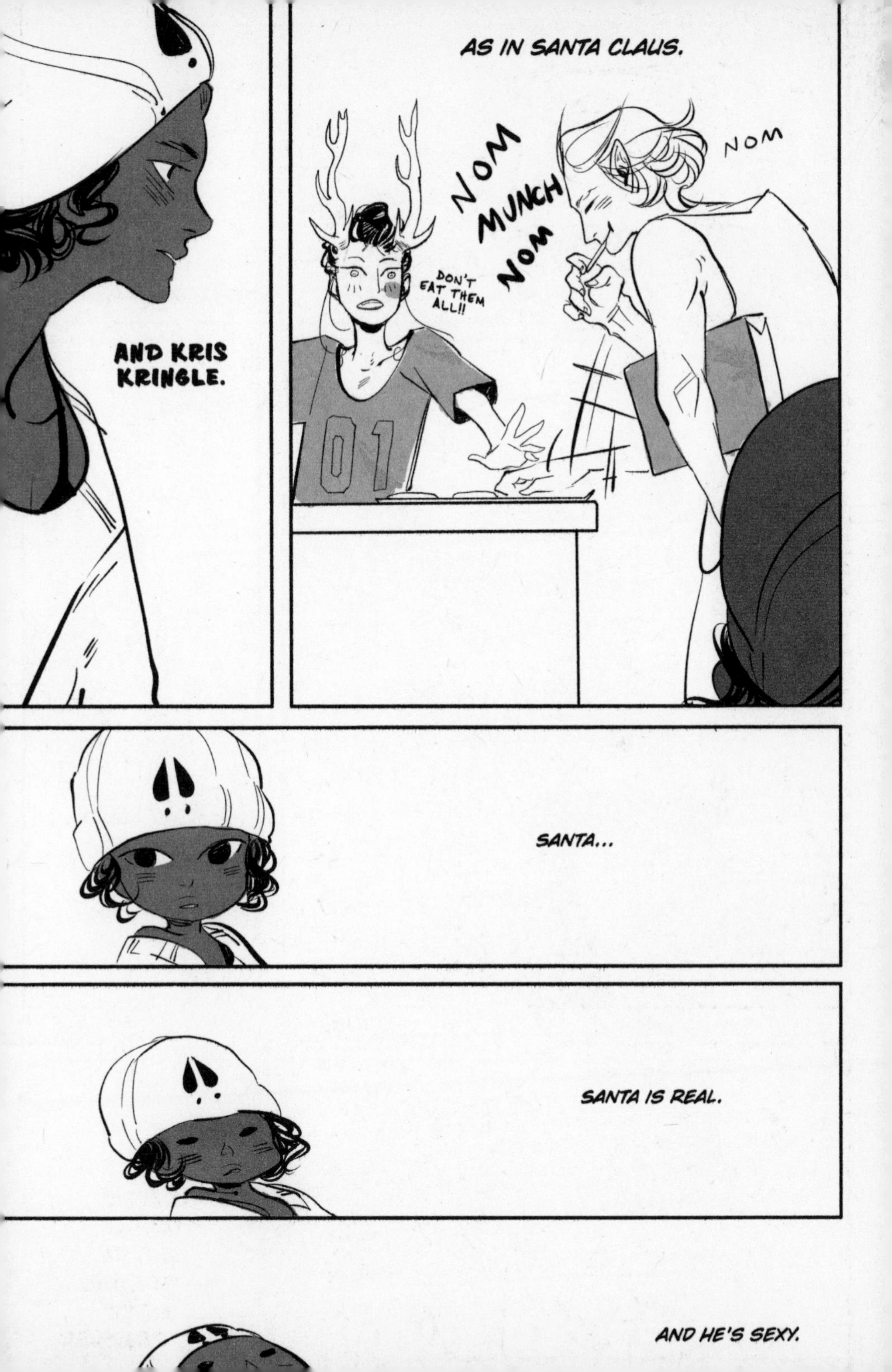
AS IN SANTA CLAUS.
AND KRIS KRINGLE.
NOM
MUNCH
NOM
NOM
DON'T EAT THEM ALL!!
SANTA...
SANTA IS REAL.
AND HE'S SEXY.

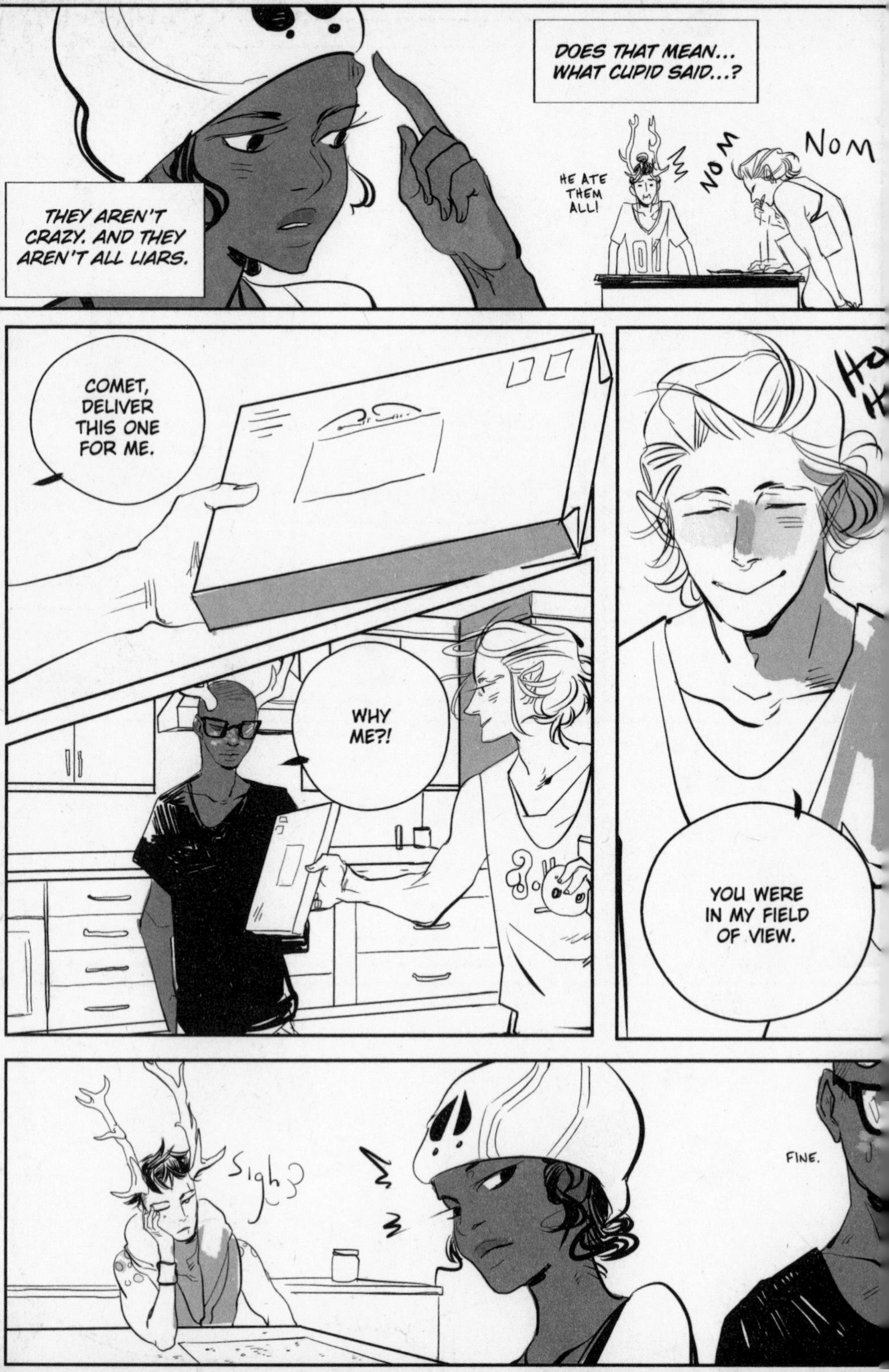
THEY AREN'T CRAZY. AND THEY AREN'T ALL LIARS.
DOES THAT MEAN... WHAT CUPID SAID...?
HE ATE THEM ALL!
NOM
NOM
COMET, DELIVER THIS ONE FOR ME.
WHY ME?!
YOU WERE IN MY FIELD OF VIEW.
Sigh
FINE.

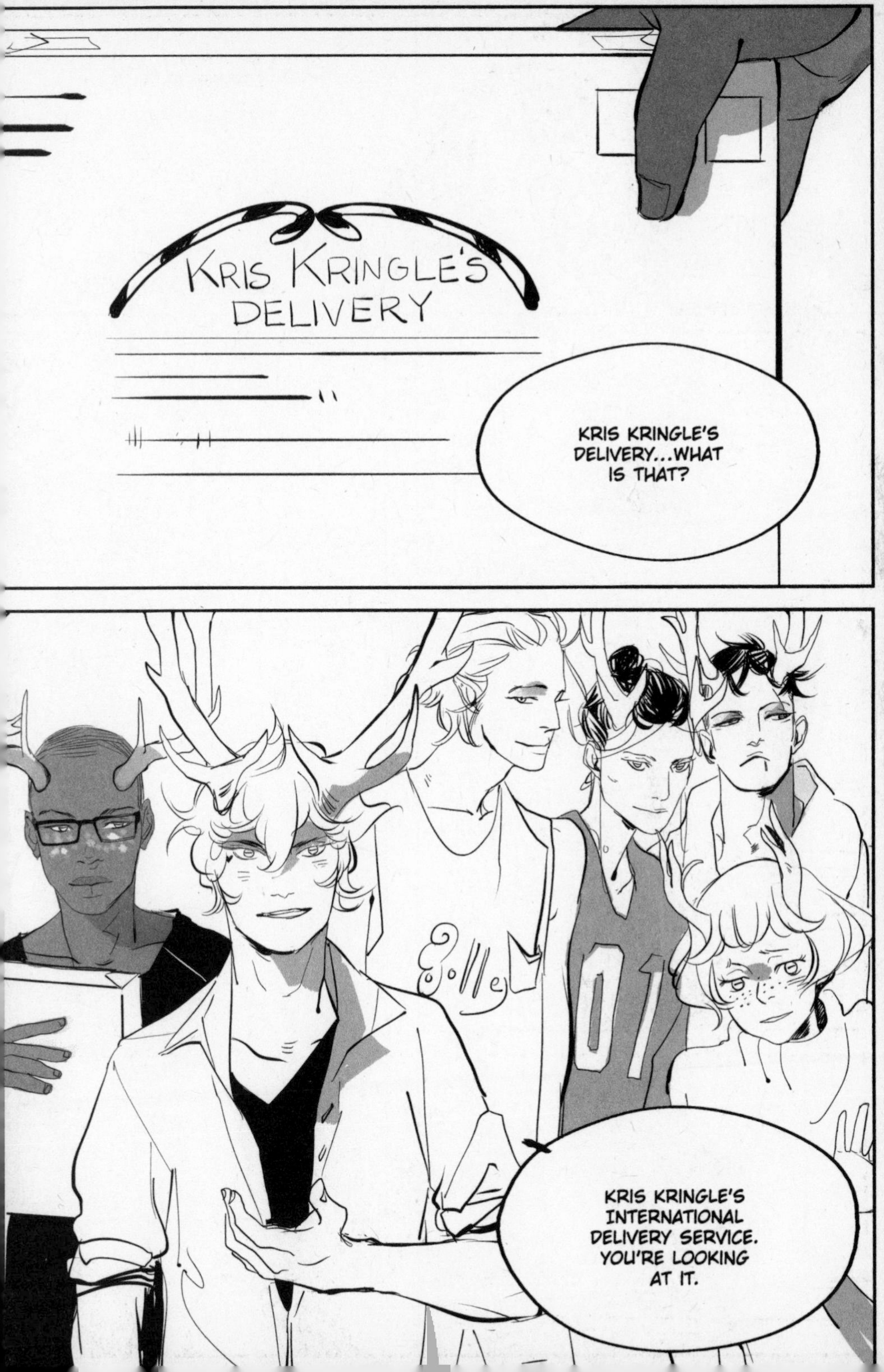
KRIS KRINGLE'S
DELIVERY
KRIS KRINGLE'S DELIVERY...WHAT IS THAT?
KRIS KRINGLE'S INTERNATIONAL DELIVERY SERVICE. YOU'RE LOOKING AT IT.

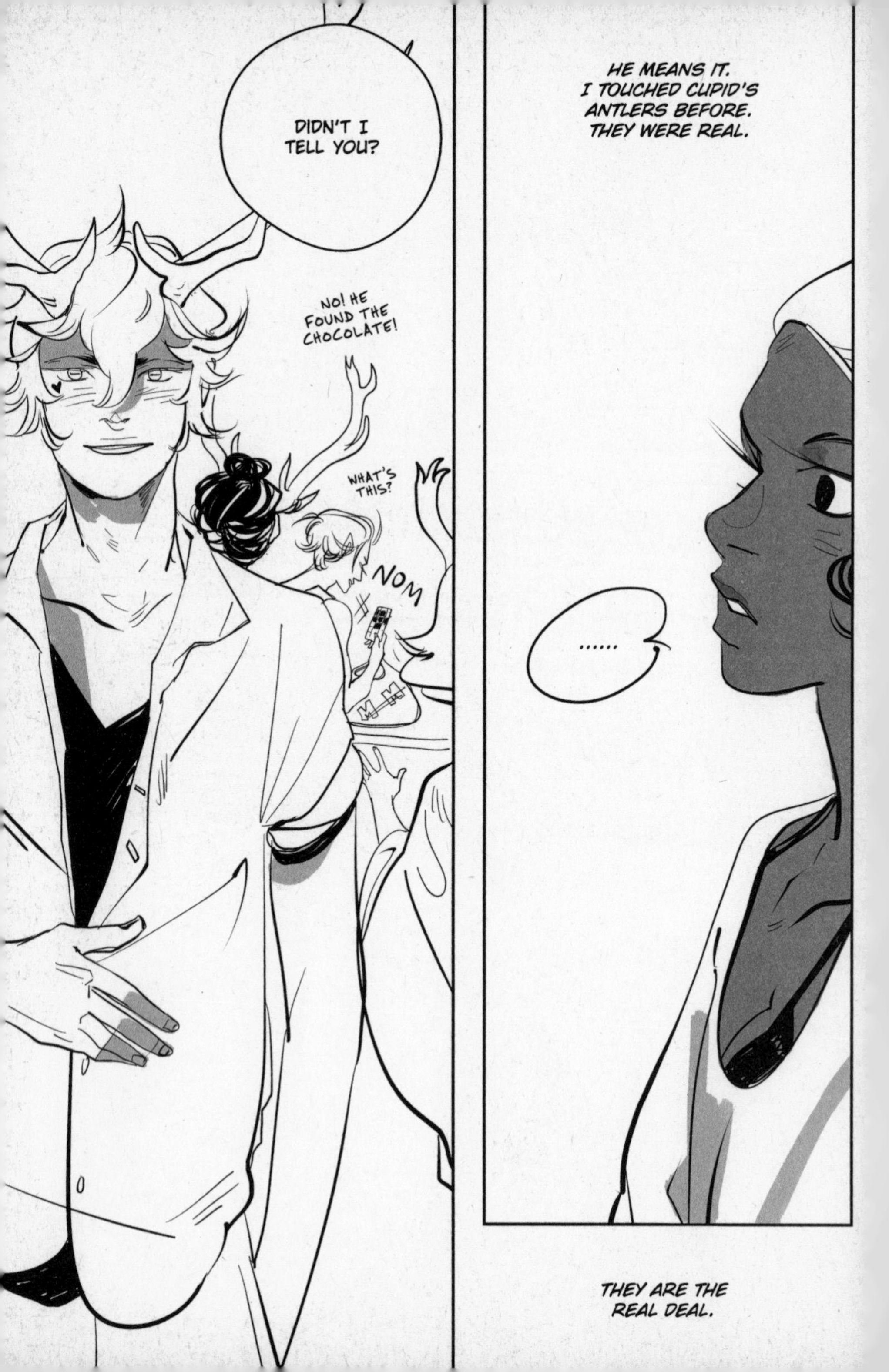
DIDN'T I TELL YOU?
NO! HE FOUND THE CHOCOLATE!
WHAT'S THIS?
NOM
HE MEANS IT. I TOUCHED CUPID'S ANTLERS BEFORE. THEY WERE REAL.
......
THEY ARE THE REAL DEAL.

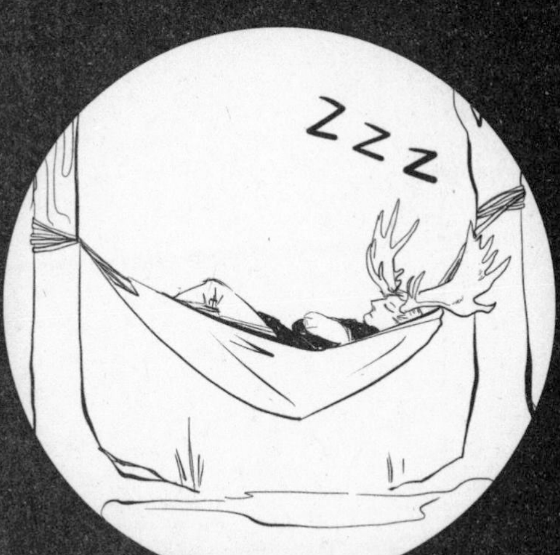
Zzz

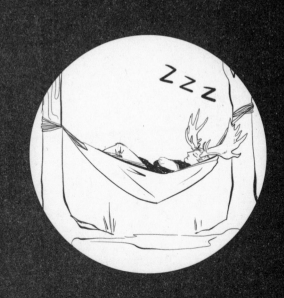

Reindeer Boy

Chapter 5

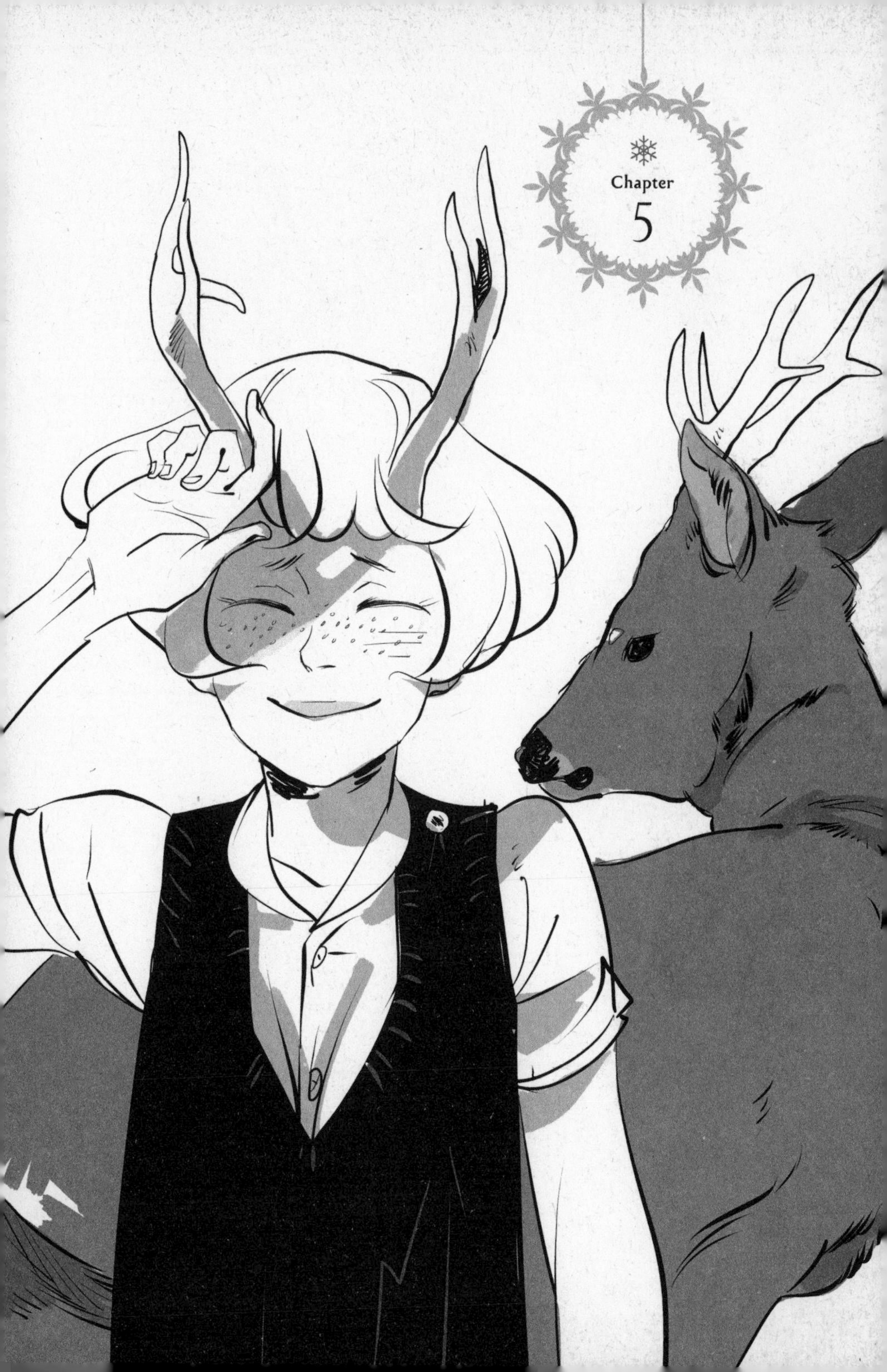

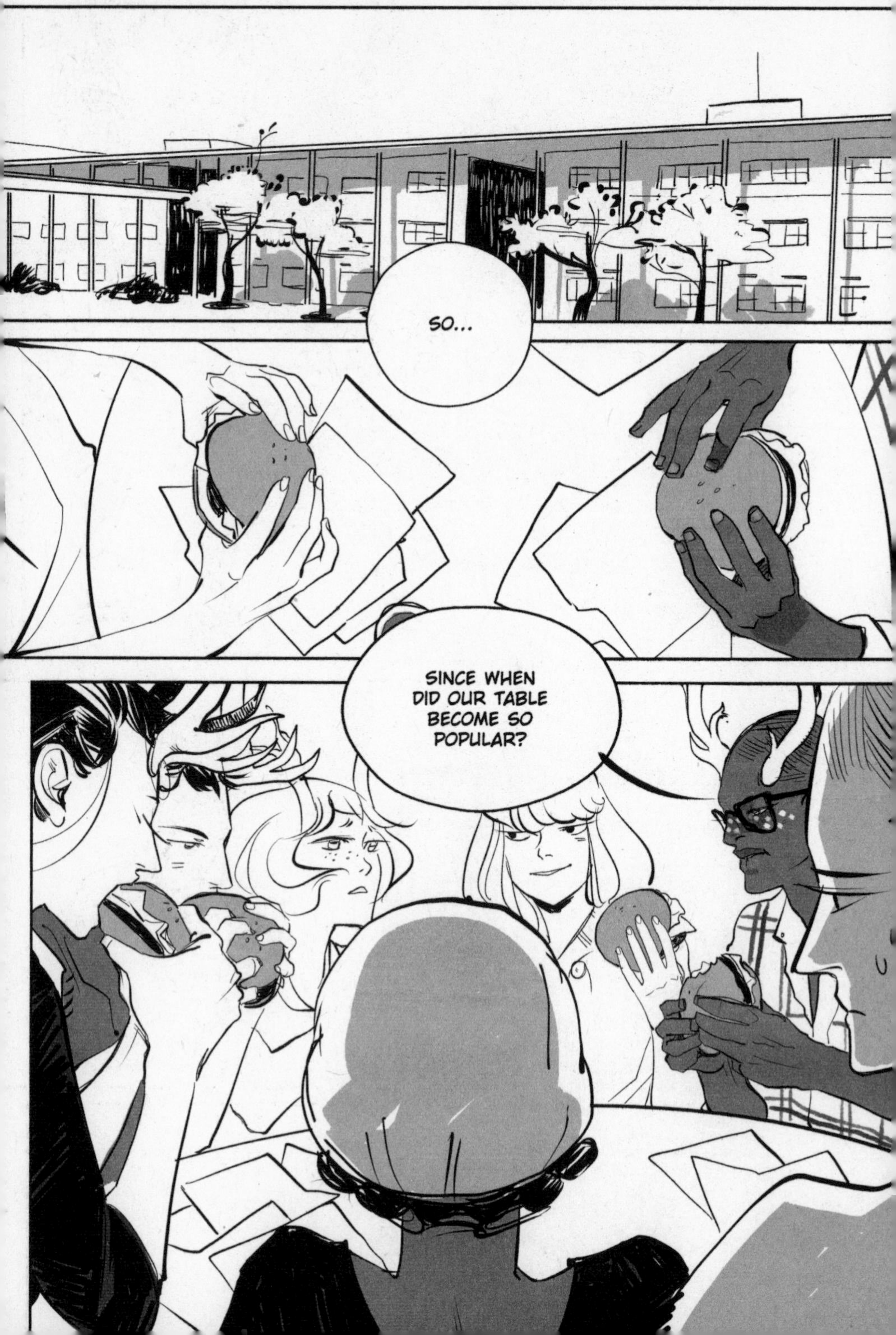
SO...
SINCE WHEN DID OUR TABLE BECOME SO POPULAR?

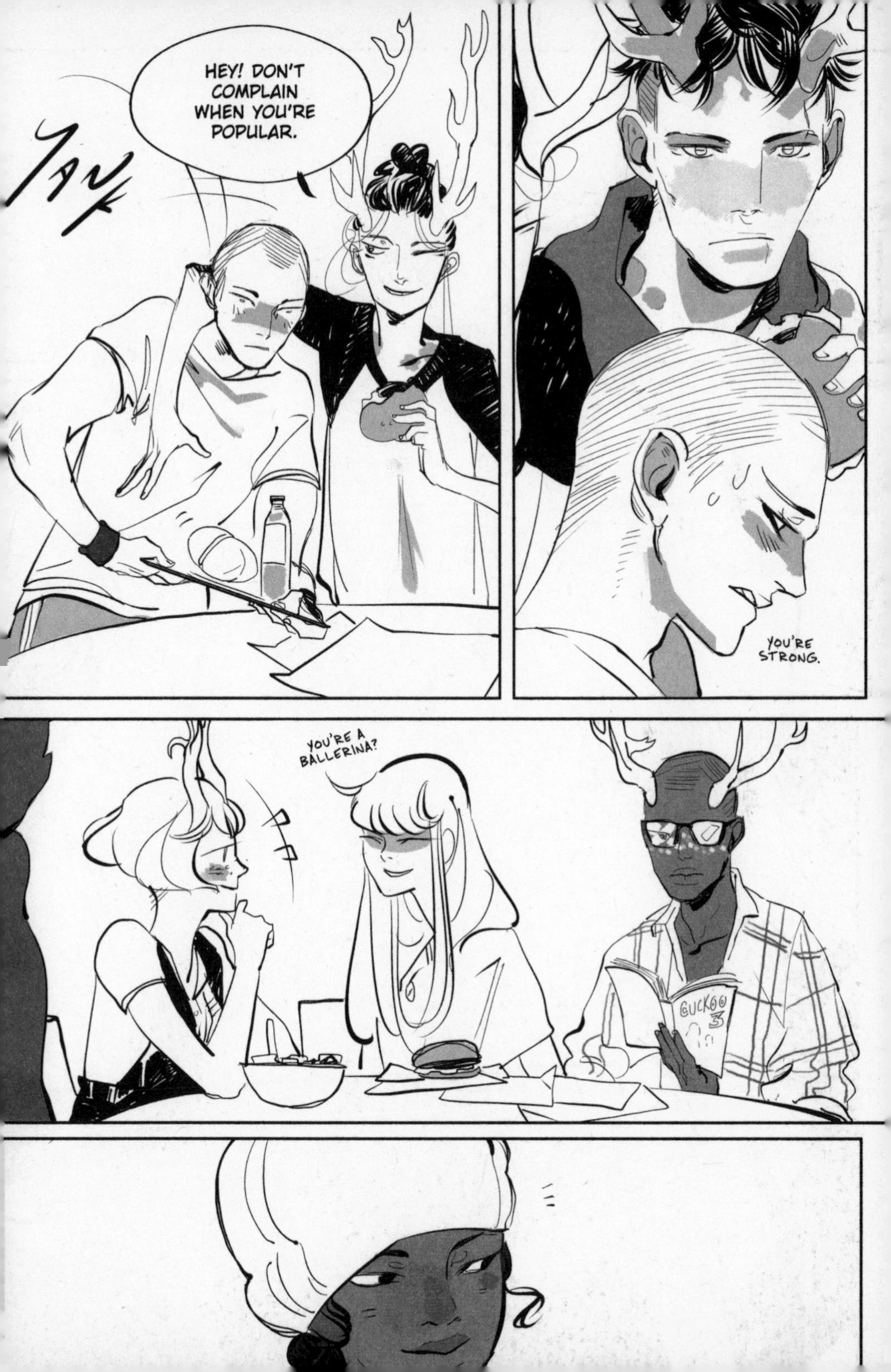
YANK
HEY! DON'T COMPLAIN WHEN YOU'RE POPULAR.
YOU'RE STRONG.
YOU'RE A BALLERINA?
CUCKOO 3

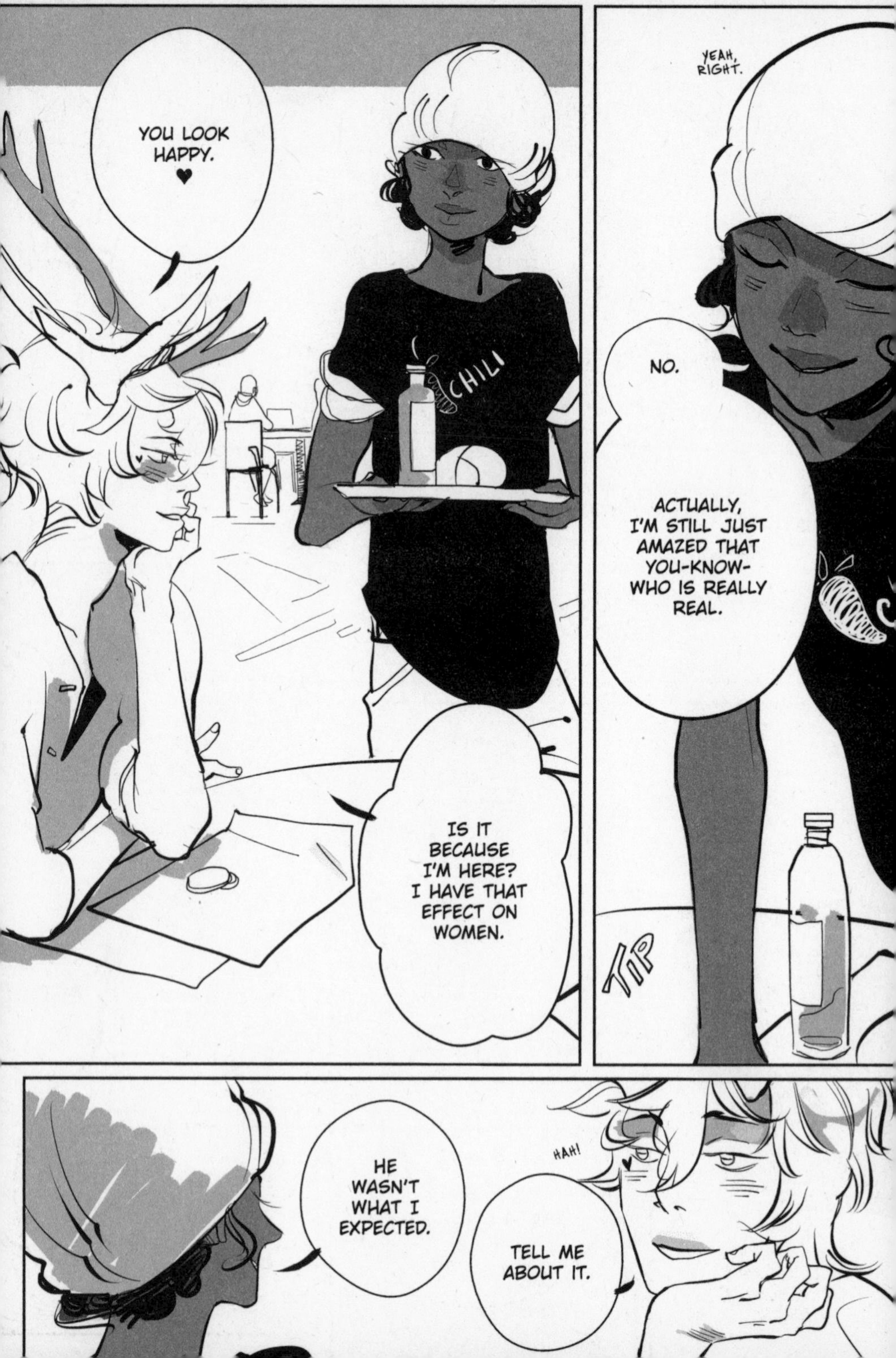
YOU LOOK HAPPY. ♥
CHILI
IS IT BECAUSE I'M HERE? I HAVE THAT EFFECT ON WOMEN.
YEAH, RIGHT.
NO.
ACTUALLY, I'M STILL JUST AMAZED THAT YOU-KNOW-WHO IS REALLY REAL.
TIP
HE WASN'T WHAT I EXPECTED.
HAH!
TELL ME ABOUT IT.

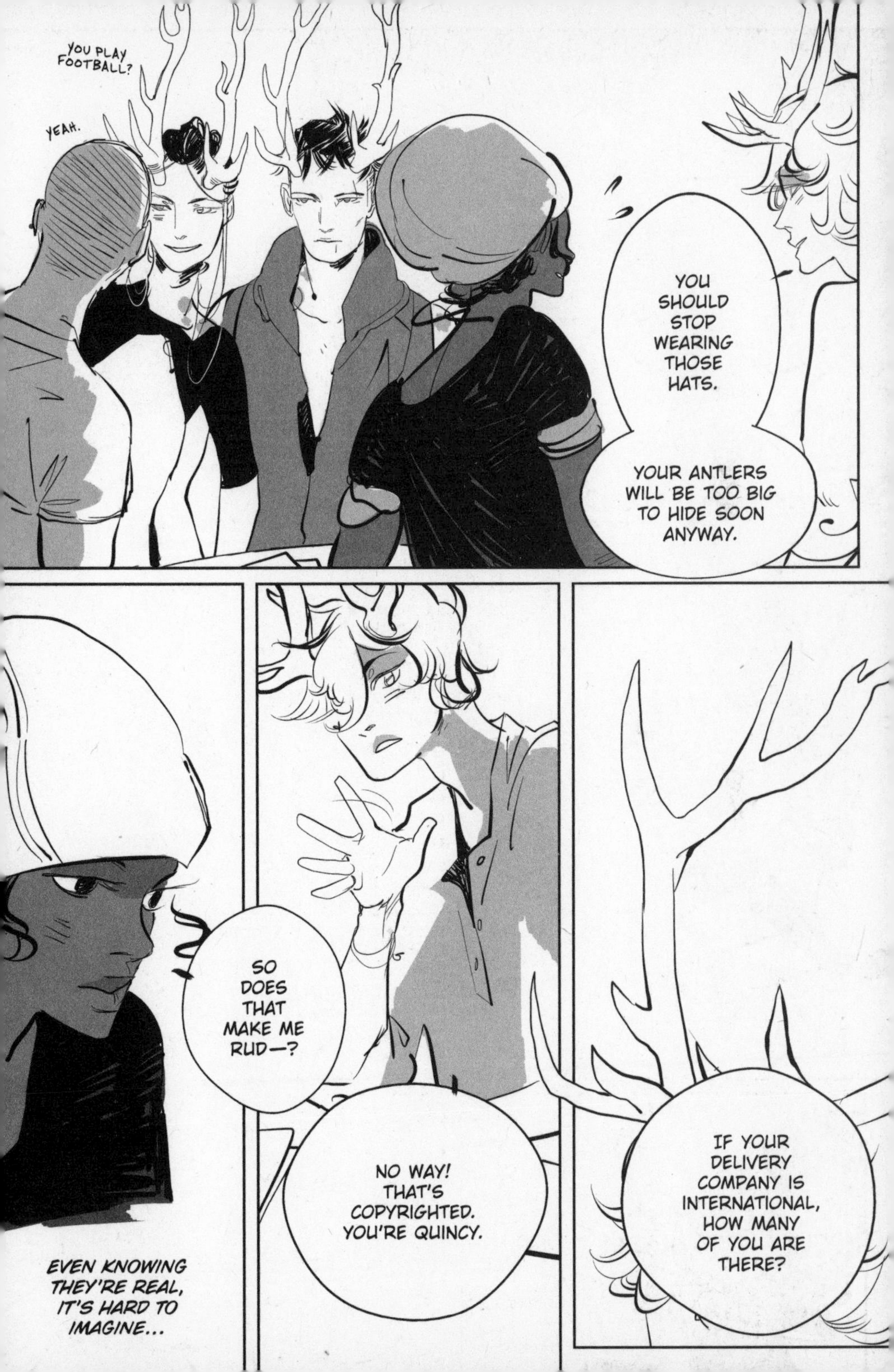
YOU PLAY FOOTBALL?
YEAH.
YOU SHOULD STOP WEARING THOSE HATS.
YOUR ANTLERS WILL BE TOO BIG TO HIDE SOON ANYWAY.
SO DOES THAT MAKE ME RUD—?
EVEN KNOWING THEY'RE REAL, IT'S HARD TO IMAGINE...
NO WAY! THAT'S COPYRIGHTED. YOU'RE QUINCY.
IF YOUR DELIVERY COMPANY IS INTERNATIONAL, HOW MANY OF YOU ARE THERE?

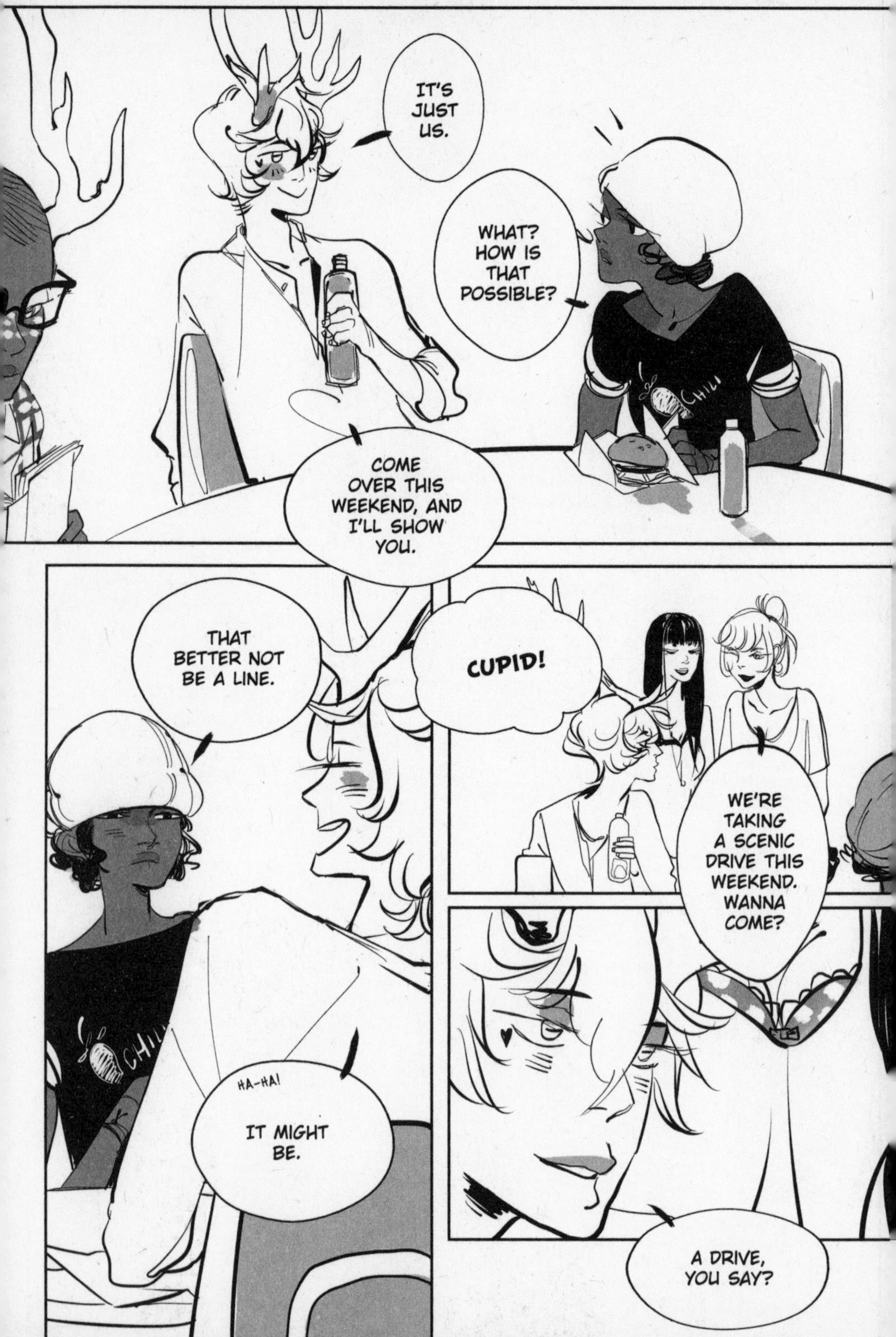
IT'S JUST US.
WHAT? HOW IS THAT POSSIBLE?
COME OVER THIS WEEKEND, AND I'LL SHOW YOU.
THAT BETTER NOT BE A LINE.
HA-HA!
IT MIGHT BE.
CUPID!
WE'RE TAKING A SCENIC DRIVE THIS WEEKEND. WANNA COME?
A DRIVE, YOU SAY?

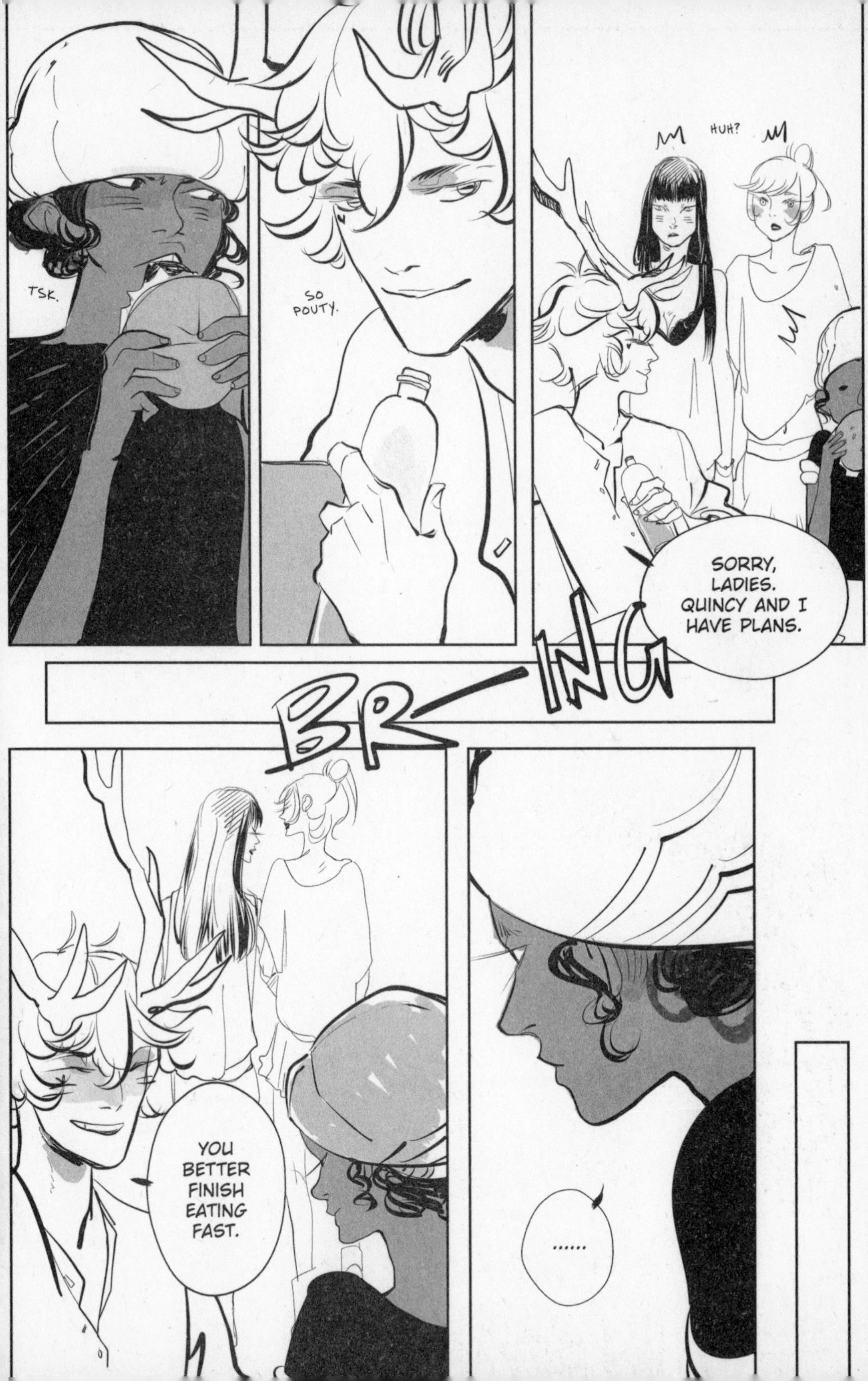
TSK.
SO POUTY.
HUH?
SORRY, LADIES. QUINCY AND I HAVE PLANS.
BR-ING
YOU BETTER FINISH EATING FAST.
......

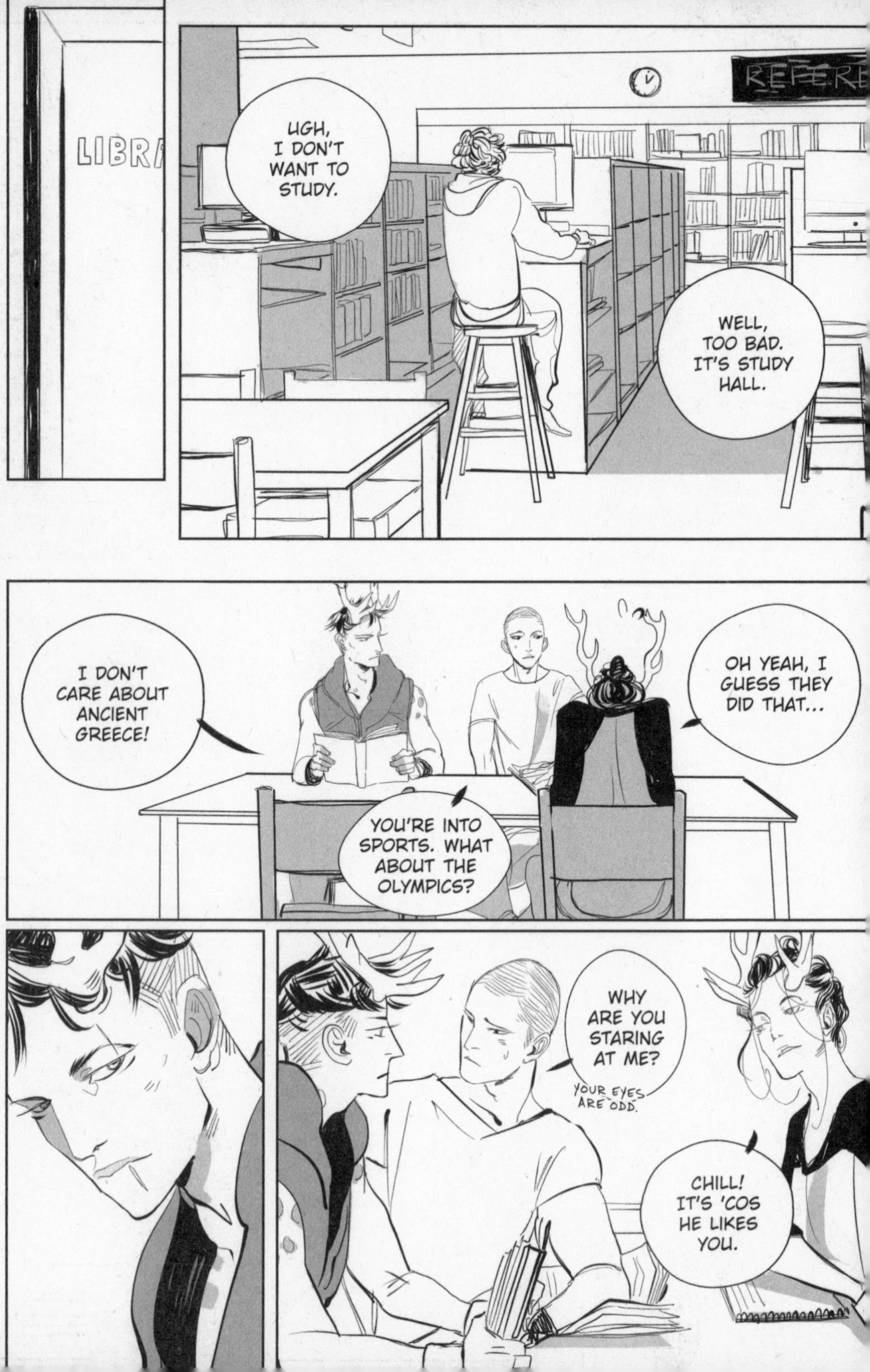
LIBR
REFERE
UGH, I DON'T WANT TO STUDY.
WELL, TOO BAD. IT'S STUDY HALL.
I DON'T CARE ABOUT ANCIENT GREECE!
YOU'RE INTO SPORTS. WHAT ABOUT THE OLYMPICS?
OH YEAH, I GUESS THEY DID THAT...
WHY ARE YOU STARING AT ME?
YOUR EYES ARE ODD.
CHILL! IT'S 'COS HE LIKES YOU.

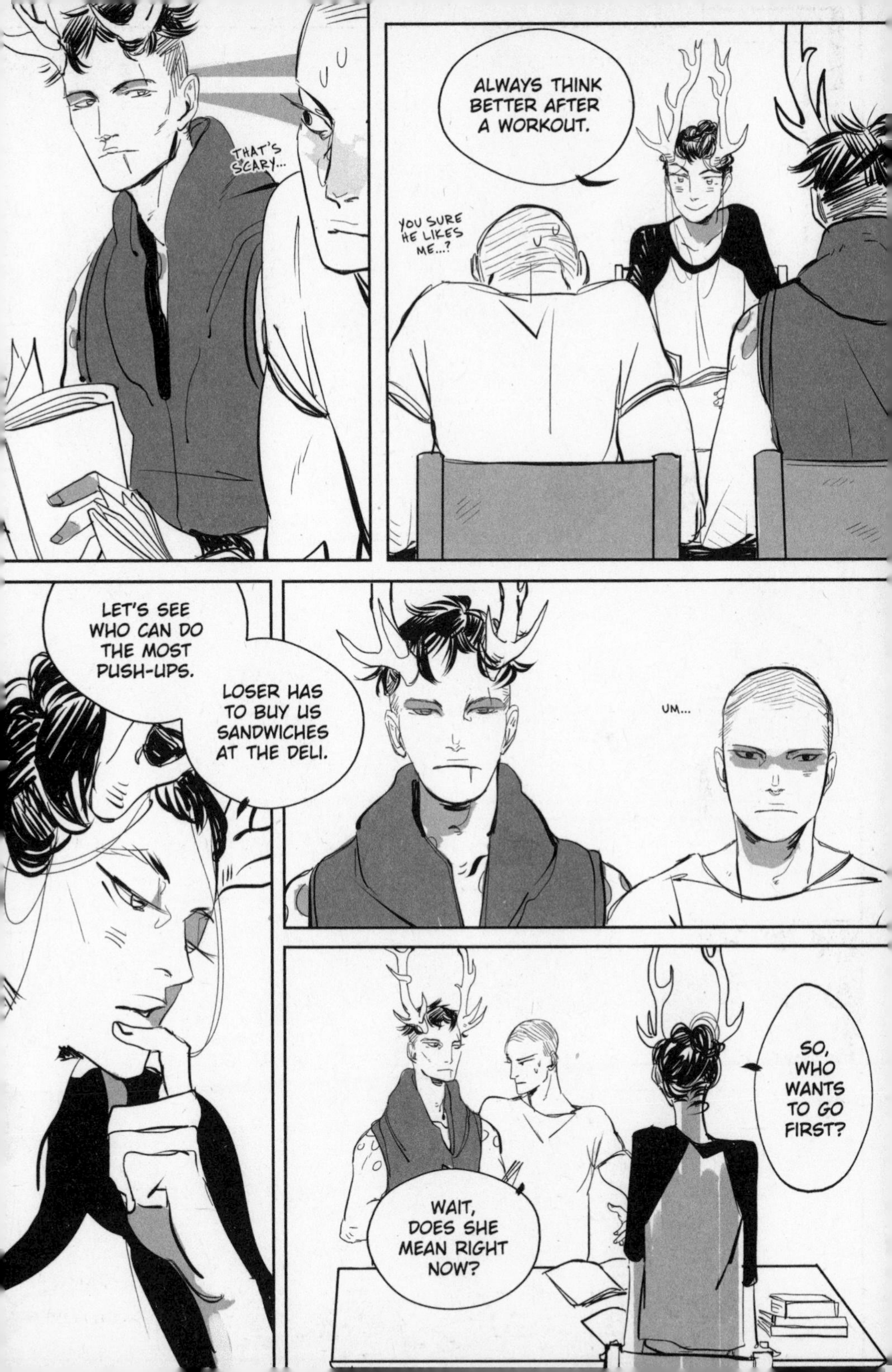
THAT'S SCARY...
ALWAYS THINK BETTER AFTER A WORKOUT.
YOU SURE HE LIKES ME...?
LET'S SEE WHO CAN DO THE MOST PUSH-UPS.
LOSER HAS TO BUY US SANDWICHES AT THE DELI.
UM...
SO, WHO WANTS TO GO FIRST?
WAIT, DOES SHE MEAN RIGHT NOW?

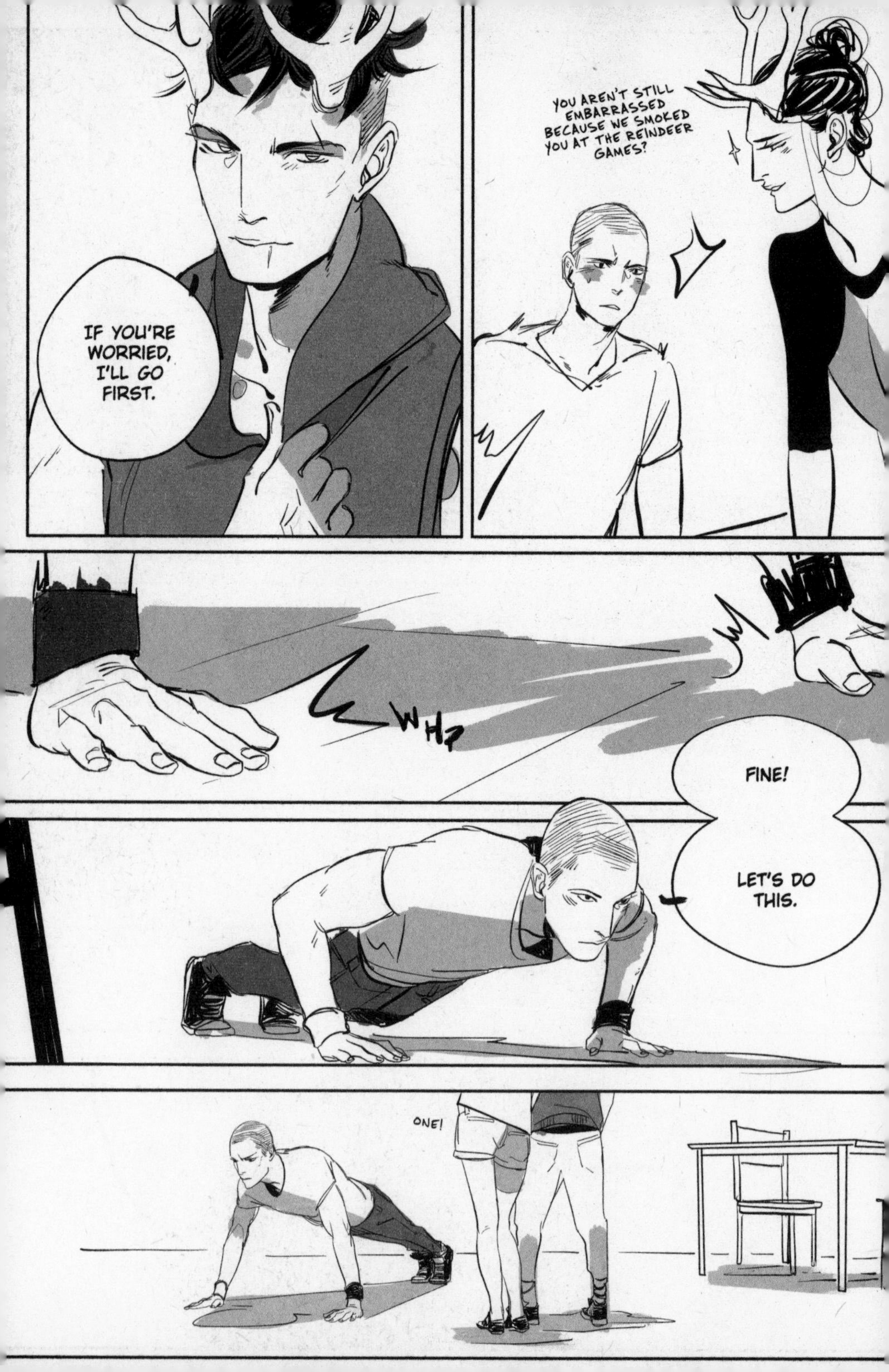

IF YOU'RE WORRIED, I'LL GO FIRST.
YOU AREN'T STILL EMBARRASSED BECAUSE WE SMOKED YOU AT THE REINDEER GAMES?
WHP
FINE!
LET'S DO THIS.
ONE!

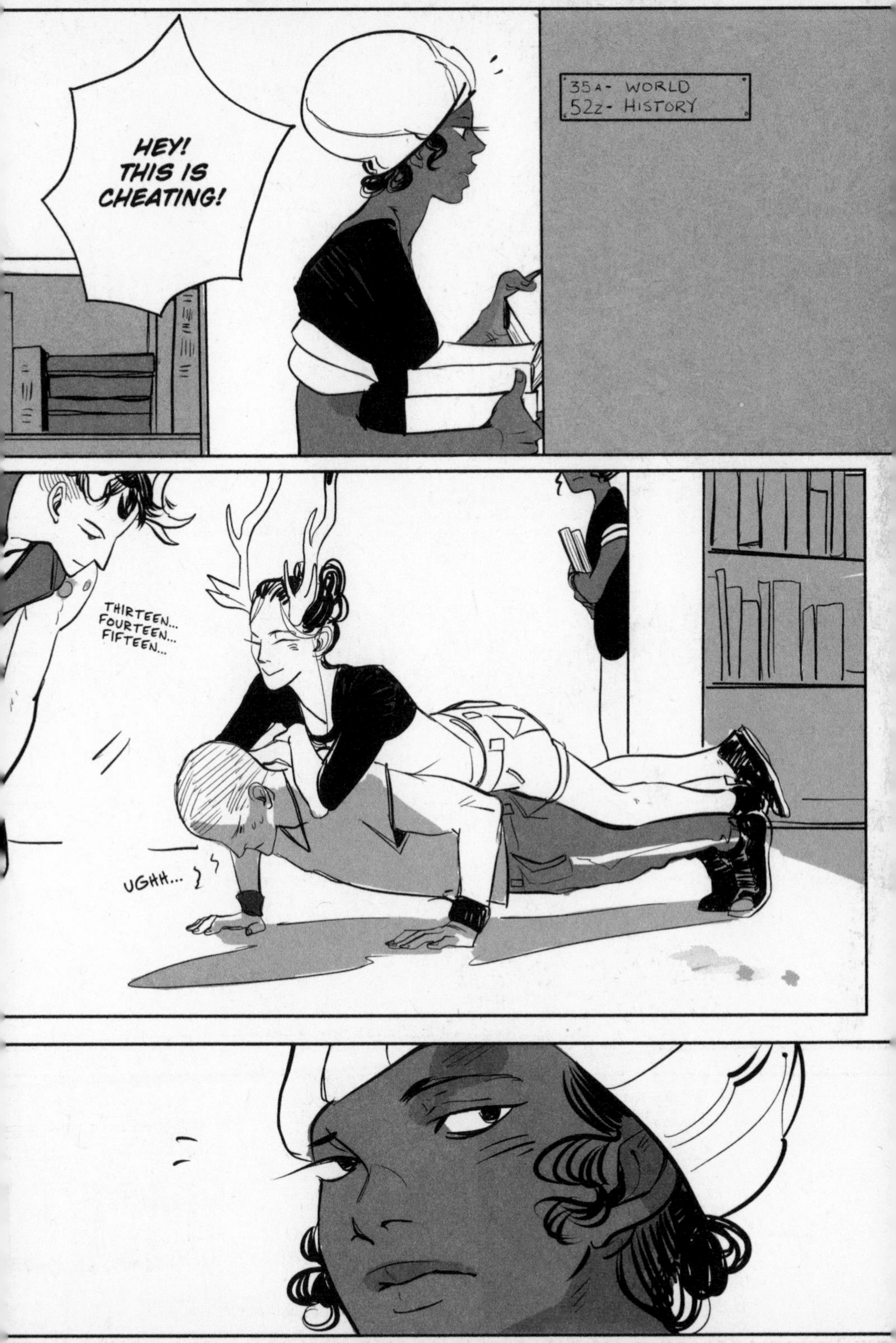
HEY! THIS IS CHEATING!
35A- WORLD
52Z- HISTORY
THIRTEEN... FOURTEEN... FIFTEEN...
UGHH...

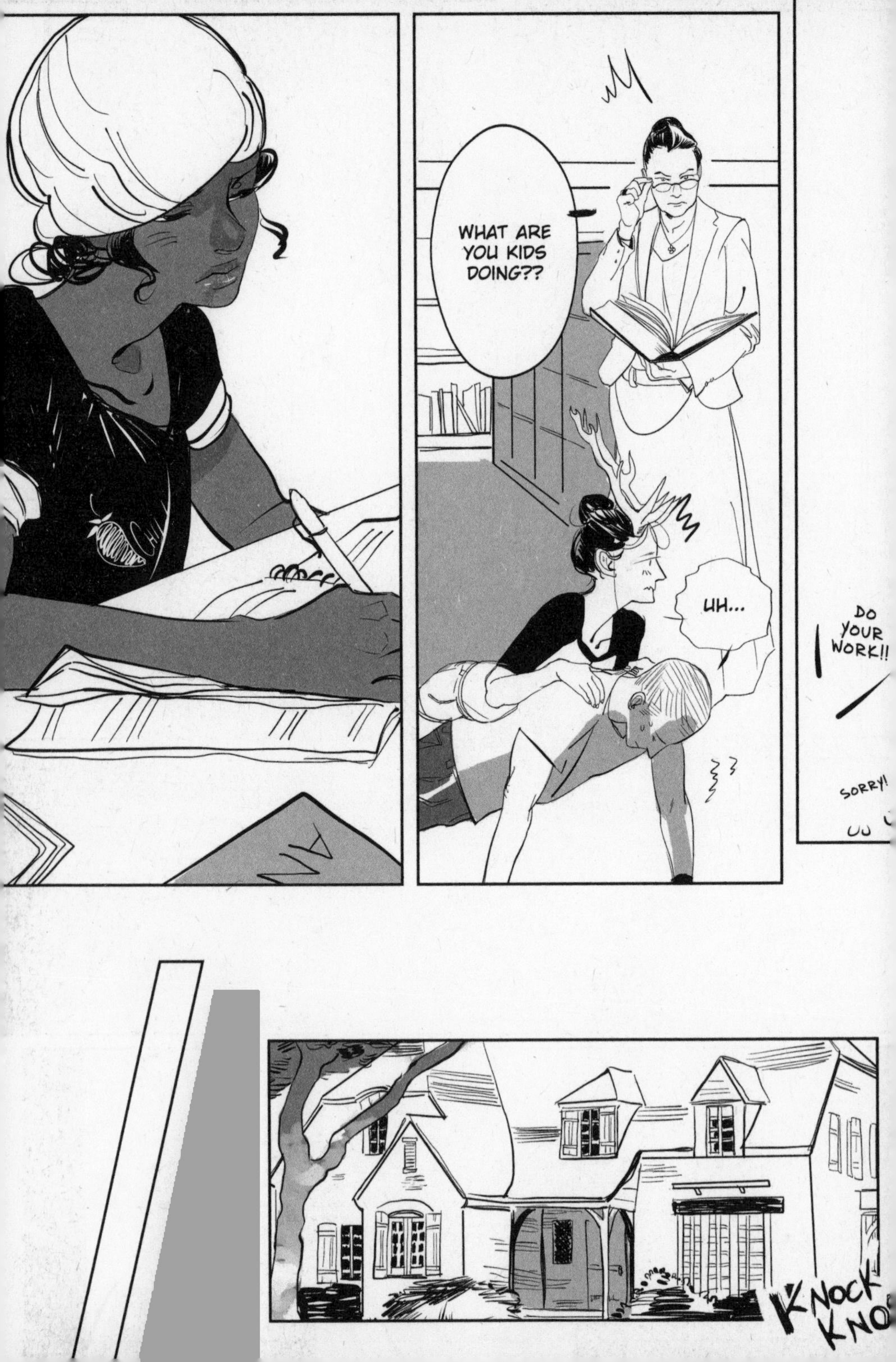
WHAT ARE YOU KIDS DOING??
UH...
DO YOUR WORK!!
SORRY!
KNOCK KNO

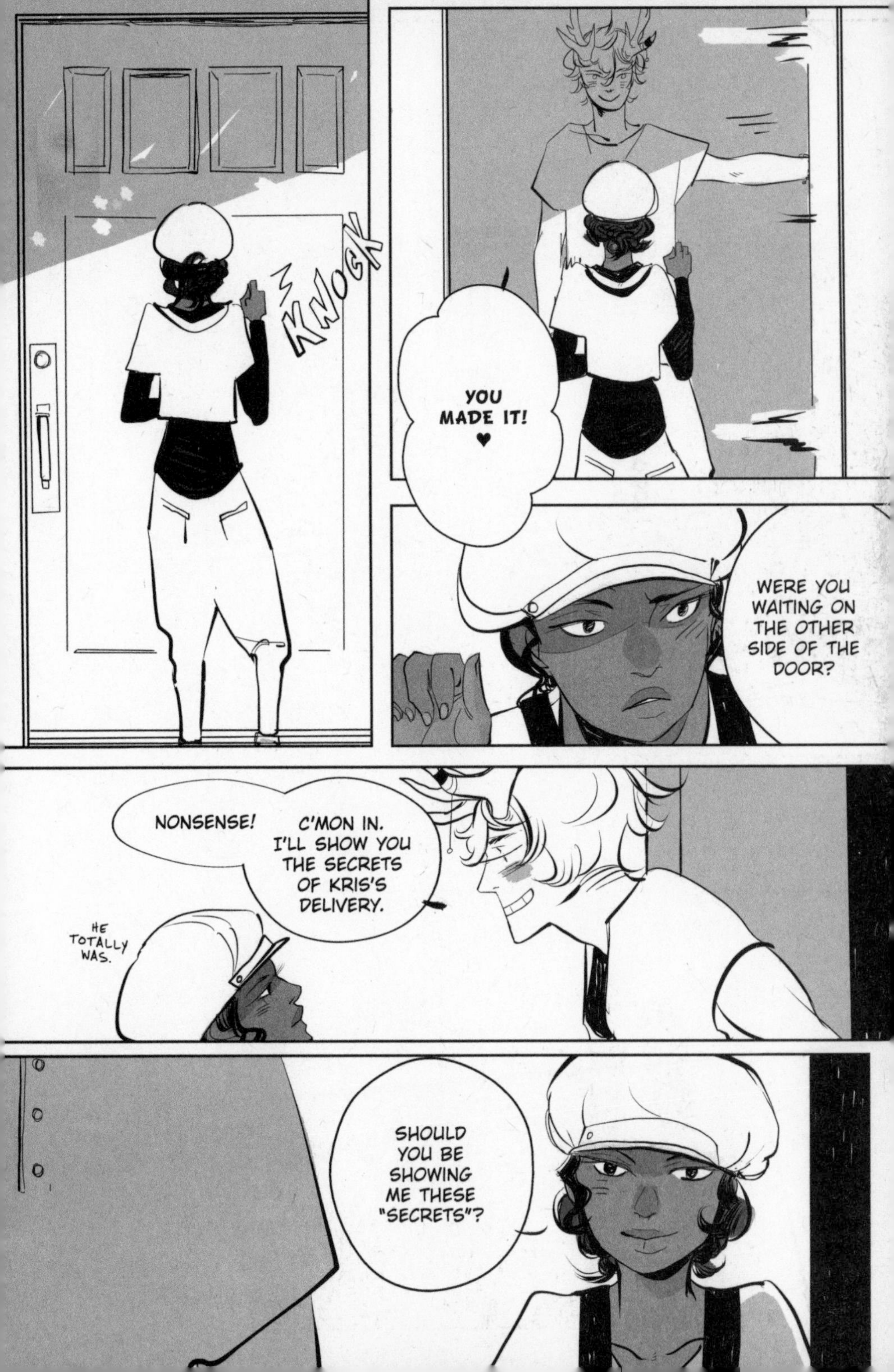
KNOCK
YOU MADE IT! ♥
WERE YOU WAITING ON THE OTHER SIDE OF THE DOOR?
NONSENSE!
C'MON IN. I'LL SHOW YOU THE SECRETS OF KRIS'S DELIVERY.
HE TOTALLY WAS.
SHOULD YOU BE SHOWING ME THESE "SECRETS"?

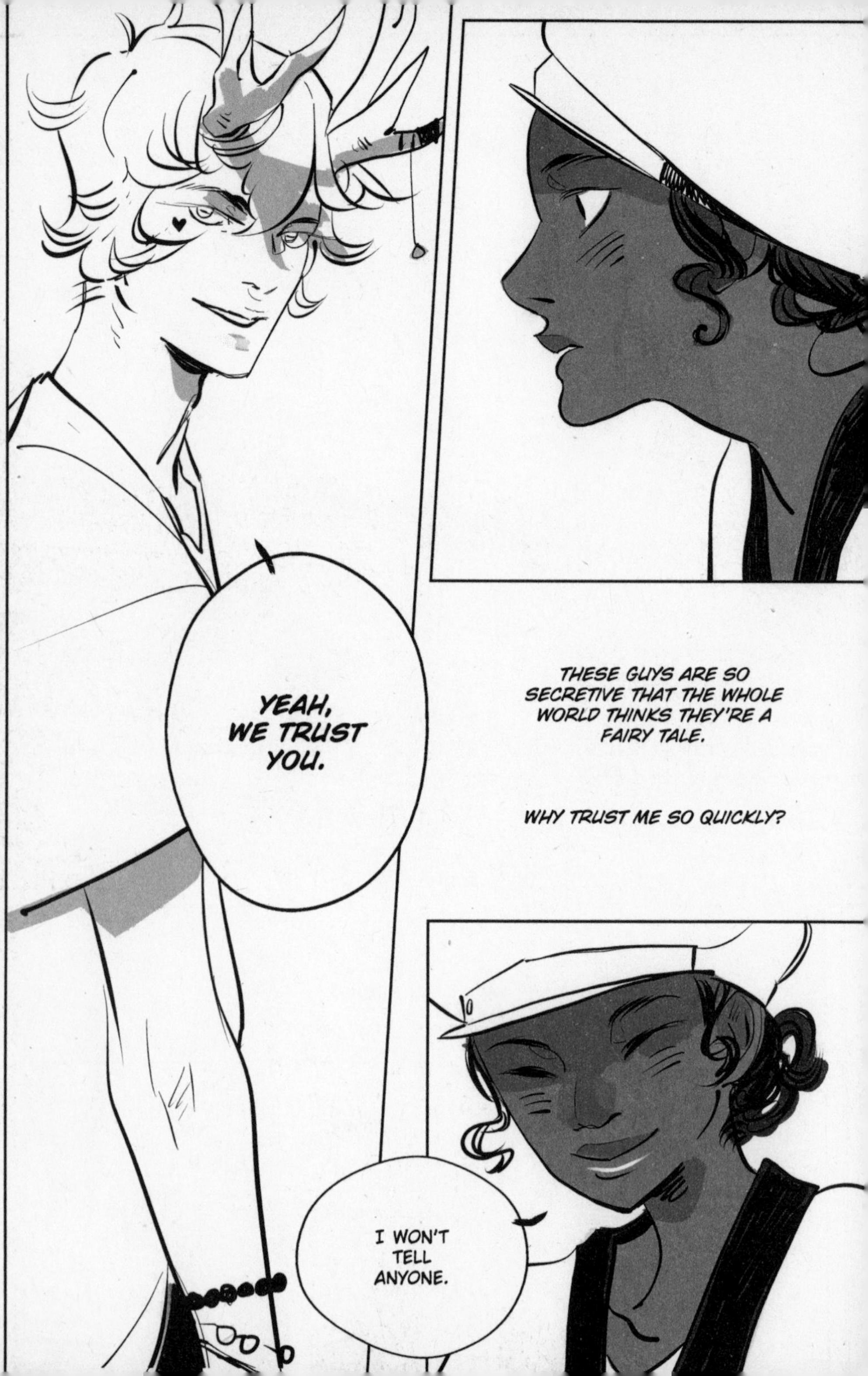
YEAH, WE TRUST YOU.
THESE GUYS ARE SO SECRETIVE THAT THE WHOLE WORLD THINKS THEY'RE A FAIRY TALE.
WHY TRUST ME SO QUICKLY?
I WON'T TELL ANYONE.

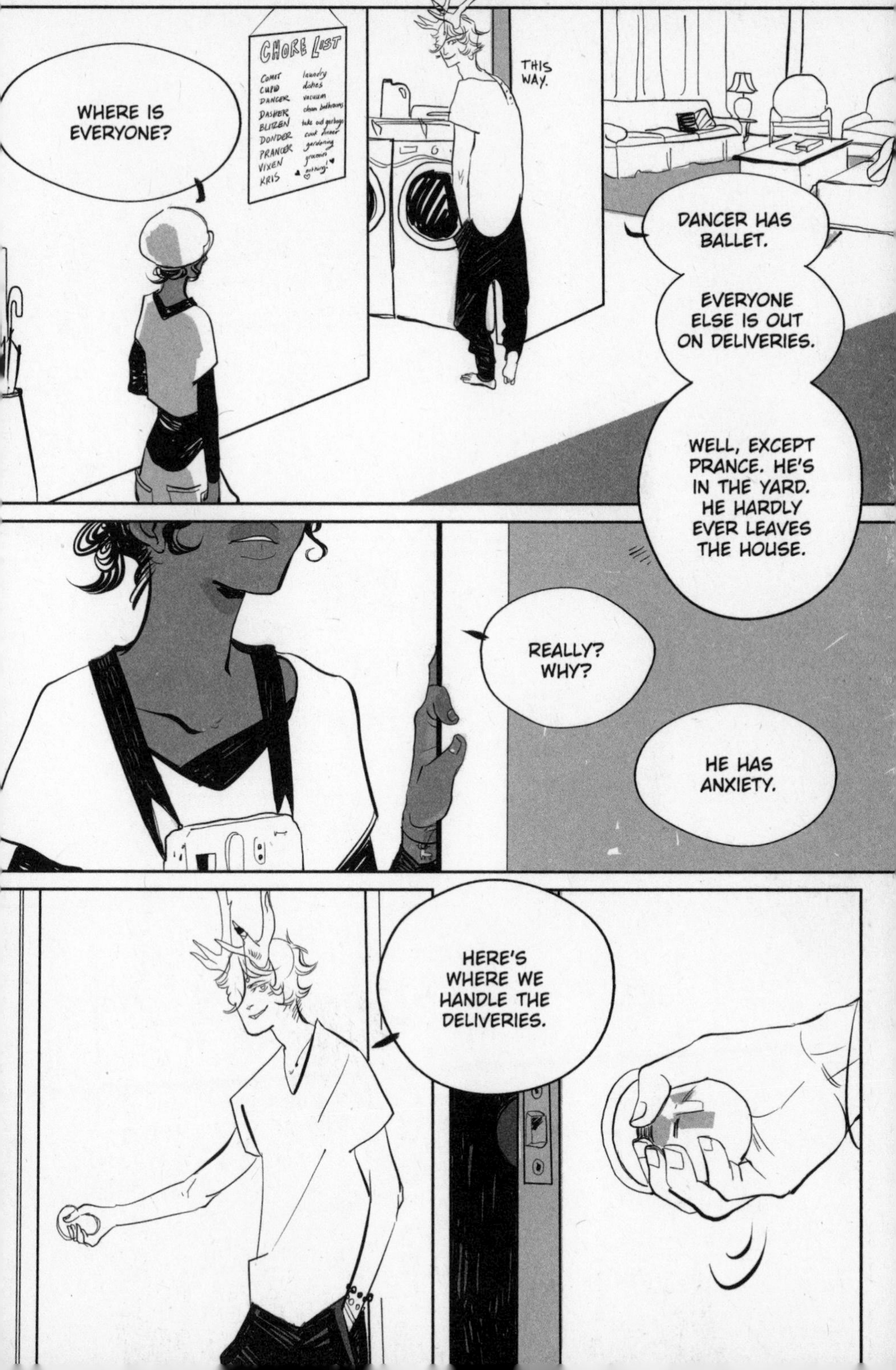
WHERE IS EVERYONE?
CHORE LIST
COMET laundry
CUPID dishes
DANCER vacuum
DASHER clean bathrooms
BLITZEN take out garbage
DONDER cook dinner
PRANCER gardening
VIXEN groceries
KRIS nothing!
THIS WAY.
DANCER HAS BALLET.
EVERYONE ELSE IS OUT ON DELIVERIES.
WELL, EXCEPT PRANCE. HE'S IN THE YARD. HE HARDLY EVER LEAVES THE HOUSE.
REALLY? WHY?
HE HAS ANXIETY.
HERE'S WHERE WE HANDLE THE DELIVERIES.

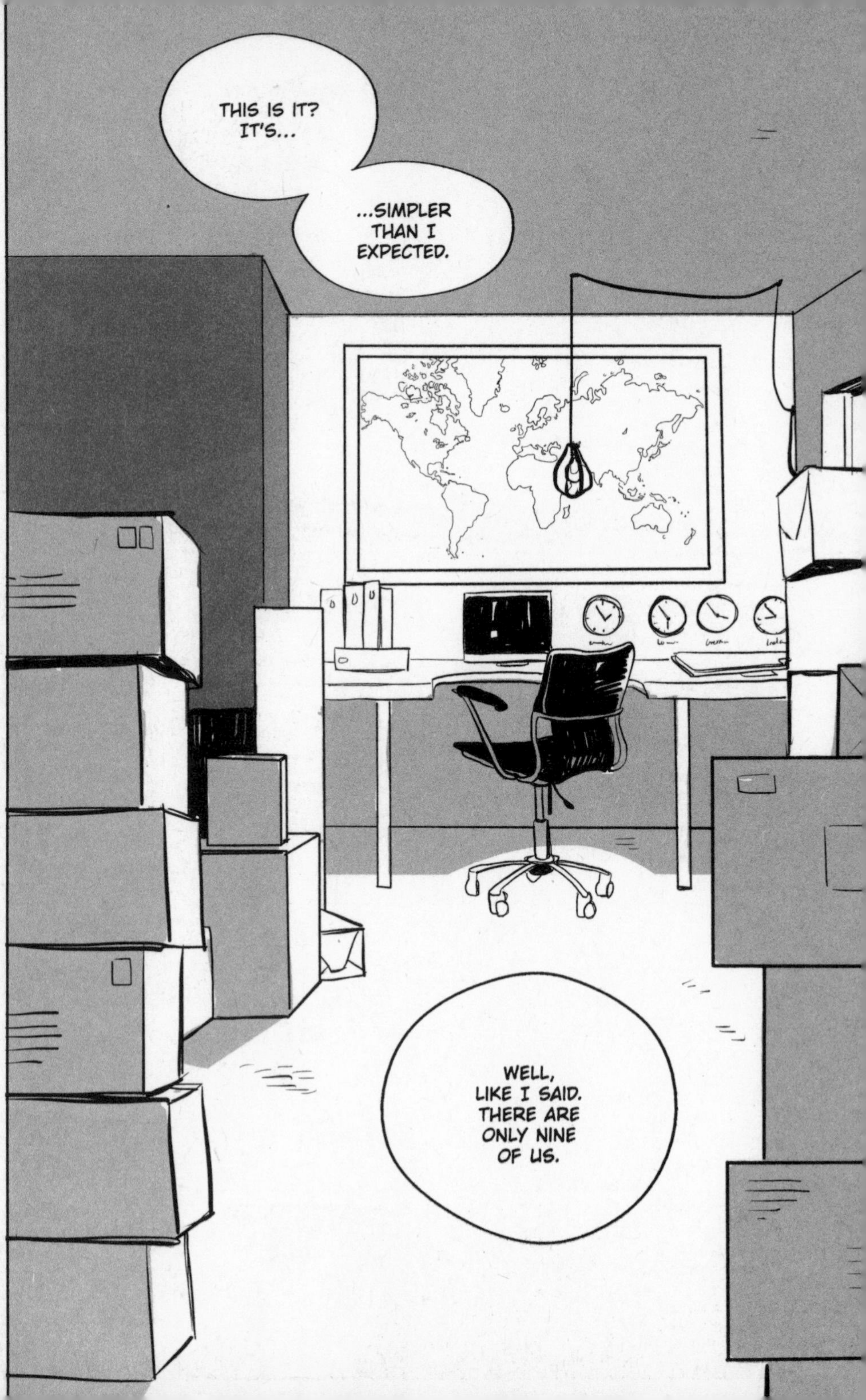
THIS IS IT? IT'S...
...SIMPLER THAN I EXPECTED.
WELL, LIKE I SAID. THERE ARE ONLY NINE OF US.

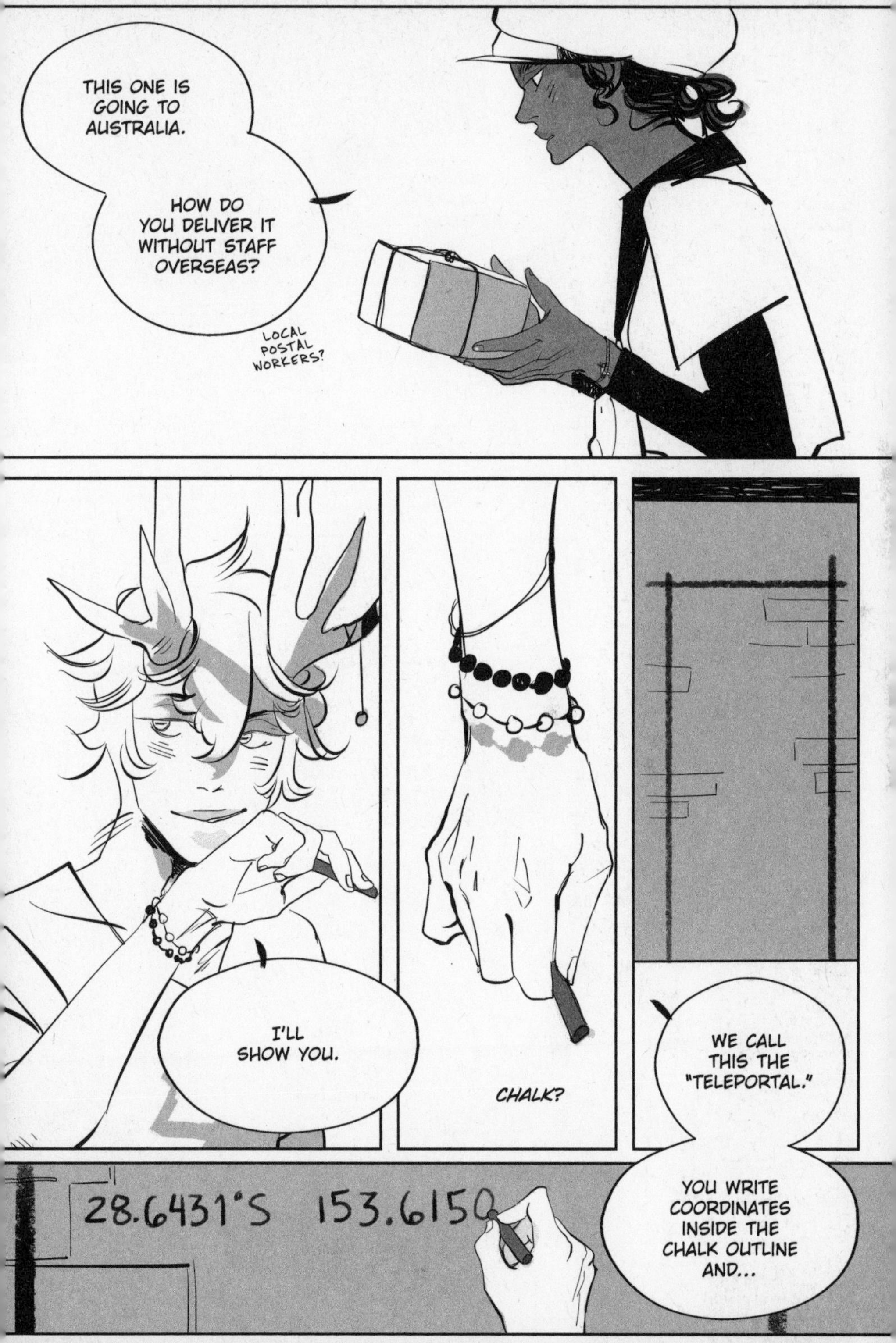
THIS ONE IS GOING TO AUSTRALIA.
HOW DO YOU DELIVER IT WITHOUT STAFF OVERSEAS?
LOCAL POSTAL WORKERS?
I'LL SHOW YOU.
CHALK?
WE CALL THIS THE "TELEPORTAL."
28.6431°S 153.6150
YOU WRITE COORDINATES INSIDE THE CHALK OUTLINE AND...

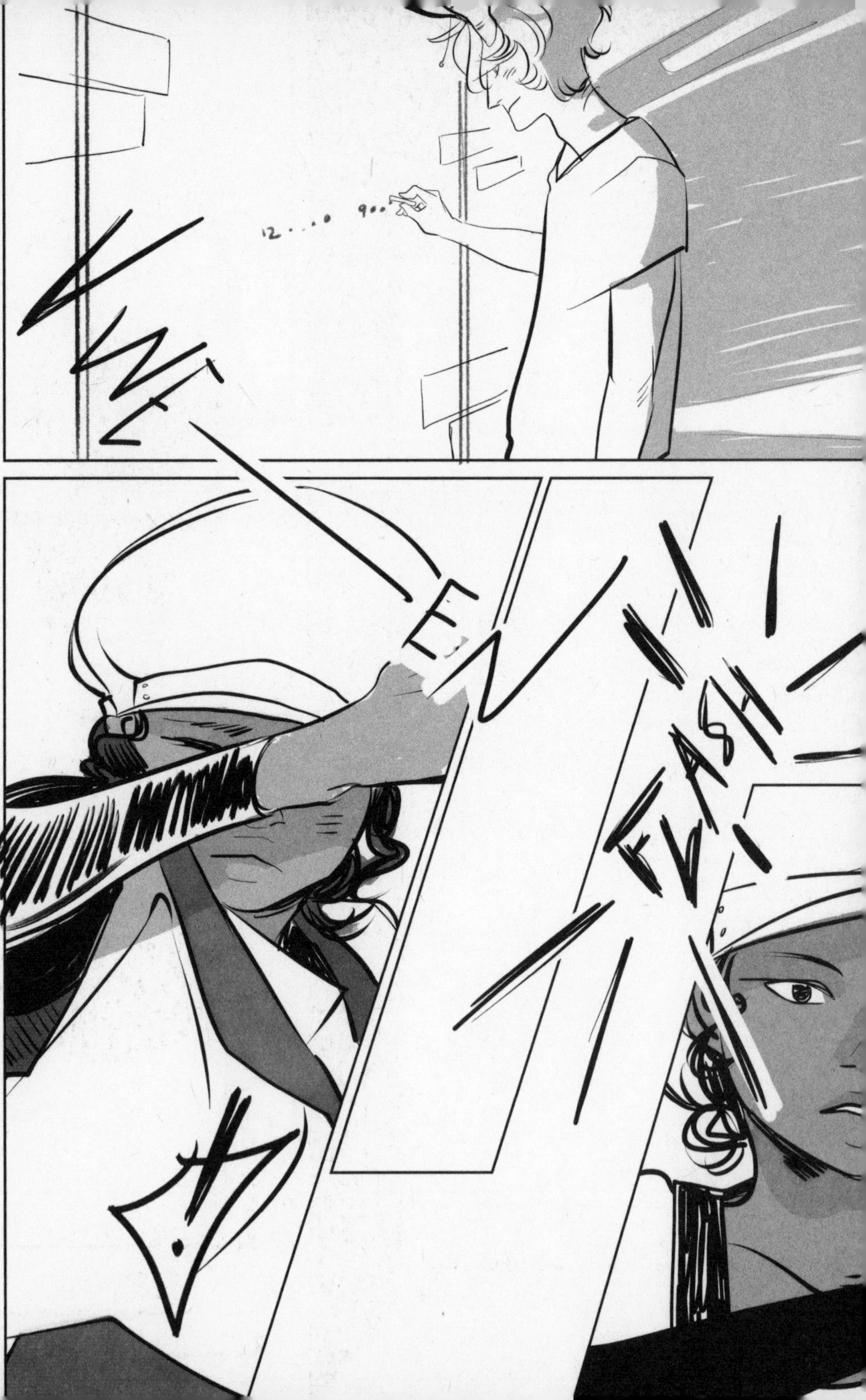

12... 9...
VWEEN
FLASH
!!

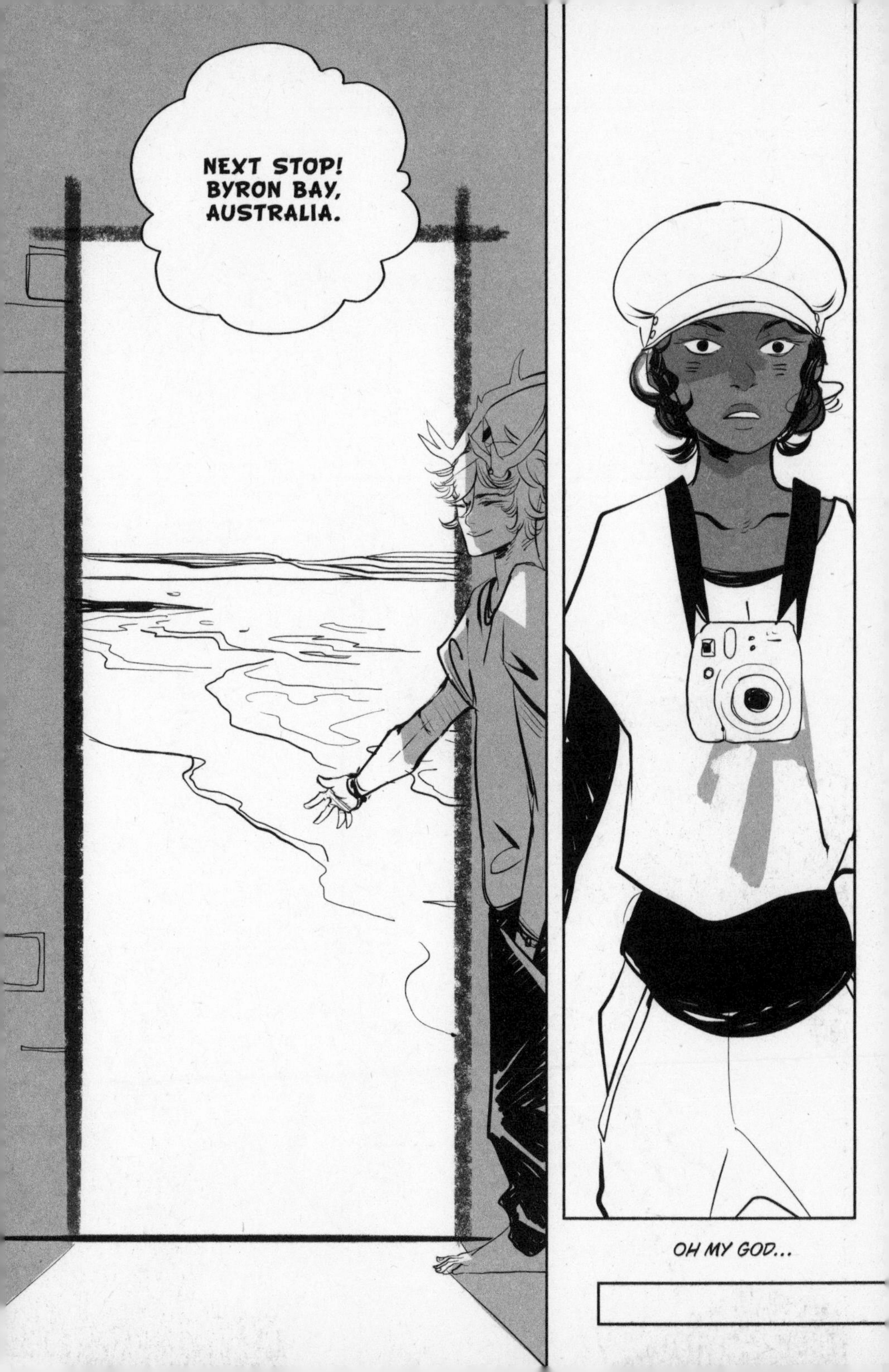
NEXT STOP! BYRON BAY, AUSTRALIA.
OH MY GOD...

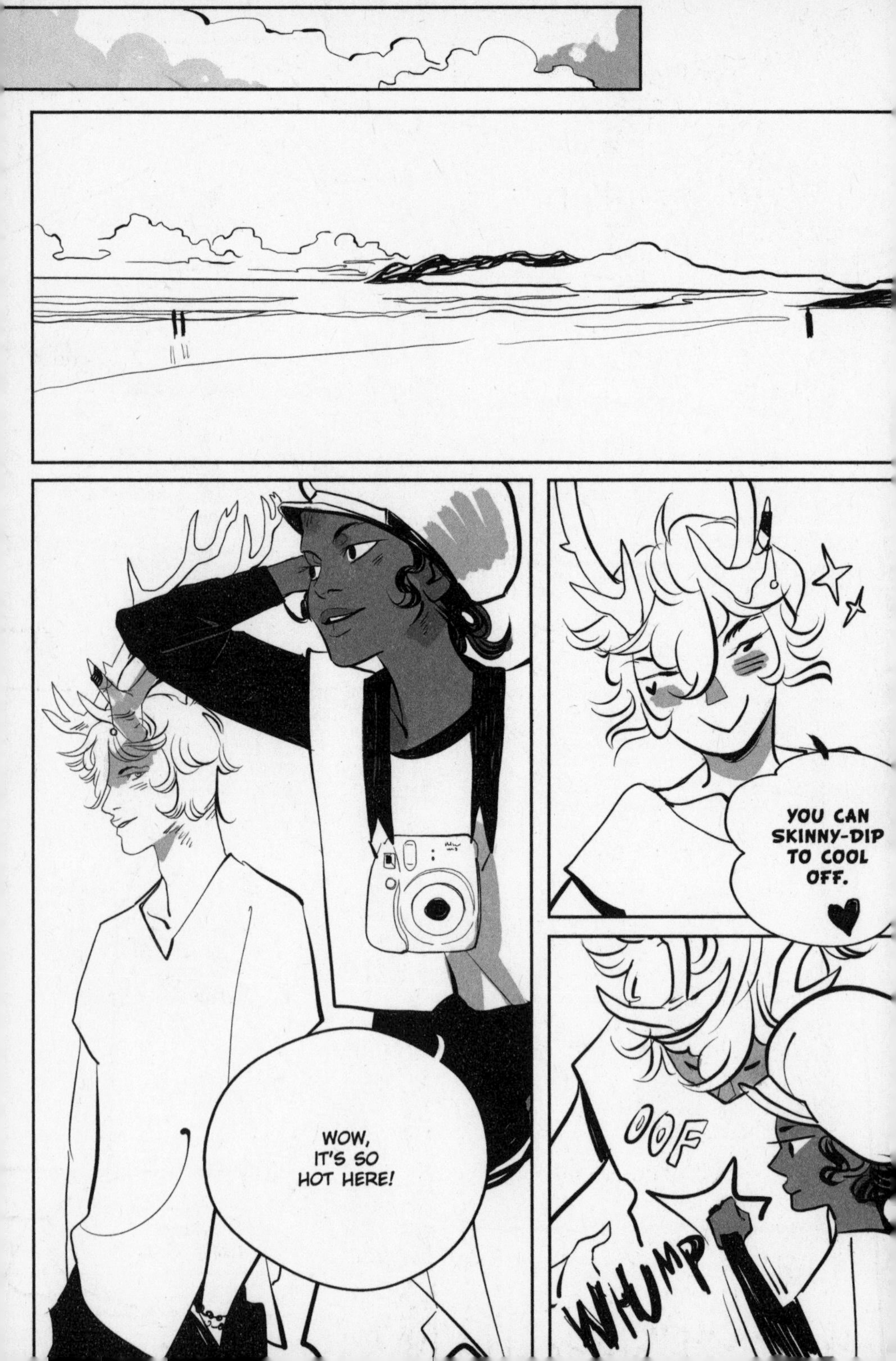
WOW, IT'S SO HOT HERE!
YOU CAN SKINNY-DIP TO COOL OFF. ♥
OOF
WHUMP

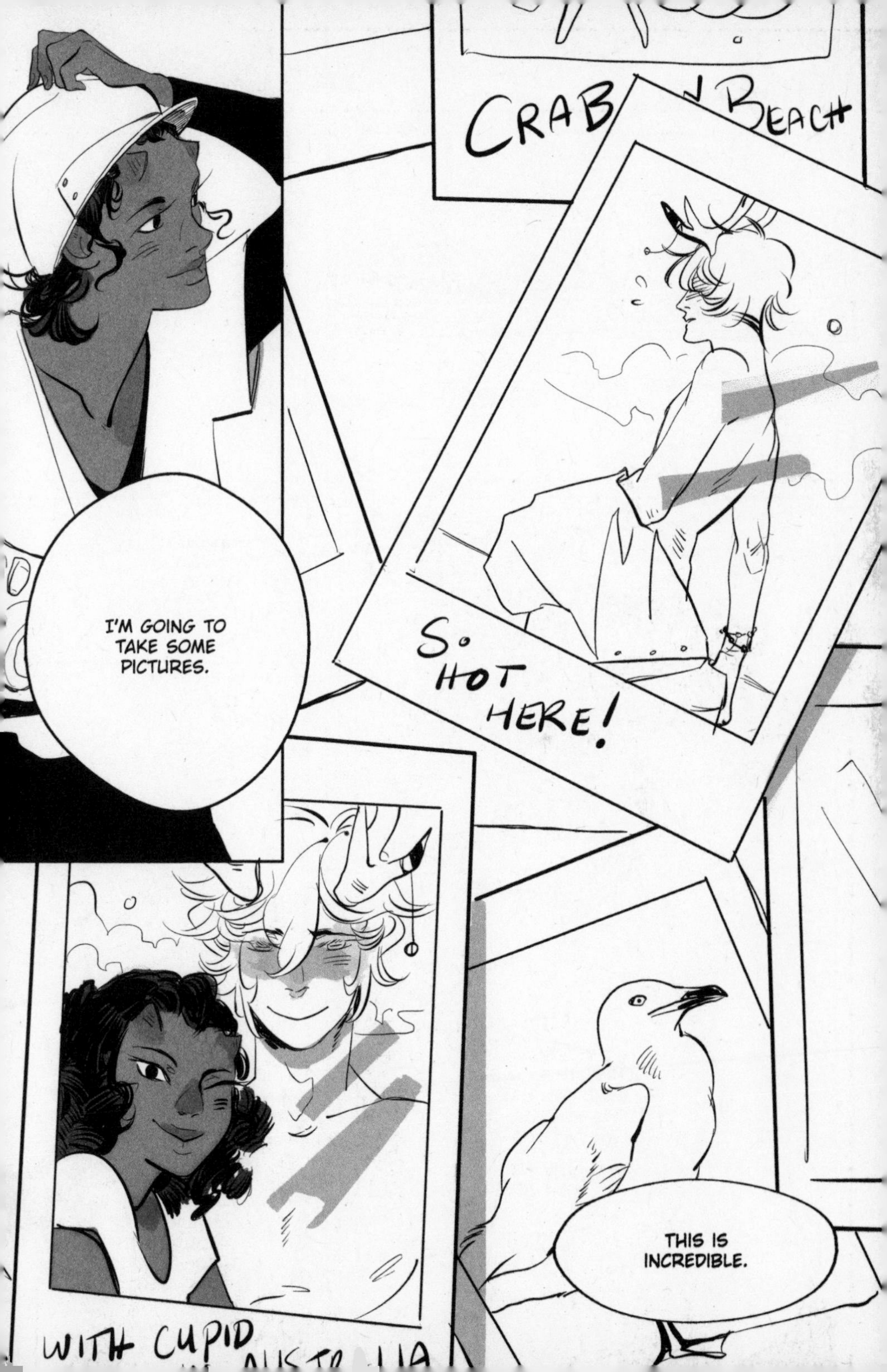
I'M GOING TO TAKE SOME PICTURES.
CRAB
BEACH
SO HOT HERE!
WITH CUPID
THIS IS INCREDIBLE.

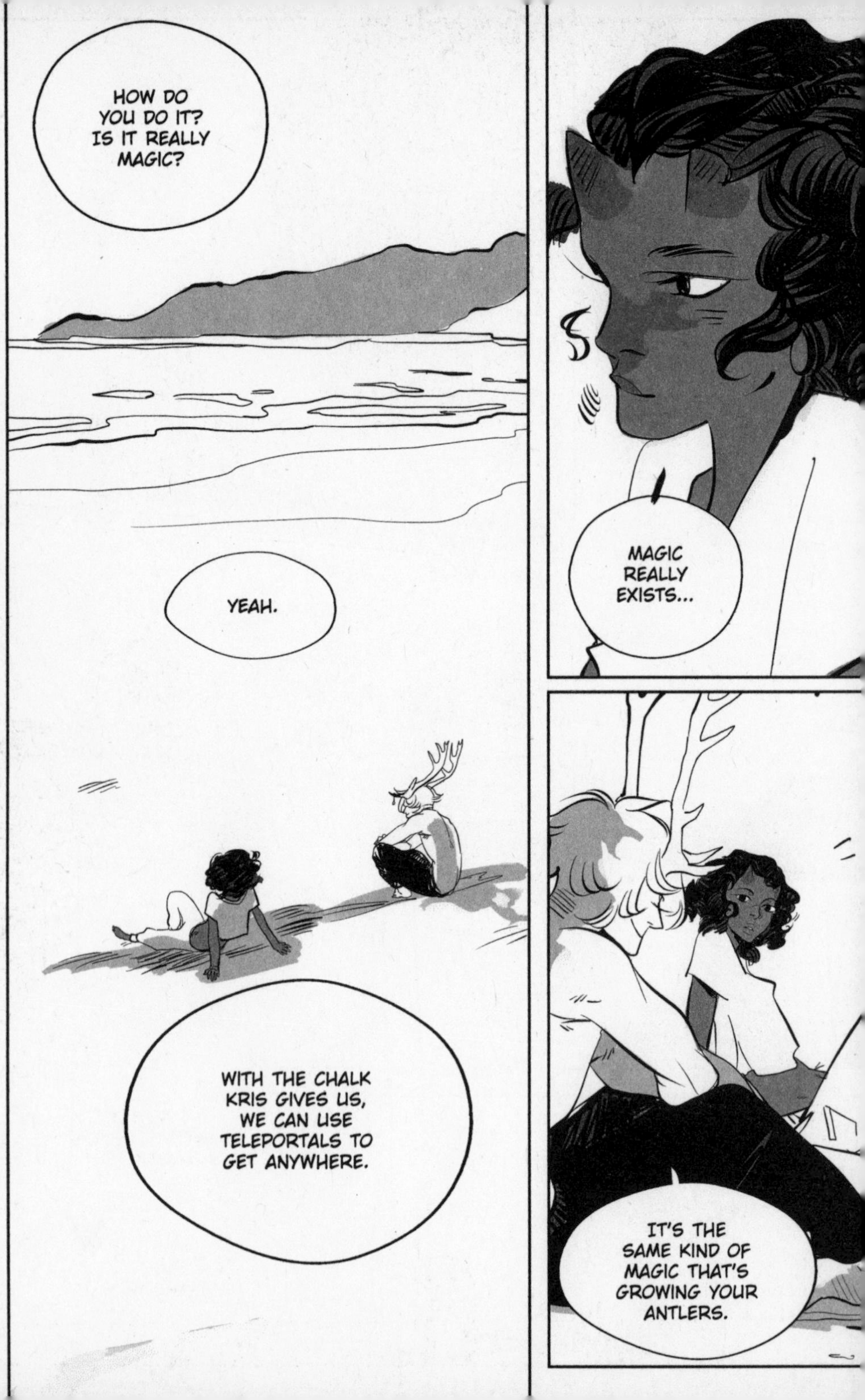
HOW DO YOU DO IT? IS IT REALLY MAGIC?
YEAH.
WITH THE CHALK KRIS GIVES US, WE CAN USE TELEPORTALS TO GET ANYWHERE.
MAGIC REALLY EXISTS...
IT'S THE SAME KIND OF MAGIC THAT'S GROWING YOUR ANTLERS.

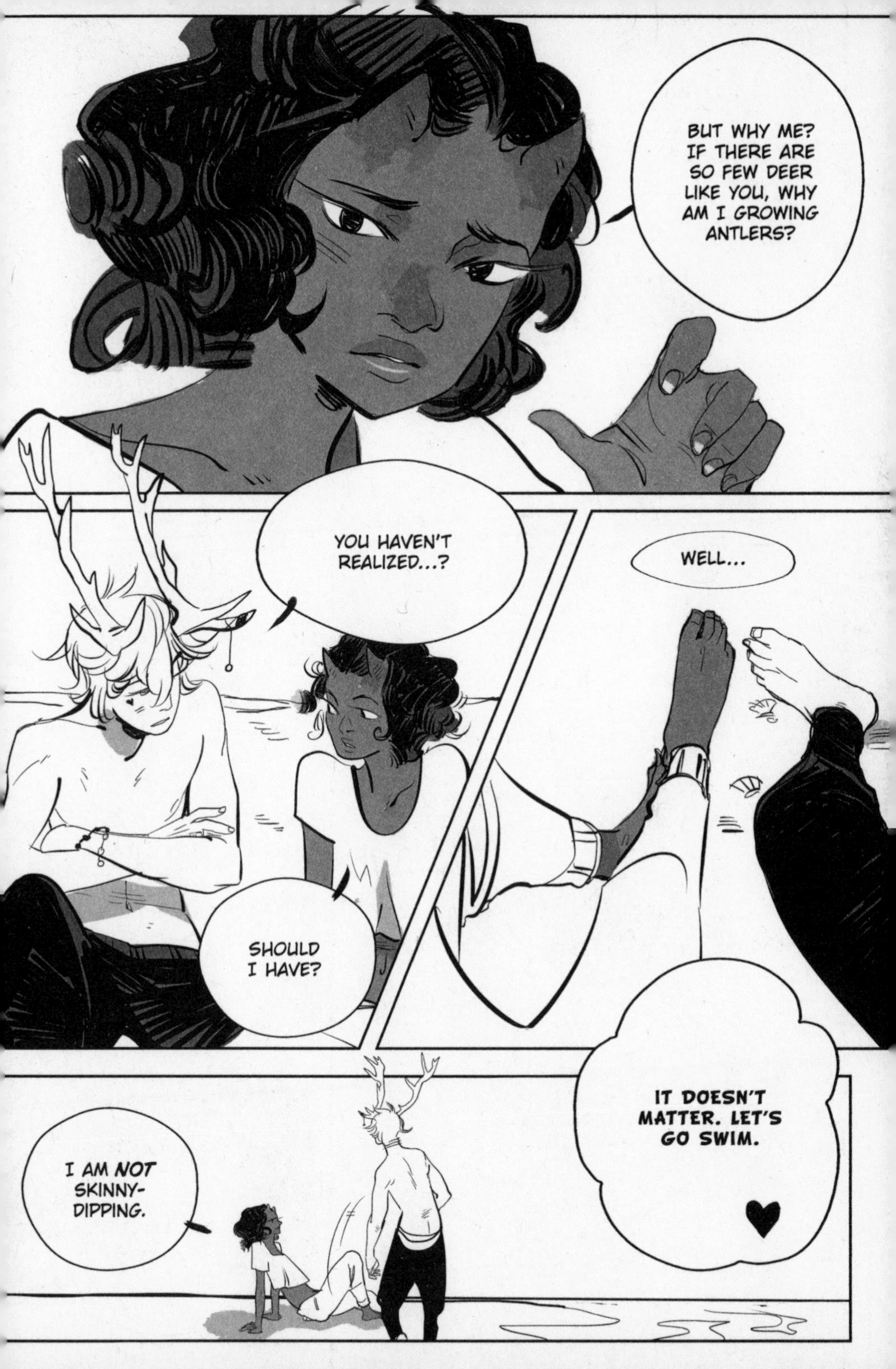
BUT WHY ME? IF THERE ARE SO FEW DEER LIKE YOU, WHY AM I GROWING ANTLERS?
YOU HAVEN'T REALIZED...?
SHOULD I HAVE?
WELL...
IT DOESN'T MATTER. LET'S GO SWIM.
I AM NOT SKINNY-DIPPING.

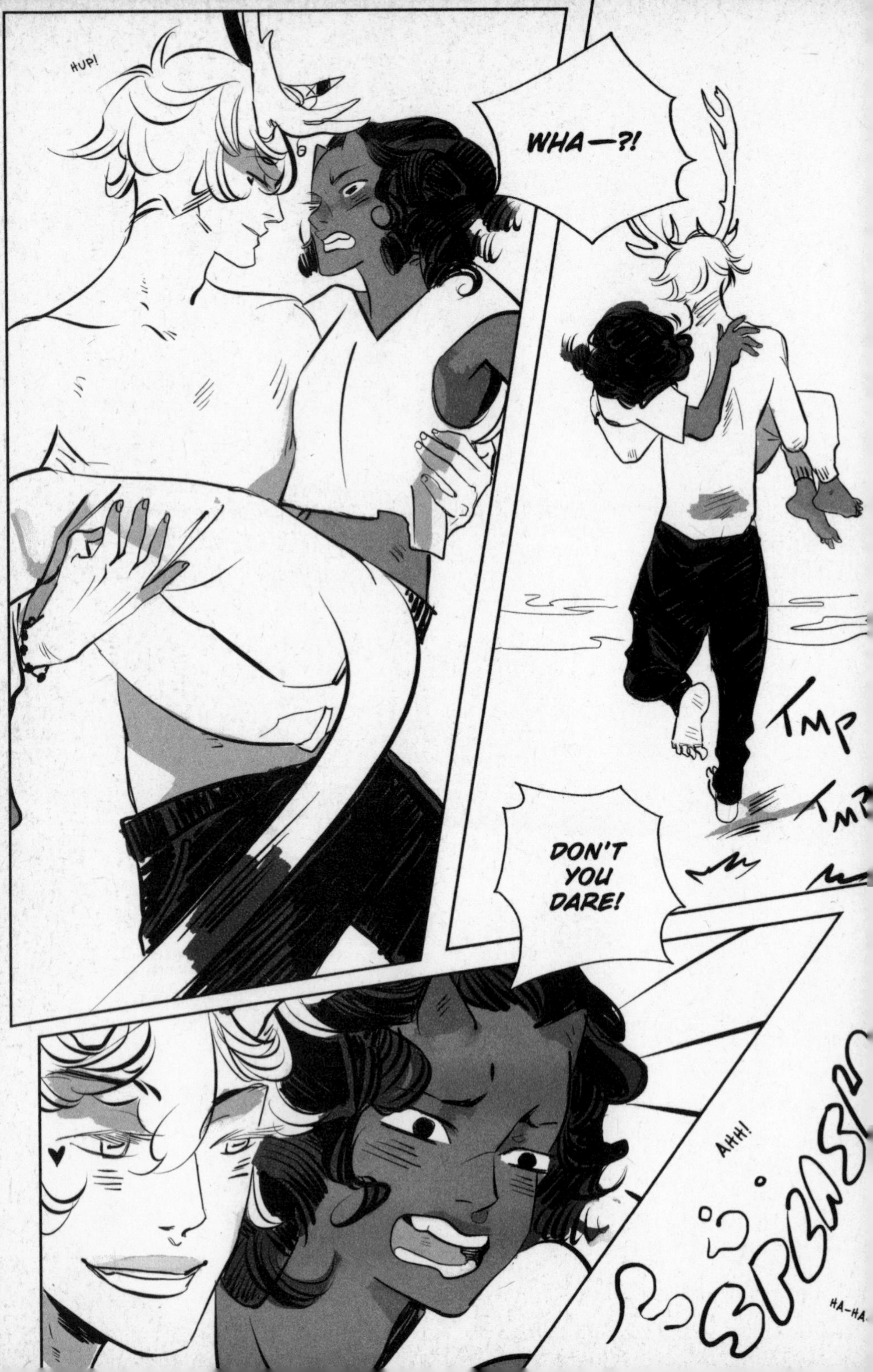

HUP!
WHA—?!
TMP
TMP
DON'T YOU DARE!
AHH!
HA-HA

Reindeer
Boy

Chapter 6

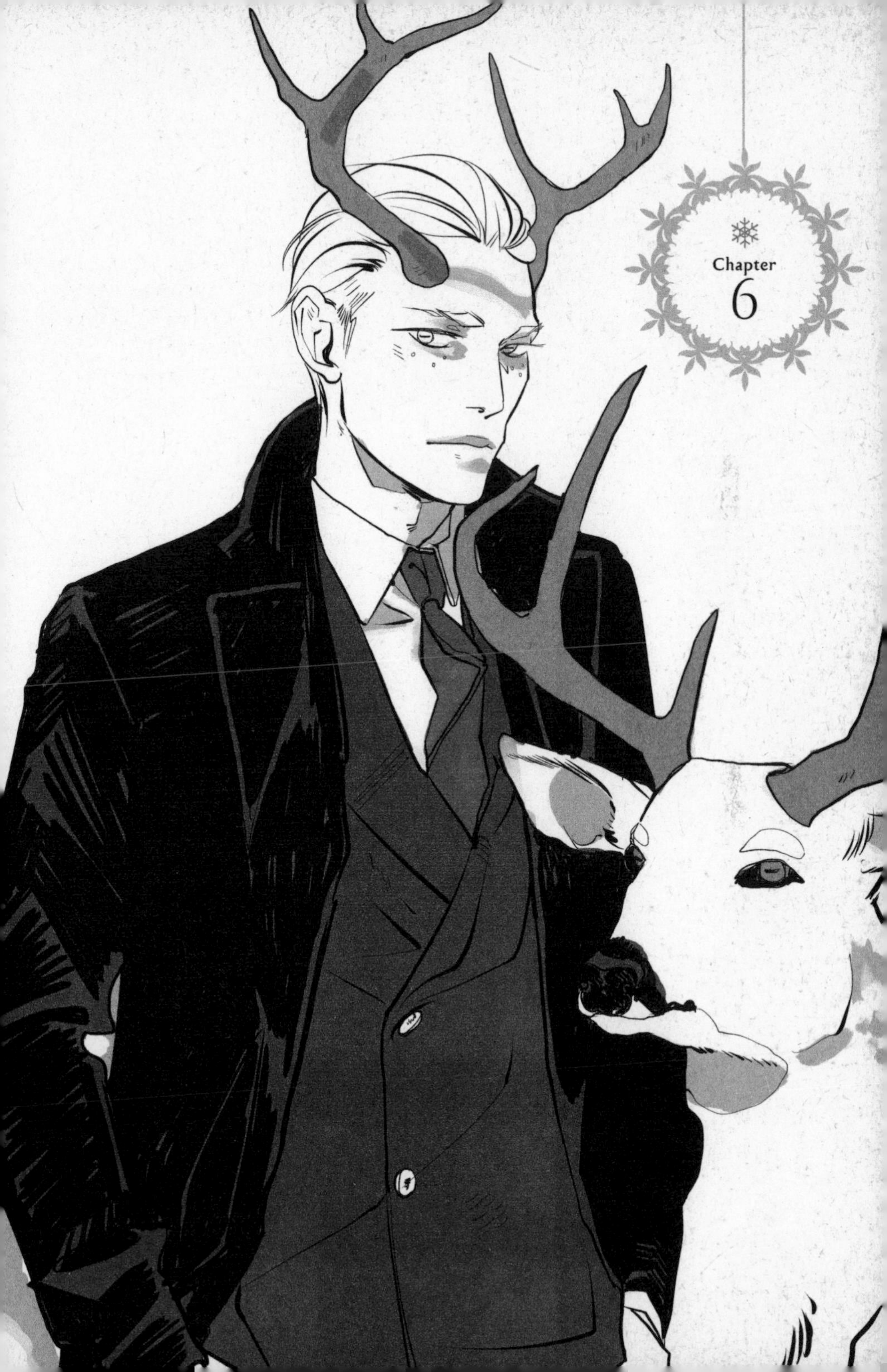

I DON'T WANNA SLEEP!

BUT IF SANTA FINDS OUT I'M AWAKE ...

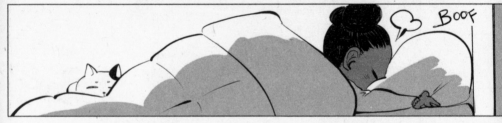

BOOF

JINGLE

SANTA!

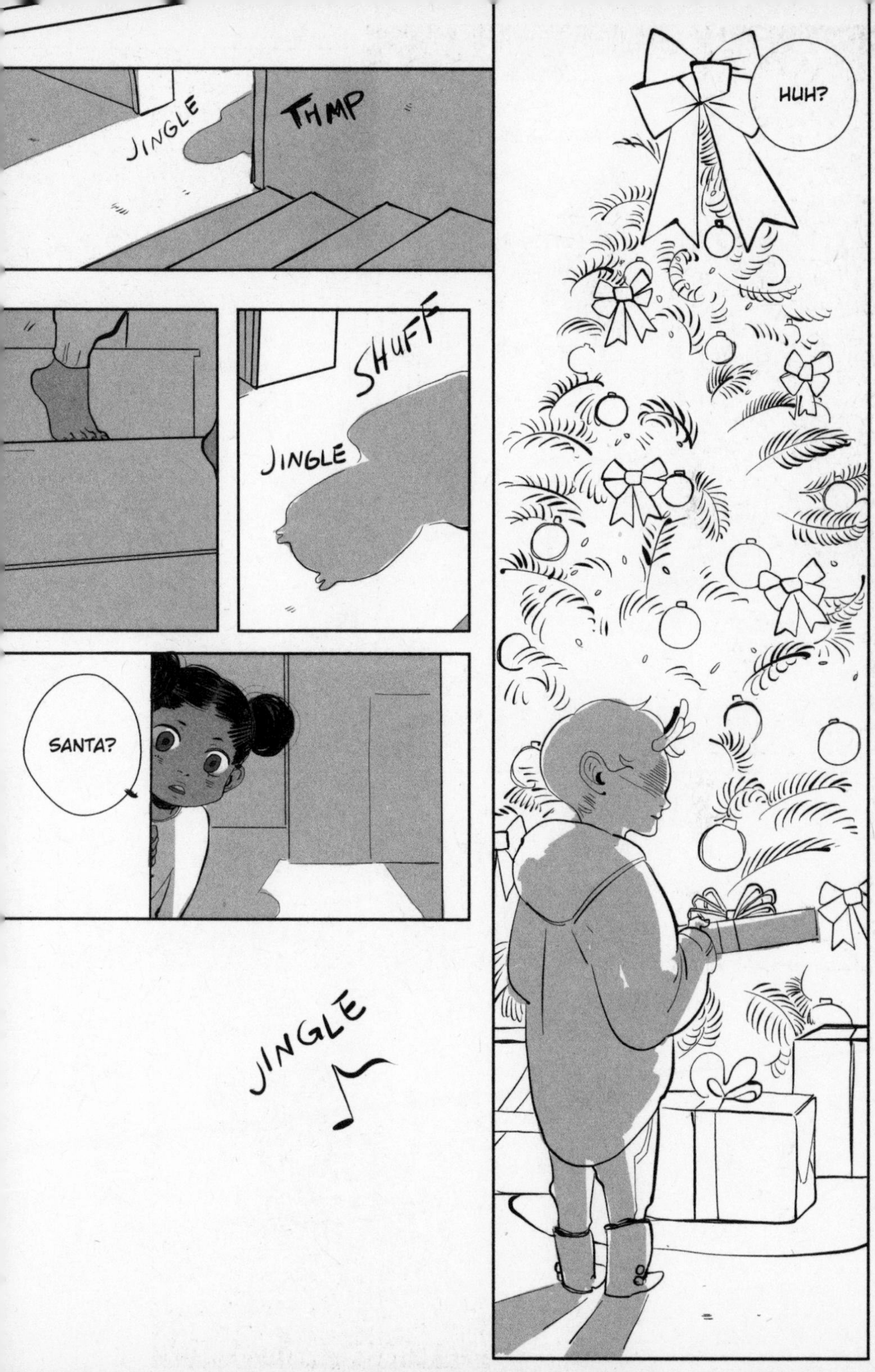
JINGLE
THMP
SHUFF
JINGLE
SANTA?
JINGLE
HUH?

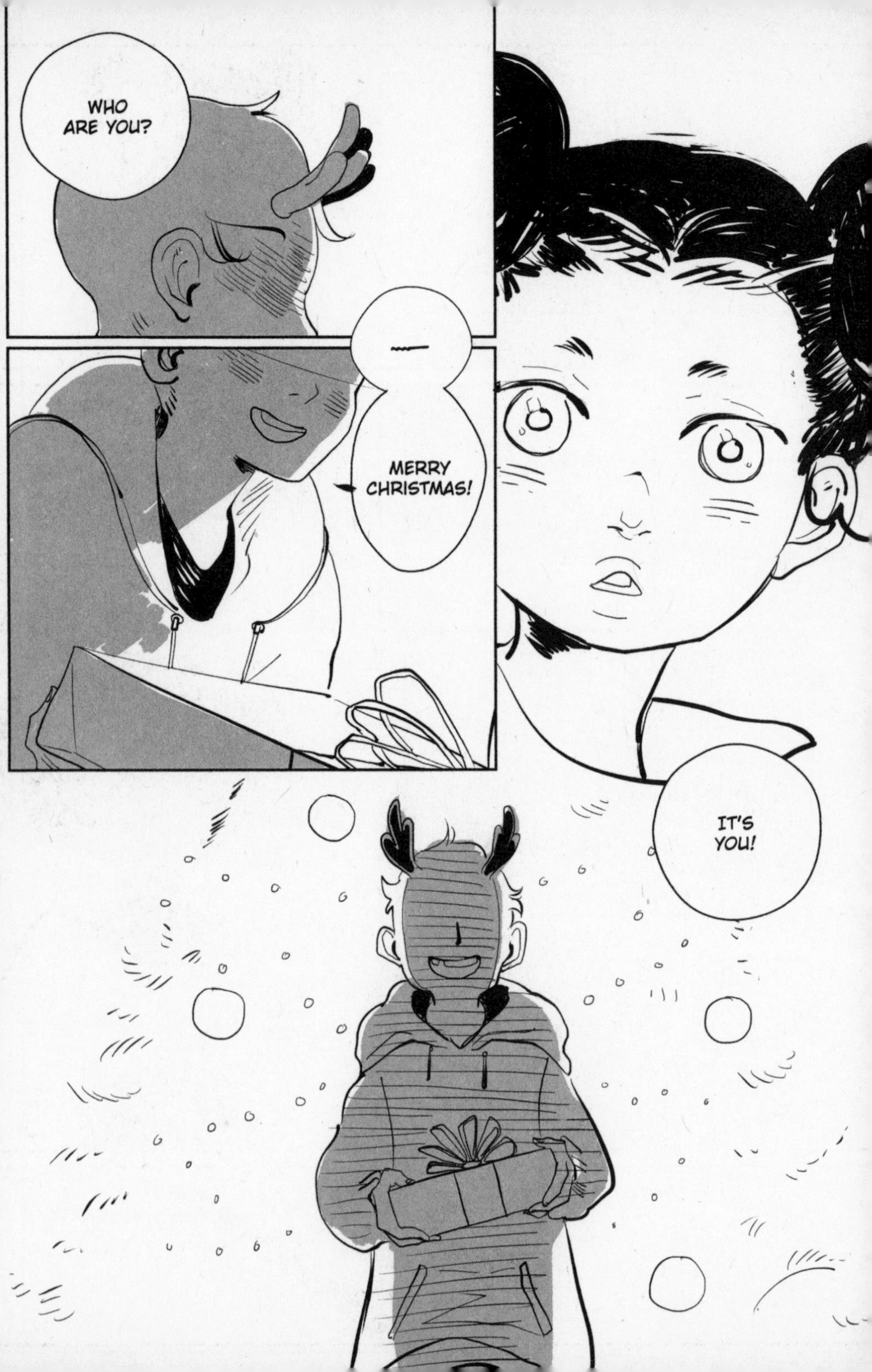
WHO ARE YOU?
MERRY CHRISTMAS!
IT'S YOU!

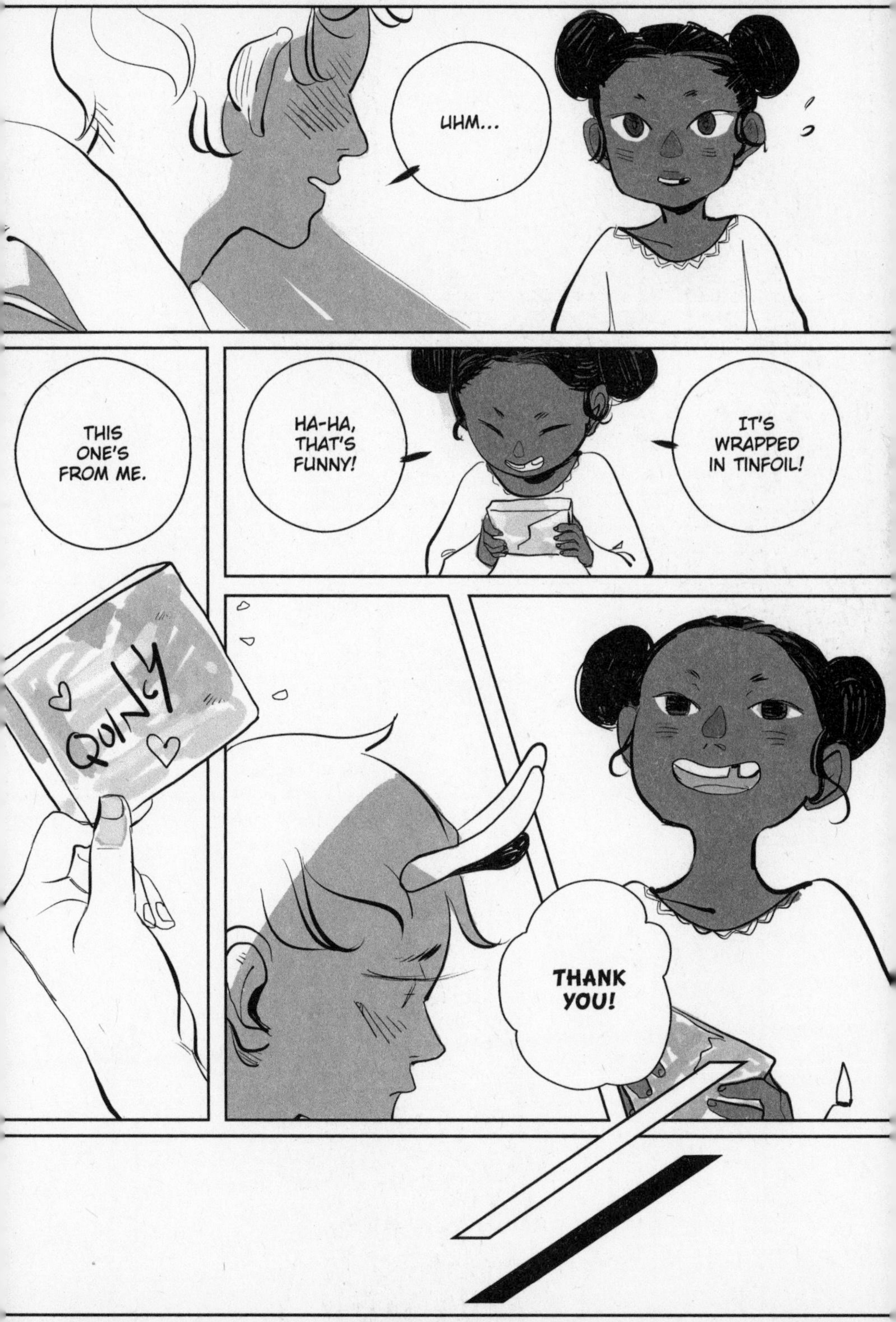
UHM...
THIS ONE'S FROM ME.
HA-HA, THAT'S FUNNY!
IT'S WRAPPED IN TINFOIL!
QUINCY
THANK YOU!

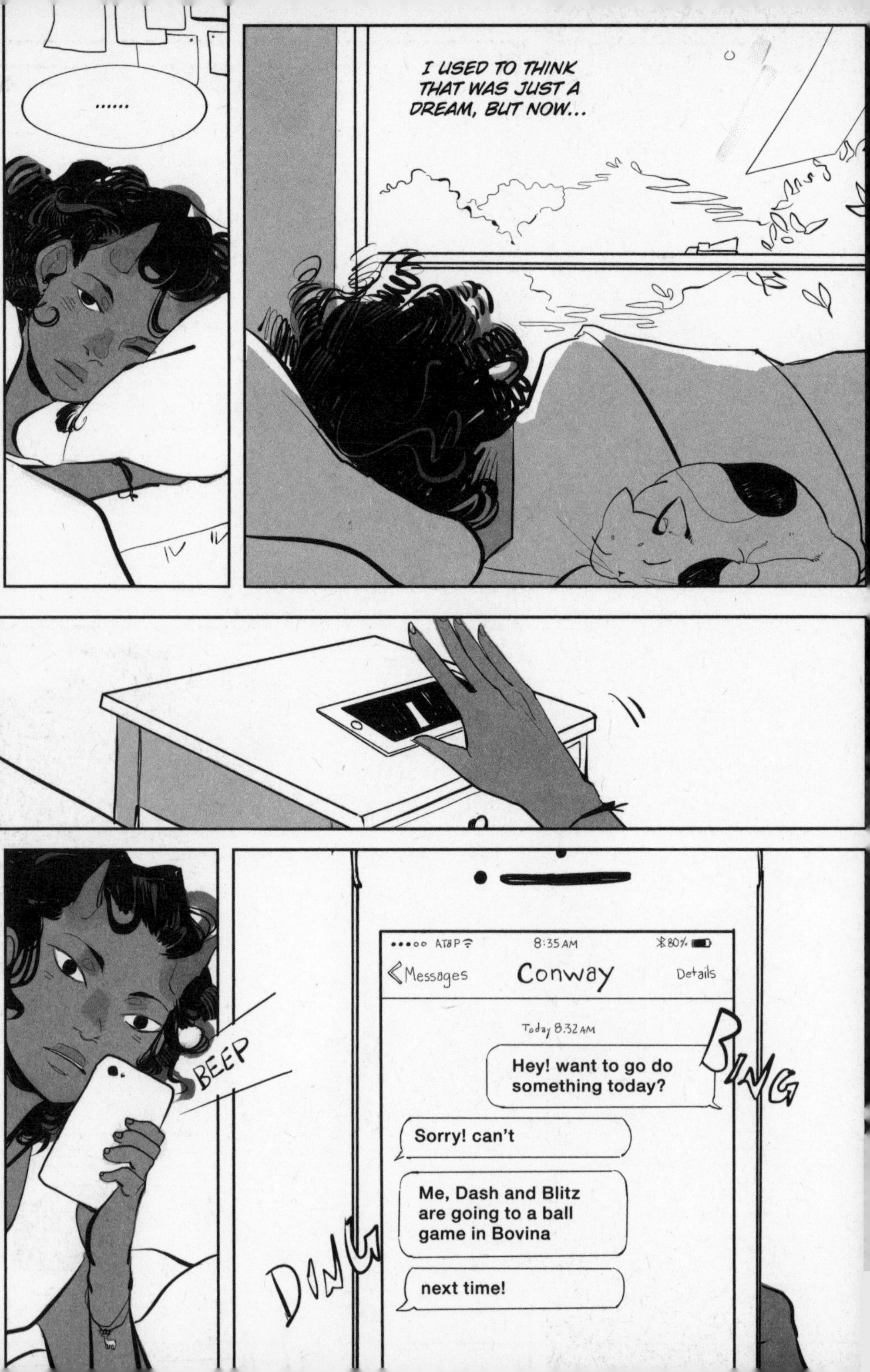
......
I USED TO THINK THAT WAS JUST A DREAM, BUT NOW...
BEEP
8:35 AM
80%
Messages
Conway
Details
Today 8:32 AM
Hey! want to go do something today?
BING
Sorry! can't
Me, Dash and Blitz are going to a ball game in Bovina
DING
next time!

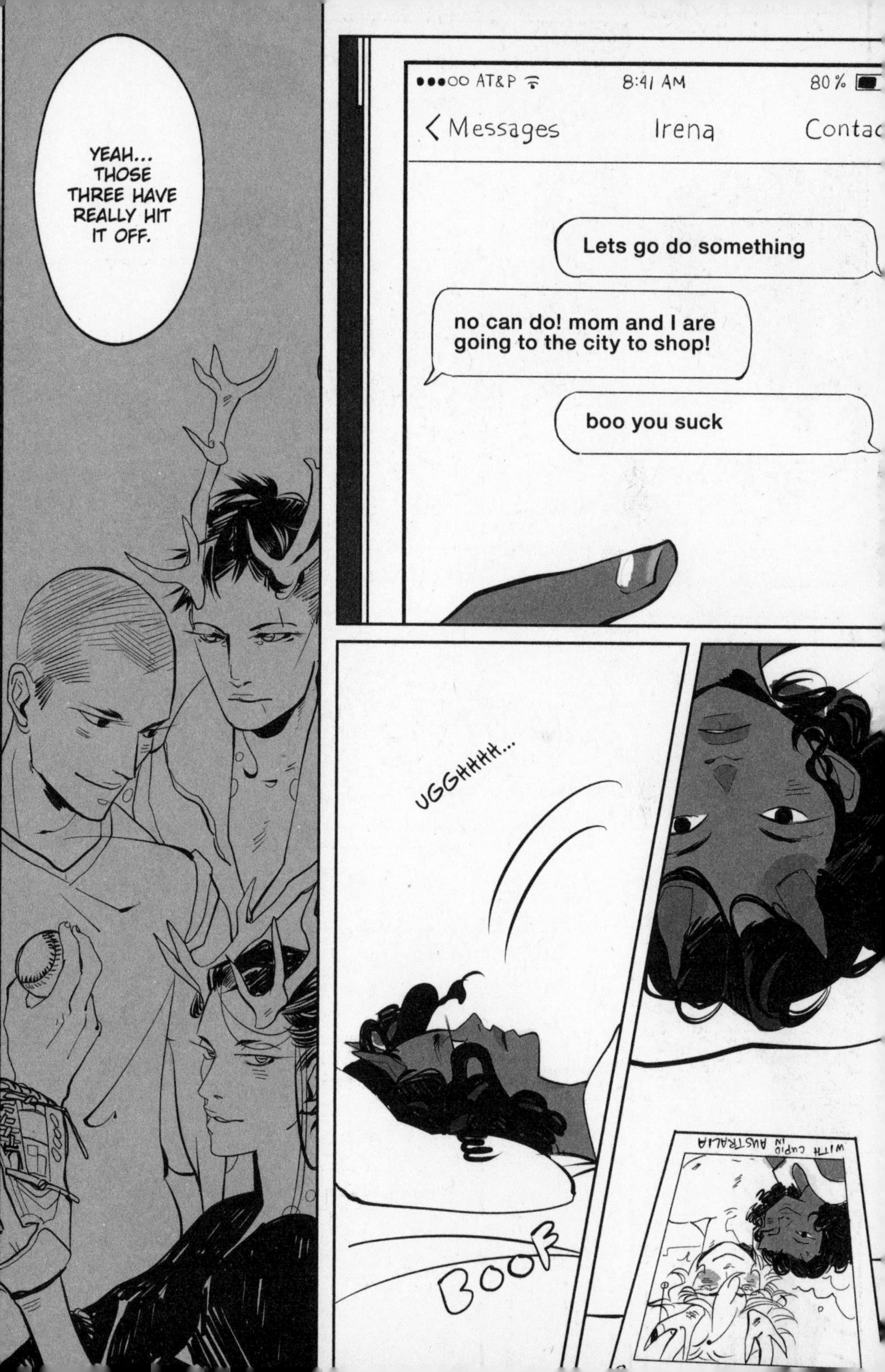
YEAH... THOSE THREE HAVE REALLY HIT IT OFF.
●●●○○ AT&P
8:41 AM
80%
Messages
Irena
Contac
Lets go do something
no can do! mom and I are going to the city to shop!
boo you suck
UGGHHHH...
BOOF
WITH CUPID IN AUSTRALIA

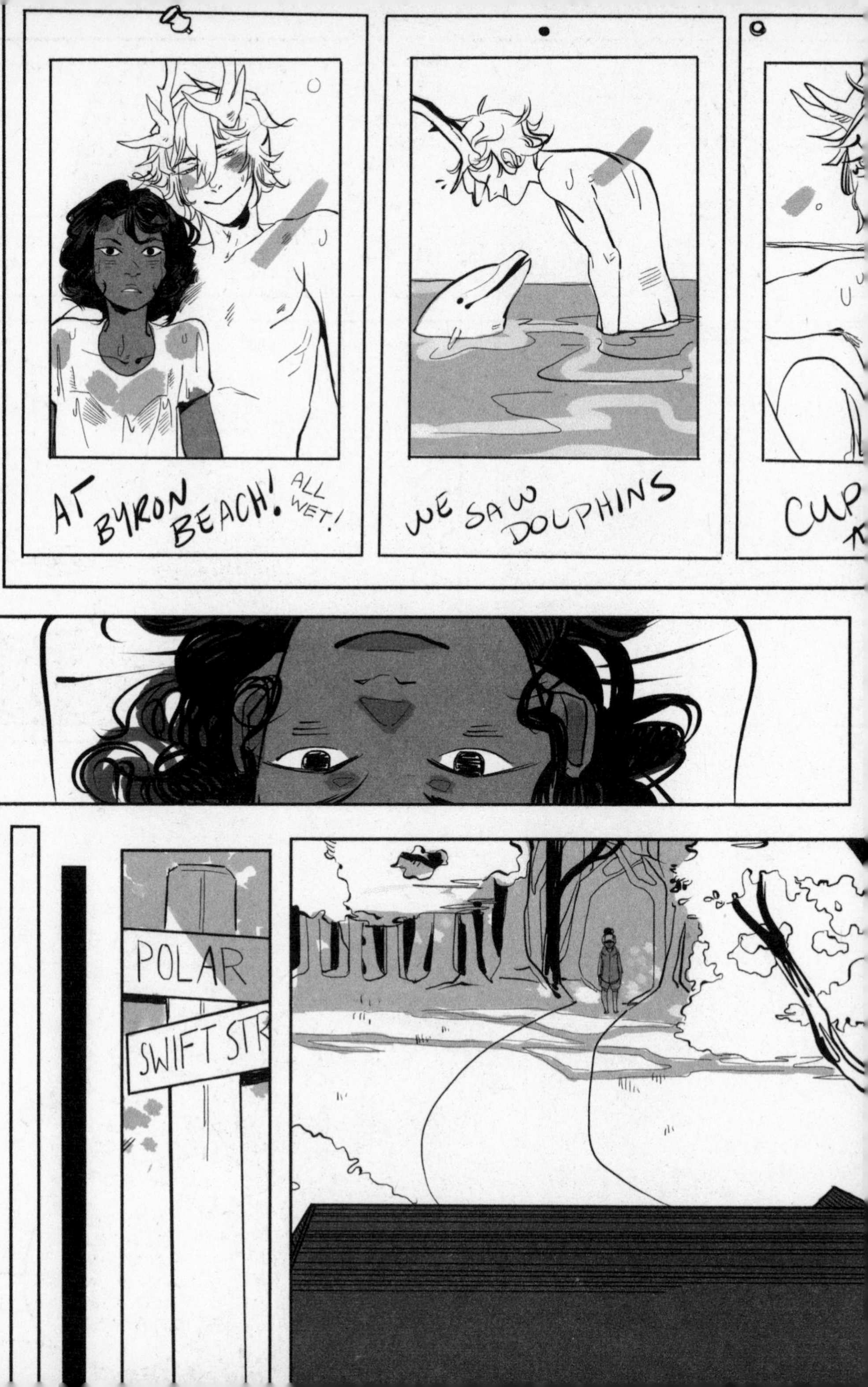
AT BYRON BEACH!
ALL WET!
WE SAW DOLPHINS
CUP
POLAR
SWIFT STR

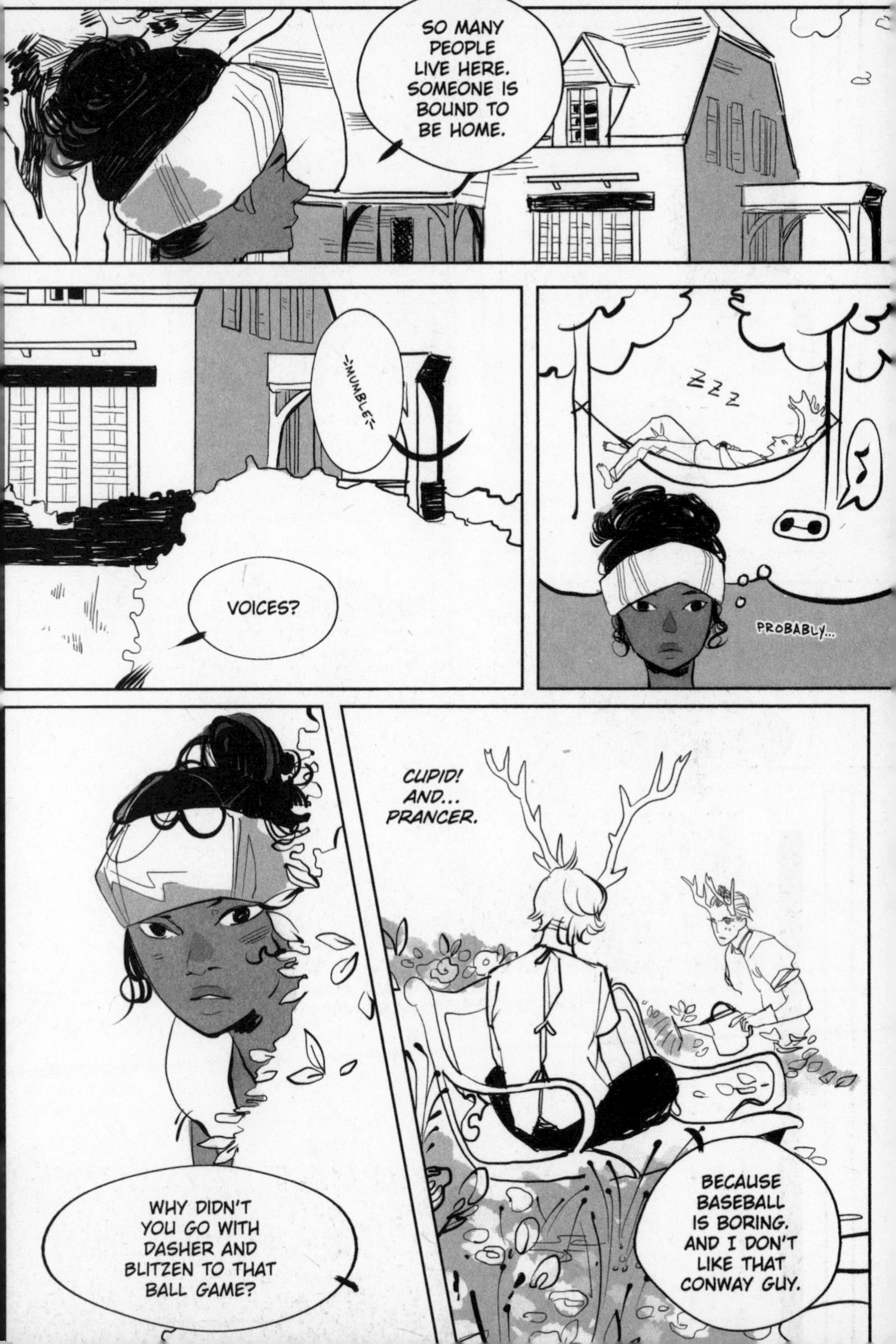
SO MANY PEOPLE LIVE HERE. SOMEONE IS BOUND TO BE HOME.
~MUMBLE~
VOICES?
ZZZ
PROBABLY...
CUPID! AND... PRANCER.
WHY DIDN'T YOU GO WITH DASHER AND BLITZEN TO THAT BALL GAME?
BECAUSE BASEBALL IS BORING. AND I DON'T LIKE THAT CONWAY GUY.

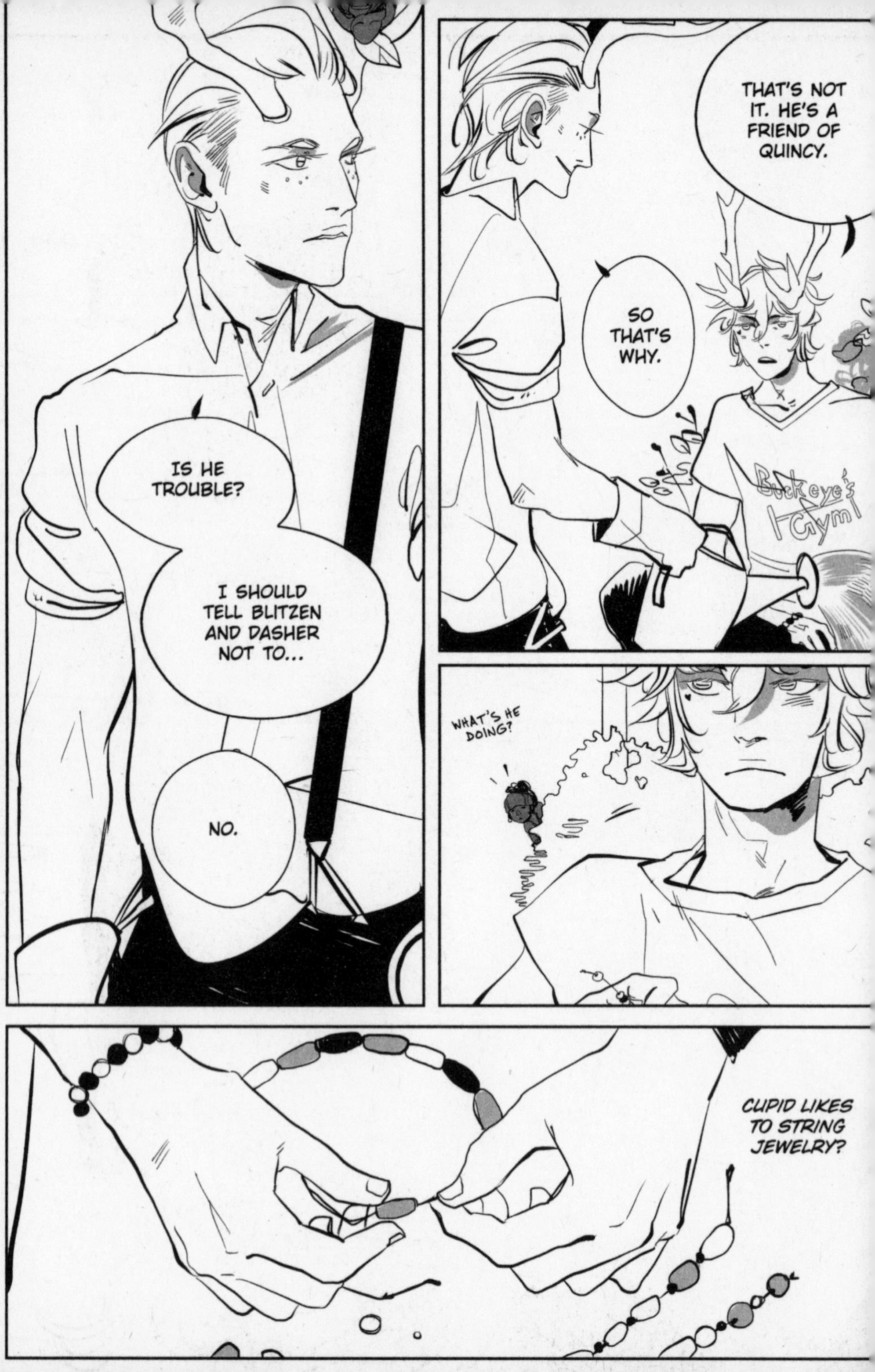
IS HE TROUBLE?
I SHOULD TELL BLITZEN AND DASHER NOT TO...
NO.
THAT'S NOT IT. HE'S A FRIEND OF QUINCY.
SO THAT'S WHY.
Buckeye's Gym
WHAT'S HE DOING?
CUPID LIKES TO STRING JEWELRY?

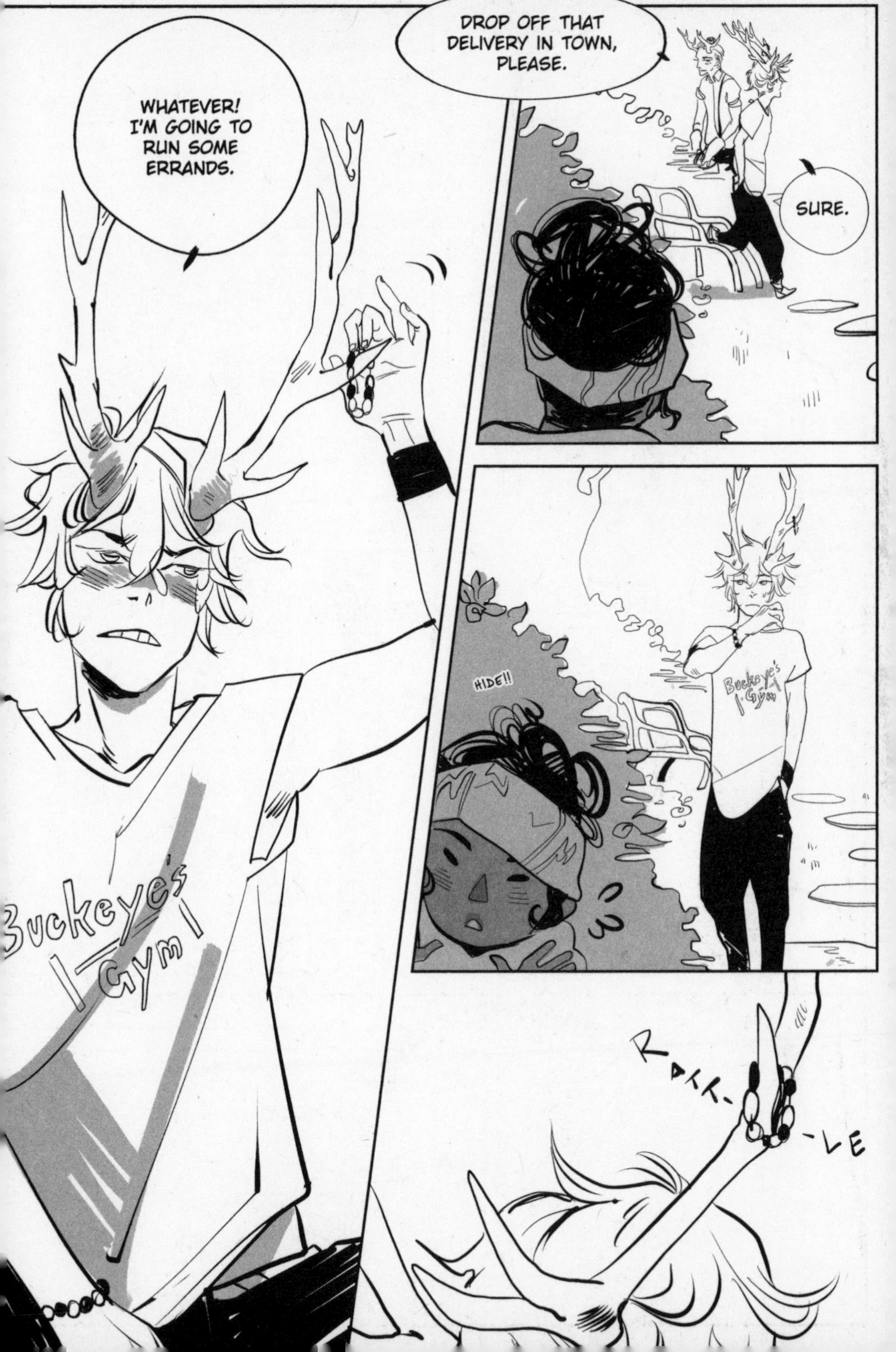
WHATEVER! I'M GOING TO RUN SOME ERRANDS.
DROP OFF THAT DELIVERY IN TOWN, PLEASE.
SURE.
HIDE!!
Buckeye's Gym
RATT- -LE
Buckeye's Gym

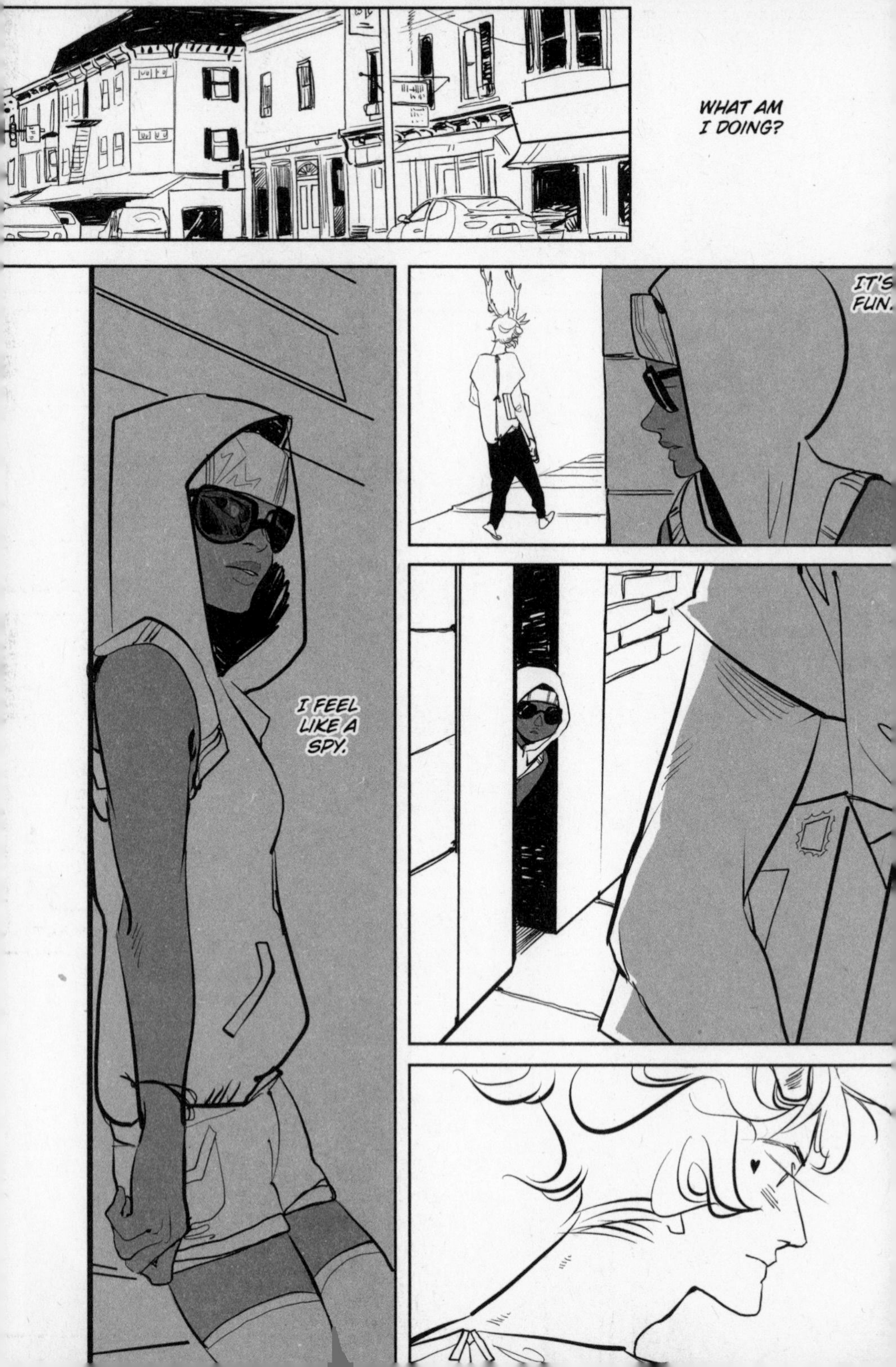
WHAT AM I DOING?
I FEEL LIKE A SPY.
IT'S FUN.

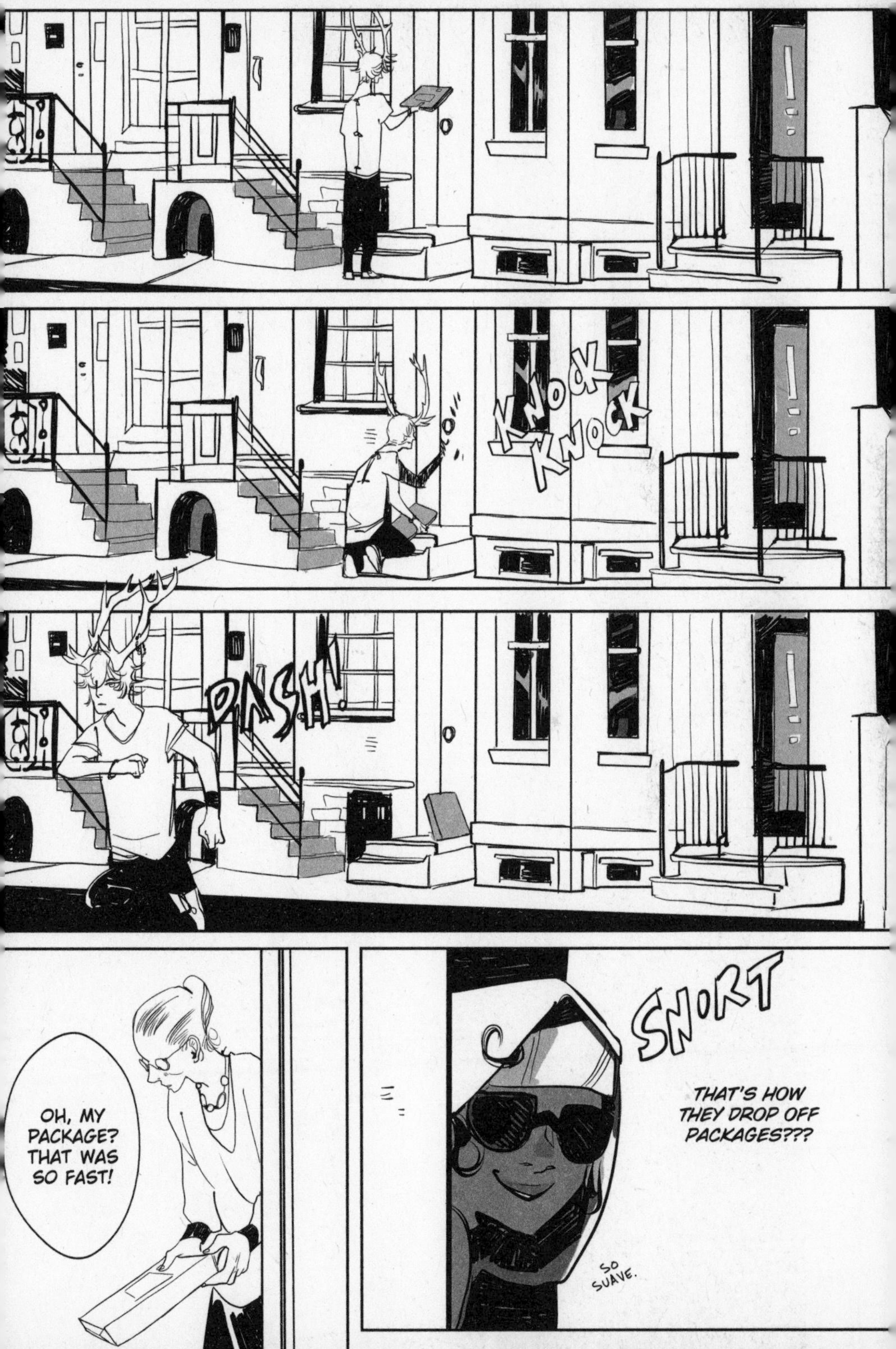
KNOCK KNOCK
DASH!
OH, MY PACKAGE? THAT WAS SO FAST!
SNORT
THAT'S HOW THEY DROP OFF PACKAGES???
SO SUAVE.

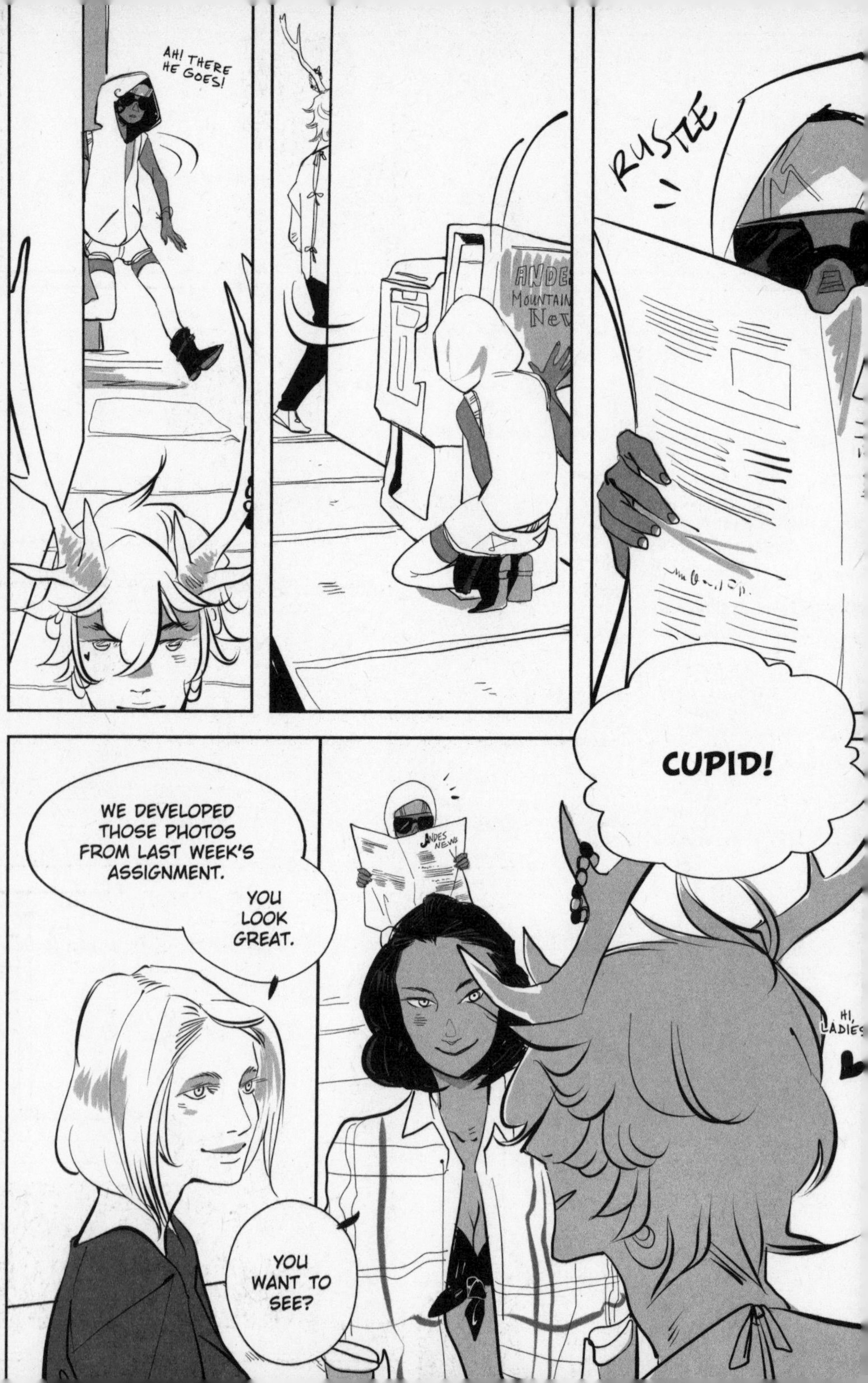
AH! THERE HE GOES!
ANDES MOUNTAIN News
RUSTLE
CUPID!
WE DEVELOPED THOSE PHOTOS FROM LAST WEEK'S ASSIGNMENT.
YOU LOOK GREAT.
YOU WANT TO SEE?
ANDES NEWS
HI, LADIES

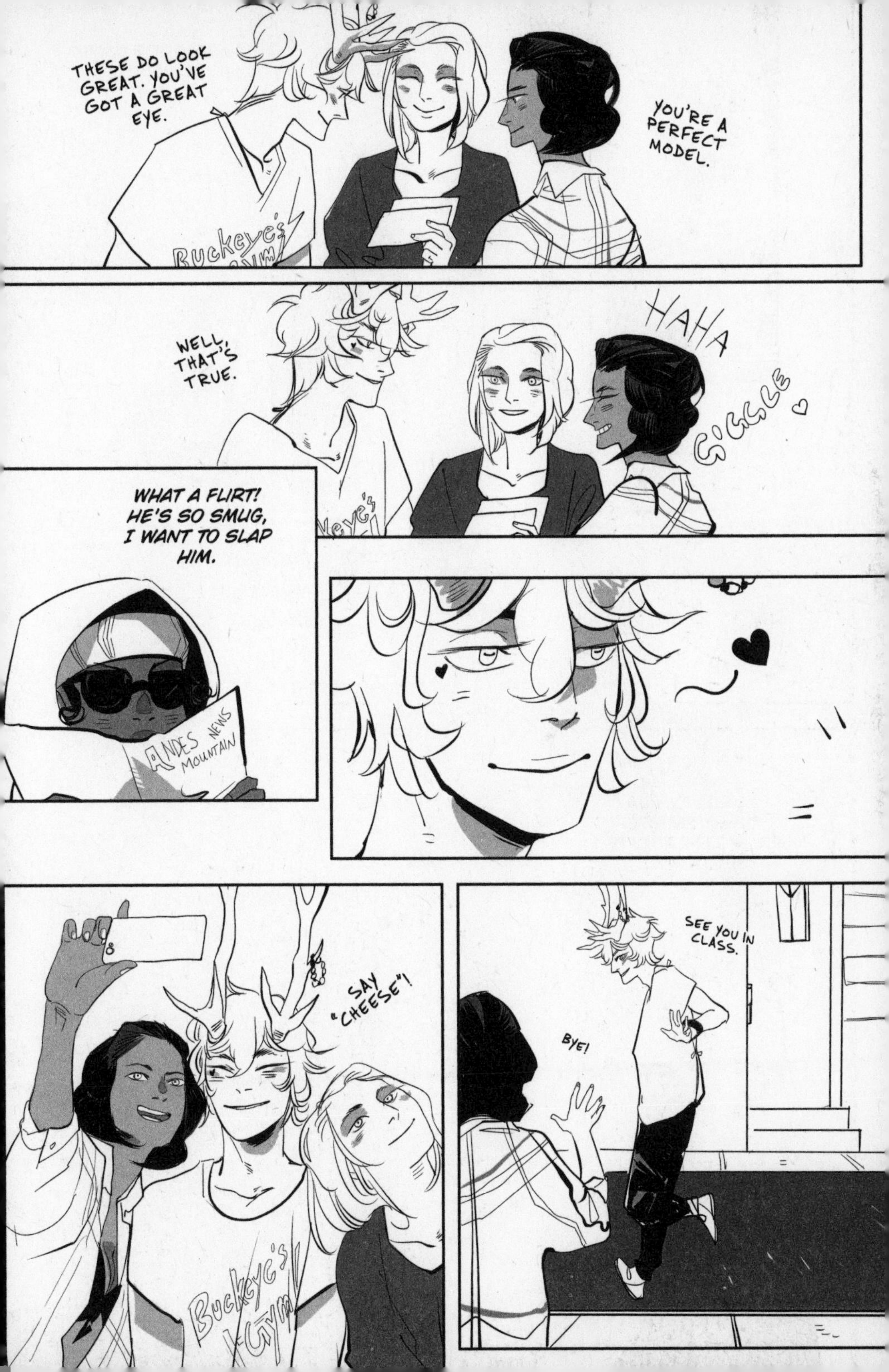
THESE DO LOOK GREAT. YOU'VE GOT A GREAT EYE.
YOU'RE A PERFECT MODEL.
WELL, THAT'S TRUE.
HAHA
GIGGLE
WHAT A FLIRT! HE'S SO SMUG, I WANT TO SLAP HIM.
ANDES MOUNTAIN NEWS
SAY "CHEESE"!
SEE YOU IN CLASS.
BYE!

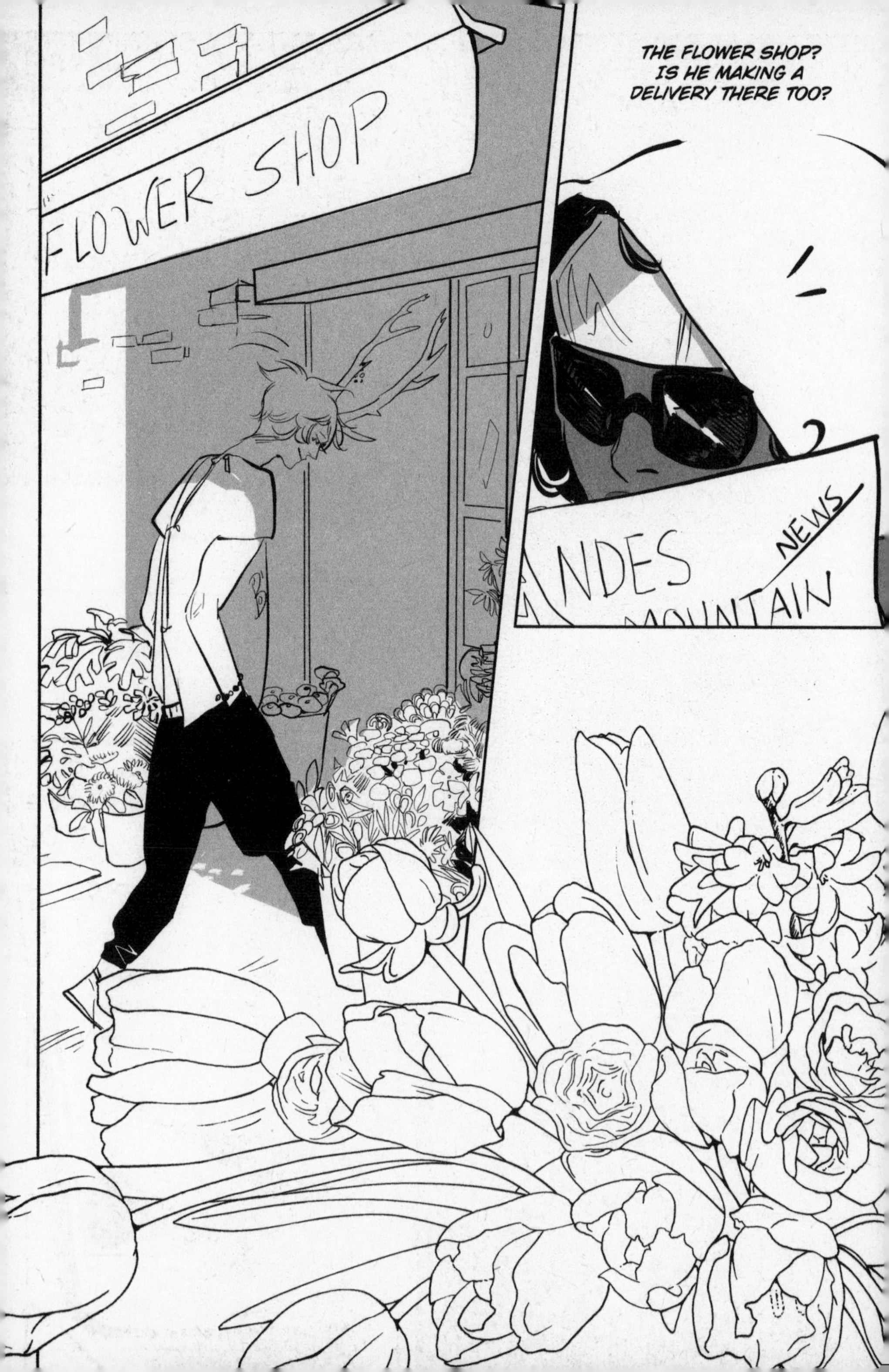
FLOWER SHOP
THE FLOWER SHOP? IS HE MAKING A DELIVERY THERE TOO?
NDES
NEWS
MOUNTAIN

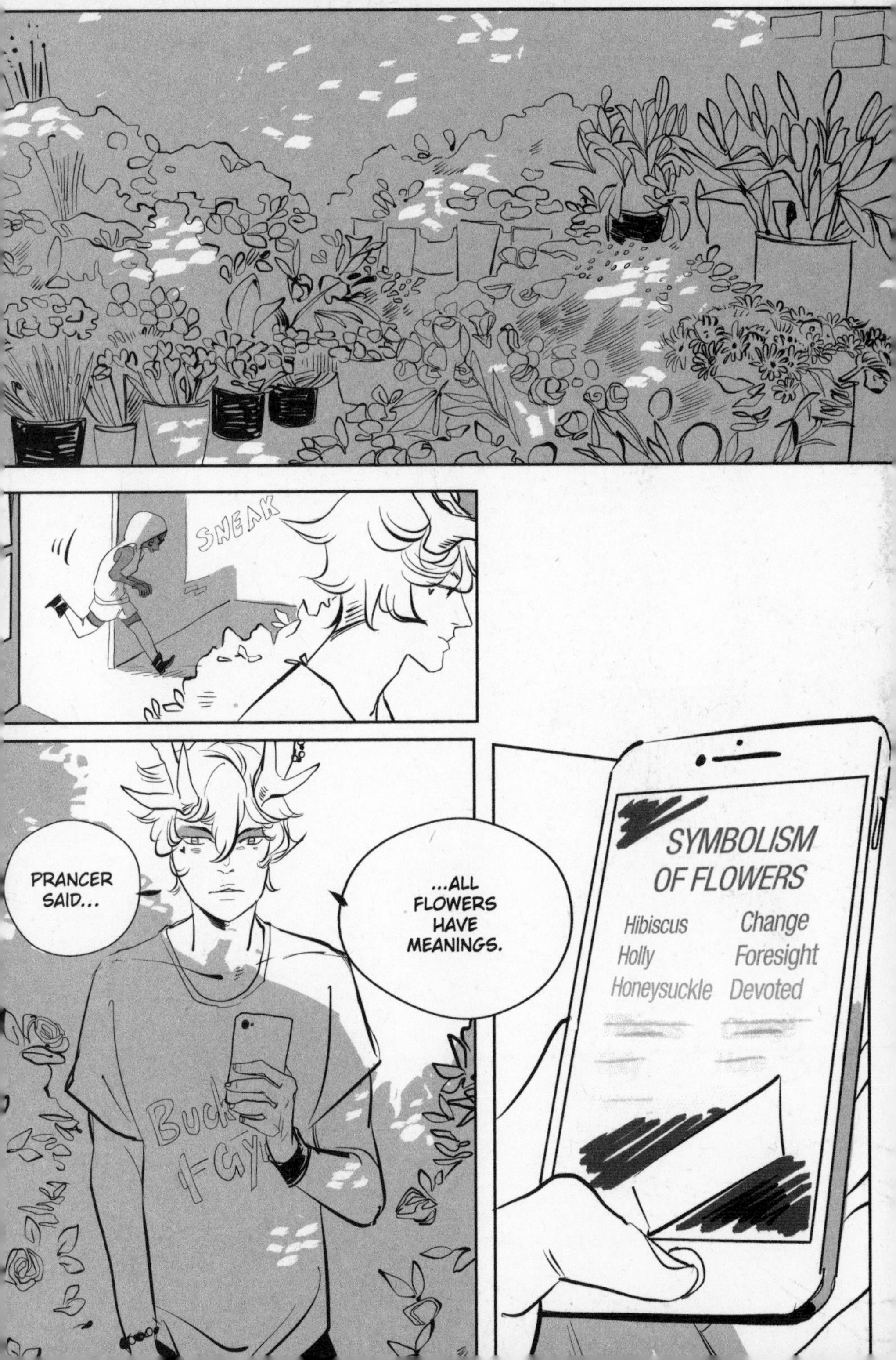
SNEAK
PRANCER SAID...
...ALL FLOWERS HAVE MEANINGS.
SYMBOLISM OF FLOWERS
Hibiscus Change
Holly Foresight
Honeysuckle Devoted

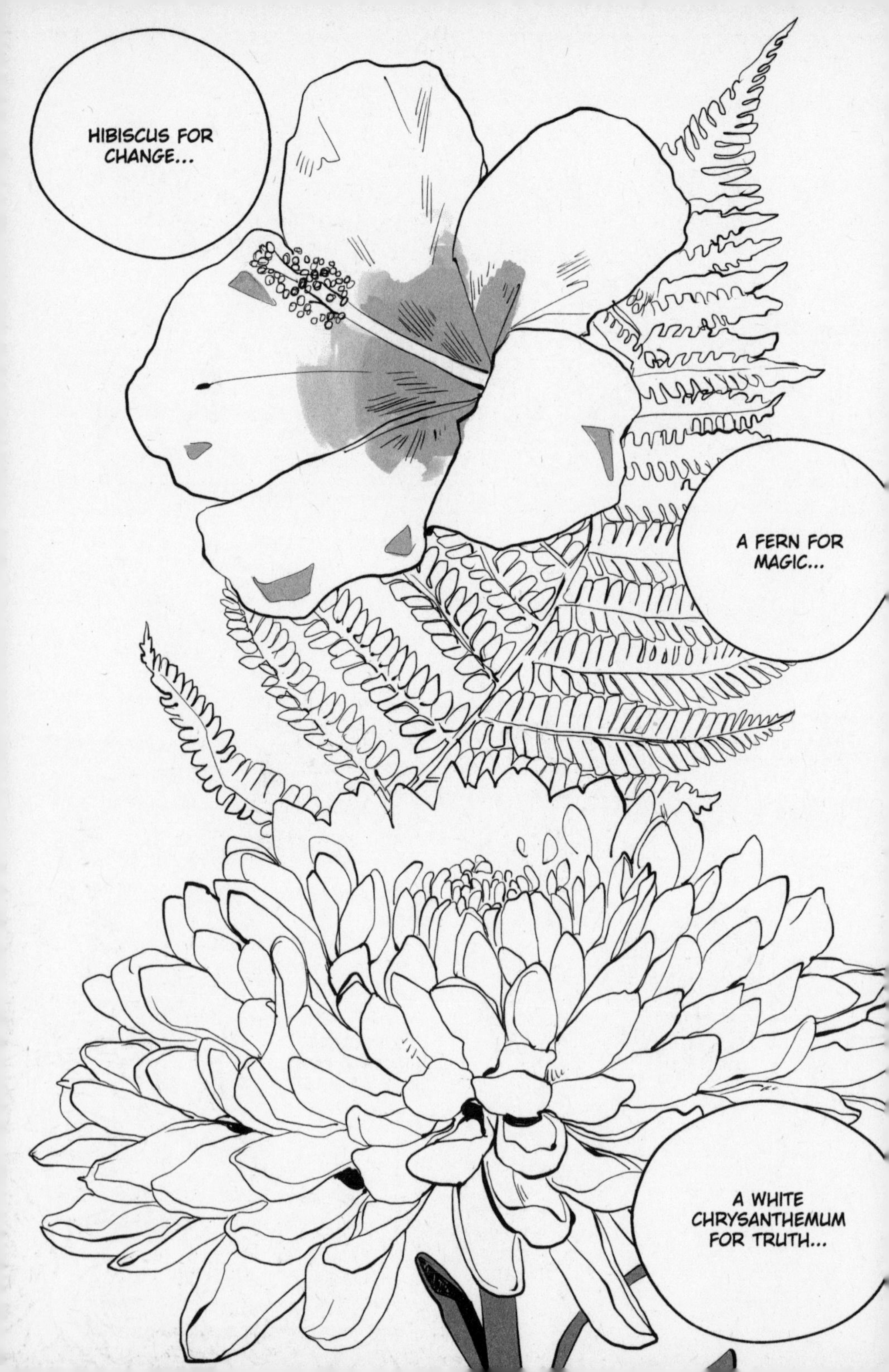
HIBISCUS FOR CHANGE...
A FERN FOR MAGIC...
A WHITE CHRYSANTHEMUM FOR TRUTH...

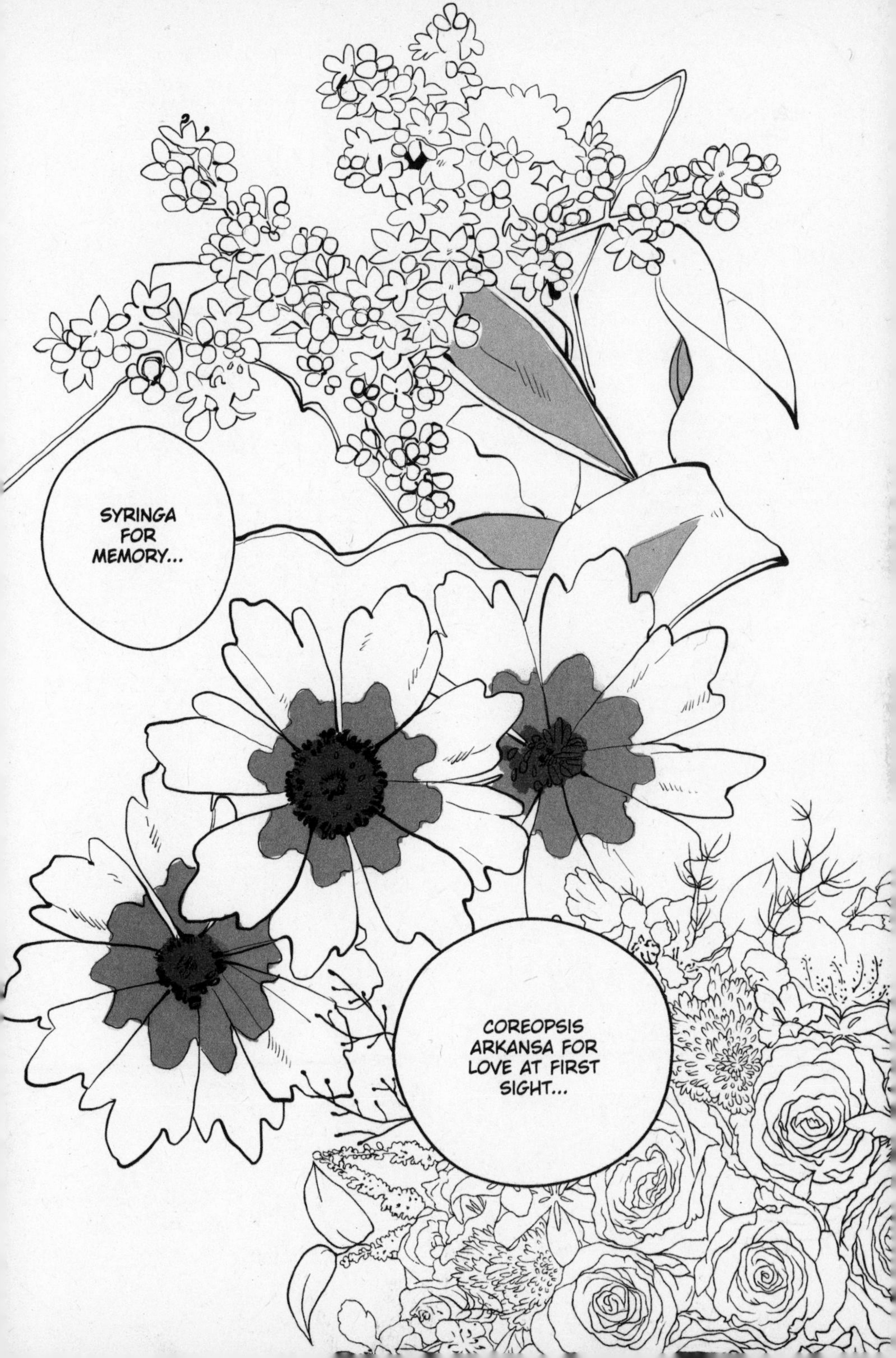
SYRINGA FOR MEMORY...
COREOPSIS ARKANSA FOR LOVE AT FIRST SIGHT...

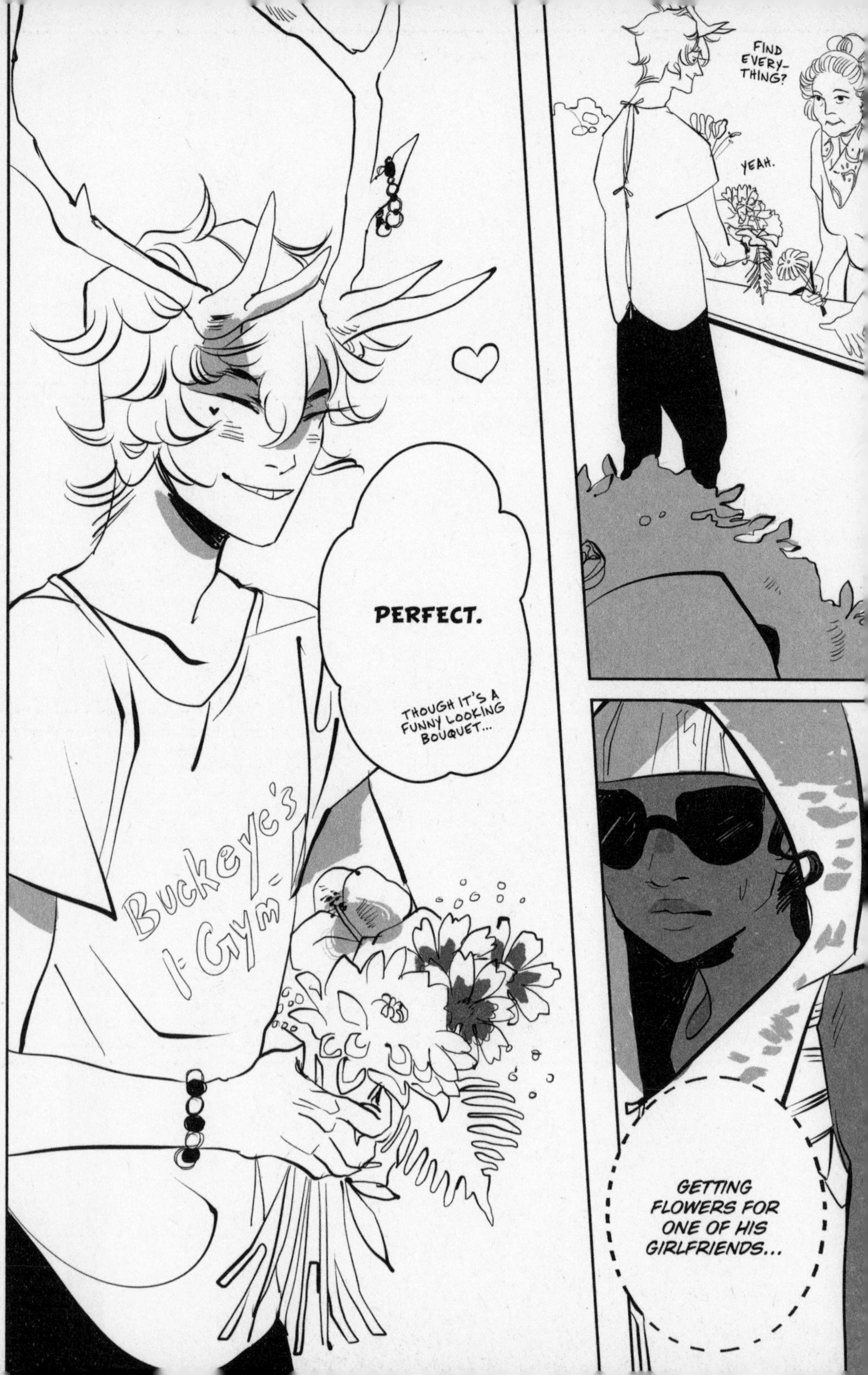
Buckeye's Gym
PERFECT.
THOUGH IT'S A FUNNY LOOKING BOUQUET...
FIND EVERY-THING?
YEAH.
GETTING FLOWERS FOR ONE OF HIS GIRLFRIENDS...

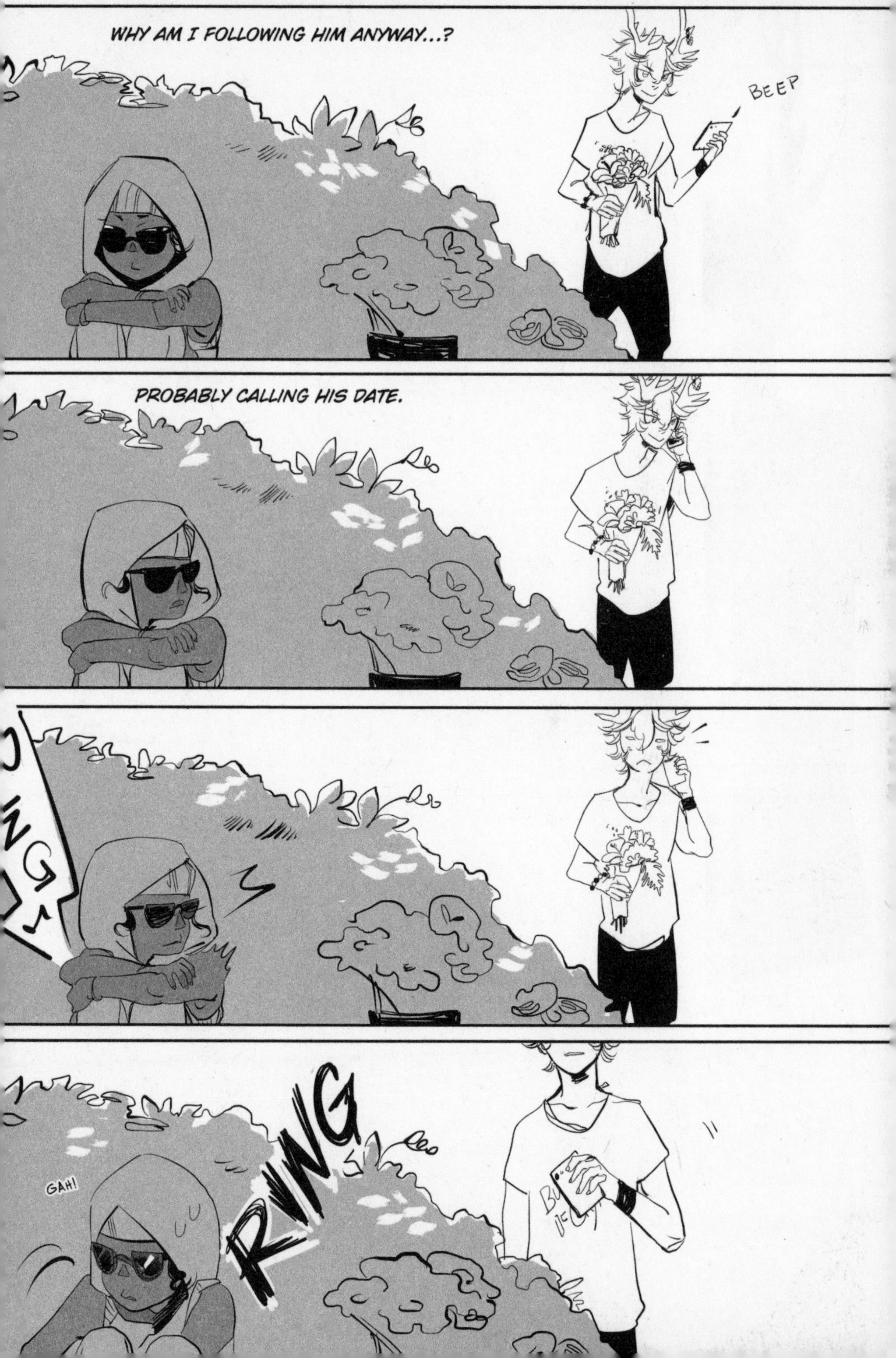
WHY AM I FOLLOWING HIM ANYWAY...?
BEEP
PROBABLY CALLING HIS DATE.
GAH!
RING

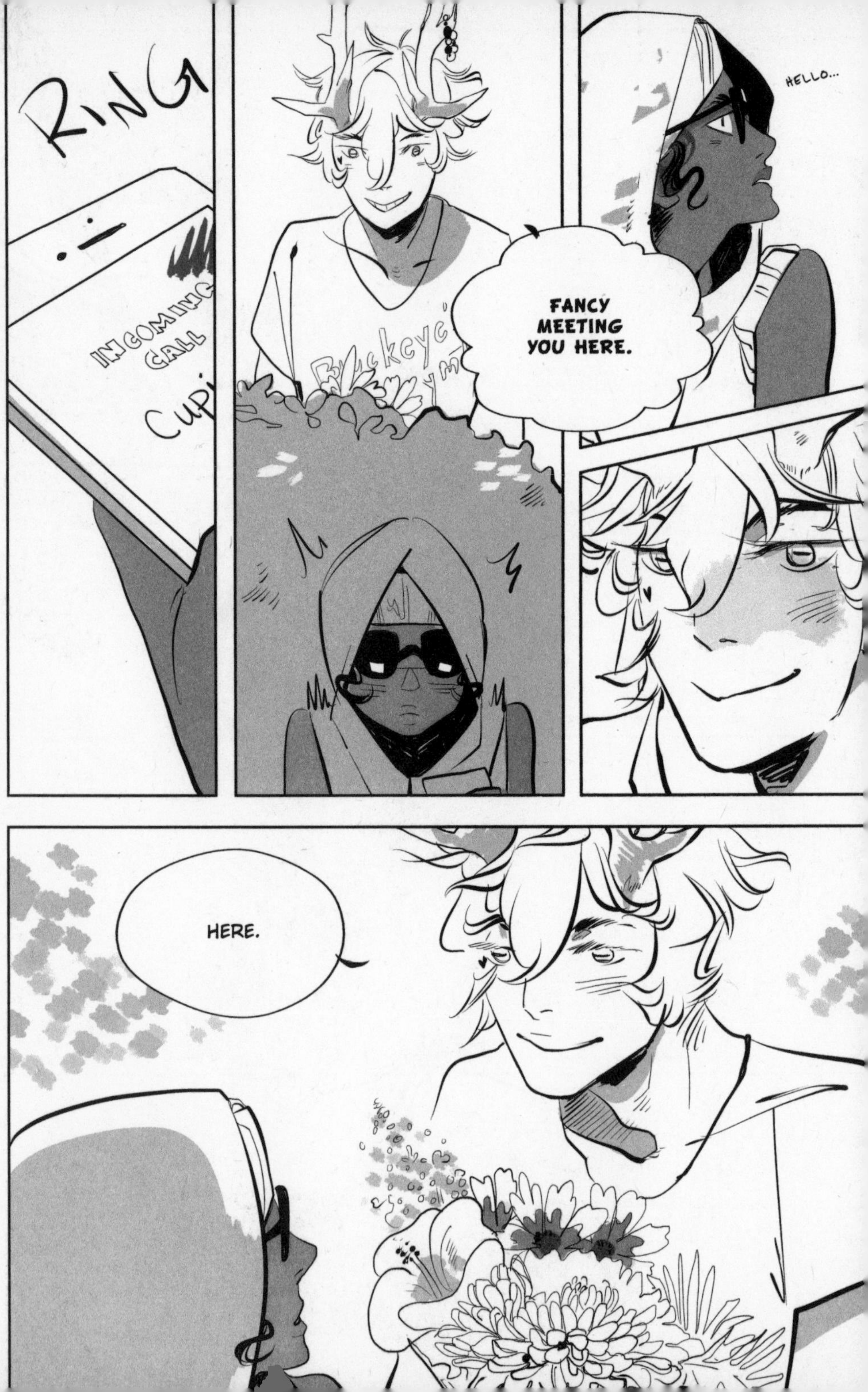
RING
INCOMING CALL
Cupi
HELLO...
FANCY MEETING YOU HERE.
HERE.

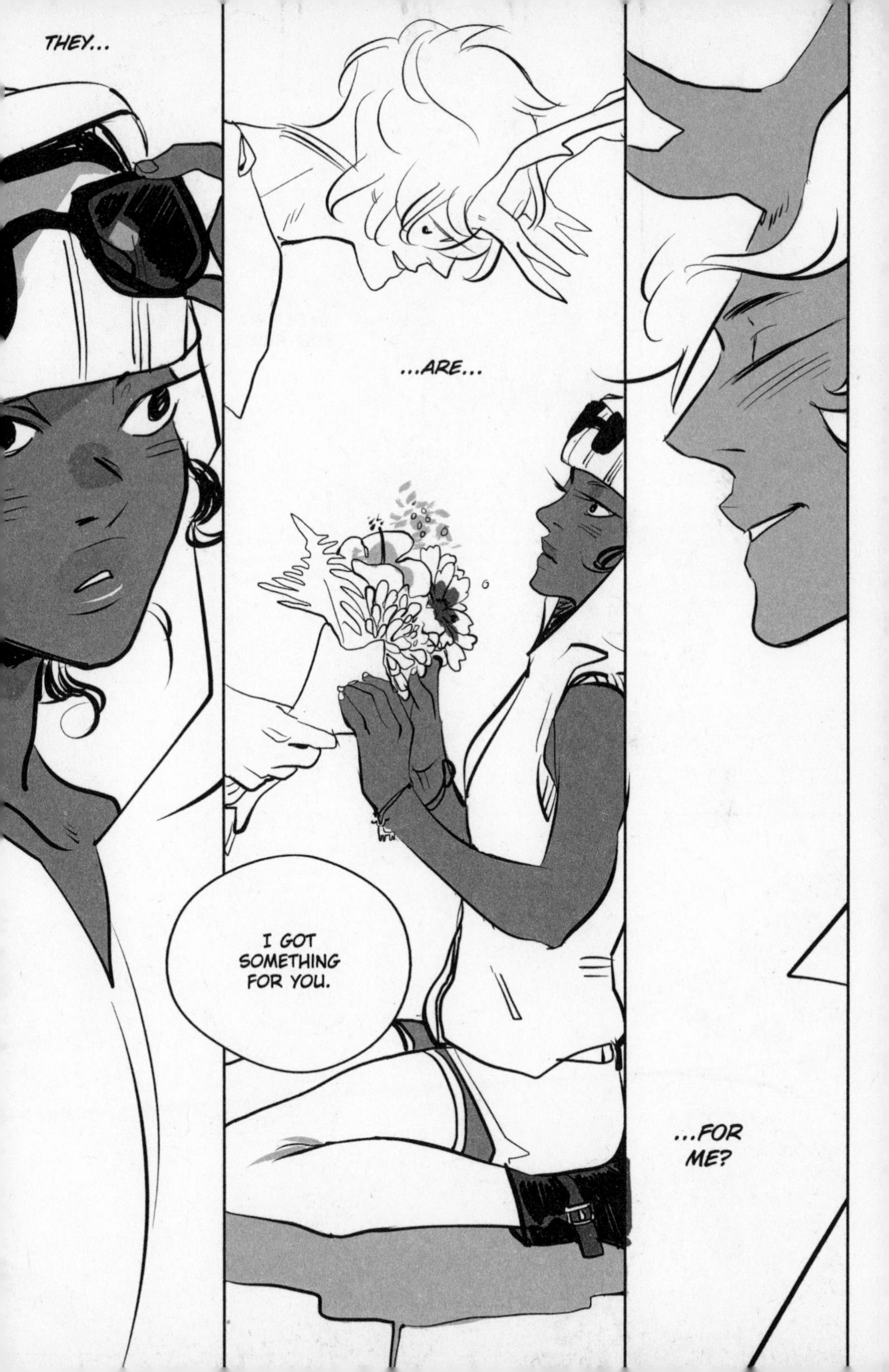
THEY...
...ARE...
I GOT SOMETHING FOR YOU.
...FOR ME?

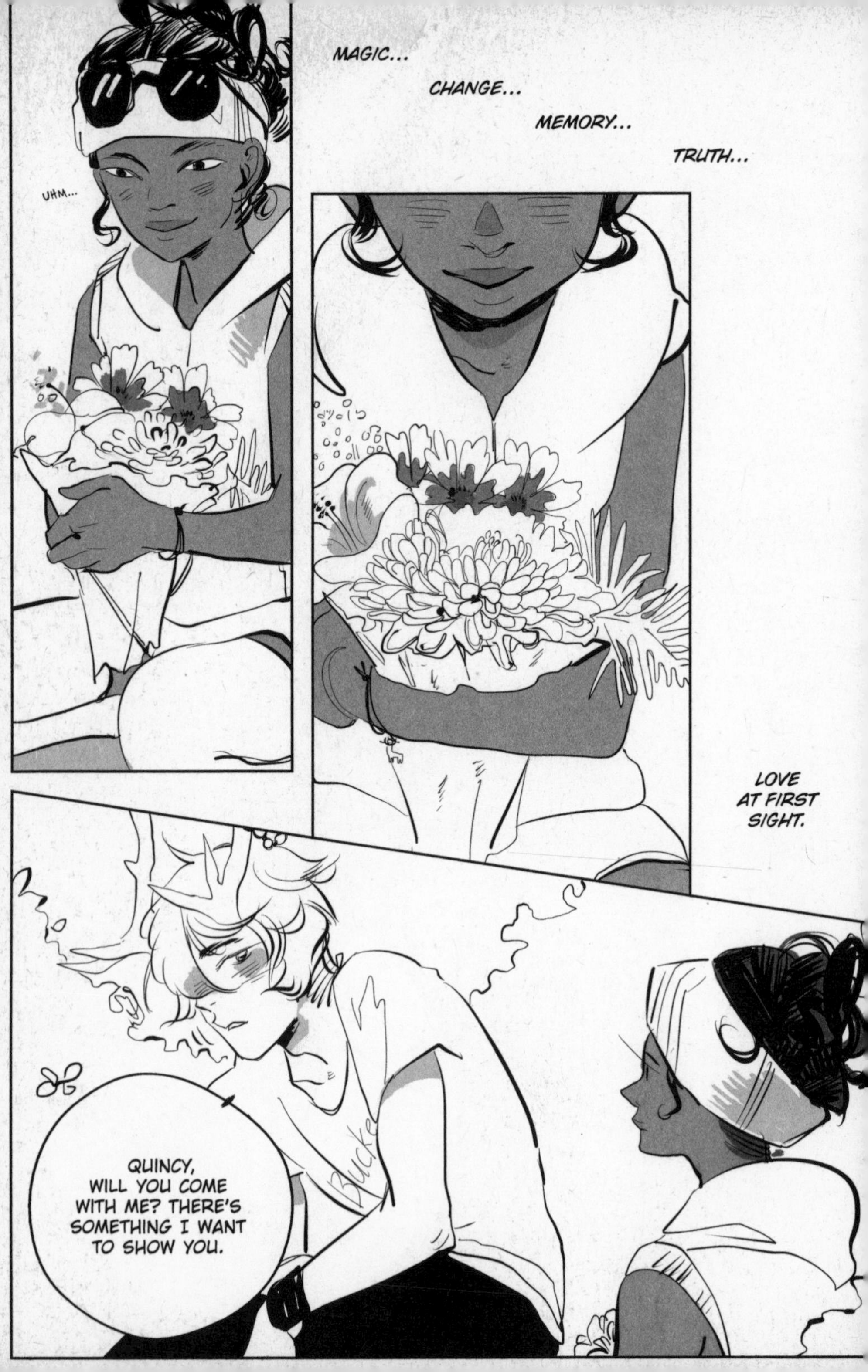
UHM...
MAGIC...
CHANGE...
MEMORY...
TRUTH...
LOVE AT FIRST SIGHT.
QUINCY, WILL YOU COME WITH ME? THERE'S SOMETHING I WANT TO SHOW YOU.

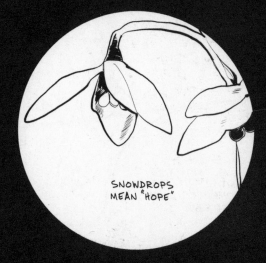

SNOWDROPS
MEAN "HOPE"

Reindeer Boy

Chapter 7

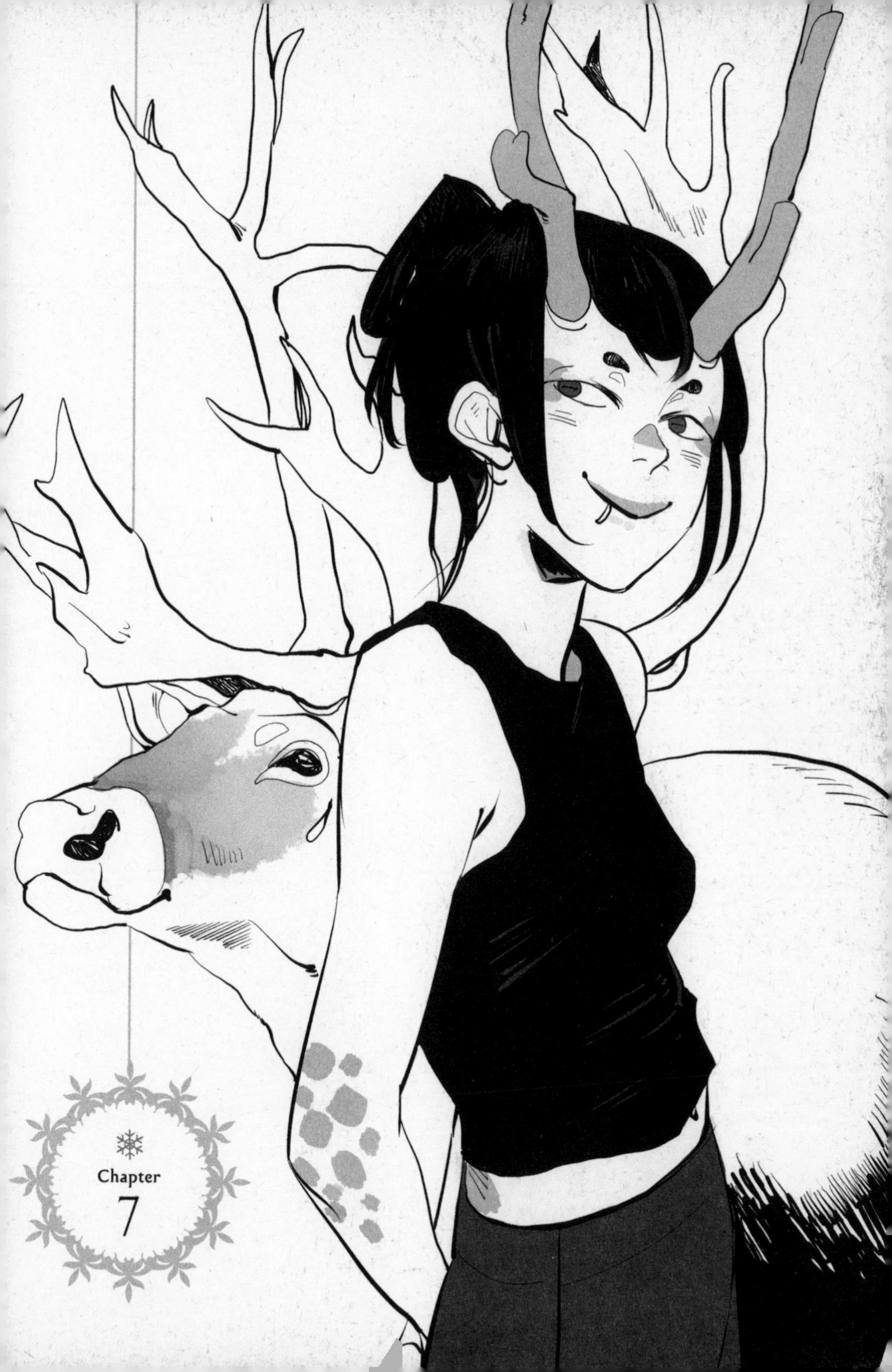

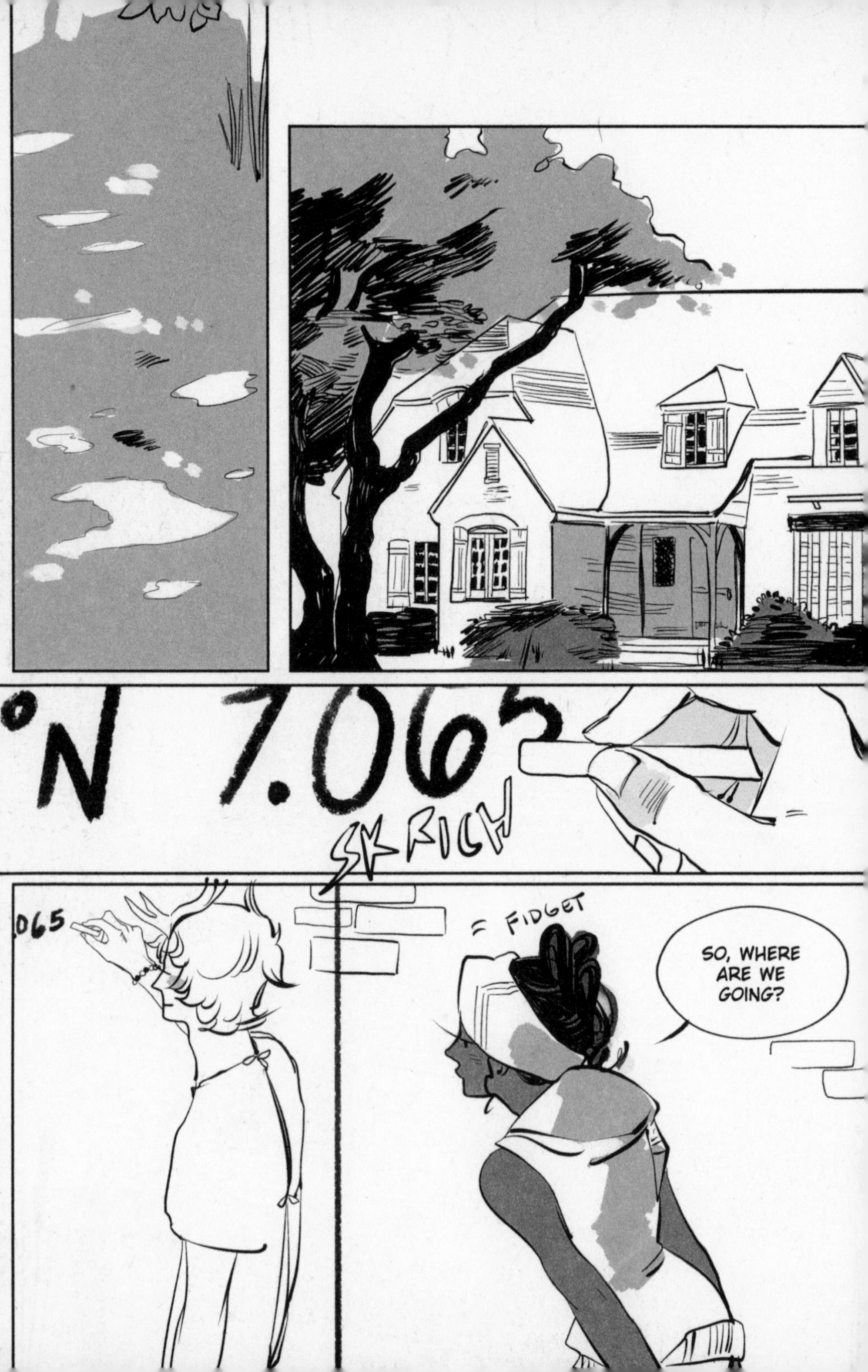
°N 7.065
SKRICH
065
FIDGET
SO, WHERE ARE WE GOING?

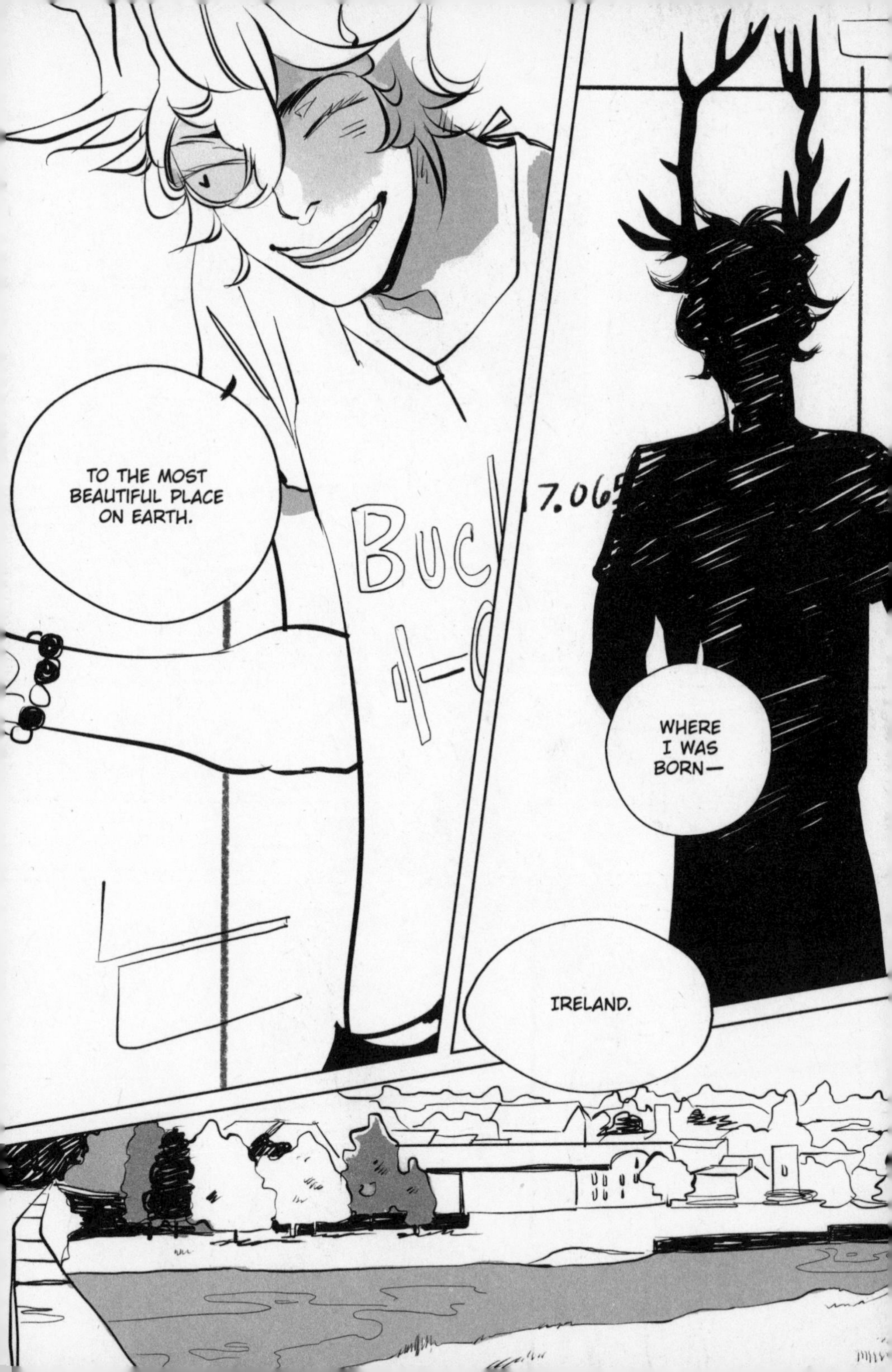
TO THE MOST BEAUTIFUL PLACE ON EARTH.
BUC
7.065
WHERE I WAS BORN—
IRELAND.

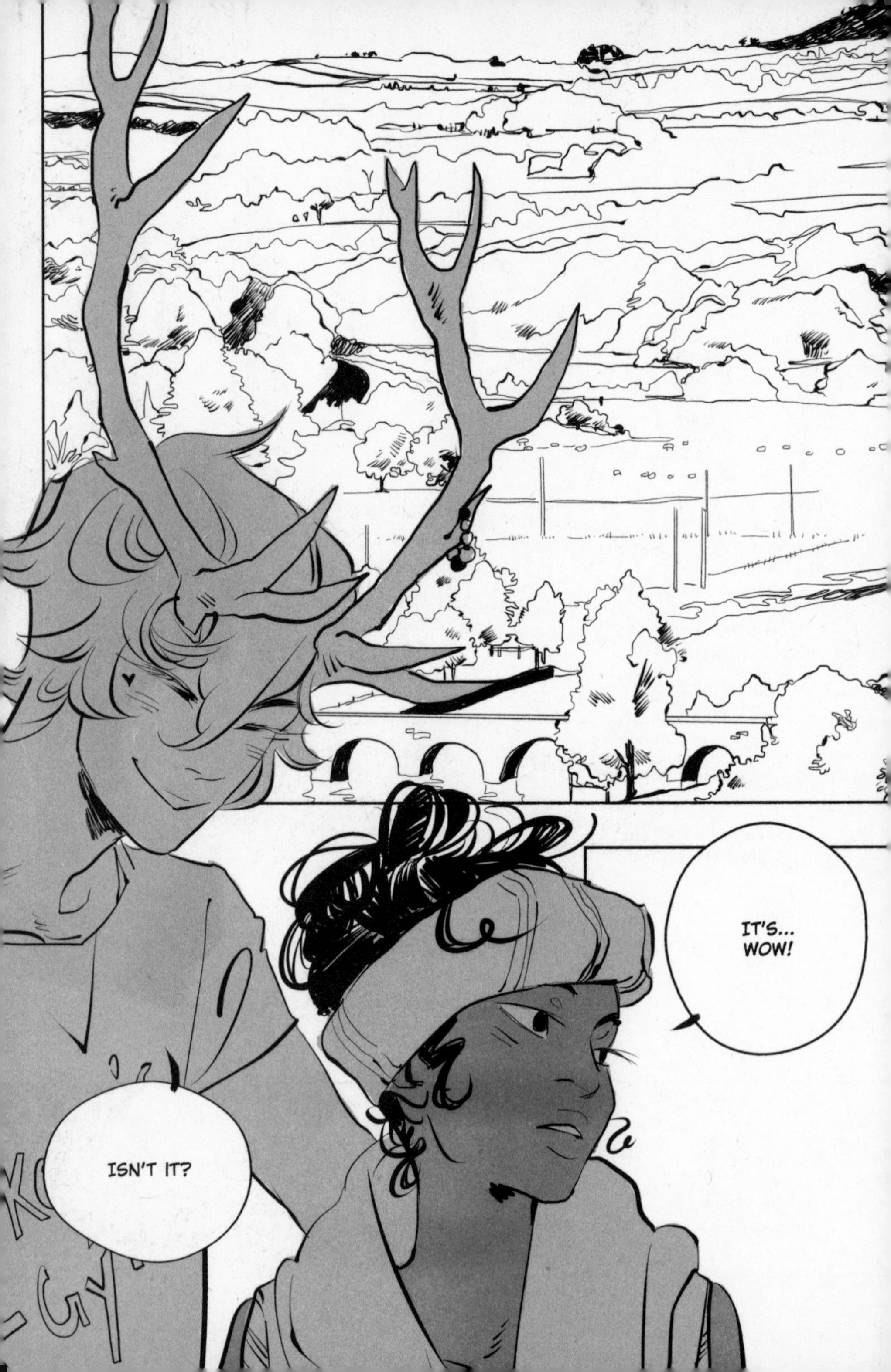
IT'S... WOW!
ISN'T IT?

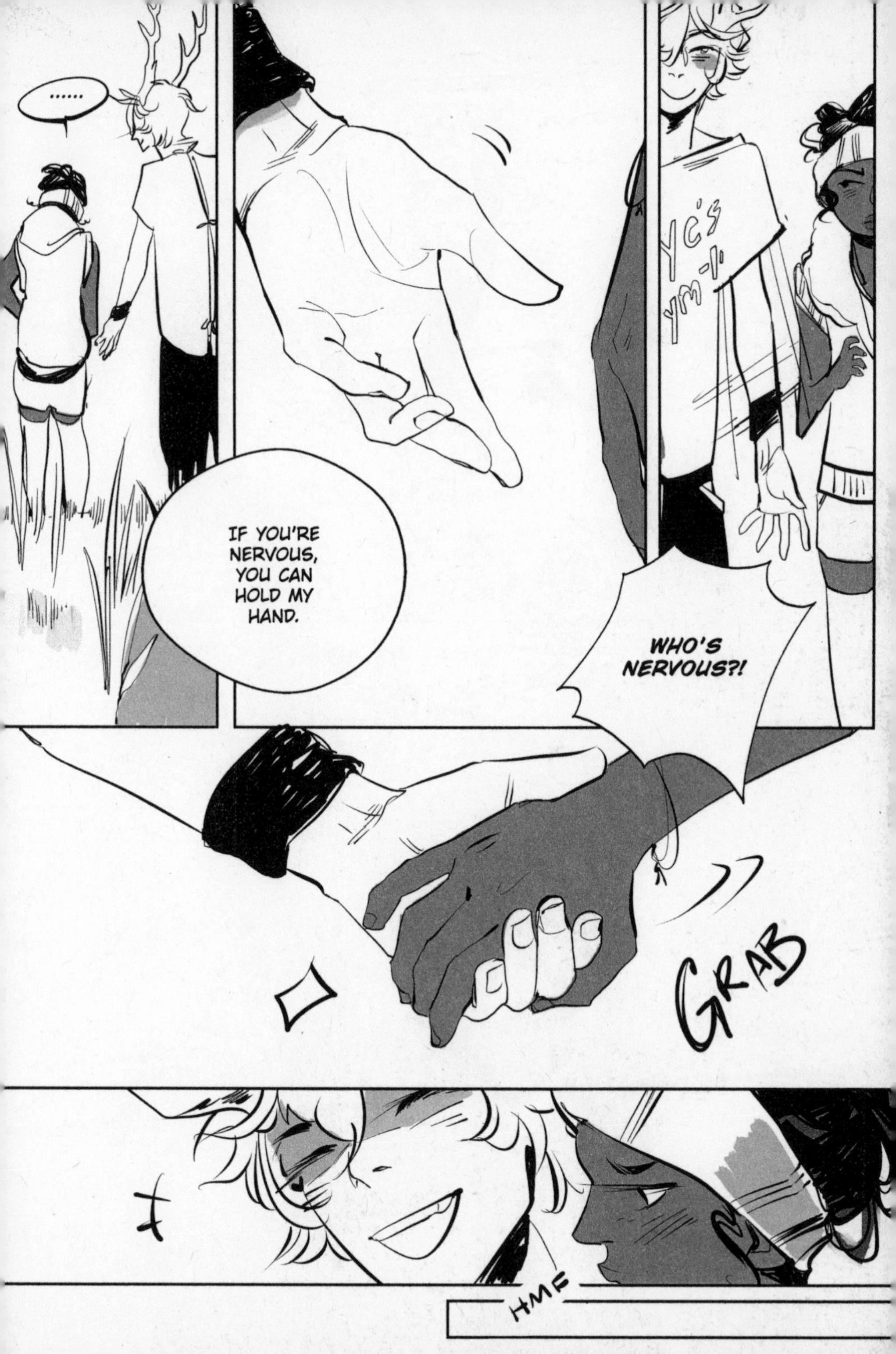
....
IF YOU'RE NERVOUS, YOU CAN HOLD MY HAND.
WHO'S NERVOUS?!
GRAB
HMF

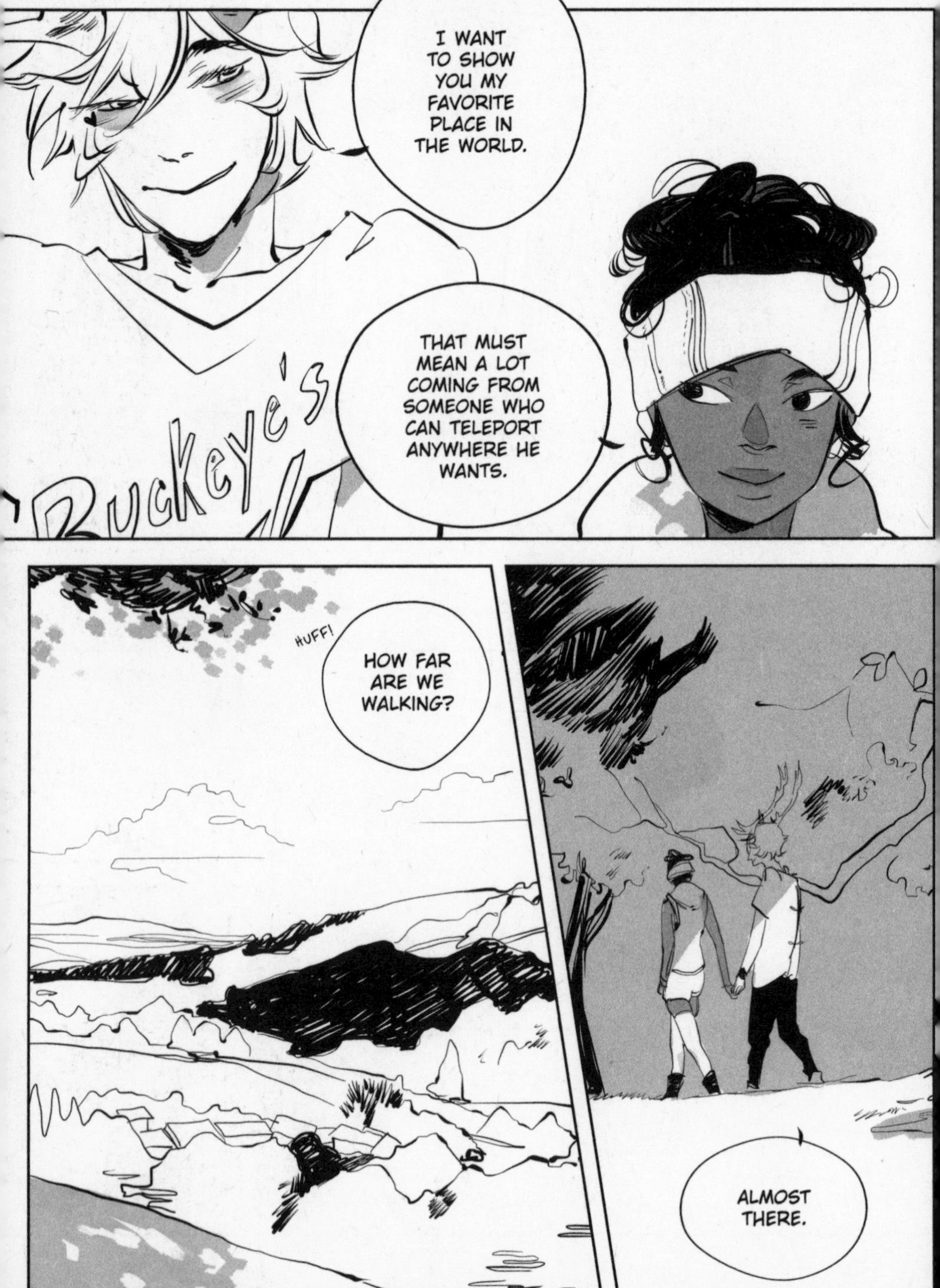

I WANT TO SHOW YOU MY FAVORITE PLACE IN THE WORLD.
THAT MUST MEAN A LOT COMING FROM SOMEONE WHO CAN TELEPORT ANYWHERE HE WANTS.
Buckeye's
HUFF!
HOW FAR ARE WE WALKING?
ALMOST THERE.

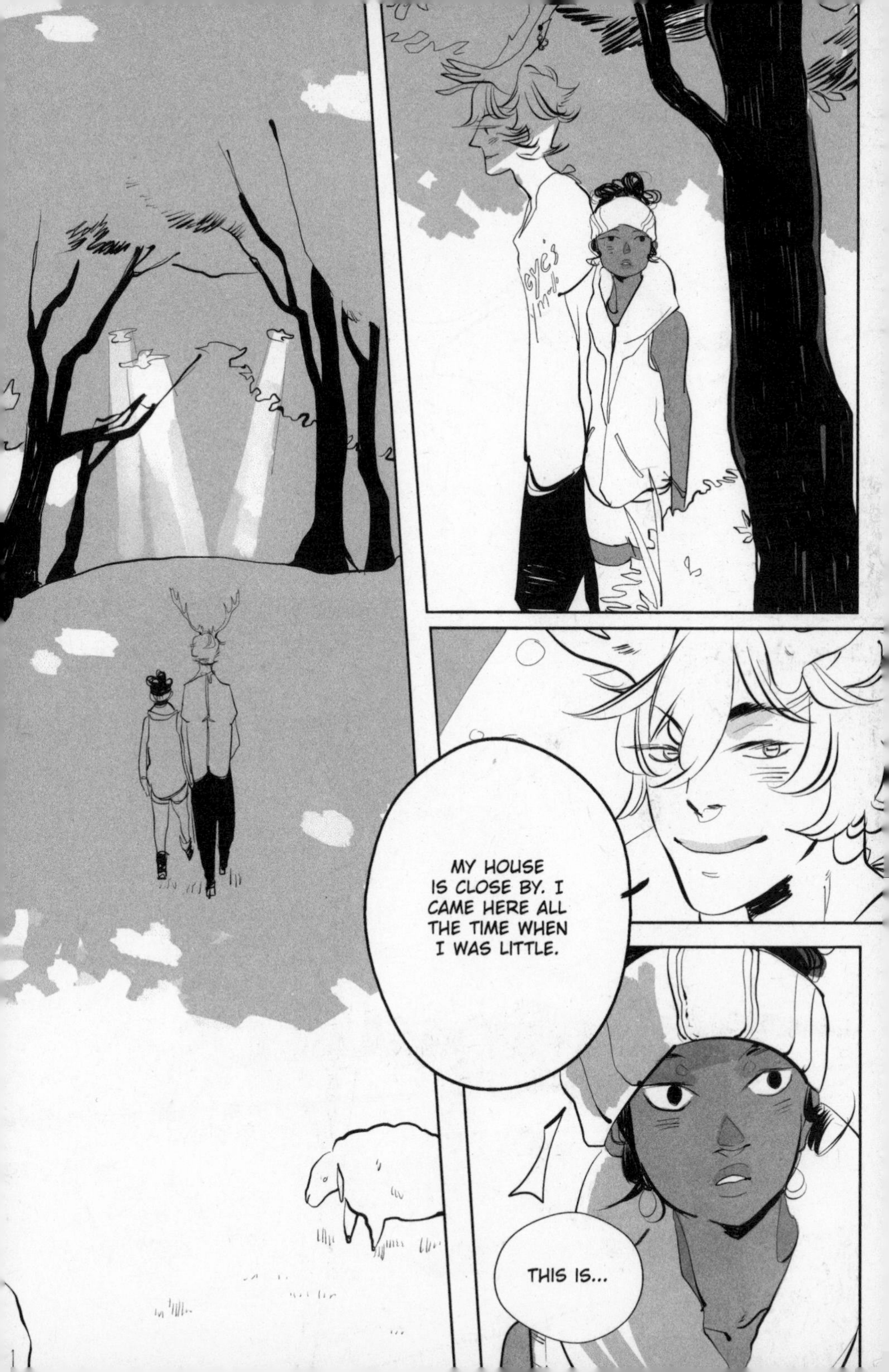
MY HOUSE IS CLOSE BY. I CAME HERE ALL THE TIME WHEN I WAS LITTLE.
THIS IS...

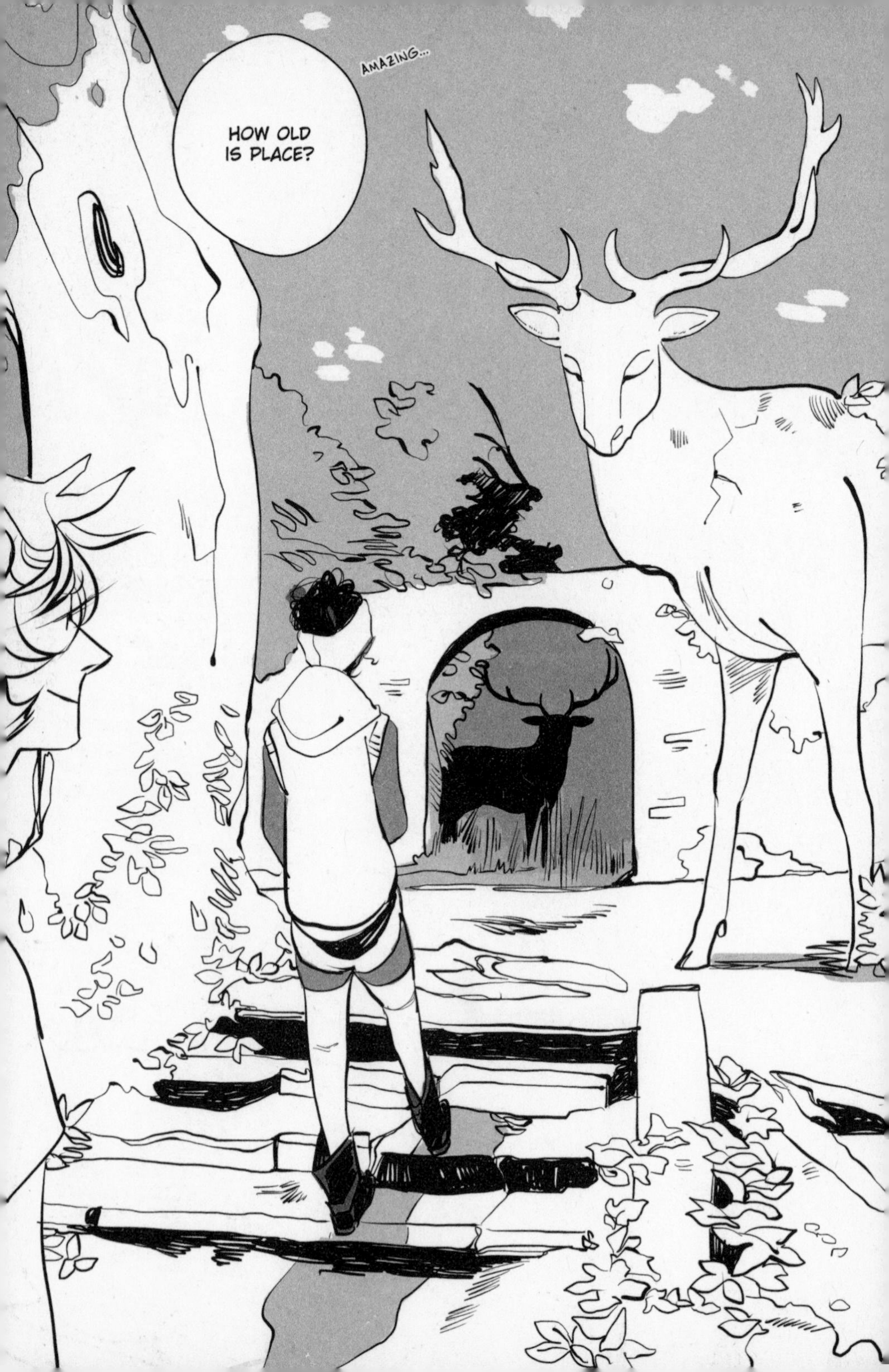
HOW OLD IS PLACE?
AMAZING...

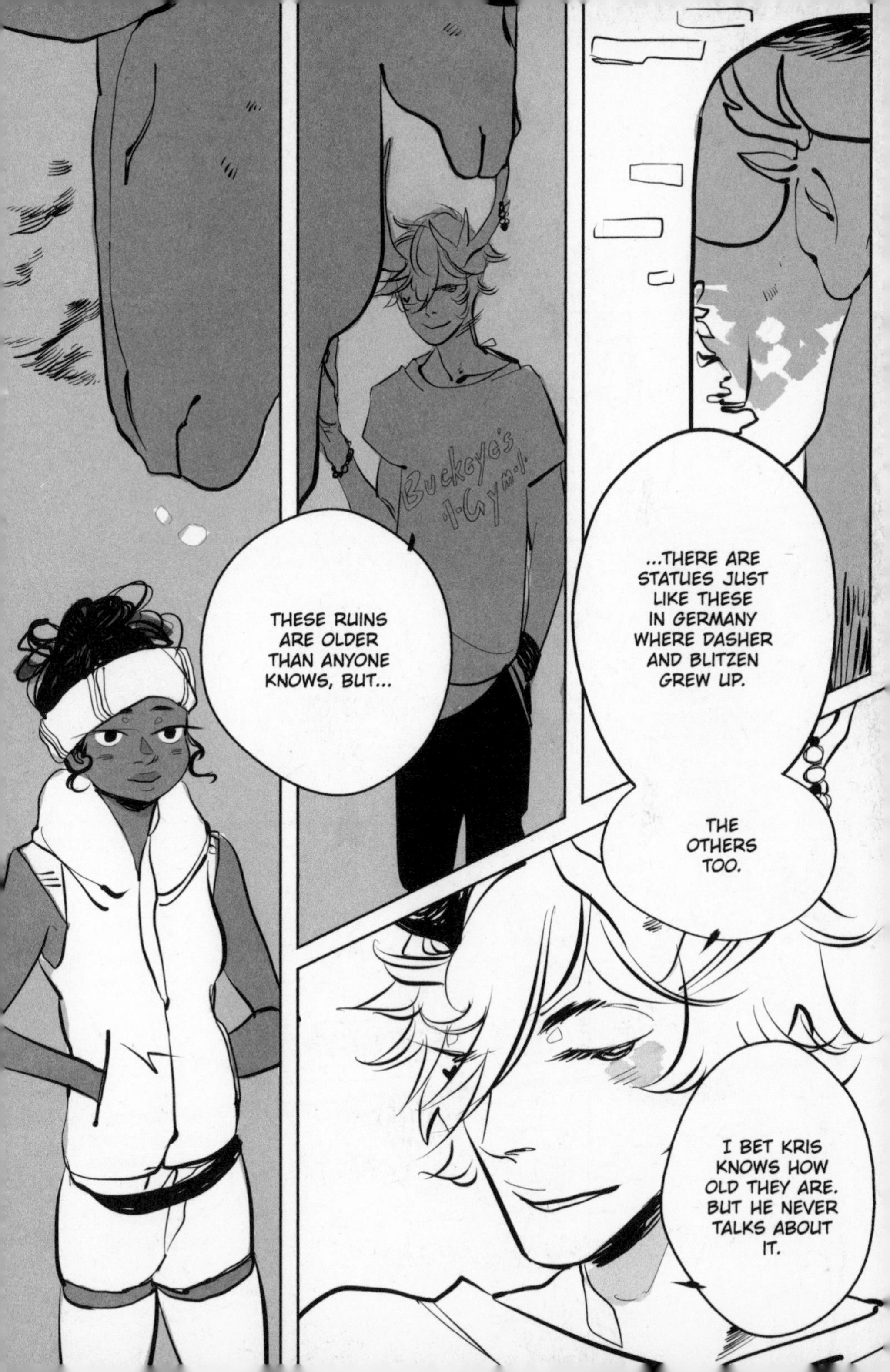

Buckeye's Gym
THESE RUINS ARE OLDER THAN ANYONE KNOWS, BUT...
...THERE ARE STATUES JUST LIKE THESE IN GERMANY WHERE DASHER AND BLITZEN GREW UP.
THE OTHERS TOO.
I BET KRIS KNOWS HOW OLD THEY ARE. BUT HE NEVER TALKS ABOUT IT.

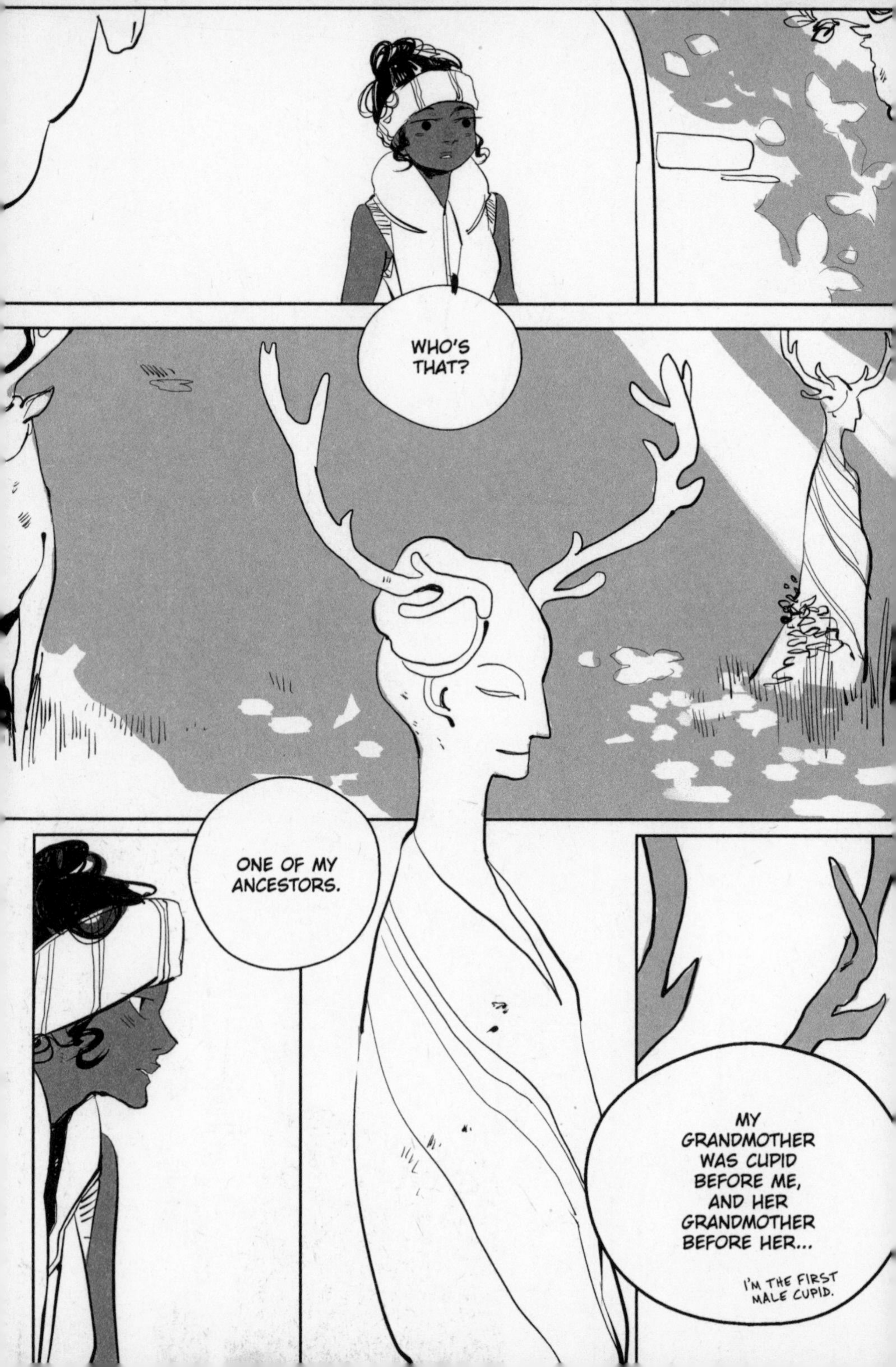
WHO'S THAT?
ONE OF MY ANCESTORS.
MY GRANDMOTHER WAS CUPID BEFORE ME, AND HER GRANDMOTHER BEFORE HER...
I'M THE FIRST MALE CUPID.

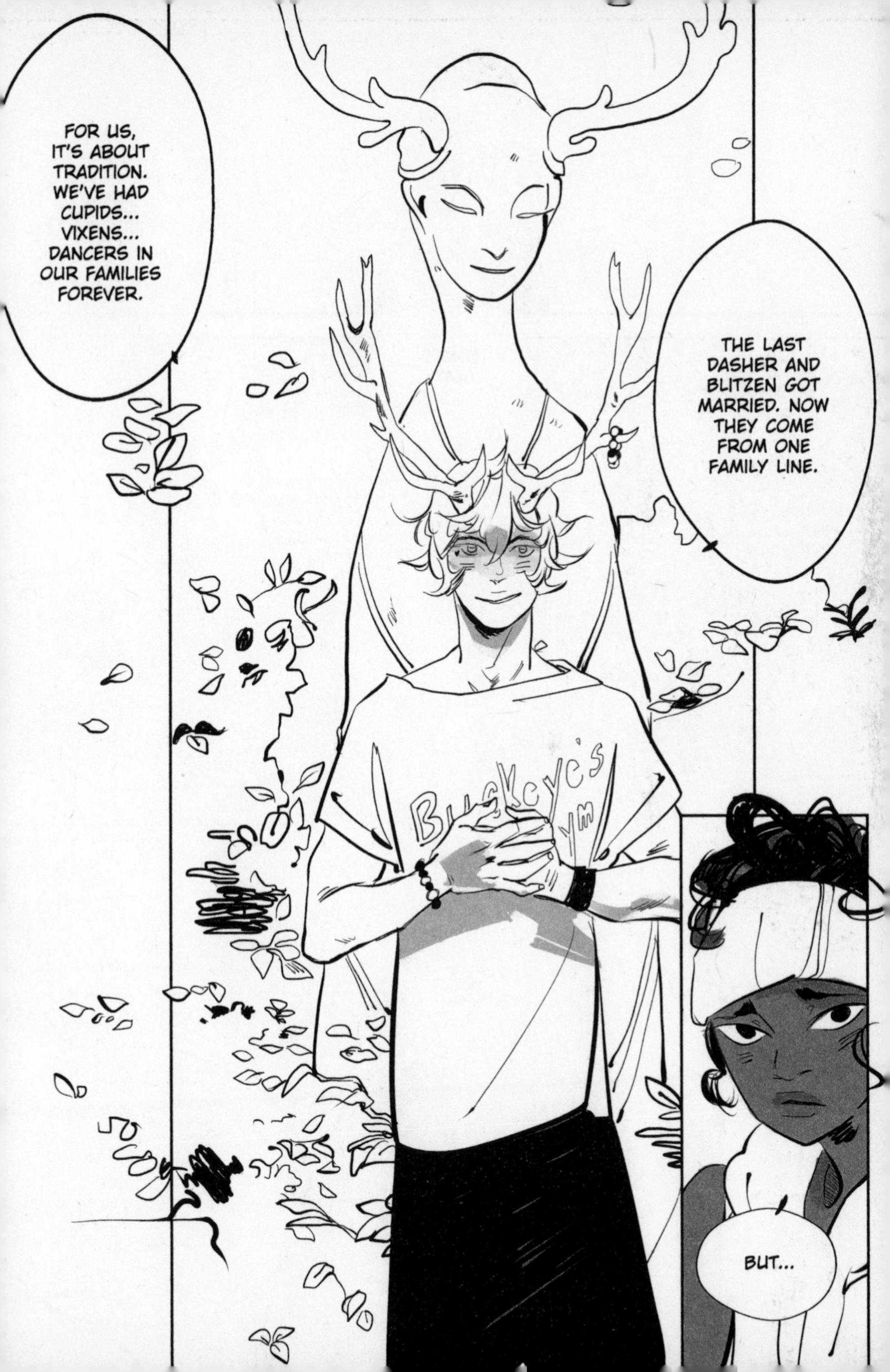
FOR US, IT'S ABOUT TRADITION. WE'VE HAD CUPIDS... VIXENS... DANCERS IN OUR FAMILIES FOREVER.
THE LAST DASHER AND BLITZEN GOT MARRIED. NOW THEY COME FROM ONE FAMILY LINE.
BUT...

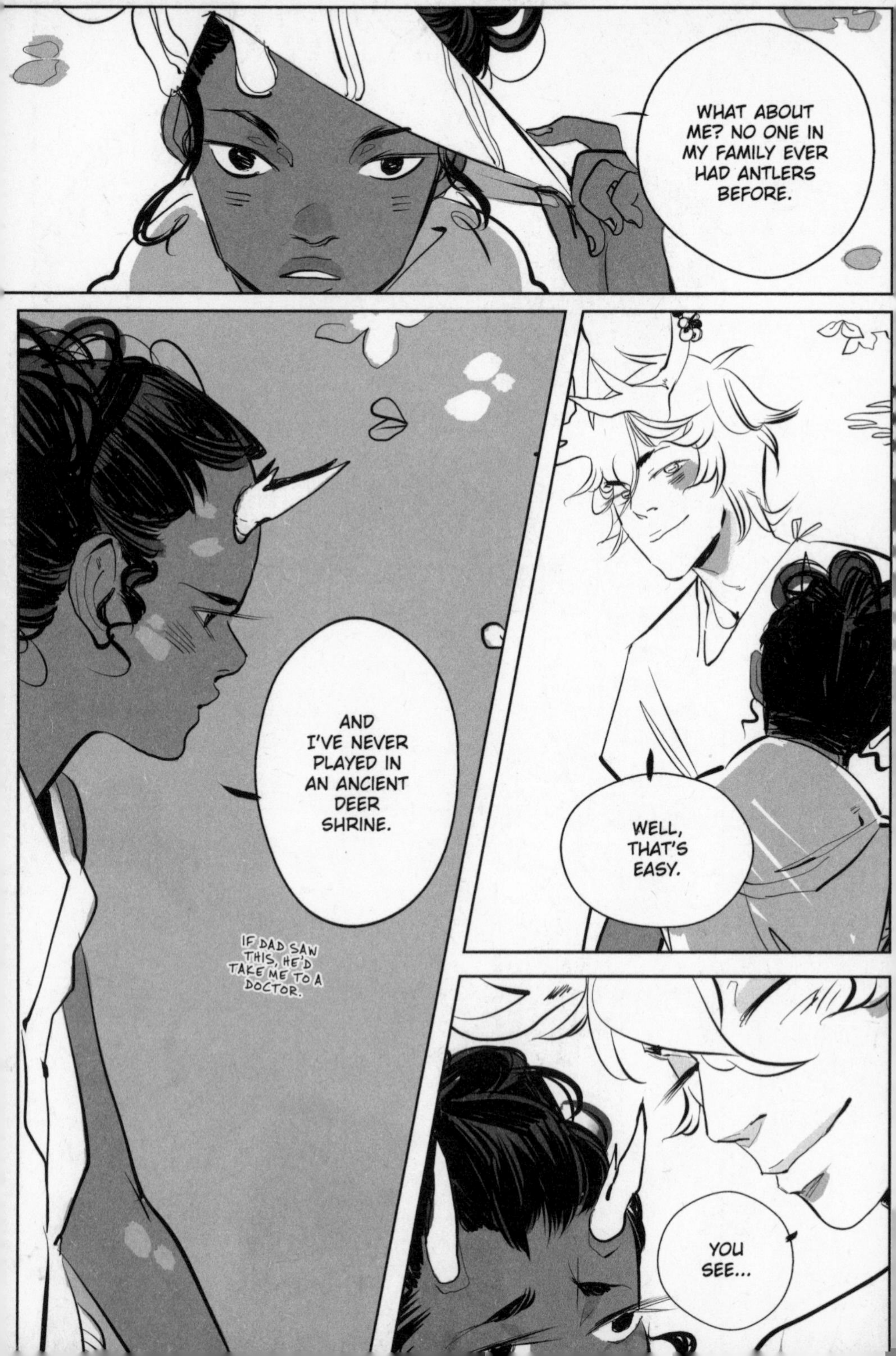
WHAT ABOUT ME? NO ONE IN MY FAMILY EVER HAD ANTLERS BEFORE.
AND I'VE NEVER PLAYED IN AN ANCIENT DEER SHRINE.
IF DAD SAW THIS, HE'D TAKE ME TO A DOCTOR.
WELL, THAT'S EASY.
YOU SEE...

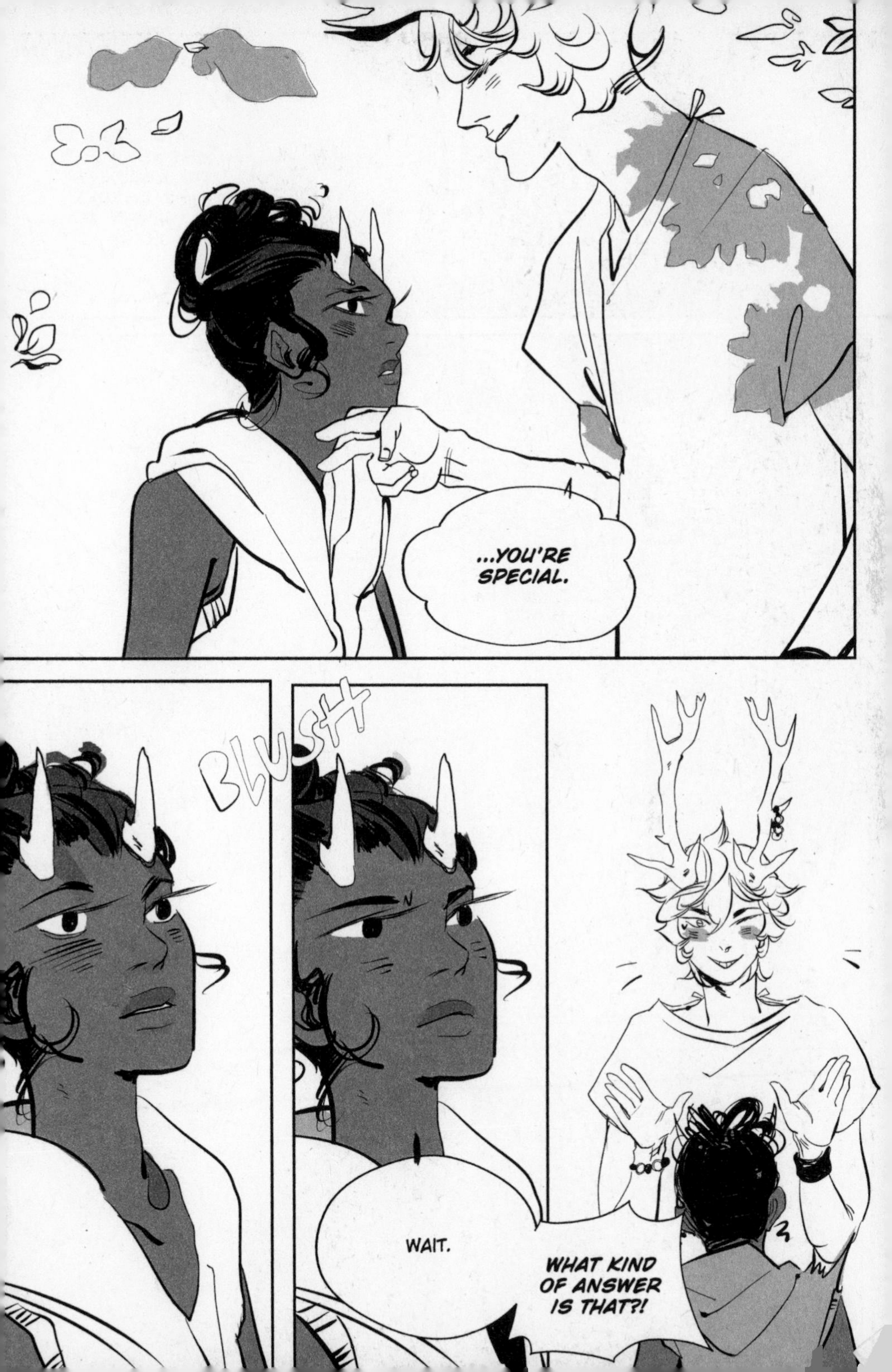
...YOU'RE SPECIAL.
BLUSH
WAIT.
WHAT KIND OF ANSWER IS THAT?!

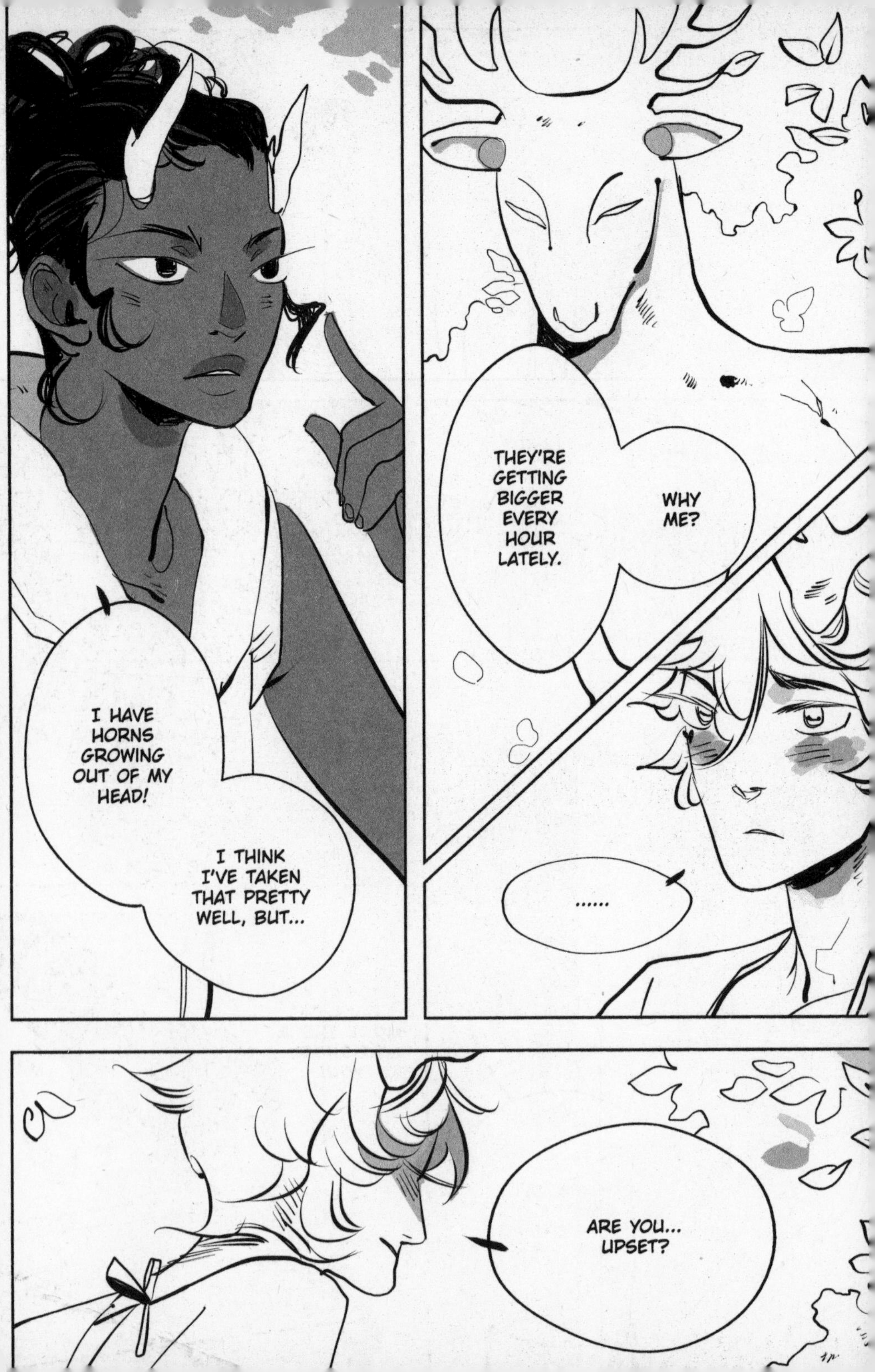
I HAVE HORNS GROWING OUT OF MY HEAD!
I THINK I'VE TAKEN THAT PRETTY WELL, BUT...
THEY'RE GETTING BIGGER EVERY HOUR LATELY.
WHY ME?
......
ARE YOU... UPSET?

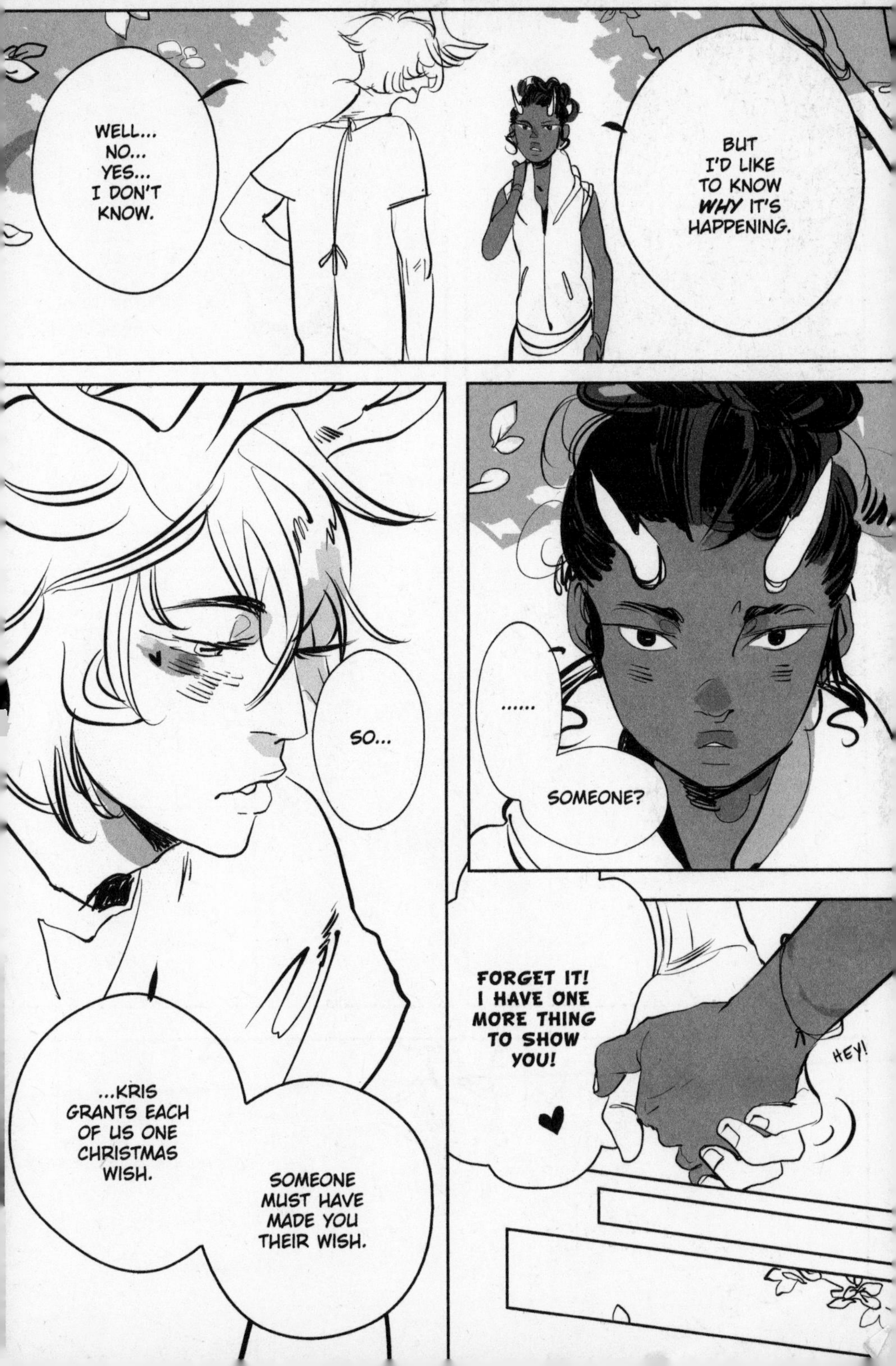
WELL... NO... YES... I DON'T KNOW.
BUT I'D LIKE TO KNOW *WHY* IT'S HAPPENING.
SO...
...KRIS GRANTS EACH OF US ONE CHRISTMAS WISH.
SOMEONE MUST HAVE MADE YOU THEIR WISH.
......
SOMEONE?
FORGET IT! I HAVE ONE MORE THING TO SHOW YOU!
HEY!

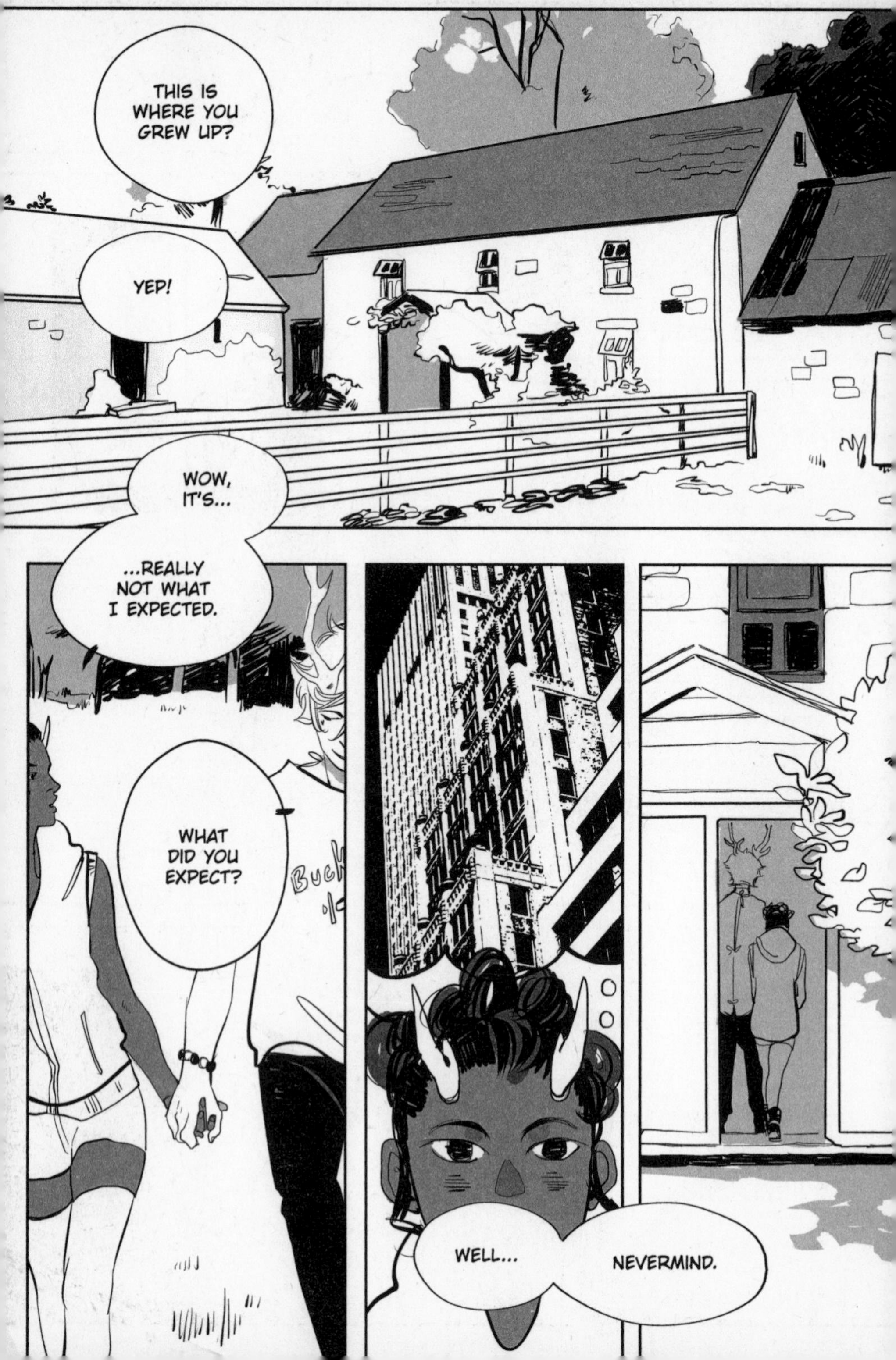
THIS IS WHERE YOU GREW UP?
YEP!
WOW, IT'S...
...REALLY NOT WHAT I EXPECTED.
WHAT DID YOU EXPECT?
WELL...
NEVERMIND.

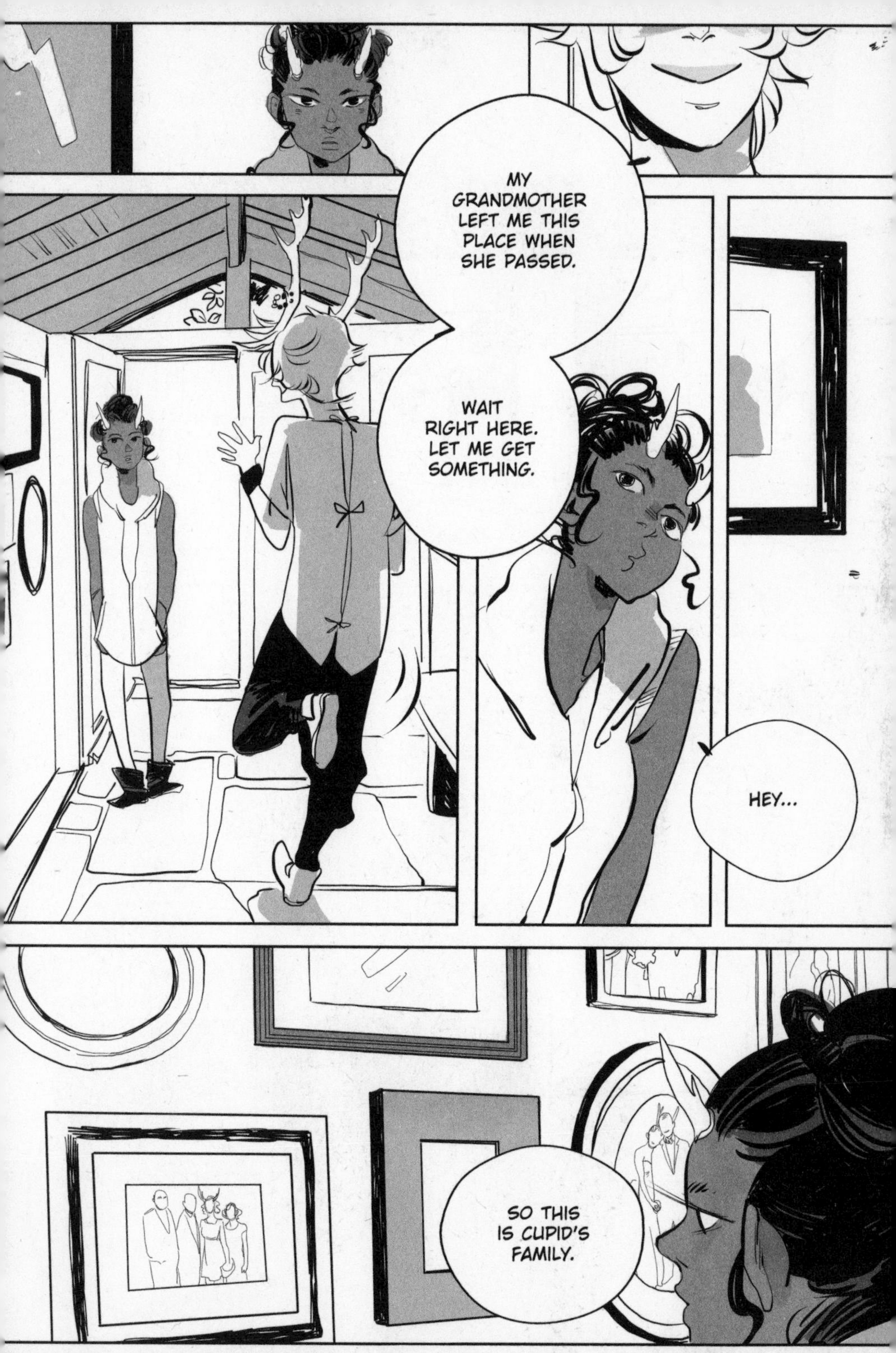
MY GRANDMOTHER LEFT ME THIS PLACE WHEN SHE PASSED.
WAIT RIGHT HERE. LET ME GET SOMETHING.
HEY...
SO THIS IS CUPID'S FAMILY.

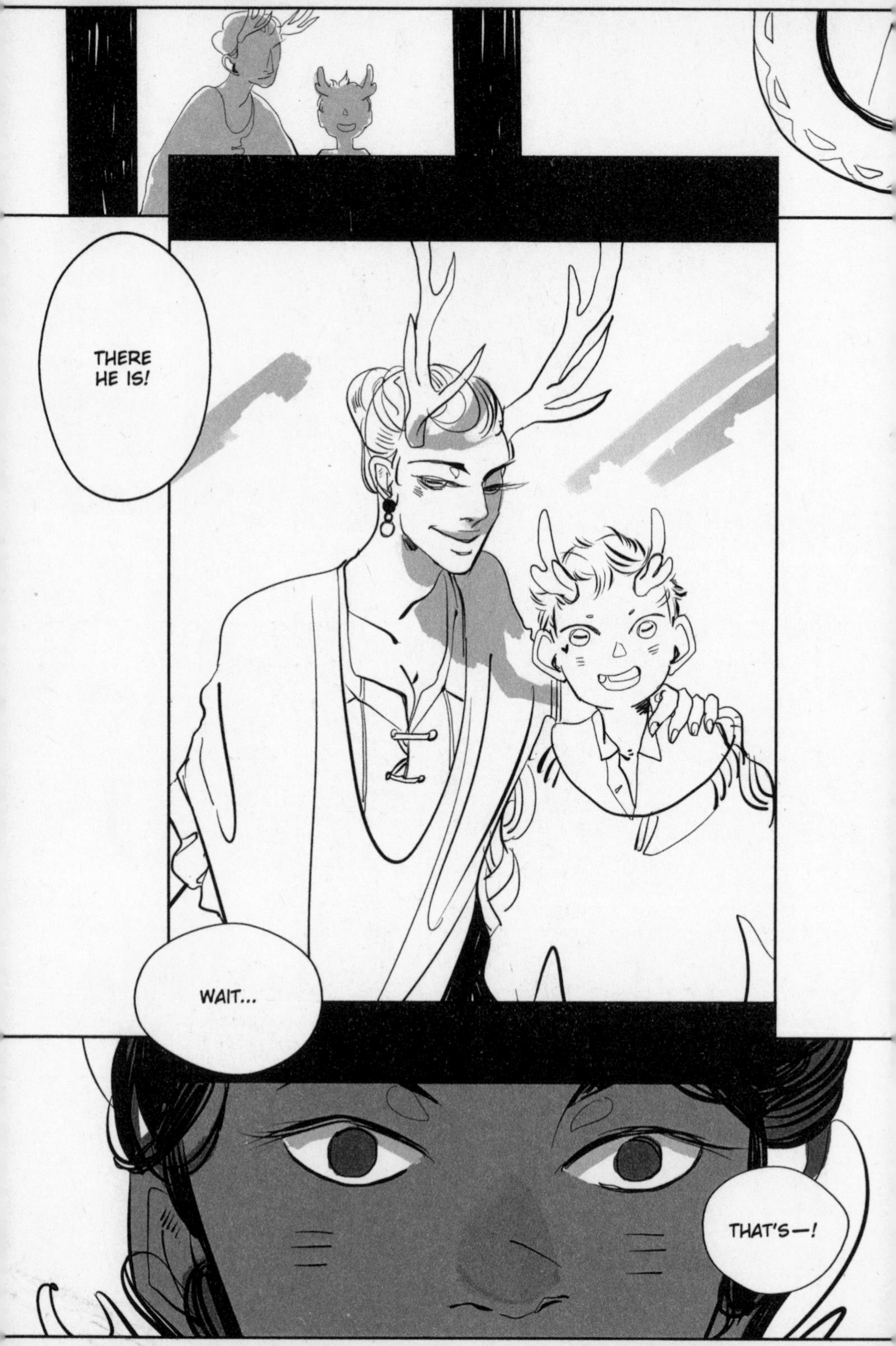
THERE HE IS!
WAIT...
THAT'S—!

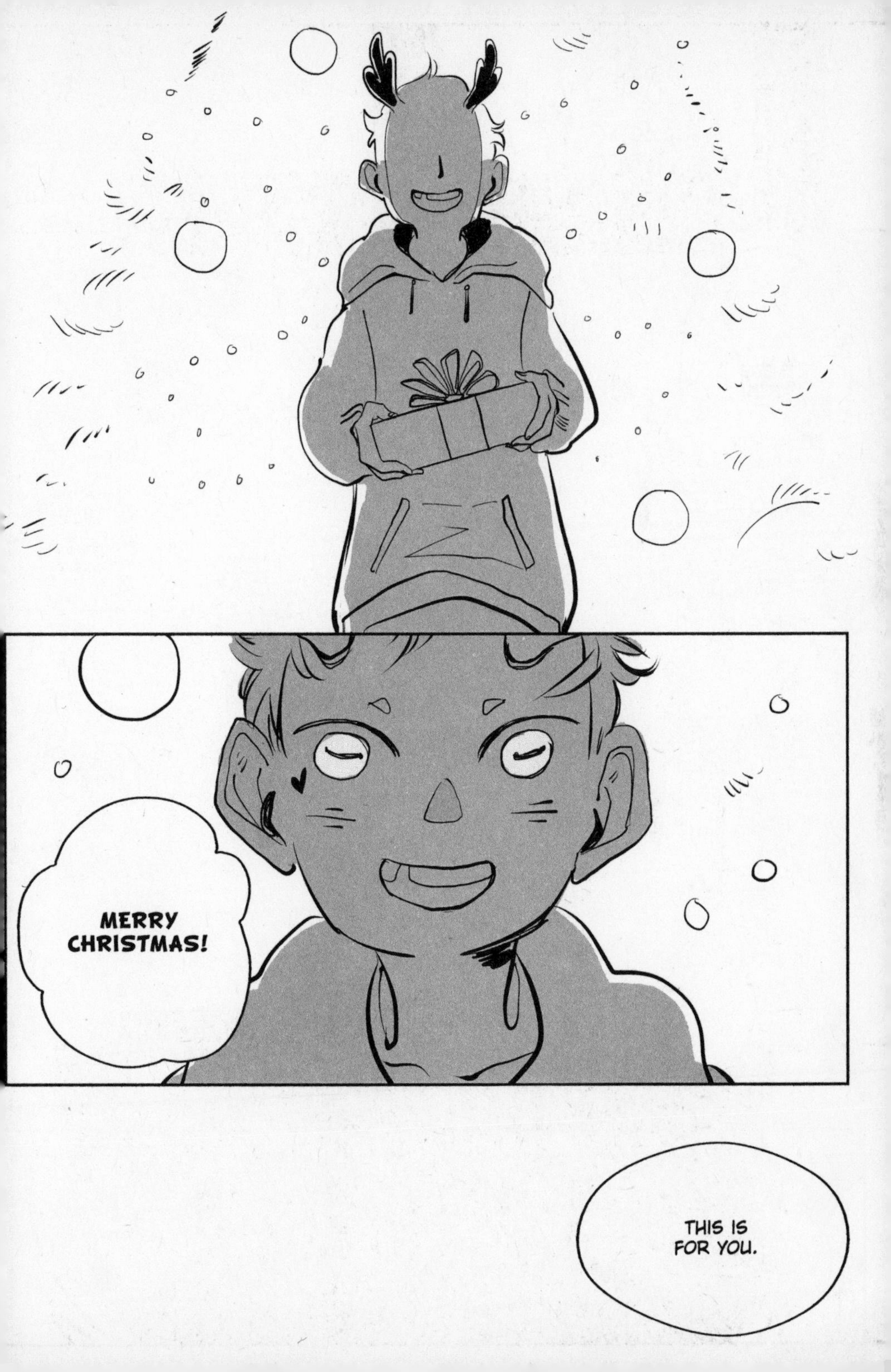
MERRY CHRISTMAS!
THIS IS FOR YOU.

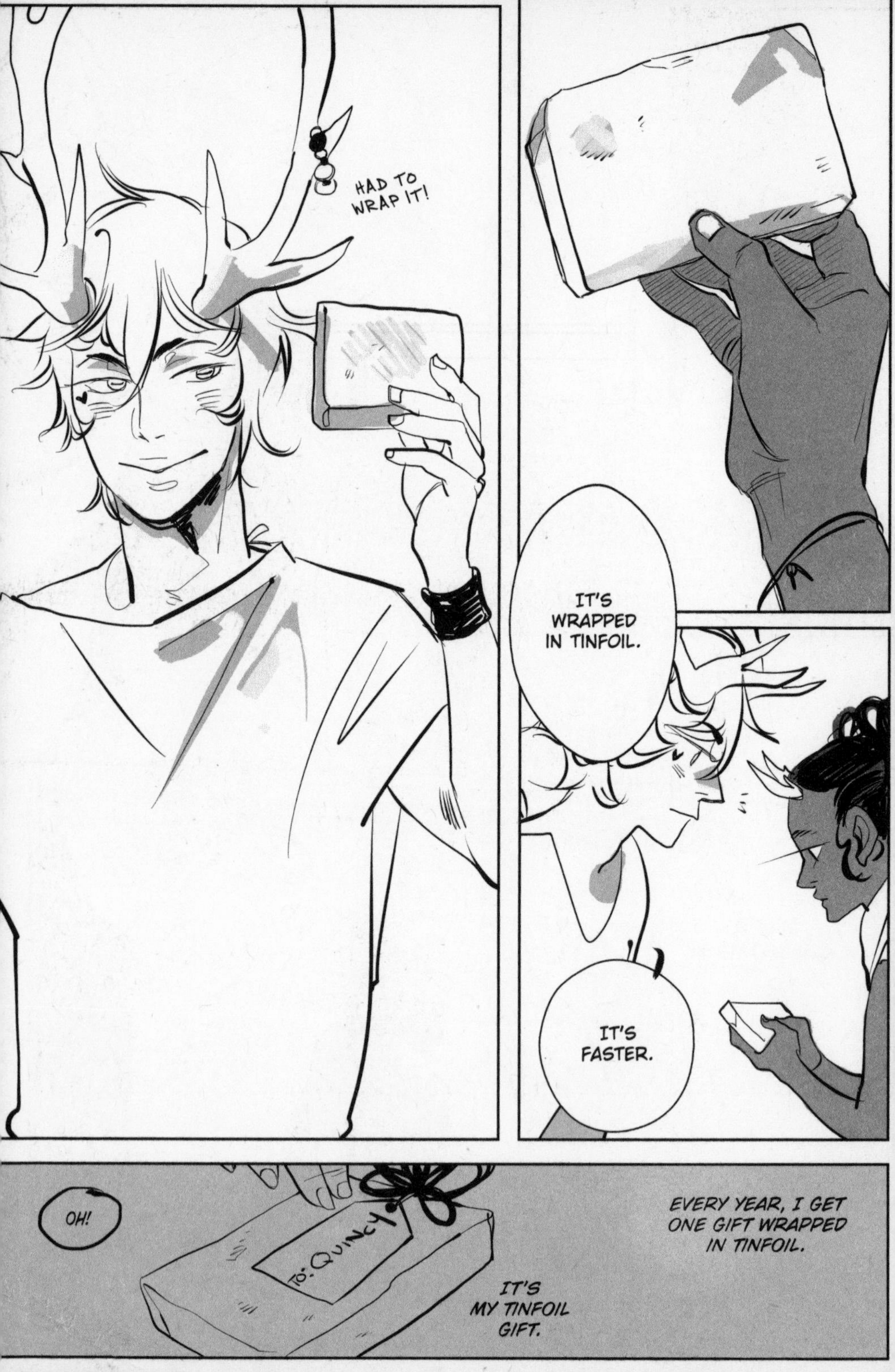
HAD TO WRAP IT!
IT'S WRAPPED IN TINFOIL.
IT'S FASTER.
OH!
TO: QUINCY
EVERY YEAR, I GET ONE GIFT WRAPPED IN TINFOIL.
IT'S MY TINFOIL GIFT.

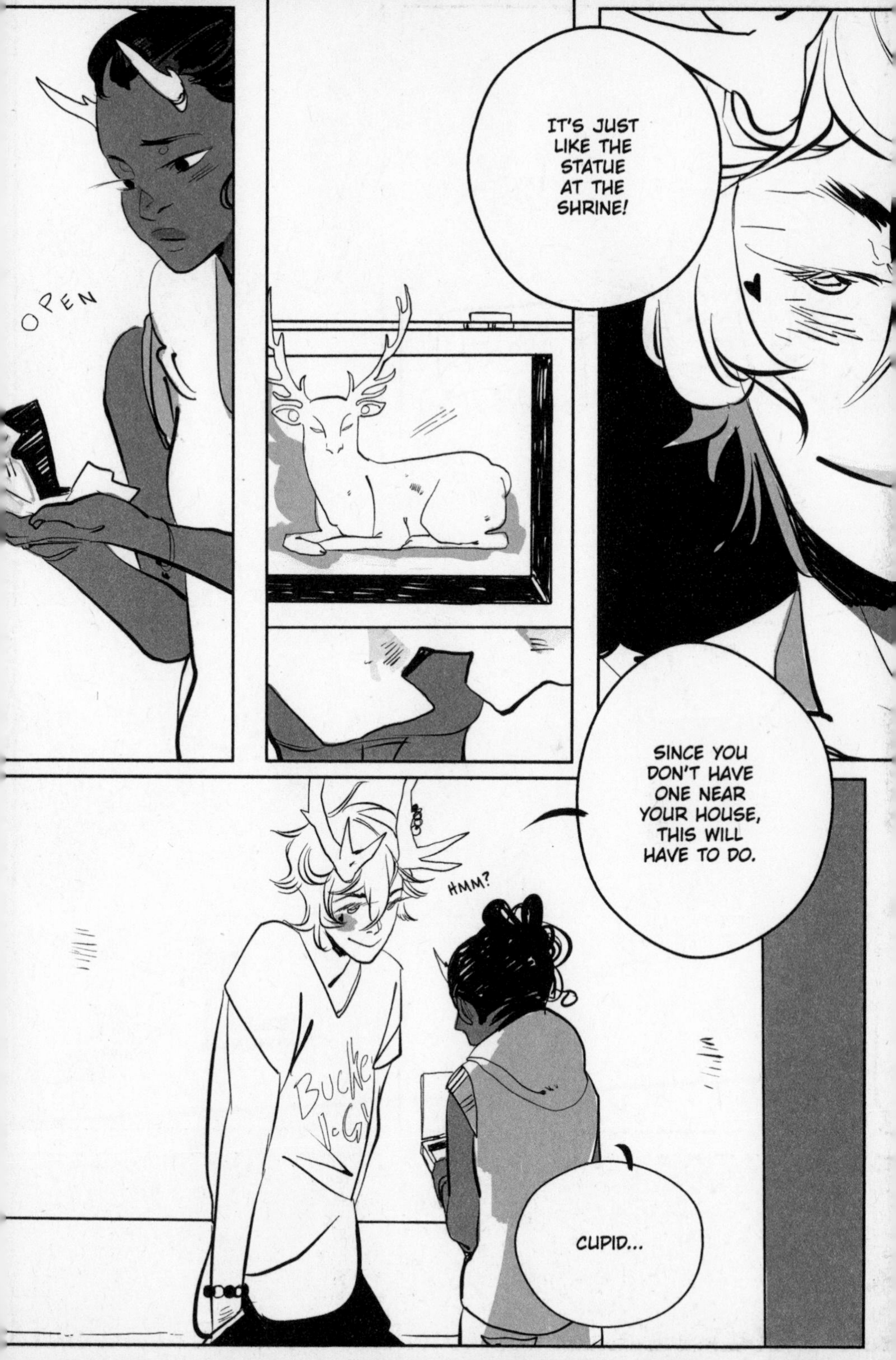
OPEN
IT'S JUST LIKE THE STATUE AT THE SHRINE!
SINCE YOU DON'T HAVE ONE NEAR YOUR HOUSE, THIS WILL HAVE TO DO.
HMM?
CUPID...

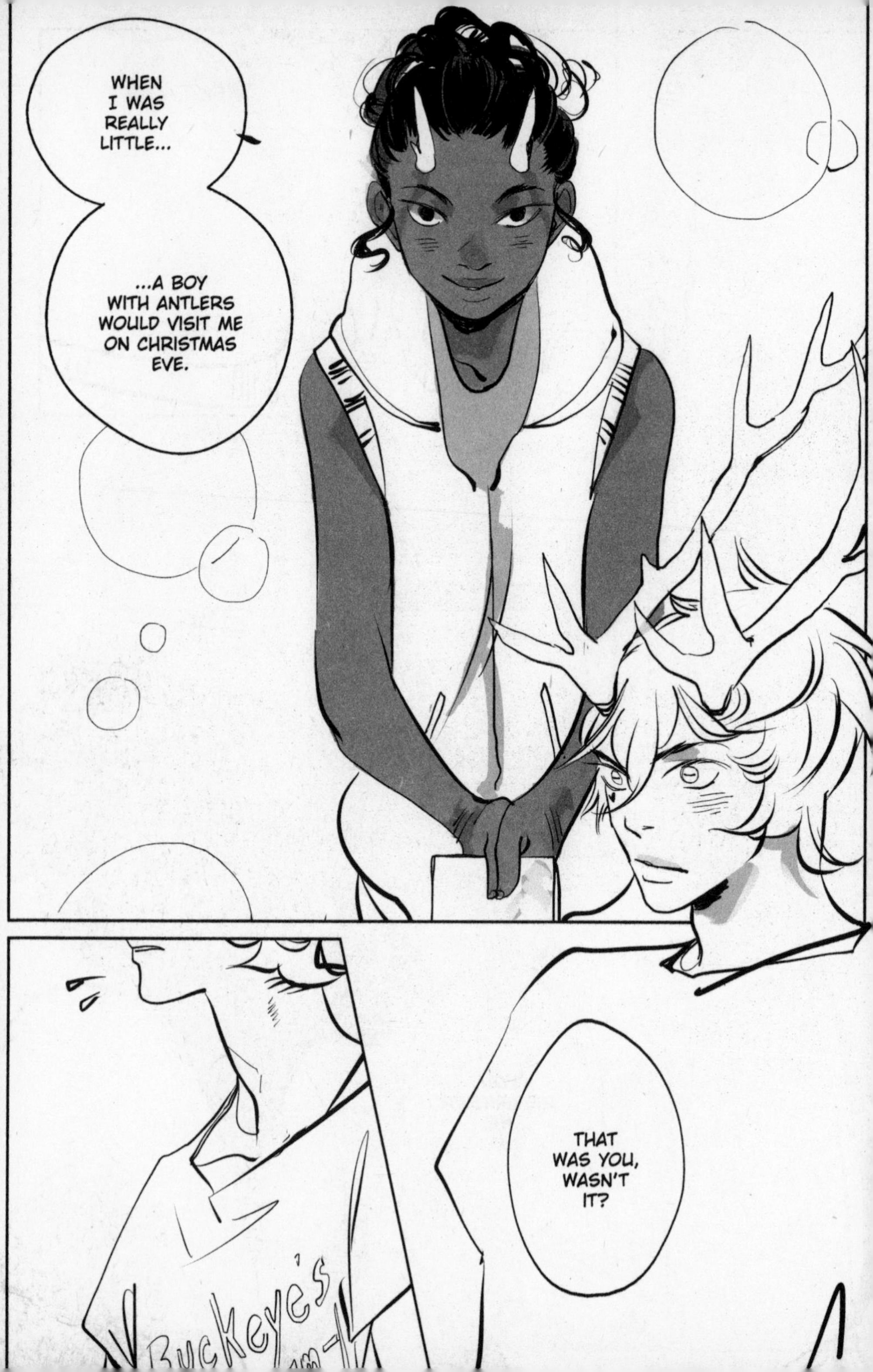
WHEN I WAS REALLY LITTLE...
...A BOY WITH ANTLERS WOULD VISIT ME ON CHRISTMAS EVE.
THAT WAS YOU, WASN'T IT?
Buckeye's

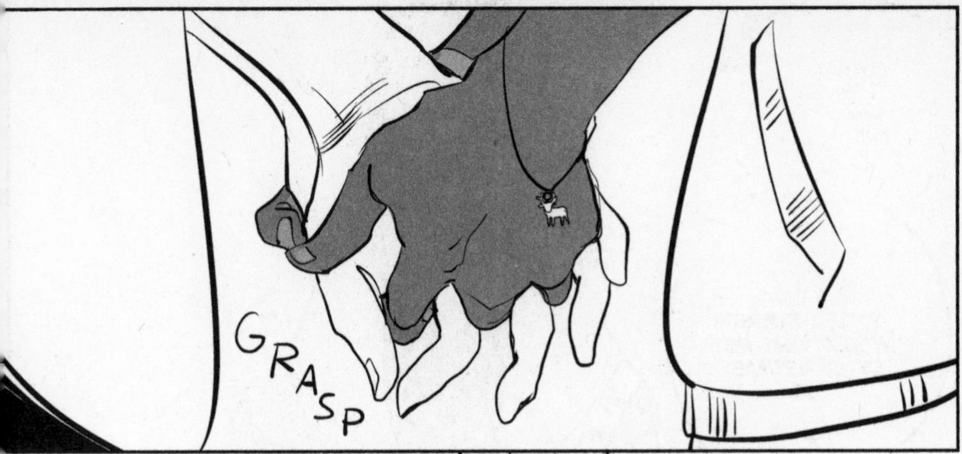
GRASP

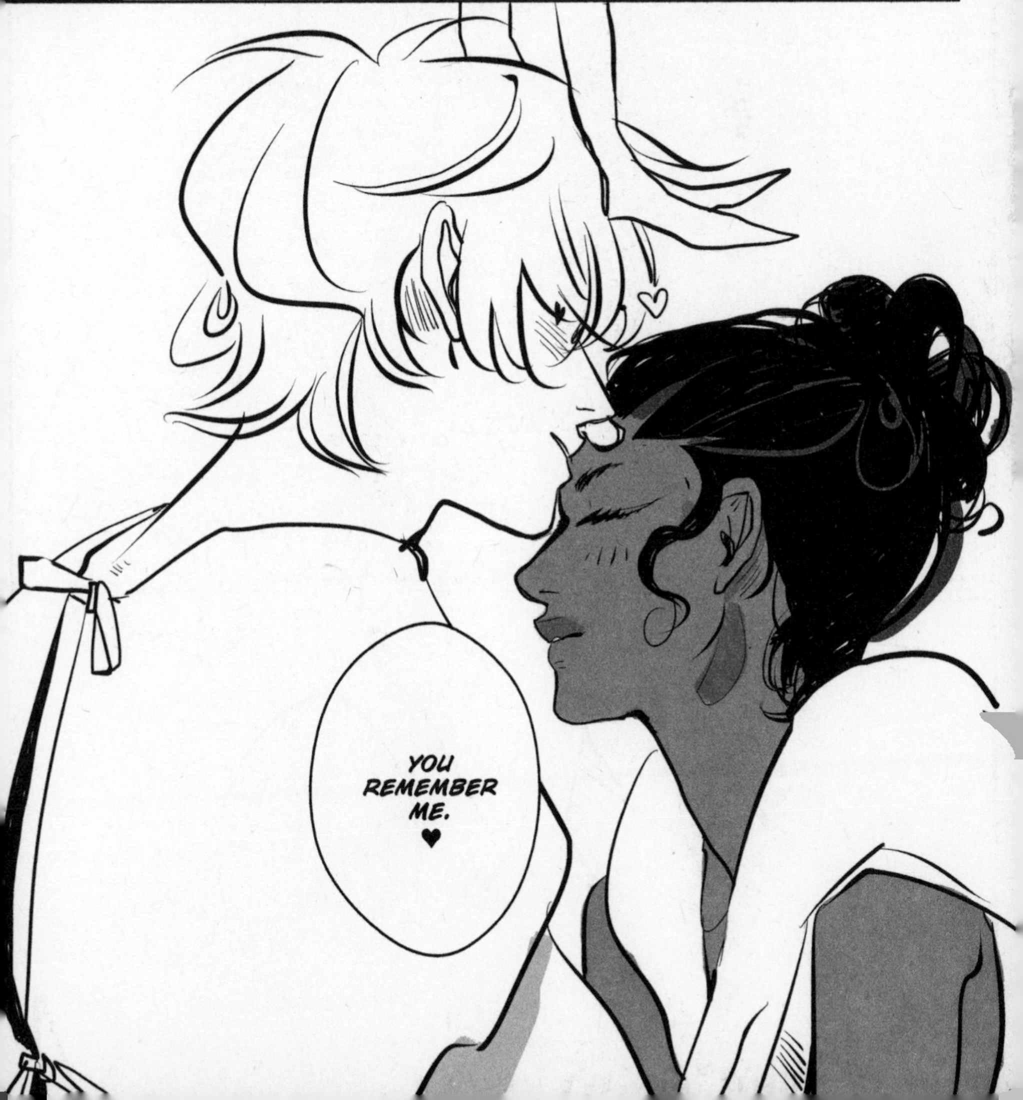
YOU REMEMBER ME. ♥

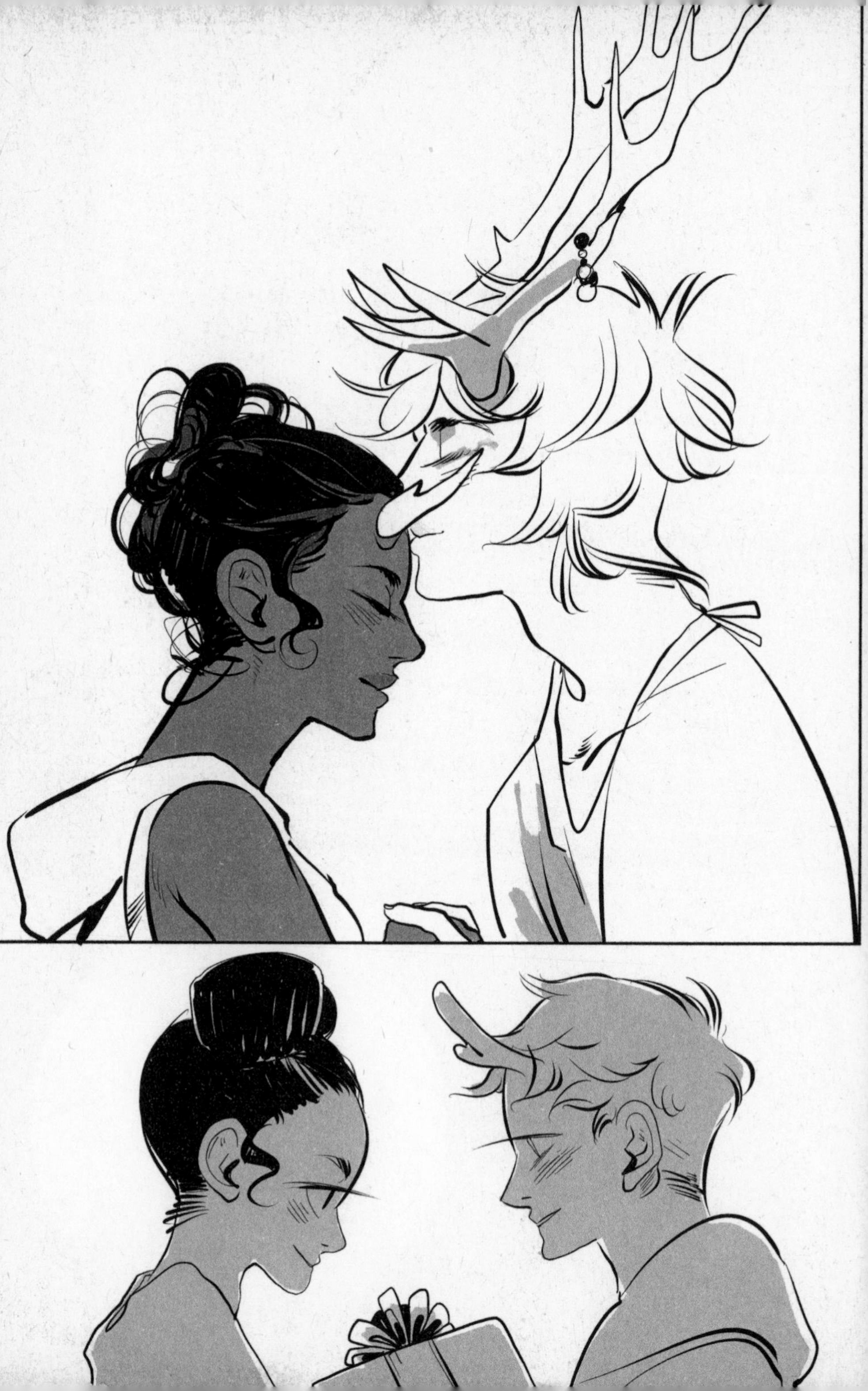

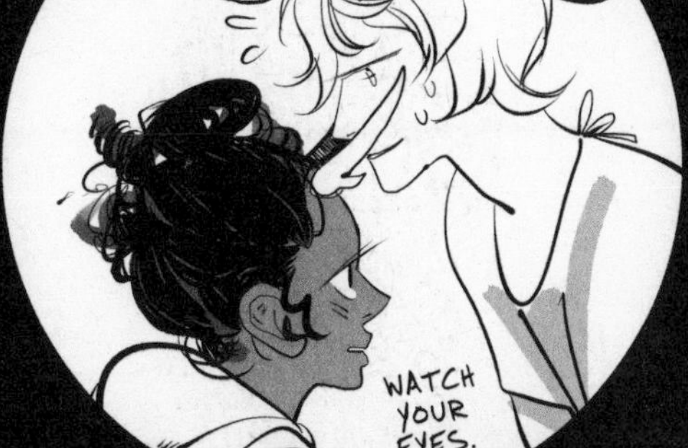
THIS IS DANGEROUS.
WATCH YOUR EYES.

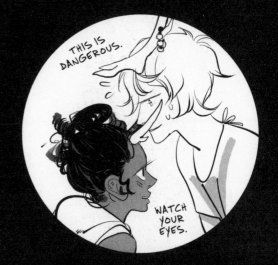

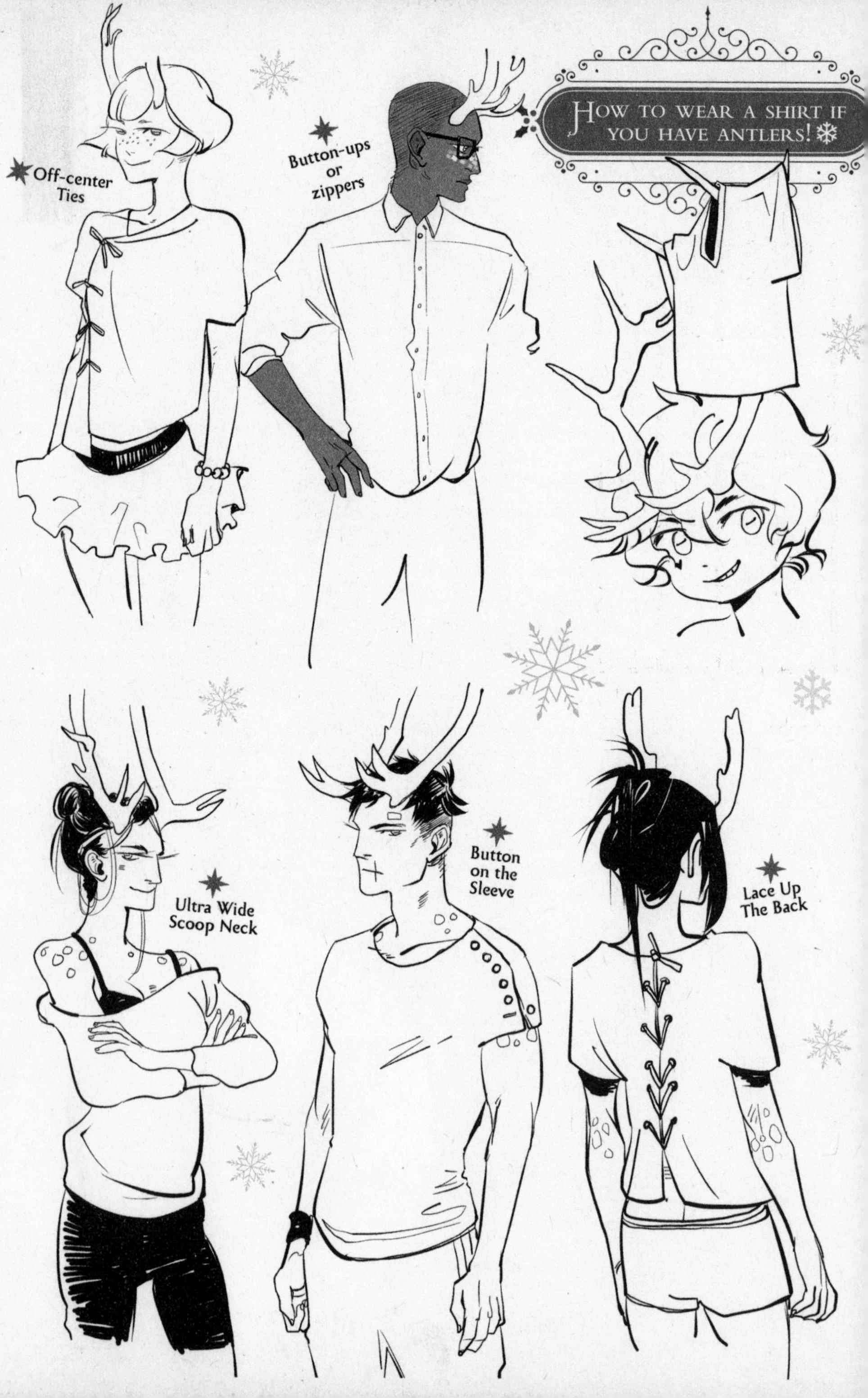

How to wear a shirt if you have antlers!
Off-center Ties
Button-ups or zippers
Ultra Wide Scoop Neck
Button on the Sleeve
Lace Up The Back